Toward a

New Deal in

Baltimore

Toward a New Deal
in Baltimore

People and Government
in the Great Depression

Jo Ann E. Argersinger

The University of North Carolina Press

Chapel Hill and London

Publication of this work was made possible in part by a grant
from the Division of Research Programs of the National
Endowment for the Humanities, an independent federal agency
which supports the study of such fields as history, philosophy,
literature, and languages.

The paper in this book meets the guidelines for permanence and
durability of the Committee on Production Guidelines for Book
Longevity of the Council on Library Resources.

92 91 90 89 88   5 4 3 2 1

Library of Congress Cataloging-in-Publication Data

Argersinger, Jo Ann E.

    Toward a New Deal in Baltimore: people and government in the
Great Depression / by Jo Ann E. Argersinger.

    p. cm.

    Revision of thesis (Ph.D.)—George Washington University, 1980.

    Bibliography: p.

    Includes index.

    ISBN 0-8078-1769-4 (alk. paper)

    1. Baltimore (Md.)—Politics and government. 2. Baltimore (Md.)—
Social conditions. 3. Baltimore (Md.)—Economic conditions.
4. New Deal, 1933–1939—Maryland—Baltimore. 5. Depressions—1929—
United States. I. Title.

F189.B157A74 1988

975.2′6042—dc19   87-21767

                                                  CIP

FOR PETER

Contents

Illustrations

Acknowledgments

During my years of work on this project, I have acquired a number of debts, which, upon reflection, serve as a pleasant reminder of the generous assistance and encouragement I received. My oldest debt is to Joseph L. Arnold, who provided direction for my vague interests in voluntarism and the Great Depression. I am fortunate to be able still to profit from his advice and support, now as a colleague. I am particularly indebted to Leo P. Ribuffo, who guided the research as a dissertation. My work has benefited from his unusual sensibilities, probing criticisms, and skillful editing. His irreverence offered a healthy antidote to the seriousness with which I approached my work as a graduate student.

A number of friends and colleagues offered advice and support throughout the various stages of this manuscript. Peter P. Hill, James O. Horton, Linda Lear, Lonna Malmsheimer, and Kathy L. Peiss made the process more stimulating and enjoyable, and for that I am grateful. Charles H. Trout read and commented on different versions of this study. His efforts— marked by skill and precision—were instrumental in my revisions and his own work served as a model of scholarship and intellectual clarity. I am also indebted to Richard Lowitt for sharing his criticisms and insights; my work benefited greatly from his careful reading. Finally, Otis L. Graham, Jr., and his NEH Summer Seminar for College Teachers in 1986 stimulated my thinking and offered many useful suggestions.

At the University of North Carolina Press, Lewis Bateman merits high praise for his encouragement and guidance. Ron Maner assisted me as my study became a book; he was always gracious and generous with his time and support. And Julia A. McVaugh demonstrated the value of a fine copyeditor.

Librarians and archivists at a number of institutions offered invaluable assistance. The staff at the National Archives was especially helpful, as were those at the Franklin D. Roosevelt Library in Hyde Park, the Southern Historical Collection at the University of North Carolina, the Martin P. Catherwood Library of the New York State School of Industrial and Labor Relations at Cornell University, and the Baltimore City Archives. I received important photographic assistance from the library of *The Sun* in Baltimore, where Fred Rasmussen deserves special mention for his efforts. I also wish to thank the Maryland Room of the University of Maryland College Park and the Special Collections Room of the Albin O. Kuhn Library of the University of Maryland Baltimore County for use of their photographic archives.

I am also grateful for typing grants from Dickinson College and the University of Maryland Baltimore County, which provided necessary assistance at different stages of the manuscript.

Carol M. Warner expertly typed the manuscript, while simultaneously struggling with the peculiarities of the Department of History's new software and personal computer. She was joined in that valiant effort by Linda M. Hatmaker. I appreciate their persistence and professionalism.

I am most indebted to my family, whose support has been unfailing. My parents, Margaret L. Eady and Buford C. Eady, have encouraged me at every step. I also deeply appreciate the kindness and support provided by Marjorie H. Argersinger and William J. Argersinger, Jr. Other members of my family have tolerated long discussions of the New Deal and have feigned interest to a remarkable degree. But no one has done as much for me or my work as my husband, friend, and colleague, Peter H. Argersinger. He has generously shared his talents as a historian and editor. And it is to him that I dedicate this book with love and appreciation.

Introduction

For years historians have argued that a fuller understanding of the New Deal requires more systematic study of the 1930s at the state and local levels. In 1969, James T. Patterson underscored that need in *The New Deal and the States* and encouraged other scholars to examine the Roosevelt record in specific states and cities.[1] More recently, a number of important studies have been completed for such cities as Boston and New York and for such states as Virginia, North Carolina, and Colorado, among others.[2]

Much of this new work focuses on the role of the New Deal in meeting the problems and needs created by the Great Depression. It attempts to explain how people responded to a long depression and to a much shorter New Deal that ultimately failed to solve the problem of unemployment. It analyzes the effects of Franklin D. Roosevelt and the New Deal on politics, labor, and the unemployed. And, specifically, these studies evaluate the success of the New Deal, asking to what extent national administrators, state legislators, and municipal officials could have done more for relief and reform. With few exceptions, these works minimize the effects of the New Deal on the society and politics of the 1930s. John Braeman, Robert Bremner, and David Brody noted this when they wrote: "Paradoxically the result of this new interest has been further to downgrade the significance of the New Deal as an instrument of fundamental changes in American life and society."[3] Operating within a shared conceptual framework, the state and local studies pursue the same questions that shaped the earlier studies of the New Deal at the national level. Accordingly, as Anthony J. Badger notes, these case studies "tend to re-inforce the main trend of New Deal historiography since the 1960s which stresses the essentially limited nature of New Deal change."[4]

No longer, however, is the primary issue one of "revolution" versus "reform" but, more appropriately, of change versus stability. By examining local prerogatives, social practices, and political traditions, these newer studies conclude that neither the New Deal's policies nor its programs were fully adopted in states and cities across the nation. In Ohio, for example, traditional politics and urban-rural divisions kept that state from "creating a workable federal-state partnership" and from providing its unemployed with adequate assistance. Strong states-rights sentiments also curbed enthusiasm for the New Deal, whereas such states as Virginia found that the "economic goals of the New Deal programs were substantially out of harmony with [its] needs." Other states simply refused to pass enabling legislation in an attempt to preclude participation in federal programs. Kentucky followed that course of action, prompting Washington to intervene, and Colorado cooperated only after bitter threats and an actual suspension of federal funds.[5] In Southern states, these problems were compounded by popular and institutionalized racism, as white supremacy frequently formed the central principle in the distribution of relief and the chief criterion in the implementation of programs.[6]

In cities, too, local circumstances impeded the effectiveness of national programs. Charles H. Trout persuasively argues that political and fiscal conservatism, ethnic rivalries, and traditional social attitudes thwarted New Deal relief and reform programs in Boston. He maintains that not only did Bostonians lag behind the New Deal, but "had the New Deal been more radical than it was, the probability is that Boston would have trailed even farther behind."[7]

But among these state and local studies stressing the essentially conservative effects of the New Deal is also a recognition that important changes occurred as a result of the Great Depression and Roosevelt's response to that economic crisis. James F. Wickens, for instance, argues that in Colorado the New Deal had "little permanent impact on state politics," but he also notes that complex modifications initiated by the depression and the New Deal transformed postwar Colorado life. These changes included the growing presence of the federal government, which made Colorado voters "proud of their connection with Washington"; a rapid growth in bureaucracy, which helped produce a modern economy; an increase in federalism, which accompanied a much-lamented decline in regionalism; and the adoption of a modern welfare system, which ensured that private charities would no longer serve as the primary custodians of society.[8] In Boston, Trout observes that "pre-Depression traits" persisted and certainly "outranked the changes"—but he also notes that as a result of the New Deal cities became more dependent on federal grants, and that the national government "assumed responsibility for an enormous welfare clientele," "revised the context in which collective bargaining took place," and "tightened the strings on the business community." Most important, the New Deal established a system of welfare that, although inadequate in Boston, permanently removed most of the burden from private charities and voluntarism.[9] And in Virginia, Ronald L. Heinemann finds that little substantive change occurred; he concludes that the Virginia of 1939 "was remarkably similar to that of ten years earlier." Yet there, too, is the recognition that the New Deal permanently altered the relationship between the states and the federal government.[10]

What emerges from these recent and important examinations of the depression and New Deal at the state and local levels is an interpretation rooted in a paradox best summarized by George Wolfskill: "The paradox, then, is Roosevelt's political successes, successes that produced in the public an admiration and approval approaching idolatry and tremendous victories at the polls, derived from economic policies that were something less than successful, that should probably be described as failures."[11] To understand that paradox, historians have offered a number of useful explanations. They have pointed to the psychological relief provided by Roosevelt's public appeals and rhetoric of compassion; they have documented the invaluable assistance provided by Eleanor Roosevelt; they have noted FDR's essentially political objectives accentuated by his wily political charms; and they have demonstrated that many citizens correctly placed much of the blame for policy failures in their communities on local and state officials.[12] All of these factors certainly help to explain Roosevelt's political and personal popularity. Yet, missing from these accounts is an explanation of considerable significance that suggests the need, not to abandon case studies, but to move beyond conventional historiographical strictures and emphasize the important role the New Deal administration maintained in encouraging and structuring citizen participation and community organization in federally based programs.

Many New Dealers, although anxious to move toward a more planned society, feared that traditional voluntarism would disappear as government expanded its authority and responsibility. President Roosevelt himself declared that "we must never lose sight of the fact that no matter what contributions the Federal government makes, local communities will always have their peculiar duties to perform." The resounding themes of the early New Deal focused on cooperation at all levels of society; Roosevelt called for a return to the "old principle of the local community" and appealed "above all [to] a spirit of neighborliness" in dealing with the problems of economic depression. Accordingly, several New Deal programs explicitly urged citizens to participate in the process of implementing federal initiatives.[13]

In some respects, the New Deal merely followed the lead of Herbert Hoover's Emergency Committee on Employment in advising citizens on how to organize and strengthen their traditions of self-help; but it also provided programs that specifically required community organization and that served to alter the relationship between citizens and the federal government. Roosevelt's government, as Otis L. Graham notes, spoke "the language of local participation." The Federal Emergency Relief Administration, for example, not only funded community efforts at providing relief through its Division of Self-Help Cooperatives but also instructed federal relief administrators to encourage "client organization" and "client participation" among relief recipients. The New Deal provided the first official recognition of community organization in national and local policies. Such legislation as the Social Security Act demanded that communities engage in social planning in order for states to receive funds, and it used the term "community organization," marking the first time, as Michael Austin and Neil Betten believe, that this phrase appeared in a federal statute. The entry of the federal government into social welfare also brought many volunteers into public and private agencies. Finally, the New Deal, through a variety of programs, facilitated the organization of the more marginal groups in society traditionally ignored by two-party politics.[14]

As this study will demonstrate, the experience of Baltimore in the 1930s largely conforms to the findings of these newer works that emphasize the conservative application of the New Deal. The local response to the New Deal was conditioned by traditional states-rights concerns, a conservative Democratic party, racial and ethnic rivalries, disdain for public relief, and a persistent belief that all forms of public assistance should be temporary in nature. But in my analysis of the "localization of federal programs," to borrow Trout's useful phrase, the twin themes of federal intervention and citizen participation will also be explored. Although I will not fully abandon the traditional approach in assessing the Roosevelt record, I will place more emphasis on examining the dynamic process of federal-local interaction, for it is within the study of that process over time that the real significance of the New Deal emerges.

What is needed, then, is a framework that can accommodate change and continuity in local and national developments without sacrificing the complexity of public policy making. For Baltimore, the most useful framework is provided by analyzing the 1930s as an episode in the process of organizational growth. The organizational theme, best developed in studies of the Progressive Era and World War I, has shown its usefulness as a tool in understanding the emergence of a more complex society characterized by business corporations, bureaucratic associations, and organized professional groups. The New Deal, especially in the areas of public welfare and organized labor, certainly advanced the pace of the "bureaucratization" of society. Gerald Nash, in his brief survey of the *Great Depression and World War II*, recognizes the organizational component of the New Deal when he refers to Roosevelt as "one of the founding fathers of the welfare state in the United States and also one of the progenitors of the organizational society in America."[15] Borrowing from notions earlier advanced by Robert Wiebe, Thomas Coode and John Bauman argue in their study of Pennsylvania in the 1930s that the "centralizing tendencies" of the New Deal transformed communities in the city and countryside. The Great Depression and the New Deal, they maintain, "altered the social relationships binding individuals and groups to their communities and the nation." Finally, in his examination of the New Deal administration, Ellis Hawley declares that the "shift from Hoover to Roosevelt" brought about "a new departure in business-government relations."[16]

Generally, however, the organizational theme has not been emphasized in the historiography of the New Deal precisely because Roosevelt's policies and programs borrowed heavily from the war experience and from the Progressive Era. The models for Roosevelt's proposed solutions were, as Hawley observes, essentially "inherited ones." Even in the area of public welfare Roosevelt acted, as Nash notes, with "characteristic caution" and the Social Security program that emerged represented "the culmination of decades of agitation and planning, rather than an innovation."[17] But to recognize the organizational changes that took place in the 1930s is not to suggest that the New Deal heralded a new era. Rather, the purpose of this study is to analyze the process of organizational change in a major city and to suggest that an integral part of those developments reflected not only the priorities of organized traditional political groups but also the activities of citizen groups that were simultaneously encouraged and restricted by federal initiatives.

The New Deal experience in Baltimore suggests that the pace of organizational growth accelerated in the 1930s and that much of the expansion resulted from federal actions and local responses. In order to examine these changes more systematically, it is necessary to analyze them on two levels. The administrative level involves the interaction of municipal, state, and federal governments in implementing New Deal programs. Much of this intergovernmental activity, while covering a wide variety of programs, from recreational activities to the construction of public works, focused on providing unemployment relief. In Baltimore, the task of establishing a municipal department of welfare from a system of private agencies proceeded fitfully, with considerable local resistance and much federal prodding.

On another, more popular, level, the organized activities of pressure groups, protest groups, and community associations tended to publicize particular issues, educate members of the communities themselves, and, on occasion, influence both local and national policy decisions. The "centralizing tendencies" of the New Deal, which unmistakably altered the role of government in public welfare, also, however, served to strengthen the local commitment and intensify the civic energy of many community groups. Citizens looked to the federal government for advice and assistance and even basked in the unprecedented attention they were receiving from Washington officials, but they did not abdicate their community responsibilities. Forced by hard times and educated by federal initiatives, these groups often widened their activities to include agitation for such new programs as public housing. For these groups, increased federal intervention provided an important means to combat the traditionalism and conservatism of local government. Consequently, they called for greater federal supervision in local policy making and attempted to use the political popularity of Roosevelt to coerce local officials into supporting the New Deal more fully. Despite Roosevelt's claim that the New Deal put "the power of government" behind "all sections of the community," there were, of course, real limits to the role and influence of citizen involvement—limits that were imposed at all levels of government.[18] And by examining those limitations, the full impact of the depression and the New Deal can better be understood.

Public reactions to New Deal programs, especially those that threatened increased taxation for unemployment relief, were not always favorable. Organized Baltimore taxpayers led periodic revolts against the prospect of paying higher taxes, and such groups as the association of Baltimore realtors espoused, with selective consistency, a credo of individualism that sharply collided with the New Deal's message of cooperation. The persistence in the 1930s of what historian James Holt calls the "anti-statist tradition" certainly characterized certain segments of the city's population.

Moreover, the failure of the federal government, despite an important beginning, to overcome local obstacles to its programs and successfully "communalize" the New Deal indicated not only the strength of municipal opposition but also the ambivalence of the New Dealers themselves in promulgating a program that lacked ideological coherence.[19]

This study documents the partially successful efforts of the New Deal to reach out to new constituencies as it unravels the complex connections between citizen activism and governmental authority. It demonstrates how the Great Depression and the New Deal served to reorganize the city in important ways that at once expanded the role of both local and national governments but also insured against more substantive change.

CHAPTER 1

The Urban Setting

Baltimore between the Wars

The prospect of a decade of hard times seemed remote in Baltimore at the onset of 1930. Only minor reverberations from the stock market crash had been felt in the city's business community. Although few businesses expected significant economic growth, still fewer anticipated a permanent decline. Reacting to what appeared to be a temporary slump, one city resident wryly observed in January 1930: "No man fears there will be actual starvation in America, but every man fears that he may have to smoke cheaper cigars and drink worse gin; and this prospect throws a pall of gloom over the whole business world."[1]

But the city's business community, and especially those activist boosters who comprised the Baltimore Association of Commerce (BAC), rejected even that restrained vision of economic retrenchment. Their optimism grew out of their view of the city's economic experience during the 1920s. Gently chided by H. L. Mencken as "boosters, boomers, go-getters and other such ballyhoo men," BAC members rarely missed an opportunity to recite the industrial advantages of the nation's seventh-largest city. Buoyed by the 1918 municipal annexation that had tripled the city's size—from 30 to 92 square miles—the association boldly, if erroneously, predicted that the city's 1920 population of 733,000 would reach the million mark in 1930. In its brochures, the BAC gave front-page billing to Baltimore's reputation as a "low-wage" town and promised prospective businesses a tractable, nonunion, predominantly white, "100% American" work force. The association reminded its audience that truly "American workers, whether white or black, are rarely found among the ranks of the Communist" and added that if labor problems occurred there was also an "ample supply" of unskilled blacks to call on for strikebreaking services.[2]

The industrial growth of the 1920s further buoyed city spirits, offering fresh evidence of a city on the move. Baltimore added significantly to its highly diversified industrial base by attracting 103 new plants, including Western Electric, American Sugar, McCormick Spice, and the Lever Bros. and Proctor and Gamble soap factories. Bethlehem Steel, which drew many of its workers from within the city, spent $100 million to expand its plant in nearby Sparrows Point; and its president, Charles Schwab, provided the BAC with a memorable quotation when he exclaimed that "there is no place in the United States so susceptible of successful industrial development" as Baltimore. The volume of foreign trade handled at the city's port facilities also grew; Baltimore jumped from a ranking as the nation's seventh most active port in 1920 to third in 1926. The dust and noise of construction became constant companions to city residents in the 1920s. Modern skyscrapers altered both the city's skyline and its image, and the construction of paved streets facilitated the flow of traffic. By 1930 Baltimore contained 929 miles of paved streets, nearly 50 percent more than at the end of the Great War. Houses were hurriedly built, filling in the newly annexed area. By the mid-1920s more than 6,000 houses were being constructed annually, and by the end of the decade the percentage of residents owning homes climbed to over fifty, representing an increase of about three percentage points from 1920. Municipal officials contributed to the building boom by authorizing the construction of larger, more spacious schools, new playgrounds, and recreational facilities. The city's private entertainment industry also expanded, attending to the needs of a commercialized citizenry. It was an era of autos and radios, with nearly 50 percent of the city's population owning a "pleasure box" and over 100,000 automobiles traveling across newly constructed viaducts, taking Sunday excursions, creating traffic jams, and increasing congestion and pollution.[3]

But there was another side to the changes occurring in Baltimore in the 1920s, one that suggested important limits to prosperity and underscored the unevenness of the city's advancements. Rarely found among the booster pamphlets were accounts of industrial setbacks. For example, although Baltimore was known as a major center for the production of men's garments, its clothing industry suffered a serious decline, dropping from third to fifth place in the nation. Large, modern factories, which had expanded only a few years earlier in order to meet the wartime demand for government uniforms, shut down entirely; medium-sized firms also closed their doors. Consequently, by the time of the Great Depression the city's garment industry had already undergone a significant transformation, as petty entrepreneurs who sweated their workers in small, cramped, and dirty shops replaced the earlier, more modern manufacturers. The change largely affected the daughters of working-class immigrant families, who endured long hours, tyrannical bosses, and pitifully low wages. And at the city's port installations, even with the hefty increase in foreign trade, the decline in the grain industry idled newly constructed elevators. In one year, 1921, wheat exports dropped from 29.7 to 21.7 million bushels, and by 1930 exports of all grains had declined to the lowest level since 1910. Moreover, despite the boosterism of the BAC, including the distribution of over 250,000 copies of a pamphlet entitled "197 Reasons Why You Should Enthuse over Baltimore," municipal authorities failed in important bids to attract major businesses into the city. The Glenn L. Martin firm, for example, was offended by the hard-sell tactics of the city and instead accepted the generous arrangements offered by Baltimore county to locate its aircraft factory there. Finally, general economic slumps, particularly in 1927 and 1928, created problems of unemployment and relief well before the depression of the 1930s; the jobless rate had risen to nearly 10 percent by 1928 (it improved slightly in 1929). By the end of the decade, although Baltimore ranked seventh among the nation's ten largest cities in the total value of its manufactured products, it ranked only ninth in wages paid its workers.[4]

The benefits of the "New era of prosperity," as one BAC spokesman championed the 1920s, did not extend to all the city's residents. For Baltimore's blacks, representing nearly 18 percent of the total population, it was not a decade of either autos or radios. Concentrated in menial and service occupations, blacks lived in the oldest and most congested areas of the city where they suffered disproportionately from unemployment, crime, disease, and infant mortality. Aside from teachers in "colored schools," blacks accounted for less than 2 percent of all municipal employees, and of that small number nearly 80 percent were classified as "common laborers." There were no black librarians, streetcar drivers, firefighters, or police officers in the entire city. Moreover, even among school teachers—and in violation of state law—blacks received less pay; white teachers in elementary schools, for example, received about twice the salary of their black counterparts. Unlike white households, where only 17 percent of the women were part of the wage economy, over 50 percent of black women were in the paid work force; and among these wage-earning black women, about 87 percent were employed as domestics or personal servants, earning no more than $6 a week. Black men also worked in service jobs or as casual laborers, relying on irregular work opportunities. Depending on the area of the city, tuberculosis struck black residents six to eleven times more often than whites (and those unfortunate blacks who resided on the infamous "Lung Block" in old west Baltimore stood at even greater risk). The rate of infant mortality in black communities ranged from thirty to fifty percentage points higher than in white neighborhoods in the city. Problems associated with disease and sanitation were made worse, according to Urban League investigators, by the practice of boarding: to supplement meager incomes and to assist recent migrants to the city, over one-third of Baltimore's black families took in boarders, compared to less than one-fourth for the population as a whole. Moreover, during the 1920s the practice increased among blacks, while it declined among white families. Finally, blacks were more likely than whites to be arrested; their arrest rate in the 1920s, for example, was about twice that for whites, and by 1934 the population of Baltimore's City Jail was nearly 50 percent black.[5]

Although the advancements that occurred in Baltimore in the 1920s certainly improved the lives of a number of blacks, the overall record fell far short of providing a "separate but equal" urban environment for them. More schools for blacks were built, but resources were not divided equally. Throughout the postwar decades, for example, authorities continued to spend more on white students than on blacks—by the mid-1930s, nearly 40 percent more per pupil. The city also maintained a facility for "feeble-minded" white children but provided no assistance at all to black children who were similarly diagnosed. The municipal building boom of the 1920s included the first public swimming pool for blacks, but the pool was not within walking distance of the nearest black residential community and was substantially smaller than the pool built nearby for white families. Blacks could not freely enter all the city's department stores, and some of Baltimore's finest stores refused to sell to blacks altogether. Movie houses in the city pursued a discriminatory policy: blacks either faced outright exclusion or were limited to seating in the balcony. The Catholic church adopted segregated seating for those few blacks who did not worship at the city's four all-black parishes. And finally, the meager wages paid to black workers meant that they did not share in the prosperity of the 1920s. Whereas 59.2 percent of the native white residents in the city owned a radio, for example, only 15.6 percent of Baltimore's blacks possessed one. Even more significantly, blacks did not share in the local reputation as a "city of homeowners": over 50 percent of the city's white residents owned their homes, but only 17 percent of the black population enjoyed that luxury.[6]

However, high rates of homeownership in white working-class neighborhoods often indicated more about the policies of industrialists and realtors than about the prosperity of the workers themselves. In the nineteenth century, New York capitalist Peter Cooper promoted homeownership to insure stability among the immigrant workers he had attracted to his east Baltimore industrial community of Canton. As a result of his efforts, workers rarely moved, even in the mobile late nineteenth century. By the 1920s, although many of the local companies attached to Cooper's industrial community had been displaced by national or regional interests, the effects of his Canton Company could still be seen in the tightly-knit residential neighborhoods. Elsewhere, too, the local tradition of homeownership encouraged working-class stability, as in the white communities of Hampden and Woodbury in west Baltimore. Strong ties within these neighborhoods, supported by the activities of the church and the tavern and bolstered by an intense pride in the local baseball clubs, promoted stable and usually inward-looking communities. The city's diversified economy provided opportunities for varied, albeit low-paying, employment, enabling sons and daughters to supplement family incomes and thus to make homeownership possible. But the price was often high, and the appealing picture of strong, stable communities drawn by the city's boosters tended to ignore the widespread practices of neighborhood bankers and realtors who, according to federal investigators in the 1930s, saddled working-class families with large mortgage payments for cheap, flimsy housing. The seemingly endless row homes that lined the city's landscape and housed working-class families too often were poorly constructed and overpriced.[7]

Residential segregation characterized the spatial configuration of the city. In 1930, for example, nearly 40 percent of the total black population resided in but four of the city's eighteen wards; in one ward, blacks accounted for 88 percent of the population—and in that same ward population densities ranged from 50,000 to 100,000 per square mile, compared to an average of 30,000 for the oldest part of the city and to a mere 3,000 in the newly annexed area. Over 30 percent of the people living in the city's oldest section were black, but blacks made up only 3 percent of the residents of the area annexed in 1918. Many of the blacks who migrated to the city from the rural counties of Virginia and Maryland settled in "Pigtown"—an area infamous for its garbage-strewn streets and severe poverty.[8]

The city experienced division along lines of ethnicity as well. Although Baltimore never witnessed a major influx of newer immigrants, as late as 1930 about 30 percent of the population had at least one foreign-born parent. The emergence of ethnic neighborhoods in the nineteenth century, their persistence into the twentieth, and the proliferation of ethnically based political and fraternal clubs, all indicated the presence and significance of ethnicity in the social and political life of the city. There was a thriving Polish community in east Baltimore, where mutual benefit associations and savings banks encouraged Poles to buy their homes and support the local parish. In "Little Italy," near the Fells Point area, political activities dominated the neighborhood clubs in the years between the wars. An enclave of Bohemians settled in southeast Baltimore at Locust Point in the nineteenth century. Bohemian men shoveled coal and pushed coal cars on the wharves of the Point; in the 1920s and 1930s their daughters worked in the garment factories and sweatshops of the clothing industry. Russian Jews, who in the twentieth century displaced Germans as the city's most numerous immigrant group, settled in the inner city in a neighborhood called Oldtown; with their arrival, the older German Jews, some of whom owned the city's garment factories and department stores, moved westward along Eutaw Place. The annexation of 1918 and the general migration to greener and less crowded suburban areas certainly affected the size and shape of the city's ethnic communities—but as late as 1940, residential segregation among immigrants remained fairly high.[9]

Although Baltimore's white ethnic groups never encountered the systematic discrimination faced daily by black residents, there were instances of anti-Catholicism and anti-Semitism. The only Jewish resident in the exclusive Guilford neighborhood was refused home delivery by the milk, bread, and newspaper services. But far more threatening to both Jews and Catholics were the activities of the Ku Klux Klan, revitalized in the city in the 1920s. Beginning in the spring of 1921, local King Kleagle H. P. Moorehead conducted a mail campaign in Baltimore to increase membership, and in 1922 robed Klansmen staged a parade in the city. The strongly Protestant, working-class community of Hampden supported an active

Klan local (#57); there the clergy cooperated with Klan members, performing group baptisms, even christening one local daughter Katerine Karlotta Knickmann—an indication of the importance of the Klan in family affairs. Led by Archbishop Michael Curley and his diocesan paper, *The Catholic Review*, Baltimore's nearly 190,000 Catholics denounced Klan activities and relied on the support of not only Catholic city council members but also Governor Albert Ritchie, who twice denied the Klan permission to use the Baltimore armory. Moreover, under Curley's aggressive leadership the Catholic community campaigned to extend the influence of the church by expanding and improving the city's parochial schools. Curley urged new parishes to construct schools even before church buildings, explaining that "the hope of the harvest is in the seed."[10]

Catholics were also active in local and state politics and policy making, sitting on the city's public school board and managing one of the most active charitable organizations in both the city and state. Archbishop Curley's preference for local prerogative and state sovereignty perfectly matched the sentiments of Governor Ritchie and Mayor Howard Jackson, who served the city for much of the period between the wars. Unlike the other private agencies, the Bureau of Catholic Charities persistently championed voluntarism in dealing with the problem of unemployment relief, opposed government intervention, and held firm to the primacy of the parish in "charitable service." Politically, the most divisive rivalry within the city's Democratic party was based in part on an ethnic-religious split symbolized by the leaders of the two factions themselves: the city's mayor, the native Protestant Howard Jackson, on one side, and the city's "boss," the Irish Catholic William Curran, on the other. Although neither faction enthusiastically endorsed President Franklin Roosevelt and his New Deal after 1933, Catholic leaders more vigorously protested the radicalism that they believed propelled the labor movement.[11]

The severe economic decline that began in Baltimore in late 1930 ultimately challenged the assumptions and attitudes of a number of groups in the city. That year the BAC conceded that the production of machinery had decreased by 20 percent, of men's clothing by 30 percent, and of petroleum products by 30 to 40 percent—but, they added, Baltimore's "industry as a whole is in good shape." Only the 1932 findings of President Hoover's Emergency Committee on Employment, placing the city's unemployment rate at just over 19 percent, jarred them into altering their platitudinous pronouncements. Although they challenged the Emergency

Committee's estimate, the BAC admitted that while Baltimore had been slow in joining the national slump, it had "arrived at about the same place."[12]

The effects of joblessness and hardship in the Great Depression, like the benefits of prosperity and urban progress in the "New Era," were not shared evenly among the city's 362,072 gainful workers. Particularly hard-hit were workers in textiles, steel, clothing, and construction. Compared to the mid-1920s, for example, when thousands of houses were constructed annually in Baltimore, in 1934 only 119 houses were built in the entire city. The black population also suffered disproportionately: representing 21.8 percent of the city's work force, blacks experienced unemployment rates approaching 50 percent and, by 1934, constituted 42.2 percent of all families receiving relief in the city. Too often, the issue of race figured prominently in all areas of employment, from work-relief programs to private business. "My only problem," solemnly observed one jobless black man, "is being colored." Black women even lost the "security" of low-paying service jobs in the early years of the depression; one employment agency reported in 1934 that only 10 percent of its calls for nursemaids were filled by black women, compared to 65 percent in 1928. A survey of newspaper advertisements for domestic jobs in March 1934 similarly found a "new" preference for whites: of the 127 requests, only 5 wanted black women. Even as late as 1940, when war orders from Europe revital-ized area industry and reduced the city's unemployment rate to almost 10 percent, blacks still accounted for 30 percent of those without jobs. But black women, unwelcome in the new wartime positions, found that they could reclaim their service jobs; by 1940, 85 percent of all wage-earning black females worked as domestics.[13]

Women in general suffered especially from the effects of hard times and scarce jobs. They experienced second-class treatment in practically all New Deal programs and often encountered overt hostility in the wage-earning world. Caught in a society that sharply divided homemaking from breadwinning and that focused almost exclusively on the "forgotten man" and the stability of the family, wage-earning women, particularly those who were married, feared for their jobs and endured public scorn. Throughout the nation, state legislatures attempted to restrict or eliminate employment opportunities for married women. Some states, although not concerned with limiting the incomes of individual men or the profits of business in the depression, placed ceilings on the incomes of married women. In 1932 the Baltimore city council passed a resolution directing the mayor and the Board of Estimates to replace married women who worked in city departments or public schools if their "husbands are able to support them." Women's gender and their primary role in family rearing, then, made them targets of discriminatory policy making, for the level of family income only became of concern when part of it came from the wife's wage. In January 1933, President Hoover's Research Committee on Social Trends concluded that in all areas of employment "the bargaining power of women was weakening." Moreover, well before the onset of serious unemployment, denunciations of working women became so severe that the Baltimore *Sun* published an editorial decrying the trend, declaring that "it is amazing to see the vindictive spleen that is vented against the poor married women. . . . To make scapegoats out of married women," the *Sun* argued, "will never solve the [economic] problems." The position taken by the *Sun* was, however, atypical, for opposition to women working was popular at all levels of society; George Gallup claimed that he had never seen people "so solidly united in opposition as on any subject imaginable including sin and hay fever."[14]

The assaults continued, but so did the entry of women into the paid work force: the percentage of women in the work force increased from 27 in 1920 to over 30 by 1940. During the depression, employers often hired women for such "men's" jobs as pressers in the garment industry and then paid them about half what men earned. An investigation into the men's garment industry in 1932 revealed that women were earning as little as $6.00 per week for 60 hours of work. New Deal programs did little to alleviate the predicament of women: although they benefited from general labor and welfare legislation, they were vastly underrepresented in work-relief programs. Moreover, these programs tended to reinforce traditional discriminatory practices based on gender as well as on race and age. White women who were fortunate enough to secure work-relief jobs found themselves in sewing rooms, but only as long as they were able to maintain the speed, and young black women were often sent to New Deal–sponsored training classes for domestic service. On the defensive throughout the depression decade, women, both with and without jobs, made few gains. The number of women in professional and semiprofessional jobs actually declined by 6 percent in the 1930s, whereas the number of men employed in those same categories jumped by 30 percent. Female-dominated unions such as the Amalgamated Clothing Workers worked to chip away at the worst abuses of the garment sweatshops, but women as a whole, after having won the vote a decade earlier, exerted little political or economic influence. The issue of equal rights for women was certainly not on society's agenda in depression America. Feminist groups tried unsuccessfully throughout the 1930s to gain for Maryland women the right to perform jury service—a right already held by women in twenty-one states—but state legislators rejected their pleas, concurring instead with a local judge who declared that "the jury has no place for women." In 1936, women prisoners were granted the right to smoke in the Baltimore City Jail, but the rationale was based, not on the grounds of securing equality, but on ending cruel and unusual punishment. And in 1937 the state employment commissioner issued a new, more restrictive maternity leave policy, explaining that the problem was "between babies and jobs" and that "we're not in the business of having babies, but of running the State government." Organized professional women denounced the ruling as still another "obstacle in the way" of working women, and the Baltimore branch of the National Women's Party threatened "vigorous opposition" against efforts to enforce "archaic masculine ideas." But the state went ahead with its new policy.[15]

Foreign-born whites, mainly from Russia, Poland, and Italy, also suffered disproportionately from the depression. They represented only 9 percent of the city's population, but they accounted for 19 percent of the relief recipients. Yet the experience of the foreign-born white differed significantly from that of the native-born black. Most of the foreign white population was either Catholic or Jewish and resided in neighborhoods that were tied to the community service network of the Bureau of Catholic Charities or the Associated Jewish Charities—both member agencies of the Community Fund, the city's chief dispenser of private relief monies. On the other hand, the black fraternal groups and neighborhood associations that assisted unemployed black families were not members of the Community Fund and had neither the resources nor the political leverage possessed by the other agencies with which to provide the same level of service to the black community. Moreover, the percentage of foreign-born residents receiving relief declined as the decade wore on, while the percentage of blacks increased. Finally, all whites, whether native or foreign-born, were throughout the 1930s consistently placed in private industry more often than were blacks.[16]

Until 1933, private relief agencies tried valiantly but unsuccessfully to meet the needs of the city's jobless, working with churches and community associations to try to feed and clothe the unemployed. Organized labor, on the other hand, did little to alleviate the situation. Representing under 10 percent of the work force, the Baltimore Federation of Labor (BFL), with which American Federation of Labor locals in the city were affiliated, rarely deviated from the voluntaristic traditions that had come to define the AFL itself. The BFL, even though it endorsed the establishment of unemployment insurance, generally avoided the political arena, and its self-help doctrines restricted its role in both labor organization and unemployment relief. When, for example, the activist president of the building trades, one of the BFL's largest affiliated unions, attempted to assist his jobless members, the BFL offered neither encouragement nor financial assistance. With the exception of the Amalgamated Clothing Workers (ACW), not until 1937 did organized labor, under the new leadership of the Committee for Industrial Organization (CIO), begin to offer programs and direct aid to jobless workers. By then the responsibility for relief had shifted from the private charities to the public agencies, and caring for the unemployed figured prominently as a major political and economic problem.

After years of unemployment and relief, social workers and public officials became concerned about the long-term effects of deprivation and the "chronic problem of idleness." Distressed by what they regarded as "family disorganization," they pointed to the city's rising divorce rate and reported cases of increased crime among both adults and juveniles, of "broken morale," of hostility toward society, and of increased aggressiveness among relief clients. They found no single profile to describe jobless Baltimoreans or the variety of ways in which the unemployed dealt with their predicament. Some of the jobless turned to political and social action, joining, for example, the Peoples Unemployment League (PUL), which was formed in 1933 to aid the unemployed by lobbying for more assistance at the national level and by pushing for a more complete adoption of programs locally. There were those who turned to illegal activity—some to petty thievery, others to gambling in the illegal lottery games that thrived in the 1930s. And hard times drove still others to risk more than small change on favorite numbers: desperate homeowners with overdue mortgage payments increasingly turned to "loan sharks" to stave off foreclosure. A scandal exposed in 1938 revealed that loan sharks had preyed particularly upon such public-service employees as teachers, fire fighters, and police officers—all of whom had suffered substantial reductions in pay. Interest rates ranged from 120 to 600 percent, and the culprits included not the usual local racketeers, who also profited from hard times, but out-of-state loan companies operating illegally within the state of Maryland. Their status as legitimate loan companies helped to attract customers but did not deter them from hiring local muscle to "threaten loan holders should they discuss their loans with investigators."[17]

To the dismay and occasional amusement of their middle-class social workers, the victims of adversity also turned to evangelical religion, flocking to revivalist meetings held in dilapidated houses, dank basements, and store-front churches. These "cult churches," as they were called, promised hope and salvation and were led by charismatic leaders such as Daddy Grace who delivered impassioned sermons. Both blacks and whites found reassurance in their neighborhood ministries, where spiritual relief seemed to have boundless possibilities and where the vagaries of economic depression faded before the powers of personal redemption. The proliferation of store-front churches in black areas disturbed the more orthodox clergy, who joined with white religious leaders in denouncing the "frenzied" spectacle of the local "prophets" and their followers. Likening the new churches to "weeds" that "spread in the depression," middle-class critics decried religious zealots for exploiting the "baffled, miserable, and hopeless." But the members of the "depression churches" celebrated their new faith, regarding their churches as a source of joy and security and finding among their new religious leaders a level of personal involvement unknown in more orthodox congregations.[18]

When Franklin D. Roosevelt took office in March 1933, city and state officials expected the new president to assist them with what they regarded as their most pressing political and economic problems: the banking crisis, the matter of prohibition, and the difficult issue of unemployment relief. But they also wanted the new administration to be ever mindful of its proper sphere of authority. Baltimore's Democratic mayor, Howard Jackson, who served the city between 1923 and 1927 and from 1931 to 1943, was especially insistent on limiting federal power, but considerably less fussy about taking federal grants. Known to drink to excess and to feud incessantly with the Curranite faction—both of which actions contributed to a Republican victory in 1927—Jackson lusted after the governor's chair throughout the 1930s. By capitalizing on the traditionally acquiescent behavior of the city council, Jackson carefully created his own local machine and staffed with his favorites such key administrative bodies as the Board of Estimates—the agency responsible for managing the city's finances. Jackson was also a successful businessman, urbane in appearance and cosmopolitan in taste; his son, he would invariably remind his audiences, even married prominent opera star Rosa Ponselle. As mayor, he consistently mixed business with politics. In his first term, for example, he slyly channeled $4 million in new insurance payments on city properties to his own insurance firm. And during his entire stint as mayor he gave city business to his favorite banks and lavished his special legal friends with accounts from the city. Jackson created a powerful alliance among attorneys and bankers, even calling upon them to staff the city's emergency relief commission, always confident that they shared his attitudes toward public assistance and fiscal conservatism. At election time, his prestigious coterie of friends repaid him handsomely by organizing business groups in his favor and persuading all who would listen, including the Baltimore *Sun*, that his able leadership and his sound financial policies provided a necessary antidote to the reckless spending practices in Washington, D.C.[19]

Unfriendly to the New Deal, Jackson identified instead with the traditional Democratic party that was not particularly receptive either to the notion of public responsibility or to the people whom such a policy would benefit. He certainly never appealed to the city's black population, which historically had been tied to the Republican party. Even the black majorities among eligible voters in four of the city's wards failed to entice local Democrats to adopt a more conciliatory approach toward Baltimore's rapidly expanding black community. In the first place, Democrats relied on political gerrymandering to minimize the impact of a potential voting bloc among blacks: the heavily black fifth, fourteenth, seventeenth, and eighteenth wards, for example, were divided among three congressional districts and along four councilmanic/state legislative lines (the eighteenth ward alone was divided among three congressional districts). Additionally, Baltimore's Democrats counted on the low voter turnout among blacks to maintain their white majorities. Blacks were politically handicapped by being neither tied to the established Democratic machine nor courted by it. In many instances, moreover, especially in the case of recent migrants to the city, they were also simply unaware of the necessary procedures involved in voting. Particularly objectionable was a 1902 law requiring all newcomers to the state to appear in court a year in advance in order to declare their intention to vote; proof of residency during that year was not sufficient without the initial declaration of intention. A study in 1934 showed that black residents strongly opposed the declaration-of-intention requirement and what they regarded as its selective enforcement. Furthermore, although blacks were linked to the Republican party in a traditionally Democratic city, on occasion they were also rebuffed by Republican candidates. The popular Republican William Broening, who exploited the persistent divisions within the Democratic party to win the mayoral position in 1919 and again in 1927, tried to widen his appeal in the city by disavowing political connections to the black population. In his unsuccessful 1923 mayoral race with Howard Jackson, Broening even allowed the KKK to march in Baltimore, issuing the parade permits that Governor Ritchie had refused to grant. In that contest, the Baltimore *Afro-American*, with little enthusiasm, recommended that city blacks bolt the GOP in favor of Jackson.[20]

The coming of the New Deal and its federal representatives, however, served to educate and politicize Baltimore's black population, attracting voters to the Roosevelt column and encouraging the organization of traditionally neglected components of the black community. Homeless groups joined together, occasionally even crossing the color line, and black tenants in public housing established, with the assistance of the federal government, an elaborate network of services for their community. Never uncritical proponents of the New Deal, blacks nevertheless called for a more active federal government to reduce the racism and conservatism that locally impeded the effectiveness of its programs. The over 400 social clubs and more than 200 churches in the city's black community attempted to spread the message of the necessity for a more enlightened and equitable government. The PUL also cooperated in this effort, taking the message of citizen action and public responsibility to all working-class neighborhoods regardless of color. It encouraged integration in all its activities, but it especially promoted the organization of black residents; of the league's twenty-five neighborhood-based locals in the city, ten were black. Finally, the City-Wide Young People's Forum—organized in 1931 in response to the problem of unemployment among blacks—expanded its activities as a result of New Deal initiatives. In 1933 the forum took its cue from the National Recovery Administration, organizing boycotts of businesses that not only failed to display the Blue Eagle but also refused to hire blacks; this "Buy Where You Can Work" movement resulted in the hiring of blacks at area A & P grocery stores, in "five and dime" stores, and in the stalls of the Lafayette Market.[21]

Recognition of what William Curran himself called "a decided Roosevelt swing" among the "laboring classes" ultimately forced local Democrats at least to posture more favorably toward the New Deal during election times. Politicians were also influenced by the less-than-subtle threats from such groups as the organized garment workers of the ACW, who in 1936, for example, warned Mayor Jackson not to do "anything against the election" of Roosevelt or else he would face their "displeasure at the polls." Beginning in January 1934, thousands of workers annually braved the winter weather to celebrate Roosevelt's birthday, waving Blue Eagle flags and shouting support for the New Deal until they were hoarse. In an attempt to secure stronger state support for the national administration, voters in 1934 even elected a Republican governor, who was purportedly more in favor of the New Deal than were the Democrats.[22]

Before losing to Republican Harry Nice in 1934, Albert Ritchie had constructed a formidable state machine, which had delivered him the gubernatorial seat without fail since 1919. Derided as "King Ritchie" because of his long tenure as governor and his genteel Virginia ancestry, the articulate and ambitious governor of Maryland shaped the Democratic party in accordance with his Southern tradition and position of privilege. His ardent commitment to state sovereignty and to limited government particularly appealed to Maryland's rural counties, where hostility toward the financing of public works in the city and toward unemployment relief, especially for blacks, ran high throughout the decade. Two brutal lynchings of black men on the rural Eastern Shore in 1931 and 1933 symbolized the racial hostility that too often distorted public policy in the state.[23]

As an adept politician, Ritchie also managed, at least in the 1920s, to endear himself to Baltimore's political leaders. He successfully pushed through legislation in 1921 increasing the representation of Baltimore in both houses of the state assembly, though the city—with half the state's population—was still limited to 15 percent of the state's representation in the Senate and 31 percent in the House of Delegates. Moreover, even in the 1930s Ritchie at least recognized, if he did not usually act upon, the demographic changes occurring in the state that were responsible for Baltimore's disproportionate share of the problem of unemployment relief. The accelerating process of urbanization in the twentieth century meant that between 1910 and 1940 many of the poorest residents of rural counties flocked to the city in search of jobs. By 1930, Baltimore not only held half of the state's people but also contained more than half of Maryland's blacks. The nation's eighth-largest city in the 1930s, Baltimore had the fourth-largest black population and contained the largest percentage of blacks of the nation's ten largest cities. The census of 1920 documented a population decline in thirteen of Maryland's twenty-three counties, and the 1930 census showed that nearly 60 percent of the city's blacks had been born in Maryland, most of them having migrated to Baltimore from rural areas. Throughout the 1930s, however, Maryland counties, gladly shed of their unemployed blacks and whites, refused to recognize their responsibility for these people, siding with the traditional Democratic politics best expressed in Ritchie's rhetoric of fiscal restraint and restricted government. Only the threats from municipal officials to return to the counties the city's new migrants, and from the federal government to halt all assistance to the state, forced county legislators to make even modest financial concessions in the area of public relief. And despite the programs that brought not merely relief but new roads, bridges, and schools throughout the state, these county legislators remained persistently opposed to the federal government's increased role in the affairs of the state.[24]

When it came to the issue of Prohibition, however, many of the state's sharpest critics of the expanded federal power of the New Deal were staunch supporters of a nationally imposed ban on alcohol. In this case, increased federal authority was both morally correct and socially necessary. Governor Ritchie's strict adherence to state sovereignty on this issue—and his renowned wetness—won him the enmity of not a few Marylanders, who labeled him "a menace to the good morals" of the entire state. And from their perspective, the city of Baltimore also deserved that epithet: dripping wet and notorious for its hostile treatment of "revenooers," who claimed to have been "thrown to the wolves" in certain neighborhoods, Baltimore remained proudly defiant of the Eighteenth Amendment, boasting of its noncompliance, advertising Crain Highway as "Bootleg Boulevard," and even continuing the illegal production of alcohol at the U.S. Industrial Alcohol plant. The struggle between the wets and the drys continued throughout the 1920s and early 1930s, frequently obscuring more pressing problems and producing what columnist Frank Kent called politics "in a sorry, soggy, sloppy state." Baltimore emerged as the battleground not only for residents and federal agents during their periodic raids but also for the war of words between such leading wet authorities as Ritchie and the acerbic H. L. Mencken, and one of the nation's most powerful spokesmen for the dry cause, Bishop James Cannon.[25]

When Franklin Roosevelt in March 1933 signed the bill legalizing 3.2 percent beer while the Twenty-first Amendment wended its way through the ratification process, Baltimoreans responded joyously with "gala welcomes for beer" throughout the city. Mayor Jackson, however, almost immediately dimmed their enthusiasm by attempting to restrict the sale of beer to city-licensed dispensaries. Local tavern owners decried the move,

railing against the proposed $250 licensing fee. Supported by city politi-
cians who relied on the carefully controlled politicking that took place in
their taverns and saloons, the owners waged a successful fight against the
mayor; Jackson agreed to drop the idea of dispensaries altogether and to
reduce the fee to a mere $50. With the licensing problem resolved, the city
began the celebration; at one minute past midnight on 1 April, beer trucks
escorted by thousands of cheering spectators delivered the first legal beer
in more than a decade to taverns and beer gardens throughout the city.
When the beer arrived, the festivities began at the Germania Turnverein
and other local clubs, where thousands of thirsty patrons waited to be
served. Noisy and happy crowds also gathered at the breweries themselves;
1,500 residents shouted their approval when loaded trucks left the Globe
brewery on South Hanover Street. Stationed at his favorite hotel bar, the
"omnibibulous" Mr. Mencken posed for cameras, eagerly downing his
first glass of new beer. It was not surprising, then, that Baltimore voters
ratified the repeal amendment by a 10-to-1 margin. Governor Ritchie
elevated the occasion to one of despotism versus democracy, touting repeal
as a "rededication of the people of America to the precepts of Democracy."
Less confident of his political support outside the city limits, Mayor
Jackson—a reformed alcoholic and, as always, angling for the governor's
chair—made no similarly lofty declarations about the significance of
repeal.[26]

Baltimoreans took particular pleasure in the return of beer, coming, as it
did, on the heels of a serious banking crisis in the city. Major difficulties
had begun in September 1931 when one of the city's largest banks, the
Baltimore Trust Company, impressively located in a thirty-two-story sky-
scraper built as part of the boom of the 1920s, closed its mammoth, gilded
doors. (Reorganized and revived by the Reconstruction Finance Corporation, the Baltimore Trust Company ultimately reopened for business—but
as late as 1936 its depositors had received only one-third of their money,
and not until after the war were the accounts settled.) Another run on the
banks occurred in 1932 when the medium-sized Park Bank failed completely; subsequent investigations resulted in criminal charges against the
bank's officers, one of whom shot himself during the trial. In February
1933, depositors, already alarmed by problems in the city's banks, pan-
icked at the news of additional failures in other cities and states: they
jammed the city's banks, lining up for blocks to withdraw their savings.
Within a few days, over thirteen million dollars had been withdrawn and
about a dozen banks were without funds. Another of the city's major

banks, Union Trust, despite its privileged position as a repository for state and municipal monies, ceased to operate for a number of months.[27]

Like the governors of some twenty other states, Ritchie responded to the crisis by calling a bank holiday. Local radio stations broadcast his appeals to depositors for patience and restraint and carried his self-styled lectures on the principles of finance. The state legislature hurriedly adopted an emergency banking bill that substantially enhanced the powers of the state bank commissioner; Governor Ritchie then extended the holiday in order to implement the legislation, which also authorized all banks to issue certificates in lieu of money to those who were withdrawing from their accounts. In early March, the focus of the drama shifted to Washington when the newly inaugurated president declared a national banking holiday, temporarily suspending all financial transactions in the nation's banking institutions. Congress then passed legislation strengthening the Federal Reserve system and extending borrowing privileges to nonmember banks.[28]

At the time, the bank holiday pleased few people save the bankers themselves. Unable to cash checks or withdraw money, many people were unable to pay bills or buy groceries. Frustrated municipal workers, with city checks they could not cash, threatened to strike until Mayor Jackson reversed his initial position that "City Hall is not in the check-cashing business" and authorized the city to cash checks for its employees. Small retailers, unable to replenish their stock, complained of "bank holiday food shortages." The certificate system irritated many bank customers, who strongly objected to having to "borrow against your own money." Hungry residents relied on credit at the neighborhood store in order to get food, and the relief agencies reported holiday-related increases in the number of people seeking assistance. The holiday created hardship for some and inconvenience for many. Even the traffic court was disrupted, for offenders were unable to cash checks in order to pay their fines until a policy of selective leniency was adopted, with no one, according to an official of the court, "detained in jail with the exception of one Negro." And the repercussions of the holiday were felt even in the city's houses of worship: area clergy complained of sharp declines in church attendance, some attributing the disappointing turnout to the inability of church members to offer their usual donations, while others worried that the decline indicated a more pervasive spiritual disillusionment and took to the pulpits and the press to instruct their followers not to "blame God for closed banks."[29]

Most people simply remained uninformed, for the city's major newspapers failed to carry the story of an inquiry that disclosed improprieties on the part of state and municipal officials, city bankers, and one of Baltimore's most prestigious law firms. At the insistence of council member Thomas D'Alesandro, Jr., who suggested that the burden of the holiday had been borne inequitably, Governor Ritchie requested and received a list of all withdrawals over $10,000 that had occurred immediately before the holiday; topping the list was Baltimore itself with a $3-million withdrawal, followed by the Baltimore and Ohio Railroad and other major corporations, the state of Maryland, and wealthy individuals—including A. S. Abell, owner of the *Sun*, which refused to print the story or the list. Only the city's Socialist paper, the *Maryland Leader*, offered full coverage and printed the list in its entirety. Confronted with enormous pressure from bankers, the press, and the state banking commission, the state assembly ultimately decided against a formal investigation. The banking crisis, Ritchie told the legislators, had passed, and he urged them to cooperate in helping to restore public confidence in the city's financial institutions. Mayor Jackson agreed. On 14 March, when banks throughout the nation opened for business, most of Baltimore's banks also resumed operation.[30]

President Roosevelt's actions on banking and beer won him the praise of many Baltimoreans, including the editors of the *Sun*. They crowed that "Mr. Roosevelt *is* a leader" and commended his "speed and initiative."[31] They toasted the new president in taverns and tea rooms and applauded his eagerness to deal with the economic depression. There remained, however, the more pressing problem of unemployment relief, and that issue proved more divisive and persistent. In the winter of 1933, Baltimoreans, to be sure, could now legally drink a glass of beer—but it now cost 10 cents, or twice what it had before Prohibition. After 14 March, they could use the city's banks with more confidence; but there were still many who had lost all their savings, and there were the painful memories of such tragedies as the case of the Italian immigrant who, upon learning of his lost savings, jumped from the Calvert Street bridge into the Jones Falls. Finally, there were the 20 percent of Baltimore's workers without jobs; one family in six was dependent on relief from the dwindling resources of the private agencies. The real challenge of providing assistance to those in need would provoke tension and resentment at all levels of government and throughout all segments of society. Rather than fostering a sense of community concern, the concept of public responsibility often strained intergovernmental relations, pitted business leaders against social workers, and divided "reliefers" from the rest of society. But the actions of the federal government also served to promote collective action among society's underprivileged groups. The welfare role of government at both the national and the local levels undeniably changed in the 1930s, but the process, as the next chapter suggests, was an uneven one, punctuated by spasms of reform and reaction.

CHAPTER 2

Private Relief and Public Assistance

The Origins of Municipal Welfare

"For the first time since the beginning of the depression," Baltimore Mayor Howard Jackson boasted in 1937, "the entire administration of direct relief is in the hands of one of the regular departments of the City Government."[1] In heralding this new era of municipal responsibility, Jackson confounded his critics and supporters alike. Committed to voluntarism, he had frequently denounced the New Deal as a dangerous departure from traditional federal policy. But in 1935, when the federal government terminated the Federal Emergency Relief Administration and returned responsibility for direct relief to the cities and states, Jackson protested, urging the federal government to continue its rightful obligations. Even with these apparent inconsistencies, Jackson perfectly illustrated the complexity of conservative change within a federal-local framework. Until 1937 he remained hopeful that the problem of unemployment would either disappear or return to a level manageable by private agencies. He consistently resisted the city's permanent involvement in the distribution of relief, preferring to rely instead on temporary measures to handle what he regarded as an emergency situation. But his own fiscal conservatism compelled him in the end to turn to the city's newly created Department of Welfare to meet the needs of the unemployed. That decision meant the institutionalization of public welfare at the local level and represented an important dimension of the rudimentary welfare state under construction in the 1930s.

The development of public welfare in the 1930s, while hardly constituting either the provision of adequate relief or the acceptance of sufficient responsibility on the parts of state, local, and federal governments, represented complex processes that included the unprecedented interaction of federal and local governments. It also suggested the growth of a popular acceptance of public assistance, despite persistent animosities toward the poor and the dole, and signaled the changing politics of fiscal conservatism and municipal responsibility. To describe these changes as conservative is accurate but incomplete, and to discount their significance is misleading.

In 1927 the national economy passed through a brief recession as investments declined and consumer consumption fell off. National recovery began early in 1928, but in Baltimore the recession dragged on throughout the year. Unemployment increased significantly, to nearly 10 percent of the work force. Relief requirements severely taxed the resources of the private charities, even forcing the city's largest agency, the Family Welfare Association (FWA), to close its doors to new families seeking assistance—marking the first "refusal" in its history. The city's other major private agencies—the Associated Jewish Charities, the Salvation Army, and the Bureau of Catholic Charities—also experienced significant increases in their case loads. Taking the lead, the FWA responded to the crisis by urging Republican Mayor William Broening to assume the responsibility for relief and to encourage area employers to help their former employees. The FWA informed municipal authorities that it no longer counted relief distribution among its priorities but "regard[ed] itself as existing primarily for the treatment and prevention of family problems." But despite its objections to being involved in relief-giving activities and its preference for comprehensive social service, it was obliged in the early 1930s to fulfill the role expected of it by the local government and the community at large: as the FWA lamented, it was viewed as "a large central relief fund into which all the community may dip for the meeting of any sort of financial need." In short, the agency that initially assumed the largest share of the burden of unemployment relief denied its responsibility only to be trapped by the historical traditions of private charity.[2]

As early as 1930, when the FWA reported that it had no funds, the city began to experience the "breakdown of local resources"—an innocuous-sounding process that in fact involved near-starvation and misery for thousands of families in the depression. The Community Fund provided emergency funds to enable the FWA, as a member agency, to resume its operations. With much reluctance the Baltimore Board of Estimates also contributed money to the FWA, allowing the agency to complete the year without a further lapse in service. But such stopgap measures failed to meet relief needs as the city's unemployment rate climbed from 11 percent in late 1930 to over 19 percent in late 1931. Workers who had been thrown off their jobs thronged police stations, relief offices, and even city hall in search of money, food, or simply advice. By January 1931, nineteen bread lines crowded the city's streets. The FWA took stock of the relief situation and its own resources and informed the city that it carried nearly 80 percent of the city's unemployment cases, that the number of families needing relief had increased 96 percent in just six months, and that the cost of that aid had jumped from $173,496 in 1930 to $614,354 in 1931. It predicted the imminent exhaustion of its funds: "Within the first few weeks [of 1931] it was evident that the FWA was expected by the entire community to carry the greater part of the burden of unemployment relief and it was equally evident that our available financial resources would be exhausted before spring."[3]

Other private agencies also complained of financial strain and inadequate governmental assistance. The Jewish Social Service Bureau, for example, which conducted the major relief activities of the Associated Jewish Charities, found the city unresponsive to the needs of the unemployed. Consequently, the bureau created its own advisory committee to study unemployment and to establish a link between industry and social service, and it helped form an Emergency Employment Bureau of the Jewish Educational Alliance. Even with a smaller relief constituency than that of the FWA, the bureau had a deficit of $133,895 in 1930 and expected worse for 1931. The agencies that had traditionally assisted Baltimore's black community felt the effects of declining resources even earlier than the other special-interest charities. Serving those struck hardest by the depression—those who had been displaced by whites "performing tasks once thought to be exclusively for Negroes"—the black charities were forced to send their needy to the FWA; by 1931, 43 percent of the FWA's 25,000 relief families were black. The Salvation Army had to reduce its food allowances and periodically close its doors to the homeless and the hungry because of its limited resources. Even the city's police stations, which had provided shelters and handouts in many neighborhoods, restricted their relief activities, and after 1 March 1931 they discontinued their assistance altogether. The police commissioner regretted the action, but he explained that the department had already conducted a campaign drive for funds and had distributed more than $72,000 in food, fuel, and clothing during the winter of 1930–31. Moreover, he noted that in certain districts, generous police officers, unaccustomed to seeing their neighbors go without food, were giving away their own sack lunches.[4]

Of all the agencies, only the Bureau of Catholic Charities (BCC) affirmed its ability to meet the needs of Catholic jobless. But, as it freely admitted, its policies did not altogether mirror those of the other agencies. Emphasizing religious faith and social tradition, Catholic charities clung tenaciously to the doctrine of private charity and particularly opposed the increasing tendency to use trained workers instead of community volunteers. In May 1933, for example, at a meeting of Maryland and Washington, D.C., social agencies, speakers routinely praised the decision of the federal government to provide relief for the unemployed and enthusiastically agreed that the government had "entered the social welfare field to stay"— but "the only speaker taking a different view" was the director of the National Conference of Catholic Charities, who warned against abandoning tradition and relinquishing private responsibility for unemployment relief, arguing that private agencies "deprived of the direct relief appeal" would ultimately lose their essential voluntary financial support. Even as late as 1936 the Baltimore director of the BCC, Rev. Edwin L. Leonard, referred to himself as a "heretic" among social workers because he favored the continued role of private agencies in unemployment relief and balked at the trend of "going public" in social welfare, adding that it was "contrary to the Catholic viewpoint and I believe it is contrary to Maryland tradition of private charity." He railed against the reliance on professionals, maintaining that volunteers frequently proved more suitable than trained workers "just out of Goucher College [who] never saw a poor family before." Unemployment relief, he concluded, had been and would "continue to be regarded as our responsibility and we want to bear it." But in 1931 that responsibility belonged wholly to the private charities, and with the exception of the BCC, they wanted to be rid of it.[5]

Accustomed to relying on private contributions and expecting little municipal assistance, the officials of the major charities appealed to the Baltimore Association of Commerce to raise money for relief activities. In February 1931 the president of the BAC, together with some of the city's philanthropic and religious leaders, formed the Citizens' Emergency Relief Committee. The committee launched an extensively advertised campaign but set its goal at the paltry sum of $300,000. Mayor Broening authorized the first contribution of $50,000 from city funds. Full-page advertisements in the newspapers, pictures of those in distress accompanied by impassioned stories of hard times, and radio appeals by local personalities brought pledges from concerned citizens and businesses and cooperation from the Baltimore Federation of Churches, which urged member clergy to appeal on behalf of the committee at their services. The committee's efforts succeeded, but within weeks the private charities had expended all the campaign money and the city had to provide additional money to forestall the complete collapse of private relief. By the end of 1931, the agencies were forced once again to appeal to the BAC's Emergency Committee. With equal fervor, the committee conducted another fund drive in December 1931, canvassing the city, advertising and propagandizing; by the end of the year, $670,000 had been provided to the private organizations. The private agencies remained desperately short of funds, however, and the committee, reluctant to appeal to the public a third time, terminated its activities.[6]

The efforts of the Citizens' Emergency Relief Committee underscored the limits of voluntarism and of business commitment to social welfare and demonstrated the need for the city to assume the responsibility for relief. But between 1928 and 1932, municipal action remained sporadic and inadequate. Mayor Broening rebuffed the FWA's pleas for municipal assistance in 1928 and reaffirmed his faith in voluntarism, although he created a Committee on Unemployment to study the problem. In late 1928 this committee proposed administrative changes, but a slight decrease in unemployment encouraged Broening to lay aside even those modest recommendations. His procrastination brought protests from the FWA, members of the Committee on Unemployment, and the unemployed themselves, one of whom observed that "declarations do not relieve unemployment, want, poverty or sickness. What we need is action. Action on the part of Congress and action on the part of the municipal and state officials."[7]

Although the October crash in 1929 helped crack such municipal complacency, the results were negligible. When, for example, President Herbert Hoover urged local and state officials to combat the depression by supporting public works construction, Maryland officials, with considerable fanfare, agreed to cooperate. But Broening's grandstanding produced little. Two years later, in an editorial entitled "Pious Hope," the *Evening*

Sun noted that, although several projects had been suggested, "not a lick of construction work has been done on any of them." Broening did succeed in establishing the city's Employment Stabilization Commission, which served as the local counterpart to the President's Emergency Committee for Employment (PECE). Like the PECE, the local commission initially attempted to promote enthusiasm and confidence in the efficacy of self-help and community responsibility. At Broening's insistence the commission was designed, not to study the unemployed or their problems, but to "direct a scientific study of industry." Accordingly, it worked closely with industrialists, not the jobless. The commission's limited focus and Broening's constant professions that it represented no cure for unemployment pleased at least the *Evening Sun* editors, who praised commission members for not raising the hopes of the unemployed, referred to its obvious weaknesses as "well meant," and called its restricted actions "honest work."[8]

In late 1930, at the request of Employment Stabilization Commission members, Mayor Broening formed the Municipal Free Employment Service. Following Broening's conventional emphasis on the business community, the Employment Service focused its activities on the "working place that wants a man." This city effort contrasted sharply with that of the Jewish Social Service Bureau, which established its employment bureau "not to stimulate business, but simply to place people who really need help." By 1932, the commission frankly acknowledged that its emphasis on voluntarism, including job-sharing schemes, and its attempts at job finding had failed miserably. Departing from its original purpose, it urged the adoption of statewide unemployment insurance, even drafting sample legislation that drew praise from such diverse groups as the Catholic church and the city's Socialist party.[9]

But the Stabilization Commission had moved toward public responsibility far in advance of most state and municipal politicians. Democratic Governor Albert Ritchie, who frequently applauded the "spirit of American initiative and self-help" and repeated his belief that "the responsibility for unemployment relief rests primarily on the people of the community," failed to endorse the insurance bill, thereby dooming it to failure. Mayor Broening also ignored the issue, focusing instead on his own unemployment program—a naive but widely publicized campaign to "Beautify Baltimore." His scheme called for homeowners to hire the jobless for household repairs in order to provide work, not charity. Responding to Broening's appeal for community participation, schools encouraged children to scour their neighborhoods in search of needed repairs, women's groups pledged to cooperate by hiring the jobless, and the telephone company inserted printed appeals in customers' bills. But in the neighborhoods where children could not attend school for want of sufficient clothing and where telephone service either had never reached or had long since been disconnected, this form of community spirit provided little relief. Despite Broening's praise of the program, the Stabilization Commission conceded that "most of the activities reported were of minor importance as regards employment."[10]

Broening's popular beautification program, timed for the 1931 municipal elections, still failed to prevent his defeat for reelection. The city's traditionally Democratic majority returned Howard Jackson to the office he had held from 1923 to 1927. Broening laid his defeat to his Republicanism, the economic depression, and the city's inadequate role in assisting the unemployed. In leaving office, he advised Jackson to do what he had failed to do as mayor: create a department to assist the jobless and eliminate "this shortcoming on the part of the city." But Jackson was not prepared to expand the municipal bureaucracy in order to provide relief. Although he promised municipal assistance "whenever the existing agencies are overburdened," he then turned down the Community Fund's request for emergency money. Like Broening, he continued to emphasize the viability of voluntarism and to denounce the dole. Jackson even proposed his own superficial scheme of having municipal employees donate a day each month of their work schedule to the unemployed because, he explained, it "is much better to give the unemployed work than to give them charity."[11]

In early 1932 the private relief agencies announced that they would be unable to provide unemployment assistance after March. Because the FWA had already reduced food budgets and restricted the number of new applicants, temporary community relief centers sprang up to ensure that neighbors were not without food. Citizen groups established barter services, ethnic communities held dances and bazaars to raise funds for those in need, and many clubs and organizations turned their activities to providing relief. Black fraternal groups were particularly important in providing badly needed assistance to black neighborhoods. These community activities scarcely obscured the severity of the problem for the FWA, but they were successful in persuading Jackson to adopt a wait-and-see approach. He responded to the agencies' official announcement of relief curtailment by denying its necessity: "I do not believe," the mayor declared, "that these agencies have all reached the limits of their abilities to meet the situation." If the problem were as grave as pictured, he challenged, the situation could be alleviated "in twenty-four hours." Citizen groups and private agencies alike ridiculed Jackson for this claim.[12]

By mid-March even Jackson believed the FWA, for it began closing its offices. When he learned that over 27,000 families or relief "cases" dependent on the FWA's meager monthly allotment of $24.87 would be left to fend for themselves, he urged the Board of Estimates to appropriate $50,000 for unemployment relief—but he announced that the city would carry the burden for only a few weeks. During these weeks he discussed the problem with business associates and municipal officials. Facing an unemployment rate of 20 percent, Jackson realized that the problem of relief could not, at least in the short run, be returned to the private agencies. By the end of the month he had assumed complete charge of relief activities, urging the city council to grant him emergency powers for an indefinite time; requesting that the private agencies cooperate with the city in administering relief assistance; discussing such long-term plans as a city-state relief bond issue; and reluctantly acquiescing in Governor Ritchie's decision to defer calling a special session of the legislature until the city had exhausted all of its resources. To oversee the city's relief program, Jackson created an Emergency Relief Committee and an Emergency Work Bureau. The committee consisted of Jackson's hand-picked favorites, including the city auditor and important businessmen such as J. Warren Belcher, who also headed the Emergency Work Bureau but received his pay from his regular employer, United Railways. At Jackson's request other major companies, like the Gas and Electric Company, donated executives one or two days per week to help organize the city's relief administration. The private charities also agreed to continue to dispense relief assistance.[13]

Although Jackson's administrative organization of relief advanced smoothly, financing that relief produced political and economic conflict. Governor Ritchie promised that in its January 1933 session the legislature would authorize a state bond issue to reimburse the city for its relief expenditures; with that understanding, Jackson borrowed nearly $3 million during the remainder of 1932 to pay for relief. Characteristically, as January approached, Ritchie sidestepped his pledge, even questioning the legality of a state bond issue for municipal relief, and instead urged greater economy in the city budget. In preparing the 1933 budget, however, Jackson had not only to deal with the uncertainties of state assistance but also to confront the complaints of over 60,000 angry citizens who had organized the Taxpayers' War Council. The council primarily represented real-estate interests, but the National Housewives League also lent its support, as did the Baltimore Federation of Labor. Increased property taxes to finance unemployment relief, the council warned the mayor, would not be tolerated. More than 4,000 irate citizens gathered at a mass meeting and heckled city council members who attempted to talk about tax delinquency, unemployment, and a shrinking tax base. The citizens clamored about their own hard times, threats of foreclosure, and assistance to unworthy unemployed.[14]

In response to the taxpayers' protests and to Governor Ritchie's reluctance to help the city, Jackson accepted the governor's challenge to find greater economy in the budget. He announced that the city had no intention of financing relief permanently, and he prepared a budget with practically no provision for relief, dramatically slashing funds for all the city's departments and even reducing the tax rate. Ritchie immediately retreated, maintaining that his comments about the bond issue had been misunderstood and reaffirming the state's responsibility to assist the city with its relief burden. When the state legislature convened, its Baltimore members introduced legislation for the state bond issue, but urban-rural tensions forced a downward revision of the bill from $15 million to $12 million and delayed passage until 3 April, the last day of the session.[15]

Until September 1933 the Emergency Relief Committee and the Emergency Work Bureau, in cooperation with the four private agencies, handled the city's relief problems. The committee allowed the agencies to investigate clients and dispense relief as they had before municipal intervention; it even accepted the agencies' estimates of relief needs, meeting once a week to review the figures and forward them to the Board of Estimates for approval. It did, however, in agreement with the agencies, enact a few economy measures—it reduced the food budget to $1.00 per person per week, decreased allotments for rent and milk, and eliminated altogether any assistance for overdue bills or back rent. The major change from the private relief system involved the creation of "made work" projects for relief clients under the Emergency Work Bureau. The private agencies and bureau members agreed that even "made work" "preserves the self-respect of the recipients of charity and prevents the growth of inertia." Although it conceded that the projects were minor—they included such tasks as clearing brush and painting hospital corridors—the bureau boasted that in December 1932 nearly 70 percent of all families assisted by the city had worked for their relief. In practice, then, because such a large percentage of clients worked for their relief, the private agencies became increasingly removed from the actual dispensation of money for food; they still investigated initial claims of need and made monthly visits to the client families, but the "working" families received their pay through the Emergency Bureau itself. Only the Bureau of Catholic Charities maintained close supervision over the "made-work" cases, visiting the families weekly and disbursing clients' wages through the parish priest.[16]

The transition from private to public relief in the city was encouraged by events on the national level. On 12 May 1933, Congress authorized a half-billion dollars in relief money for state and local relief agencies. President Franklin Roosevelt selected Harry Hopkins to head the Federal Emergency Relief Administration (FERA), which was to be in charge of dispensing funds. Because federal regulations required that money be given only to public agencies, the organizational structure of Baltimore's relief system had to be changed in order to be eligible for FERA money. Mayor Jackson immediately authorized a "comprehensive survey of private and public social welfare work and needs" to determine "the line between private and public social work." The *Sun* correctly noted that the federal government wanted a municipal welfare department that would follow uniform procedures in the processing and distribution of relief; as that was not the situation in the city, the *Sun* predicted "revolutionary changes" in "Baltimore's machinery for handling unemployment relief."[17]

What emerged was hardly revolutionary but represented a compromise between Baltimore's traditions and federal policy dictates. Despite the federal requirement, Jackson consistently opposed the creation of a welfare department to handle an "emergency" problem, fearing the permanent institutionalization of unemployment relief: "If ever unemployment relief," he warned, "becomes a definite part of the city's governmental machinery it will cling there as a budgetary barnacle most difficult to scrape off when normal business conditions are restored." Jackson instead created the Baltimore Emergency Relief Commission (BERC), which, in effect, merely combined the Emergency Relief Committee and the Work Bureau.[18]

On 1 September 1933 BERC, established as part of the Maryland Emergency Relief Administration (MERA), took charge of relief in Baltimore. Unemployment registered at over 20 percent of the work force, and more than 10 percent of the city's 804,874 people were on relief. Members of BERC were predominantly business leaders and bankers who pledged a "businesslike" administration of relief. They shared Jackson's concern

about the proper disposition of the money provided by the federal government. Likening themselves to a board of trustees, they described their
function as primarily policy making and left the actual relief distribution to
BERC's two chief executives—J. Warren Belcher, the former head of the
Emergency Work Bureau who became BERC's new administrative secretary, and Anna Ward, the former executive secretary of the FWA who
became BERC's new director of social work. Like its predecessor, BERC
worked with the private agencies, even incorporating most of the staffs of
all four agencies into its organization. Earlier eligibility standards were
also adopted: to obtain relief, a client had to be a city resident of at least
one year's standing, in visible need without additional resources, and
willing to work, if able, for assistance. Assistance was awarded only after
scrutinizing family and financial records, and the amount of relief continued to be based on family size and degree of need as determined by the
social worker investigating the case.[19]

This emphasis on the practical continuity in relief distribution, however,
obscures the important changes that BERC represented. Not only did it
officially mark a break with voluntarism, but the basis of decision making
changed significantly: relief policies for the next four years would no
longer be made by social workers but by business leaders. Of course, the
stage had been set for these changes with Jackson's establishment of the
Emergency Relief Committee and the Work Bureau. But under BERC,
officials' salaries would no longer be paid by corporations. From the
outset, moreover, BERC attempted to supervise the practices of the social
workers themselves and to wage a more vigorous campaign against possible relief fraud. Consequently, the commission's members spent considerable time and money to detect "chiseling" and to conduct "client eligibility" studies, and these studies convinced them that the private agencies had
been too "liberal" in accepting relief clients. Particularly in "congested
colored areas" and a "slum area in an Italian section" of the city, according
to BERC, too "little emphasis had been placed upon the financial investigation," too "many families were receiving relief who might provide for
themselves," and, most distressing, "the attitude of the client was a passive
acceptance of relief as their due." Anna Ward denied the charges and
defended the record of the private agencies, but other BERC members
accused the social workers of pampering the jobless and initiated a new
system involving a "second check" of each applicant's background. These
attitudes and policies contrasted sharply with those of the earlier Emergency Relief Committee, which had merely rubberstamped the private

agencies' assessment of relief needs and had concurred with their belief that "undeserving cases receiving aid are so few in number as to be negligible." Mutual suspicion, not cooperation, now characterized the relationships between BERC and the private agencies; some social workers even feared that BERC members shared the sentiments of one city council member who denounced the private agencies as "a group of racketeers handling city funds."[20]

Despite BERC's determination to improve the distribution of relief, to be more efficient than the private agencies, and to reduce the case load, within seven months after taking over, its own load had nearly doubled to 42,425 cases, representing 20 percent of the city's population. The increase resulted directly from declines in employment in manufacturing and construction, from the extensive national publicity advertising relief assistance, and from the willingness of "many self-respecting needy persons" to "apply for relief from a governmental agency financed by taxation" rather than from a "private 'charity' "—and it resulted, too, from Baltimore's incomplete participation in the New Deal's Civil Works Administration (CWA) program, which was started in November 1933 to provide temporary emergency employment. But responsibility for the latter failure also belonged in large measure to BERC itself. Local officials resented federal control of the CWA program and complained of the speed that federal officials demanded in putting people to work. Mayor Jackson repudiated the program; apparently forgetting the city's own earlier make-work program, he harshly objected to hastily devised projects like the elimination of rats in the city and denounced what he termed the excessive wages paid to CWA workers. Officials of BERC very reluctantly reassigned their relief recipients to CWA jobs, preferring instead to provide CWA jobs for the newly unemployed, who were traditionally unaffected by idleness and were therefore considered by BERC to be more worthy of the relatively high-paying jobs; consequently, only 26.5 percent of BERC heads of households held CWA jobs. But in March 1934, when the program was terminated, BERC had to take the entire CWA population onto its rolls, pushing its relief load to 64,876 cases (or roughly 30 percent of the city's total population). Neither the public-private arrangement of BERC nor its record case load pleased federal authorities.[21]

Although the establishment of BERC had effectively displaced the leadership of private charities, federal officials did not believe that it adequately distinguished between public and private relief activities. In 1933 and 1934, FERA field observers visited Baltimore and reported that the city had not moved beyond its tradition of private relief. One observer informed Hopkins that the problem of "deepest concern" and "most acute in Baltimore where a public welfare department has never been established" was "the relationship of the private agency to the emergency relief forces." Another field reporter criticized the bookkeeping methods of the Bureau of Catholic Charities and condemned its practice of assisting blacks only through its three "colored parishes"; the connection between public assistance and the private agency, he wrote, formed "a serious matter in Baltimore, where racial and church alignments in relief work are pronounced." Almost all the FERA investigators found the city's neighborhoods sharply defined by strong loyalties and traditions, prompting one official to argue that the city's refusal to establish a municipal welfare department reflected its desire to continue past relief practices and personnel so that "neighborhood traditions shall be preserved." Such a continuation, he warned, would involve the maintenance of a network of "established contacts and traditions" in determining the eligibility of relief clients and the level of assistance granted. Consequently, factors such as race, ethnicity, friendship and kinship networks, and community status—instead of simple need—figured prominently in the process of distributing relief assistance. Few observers expected the city to change the system voluntarily and create a centralized public relief agency because, they noted, "city officials do not appear to wish this result."[22]

Federal officials continued to press for the establishment of a public welfare department in Baltimore. Citing "too much overhead," they charged that BERC had failed "to construct an efficient organization" and was simply "incompetent to handle the relief situation." The public-private tension became more of a problem for BERC when charges of incompetence took on added credibility as its relief rolls skyrocketed. To determine "why Baltimore has such a large caseload which has been steadily mounting," the FERA began in the summer of 1934 an investigation of the city's peculiar relief administration. There was, however, a time lag between actual practices in Baltimore and decisions in Washington, for by late spring of 1934, BERC officials had in fact already begun slashing the city's relief rolls in response to federal concerns and state budgeting problems. Still, when the FERA began its study, it found Baltimore's relief load of 20 percent of the population to be out of line with the 15 to 16 percent relief load in such cities as St. Louis and Buffalo. The investigators attributed the discrepancy solely to Baltimore's unsatisfactory relief arrangement. The establishment of BERC, they explained, had little effect on the distribution of relief because "the set-up in actuality remained practically unchanged." Their findings corroborated the earlier reports filed by field investigators, which had emphasized the problems created by untrained relief staffs, neighborhood-based private agencies, and an overabundance of businessmen-administrators whose policies dangerously smacked of favoritism for fellow businessmen.[23]

The major problem with the relief administration in Baltimore, according to the FERA study, was the uneasy division between its business leadership and its private social service, which resulted in "a lack of coordination in the whole operation." Aptly describing the city's transitional phase in its development of public welfare, the study referred to BERC as "both a large social work job and a large business enterprise." The reliance on private volunteers to conduct client investigations led to serious questions about professionalism and impartiality. In particular, federal officials, relying on the testimony of black residents and discounting the denials of local officials, strongly suspected that black families received smaller relief allowances than white clients. Still, the sample survey of relief cases completed by the FERA administrators suggested their own problems in observing professional standards: they, for example, regularly accepted rumor and innuendo within the neighborhood as reasonable evidence for removing a client from the relief rolls, and they routinely agreed with local decisions against clients who were found to be "immoral" or "of a very low type." Far more disturbing to federal investigators than the selective professionalism of the city's caseworkers were the arbitrary and idiosyncratic record-keeping methods of the separate private agencies. Even worse, BERC administrators failed to coordinate the reports of private agencies or to provide comprehensible summaries of the data they received. Finally, FERA officials singled out for sharp criticism BERC's practice of direct payment of rent, arguing that such a policy enriched certain BERC officials and their business associates who controlled many of the rental properties in the city's poorest neighborhoods. Indeed, one of BERC's chief administrators also served as the local president of the realtors' association.[24]

As city officials had expected, the FERA study recommended a uniform welfare program directed solely by a public department. Calling for a "sound training program," the report urged the city to abandon its reliance on private agencies, whose policies had produced an unhealthy "paternalism" in the distribution of relief. The study also suggested separating clerical work from public assistance, using uniform case records, observing greater care in granting assistance, and providing more work relief.

This last recommendation underscored the fitful nature of Baltimore's relief policies. Before the introduction of the FERA, when the city distributed relief through the Emergency Work Bureau, most of the relief recipients performed some task in order to receive assistance. With the availability of federal money, however, local officials under BERC merely provided direct relief to their clients and the make-work program declined significantly. The explanation for this policy change was, of course, simple: it was cheaper for the city to provide relief at federal expense than to supply the necessary materials for work projects at municipal expense. Accordingly, FERA officials urged BERC to increase its percentage of work-relief cases and strongly suggested that the city cooperate more closely with the national government in its administration of relief. With federal assistance, the report indicated, Baltimore could move toward adopting a more specialized, efficient, and professional welfare program.[25]

Several factors conditioned BERC's response to the FERA study and helped shape the course of the city's developing system of social welfare. First and foremost, the federal government, also fearful that unemployment relief would become, in Jackson's words, a "budgetary barnacle," attempted to make the nation's cities and states assume a greater share of the relief burden. In Baltimore that effort began as early as December 1933. It involved endless haggling with local and state officials. The ultimate termination of the FERA in 1935 and the delayed establishment of its substitute—the Works Progress Administration (WPA) and the Social Security programs—served in some ways to exacerbate the problem of relief. Secondly, the city and state governments, divided by economic interests and by urban-rural conflicts, failed to agree upon the proper areas of relief responsibility. Finally, organized citizens worked consistently to remind state and national officials, as well as BERC administrators, of their responsibility to assist the needy. Officials of BERC faced a difficult job in attempting to harmonize traditional policies with unprecedented problems.

Angered by the FERA attacks on its managerial efficiency and "business-like" methods, BERC determined to modify its policies, reduce its case load, and reorganize its administration. The financial clash over relief contributions occurring on the local, state, and national levels was even more compelling in altering BERC's practices. As early as December 1933, federal officials had demanded that the state contribute more money toward unemployment assistance, but between October and February, notwithstanding the city's appropriations, Maryland had failed to provide even a penny for relief. In February, Hopkins warned that no more federal money would be forthcoming until the state at least sold the remaining $4 million of the original $12-million bond issue. Governor Ritchie and Mayor Jackson, both courting the 1934 Democratic gubernatorial nomination, regarded the Hopkins announcement not as a directive for action but as an opportunity to swap insults. Irresponsible politicking infuriated federal officials, who stopped short of cutting off federal funds only because of the entreaties from citizen groups and from the director of the Maryland Emergency Relief Administration, Harry Greenstein. The petitions of religious and charity groups and the visits to Washington by members of the Peoples Unemployment League—a Socialist-led but nonpartisan group of about 15,000 members—persuaded the federal government to make a deal with the state and city. Hopkins then agreed to carry the relief burden until 1 June 1934 but demanded that on that date state and local officials present a plan detailing their future contributions to the relief budget. He barely concealed his disgust for the city's and state's sorry performance and warned that it would not be allowed to continue. As one field reporter commented: "Mr. Hopkins has informed the Maryland crowd that they have to put some money into the relief pot, as he does not intend to continue to pay the entire bill."[26]

Yet despite the deals, threats, promises, and investigations, little was accomplished by the 1 June deadline. The *Sun* described the predicament: "Greenstein is waiting for Ritchie and Jackson to do something; Jackson is waiting for Ritchie to do something. And Ritchie is waiting for Greenstein to do something." The state director of the National Emergency Council decried the whole situation, declared the local and state officials to be "at sea," and urged Hopkins to take over the state's entire relief program.[27]

The June meeting with Hopkins produced an uproar. Arriving without the promised plan, local and state representatives still expected to receive federal handouts. But Hopkins was in no mood for further delay. He criticized city and state officials for abusing federal generosity and announced that henceforth all relief expenditures would be evenly shared. Estimating that Maryland would need $18 million for relief in the coming year, he declared that the federal government would contribute half of that amount. He agreed to advance the state $1.5 million to meet current expenses, but even that concession failed to cushion the shock to local and state officials accustomed to federal contributions of over 90 percent of the total cost. One local official bitterly complained that Hopkins, and not the city, would be controlling local relief programs.[28]

In response to this meeting, Governor Ritchie appointed a committee to study the relief issue and Mayor Jackson instructed BERC to slash relief rolls. Both politicians announced that they could not meet the new financial demands, but neither attempted to cooperate in creating a city-state plan for relief. Ritchie instead denounced the city for not upholding its relief responsibilities and suggested increasing taxes to pay for relief. Pointing to the city's sizeable relief population, he added, "When the people once begin feeding at the public trough, it's a hard matter to get them away from it." While Jackson and Ritchie bickered, Maryland Senator Millard Tydings, although no supporter of unemployment relief, attempted to bridge the gap between the state and federal governments, persuading Hopkins to reconsider the fifty-fifty arrangement and work with Ritchie's new committee. On 31 July the FERA and the Ritchie committee reached an agreement on relief contributions for the remainder of the year: the state would sell its remaining bonds and Hopkins would carry 75 to 80 percent of the total relief costs.[29]

At the local level, BERC proceeded with its case-load reductions and administrative reorganization. It first sharply cut relief distribution in the "congested colored" and "slum areas"—places earlier targeted in its eligibility studies. Citizen groups protested the reductions with petitions and demonstrations. City ministers, for example, organized to protest the cuts made at the expense of single men and black families: "Thousands of single men were indiscriminately taken off the roll, leaving them to starve or steal," but "the heaviest portions of the burden caused by the drastic cuts were placed upon the Negro. A group that has suffered most heavily in the economic crisis was made even more miserable." Ignoring the public protest, Jackson directed BERC to continue cutting its rolls and to reduce relief payments. In the first two weeks of July 1934, BERC dropped over 1300 cases. And by mid-month Baltimore exceeded the U.S. average in relief cuts, reducing cases by 9 percent and costs by 18 percent; other cities averaged 2 percent and 4 percent, respectively (indeed, of the nation's thirty-five largest cities, twenty-three increased their case loads and thirty-two increased both cases and costs). By the end of July, Baltimore had only 15.4 percent of its population on relief, down from 16.9 percent in May, whereas other cities averaged 15.6. It had also reduced the size of its weekly relief payments, from $9.99 in May to $8.93 in June. Finally, to cap its retrenchment program, BERC announced that it would no longer directly pay the rents of those on relief but would incorporate rent money into the client's cash budget. The announcement disturbed not only relief clients but also the city's 20,000 landlords who had been regularly receiving BERC payments. The Real Estate Board labeled the new policy "discriminatory and unfair to landlords." The BERC decision to compute rental payments on the basis of 7 percent of the assessed value of the property outraged landlords long accustomed to underassessments and high rents; they denounced the 7 percent rule as "equivalent to confiscation" and threatened to evict families on relief. Even BERC chairman Joseph Healy conceded that the new policy would "result in a number of evictions."[30]

Officials of BERC defended the cuts by pointing to the financial difficulties between the federal and the state and local governments, and to the findings of the FERA study. Discontinuing the direct payment of rent and adopting a policy of "cash relief for all items" represented, according to the commission, a "first step" in the elimination of "paternalism." But not all FERA officials accepted this explanation. Aubrey Williams, assistant FERA director and a liberal New Dealer, for example, denounced the new rental policy as fraudulent. He attacked the percentage rule as sheer "gravy for landlords" and complained that BERC's agreement "to pay those 'chiselers' a certain sum for those conditions which on open market wouldn't rent for anything" really "knock[s] the bottom out of us about Baltimore. . . . We want a new administrator up there," Williams asserted; "we don't make any bones about it."[31]

In July 1934 BERC began its administrative reorganization, creating a new office to supervise all BERC branches in an attempt to conform to FERA recommendations. Howard C. Beck, Jr., a successful businessman and the city auditor, assumed the new post of supervisor in early August. The change sharply diminished the authority of Anna Ward, BERC's director of social work. As the major representative of private relief in BERC, she was an easy target; her displacement offered a simple solution to the FERA's complaint of continued private involvement in public welfare. State relief administrator Harry Greenstein, although himself an official of the Associated Jewish Charities, continued the attack on the private influence by registering his agreement with the FERA study on the "striking shortage of trained workers." He started a new training program in the city and shrewdly appointed a federal official earlier involved in the FERA study to direct the effort. In light of these developments, Ward's departure resulted not only from BERC's distrust of social workers but also from FERA decisions that had made clear the need to establish a truly public department of welfare; ironically, however, with her resignation, BERC lost its most vocal proponent of such a department. Ward's professional training and quest for efficiency had impressed even business-minded BERC, but her connections to private relief and her defense of private social workers and volunteers had made her vulnerable. The influence of the private agencies in relief work continued to decline as graduates of Greenstein's training program replaced private social workers and volunteers in the BERC administration.[32]

But the emergence of a public welfare system did not mean the demise of private charities. Although they had been displaced, private agencies, in many cases even at the instigation of the federal government, continued to assist the city's unemployed by shifting their efforts from distributing relief to advising public authorities, providing counseling and other services for needy families, and joining other organized citizen groups to lobby for better treatment of the unemployed. The scope of the unemployment problem, the private agencies' own disavowal of responsibility for unemployment relief, the city's preference for businessmen over social workers as policy makers, and the intervention of the federal government—all led to the development of a public welfare system and a new role for the private charities and their volunteers.[33]

Despite the administrative reorganization, by the late summer of 1934 Baltimore's relief situation was critical. While BERC continued to slash relief rolls, petitions and letters flooded the offices of both BERC and the FERA, describing children without sufficient food or clothes, homeless families, and ailing jobless. The reduction of milk allotments prompted the city's health commissioner to warn that the "consumption of milk [among children] has reached such a low point that it is having a direct effect in increasing the incidence of rickets." The Socialist newspaper, the *Maryland Leader*, further condemned BERC's milk policies, especially its practice of purchasing milk at 6 ½ cents per quart but charging relief clients 11 cents per quart. Reports from the city schools that children could not begin school because of a lack of proper clothing prompted the Socialist party to establish the "Socialist Party Relief Committee" to collect "money, clothing, shoes, and other such things the givers can afford"; at the insistence of the Peoples Unemployment League, BERC officials cooperated with this effort. To publicize the relief cuts, the PUL daily picketed BERC headquarters, and in August it held a major protest rally. Wearing red arm bands, over one hundred PUL members denounced BERC's practices with signs that read, "Ritchie gets relief in Europe; we can't get it here"—referring to the governor's six-week vacation on the Normandy coast. Retiring BERC director Anna Ward defied the other BERC officials by meeting with the demonstrators; she acknowledged the inadequacy of the relief payments but pointed helplessly to the commission's limited and uncertain funds. Other BERC officials, however, responded to the demonstration by calling the city police. Twenty of the pickets were arrested, including Adelaide Mitchell, a Socialist agitator, PUL member, and wife of the Socialist 1934 gubernatorial candidate, Professor Broadus Mitchell of the Johns Hopkins University. Attorneys for PUL attempted unsuccessfully to get an injunction prohibiting police from arresting "peaceful picketers," and Ward acidly observed, "I don't see any point in arresting them." Apparently neither did the court, which dismissed the charges. Irritated by BERC and police actions, the PUL renewed its protest the following day, even gaining the additional support of two of the city's most respected ministers. The *Sun* barely disguised its incredulity in a story entitled "Pastor to be Picketer."[34]

The relief situation thereafter provided little encouragement to either the jobless or the organized citizen groups. Financial problems persisted, as did uncertainties over proper governmental responsibility. In early 1935, federal officials began pressuring the Maryland Emergency Relief Administration for an agreement on state contributions for financing relief. Anticipating jurisdictional disputes, MERA officials instructed BERC to stop taking new applications for relief and to prepare for even more reductions. Then MERA turned to the state legislature and to the new governor, Harry Nice.

Although a Republican, Nice had defeated Democratic Governor Ritchie in 1934 on a platform favoring a stronger, more complete New Deal in Maryland. At least rhetorically, Nice proved more sympathetic to the needs of the unemployed and contrasted sharply with Ritchie, who had criticized the federal government for robbing the states and cities of their "initiative and incentive" (but, as the unemployed were to learn, the city and state had neither the initiative nor the incentive to help the unemployed when the federal government later withdrew from the arrangement).[35]

In January 1935, Nice drew up plans to meet the "greatest human problem Maryland has ever faced" and then urged the General Assembly to appropriate immediately sufficient money to assist the unemployed: "It has been said that no Maryland legislature is capable of the performance of serious business prior to the middle of its session. Let us disprove this assertion." The legislature responded by adjourning for a week, and months passed without action on the relief issue. The state's behavior outraged federal officials. Hopkins fired off a telegram to Nice complaining of the state's persistent failure to cooperate and warning that "the responsibility for not providing relief will be upon the legislature for the Federal Government cannot furnish funds unless you too are willing to do what you can to carry your proportionate share." Nice attempted to placate Hopkins with assurances of imminent state action, but many legislators denounced Hopkins's thinly veiled threat and called for even greater reductions in the state's contribution for relief. And in a move against both Governor Nice and the city of Baltimore, county legislators pushed through a bill authorizing an investigation of the relief administration, rejecting the "house cleaning" of all agencies that Nice had proposed and focusing only on relief in an attempt to expose suspected fraud in the city.[36]

Although the state delayed taking action on financing relief, it moved ahead with the administrative reorganization of its system of public welfare. Stung by federal charges that Maryland's welfare administration was backward and cumbersome, state legislators created a "comprehensive and coordinated administration of relief" that finally provided for a municipal Department of Welfare. The state also approved new programs, such as aid to dependent children, and placed all assistance programs under the jurisdiction of the new welfare system. In Baltimore, Judge T. J. S. Waxter was appointed director of the welfare department and authorized to handle all the insurance and assistance programs with the exception of unemployment relief—which Mayor Jackson insisted must remain under the supervision of his handpicked, quasi-public agency, BERC. The state's new welfare system drew praise from federal officials, and state leaders boasted that Maryland was no longer outmoded in its administration of relief. The federal government's criticisms had in fact served as an important catalyst in the reorganization of the relief system in both the city and the state; at the same time, however, the effort toward creating a more modern, efficient welfare program was undermined by the state's refusal to fund the program. That apparent paradox mattered little to legislators more sensitive to charges of inefficiency than to those of inhumanity, and more determined to maintain state sovereignty than to allow increased federal supervision. Indeed, certain assembly members balked at participating in the Social Security program enacted by Congress in 1935 precisely because it required modifications in the state system and because it involved large financial contributions. As one member of the House of Delegates naively put it, "Every time Washington gives us money we have to match it; mightn't we be better off without the Federal government?"[37]

Major administrative changes had finally occurred. New programs were under way and a public system of welfare had been achieved. The city now had a Department of Welfare to oversee and coordinate its social programs. Goaded by the federal government, Maryland had reorganized its system of social assistance, accelerating the pace of organizational growth and advancing the "bureaucratization" of state and local government. But the growth of the welfare state at the local level did not necessarily mean an improvement in the lives of the city's dependent populations. The practical effects of the changes were barely detectable among the jobless, for, although changing notions of public responsibility had helped produce a new administrative framework, they failed to alter conservative fiscal policies. To squeeze more money from the city and the state for relief, the unemployed had to rely on themselves and other organized citizen groups. They were not always successful, for even the federal government had but a spotty record in dealing with the parsimonious policies of the city and state. Still, these organized groups carved out an important role in shaping the emergent welfare system.

Toward the close of the 1935 state legislative session, the state and the federal government finally agreed on Maryland's contribution. The compromise represented only about 60 percent of what Hopkins had earlier demanded, but it still failed to satisfy county legislators, who denounced the deal, objected to assisting Baltimore's "unworthy cases," and steadfastly refused to acknowledge that Baltimore's 80 percent share of the state's total relief burden resulted in part from the influx of jobless county residents now "stranded" in the city. To finance the state's contribution, the legislature enacted a gross-receipts tax with a one-year expiration date. Both Nice and Hopkins fully understood that in March 1936 the legislature would have to reconvene in special session for an unfortunate repeat performance.[38]

The city government also remained reluctant to assist the unemployed. Jackson maintained that relief was a state and federal obligation, and the city council disclaimed responsibility as well, saying that Jackson and the Board of Estimates controlled city finances. Baltimore's refusal to help caused considerable controversy and much misery in late 1935, when the federal government began reducing its FERA payments in order to phase out the program entirely. Neither the WPA nor the Social Security program took effect rapidly enough to offset the decreases in FERA funds. Facing a serious crisis and accustomed to local and state indifference, organized citizen groups appealed directly to the FERA, prompting one federal official to quip that the FERA had more contact with the city's unemployed than it did with the local government. When they were told to meet instead with the local and state authorities, such groups realized that representation in BERC was needed in order to get adequate relief. The Baltimore Building Trades Council, for example, petitioned BERC for a labor representative, saying that BERC's composition of "all employers is, in our opinion, improper and unfair to labor." The Ministerial Union of Baltimore complained to Jackson and Nice that BERC was "now composed entirely of members of the Baltimore Association of Commerce," and it requested new members "peculiarly qualified to understand the problems and needs of those on relief." The PUL, too, intensified its campaign to get a representative of the unemployed on the commission. By demanding citizen participation in relief decisions, these groups were calling for a public system of social welfare that represented its constituencies.[39]

In closing its operations, the FERA announced that no more funds would be provided after 30 November 1935. The WPA, Hopkins explained, would handle work relief for the able-bodied jobless while the cities and states supplied direct relief to those who were unemployable. Yet even by the end of November, few people on BERC relief rolls had been certified by the National Reemployment Service as eligible for WPA jobs. State relief administrator Greenstein pleaded with Hopkins to provide additional funds, explaining that the WPA was not yet "able to take care of the [relief] situation." Church groups, private charities, the PUL, and even BERC officials echoed these sentiments. But federal authorities stood firm. Speaking for Hopkins, Aubrey Williams reminded Greenstein of the "small sum" spent for relief by Baltimore and Maryland, and added, "I think this thing rests squarely on the doorstep of the state." Responding to a PUL delegation at his Washington office, Williams praised the actions of the organized unemployed, telling PUL chairman James Blackwell, "I'm glad to find somebody in Maryland who seems to be interested in the unemployed," but he suggested they were at the wrong address: "We have done our share— let the state do something for their own people." Referring to state and local inaction, Williams noted that "there's been a great job of buck-passing" and called upon Nice and Jackson to "do the decent thing" and assist the unemployed. Williams's statements to the PUL forced Nice to respond publicly; he weakly objected to Williams's description of state relief policies and appointed a committee to investigate the relief situation. But he failed to summon a special session of the legislature, following instead the advice of a state senator who cynically observed that "the State has received one 'ultimatum' after another that Federal funds were to cease as of certain dates, but it has continued to receive relief grants regularly." Jackson ignored all the charges and dismissed the hardship involved in the transition from the FERA to the WPA as a "federal matter."[40]

Social workers, religious leaders, and PUL members complained publicly of conditions that BERC officials acknowledged only privately. In response to criticisms of "food allowances below [the] health minimum," unprecedented "hardships for thousands of families," and increased absenteeism in schools "for lack of clothing," the commission boasted that its relief standards were "far in excess" of those earlier "maintained by the private agencies" and affirmed that it was "meeting the needs of its clients"—but privately, BERC's chairman warned Governor Nice that "it has recently been necessary to cut the standard [of relief] below the minimum requirements" and urged him "to relieve what in our judgment is a serious crisis." Still another BERC official wrote Nice that the city's relief load "has been reduced too far already," advised against additional cuts, and—to underscore the severity of the problem and his own credibility—added, "I think you know that I represent no extreme social service point of view." He continued, "I truly believe that we are sitting on a volcano, whether you look at it merely as the tragedy of having a hundred thousand citizens starving to death, or whether you consider the resulting disorder." By early January 1936, BERC administrator Howard Beck had recorded twenty-five cases of "actual starvation."[41]

The 1935–36 relief crisis forced private agencies and community groups to resume their relief-giving activities. Some predicted the return of "apple-selling, bundle days and soup kitchens." The FWA reported a significant increase in clients in early 1936 as "the result of cutting off Federal funds for general public assistance." When the city's superintendent of public education declared a "real emergency" in the schools, the parent-teachers association and the PUL once again began collecting clothes and food. To supplement the effort, the WPA launched a program to serve 4,000 free lunches to undernourished children. The city police department renewed its efforts to assist the unemployed as the stations again became centers for food and shelter, with police officers contributing "money they had saved up to buy funeral flowers for brother officers" in order to buy food for needy families. Desk sergeants even warned officers to limit the money they brought to the station, explaining that they "can't resist the pleas" and "usually go home broke."[42]

The relief crisis also served to unite various citizen groups in their opposition to state and local relief administrators. In response to the crisis and to the federal passage of the Social Security Act, a number of civic, trade-union, fraternal, religious, and social-welfare organizations joined with the PUL to form the Citizens' Alliance for Social Security. The alliance promoted municipal acceptance of, and responsibility for, an "adequate social insurance and relief program." It staged protests against BERC reductions and municipal inaction, drawing enough publicity to force Jackson to pledge that "no one will starve" in Baltimore. On a more informal level, groups met and communicated as never before. The Baltimore Federation of Labor, although known for its antiradicalism, gathered with the PUL, the Baltimore Building Trades, and the Church League for Industrial Democracy to discuss proposals for raising relief funds and urging the legislature to increase inheritance and corporate taxes. In another instance, when Jackson and BERC attempted to alleviate the relief crisis by suggesting that city churches and civic organizations feed over 2,000 needy families, religious leaders called the scheme "impractical" and "unintelligently made," denounced the city for "jockeying . . . with human suffering," and invited the PUL, the Socialist party, and organized labor to join them in a mass protest meeting against Jackson and BERC.[43]

The city's relief predicament resulted primarily from Jackson's refusal to recognize unemployment as a permanent problem and to treat it accordingly, and from the state's niggardly contributions to relief assistance. Moreover, the city and state preferred to blame each other or the federal government rather than to initiate any coordinated program of relief. Baltimore's liberal rabbi, Edward Israel, accurately summarized the situation: "We find our relief problem in a miserable mess. The 1935 Legislature was inconceivably inept in facing the problem. And now in the midst of a crisis, we have men making a survey, while people are at the point of starvation. To complete the incongruous picture, we have a Governor and a Baltimore City Mayor, both of whom are proud anti-New Dealers and States righters, insisting that the job of meeting this relief emergency is the responsibility of the Federal Government. It would be laughable if it were not tragic." Another religious leader concurred, adding that "while everybody is disclaiming responsibility, people go hungry."[44]

But by the end of January 1936 even Jackson had become alarmed by the relief situation. In response to public protests and the prospect of no state financial assistance, he appointed two committees—the first to untangle the immediate financial imbroglio, the other to devise a more permanent municipal policy for relief. He also appealed to Nice to call a special session of the legislature in order to determine the state's relief plans after the March expiration date of the gross-receipts tax. Nice refused to call the session before March, but he advanced the city $100,000 from the tax fund and reminded Jackson of the 1933 legislation allowing the city to borrow to pay for relief. Jackson curtly replied that he would not use city funds until the state offered its own plan to finance relief. Referring to the relief situation, Jackson moaned, "after five years we are practically where we were when we started." His critics and the unemployed agreed completely.[45]

Poor relations with the federal government further damaged the city's relief situation. Except during elections, Jackson and Nice denounced federal interference and warned that New Deal programs eroded individualism. At the national governors' conference, for example, Nice spouted, "No possible emergency can justify the philosophy which has been injected into our national government for scrapping the states and filling the land with federal agents." Shortly thereafter, however, he protested the termination of the FERA and requested additional federal money. Jackson regularly attacked the New Deal and referred to the Social Security Act as "the most asinine thing I have ever read in my life." But he, too, demanded continued federal assistance after 1935. Of the two, Jackson more consistently used the federal government as a cover for his own irresponsibility. And his failure to assist the unemployed particularly irked federal officials. Under the FERA, Jackson's refusal to provide material for work-relief projects not only produced federal criticism but had also resulted in the placement of thousands of families on direct relief for over two years. Reassured by promises from city officials, federal administrators looked to the reorganization of BERC under Howard Beck as an opportunity for Baltimore to establish a "substantial work relief program"—but city policies remained unchanged; in September 1935 BERC even terminated its limited work-relief program altogether, describing it as "more expensive than direct relief." However, when the federal government began its WPA program in November, state director Francis Dryden regarded many of the city's long-term recipients of direct relief as unemployable, charging local officials with avoiding their own relief responsibilities by "load[ing] them on our necks." In short, the city's maneuvers under FERA backfired under the WPA.[46]

The city's own demands on the WPA program further restricted its effectiveness. Mayor Jackson insisted that Baltimore's WPA be used, not so much as an emergency works project, as a major construction program. To that end, he secured from the federal government an agreement combining the funds of the WPA with those of the Public Works Administration (PWA), created in 1933 to fund substantial construction in cities and states. Baltimore was the only city in the nation with such an arrangement. But delays caused by winter weather and insufficient materials hampered WPA projects. Although by the end of February 1936 the WPA had found work for nearly 14,000 of BERC's cases, it had taken responsibility for less than half of the commission's load as tabulated in the summer of 1935; BERC itself had dropped 5,000 cases but still had nearly 10,000 on its rolls.[47]

State legislators remained unreceptive to Baltimore's pleas for increased relief funds. At the March 1936 special session, Governor Nice presented the findings of the committee that he had earlier appointed to study the relief situation: under the leadership of William J. Casey, the study group called for relief retrenchment, warned against continued participation in federal programs, and suggested that the state raise $7 million through a 10 percent consumer's tax to meet relief needs. Rural legislators from the Eastern Shore and Southern Maryland agreed with the committee in principle, but they found the $7-million figure too liberal and opposed assisting the unemployed in the city, referring to Baltimore's relief system as one of "the greatest modern-day rackets." Within five hours, they defeated the Casey proposal. Delaying action until the end of the session, the legislature appropriated $3.3 million, with $1.7 million for direct relief and the remainder for the state's programs for pensions and aid to dependent children. Baltimore's 60 percent share of the $1.7 million hardly matched its direct relief needs, which accounted for 84 percent of the state's direct relief cases. Moreover, it was barely enough to allow BERC to continue operations for another three months. After consulting with his own unemployment committee, Jackson called for the dissolution of BERC at the end of those three months.[48]

The liquidation of BERC represented a painful process for the unemployed. Between 1 May and 1 June 1936, when the commission officially closed its doors, BERC reduced its case load from 9,570 to 3,764. Over 2,000 of those dropped had been employables, eligible for WPA jobs, but full WPA quotas precluded their certification. Not one of the heads of households found work in private industry. Administrator Howard Beck also reported that BERC turned down more than 3,000 new applicants daily. He conceded that people would have to fend for themselves, finding hit-or-miss assistance at private charities or police stations. But, he added, more and more of the jobless "filled the headquarters of the Peoples Unemployment League."[49]

Mayor Jackson, although uncertain as to what should replace BERC, remained "absolutely opposed" to the assumption of an emergency problem by the city's Department of Welfare. In June 1936, therefore, he formed a private, nonprofit organization to care for those who had been receiving direct relief from BERC. To be funded entirely by the city, the new organization—named the Emergency Charity Association (ECA)—included representatives from both the business and the social-service communities; the real power, however, rested with the ECA's Citizens' Board of Review, comprised of representatives of the city's business organizations, which scrutinized each case transferred from BERC to the ECA. The *Sun* praised the new arrangement for direct relief as "businesslike" and a "safeguard against unnecessary expenditure." By wiping the relief slate clean, the *Sun* continued, the ECA would ensure that all clients were "carefully re-examined"—and that, the *Sun* affirmed, should "check chiseling." Meanwhile, members of the new association gathered to decide their primary objective in relief giving: "simply to keep people alive or to do more than merely maintain life." But the conservative financial policies of the city effectively made that decision for them.[50]

Working with officials from the city's welfare department, the ECA revised BERC's application procedures in order to make "intake policies . . . more stringent." The welfare department's director, Judge Waxter, suggested the adoption of the "St. Louis questionnaire" with its "searching" questions in order to facilitate a "purging of the rolls." The ECA agreed and mailed its lengthy relief application to BERC's 3,764 families, all of whom had been without any assistance for nearly three weeks. Of the cases reviewed, the Citizens' Board found only 57 percent worthy, another 32 percent questionable (in need of additional investigation), and 11 percent ineligible for ECA assistance. At the end of June the ECA began accepting new applications for relief, but degrading procedures and stiff regulations prevented more than 25 percent of all applicants from receiving aid. The PUL, the Citizens' Alliance, and private agencies all protested the ECA "purges" and called for additional assistance to large families unable to survive on the WPA work-relief allotment. To quiet the outcry, the ECA announced that it would supplement the WPA wages of large families. But the policy rarely became practice, as ECA members conducted investigations of need that usually lasted from three to six months. Thus, from the perspective of the unemployed, bureaucratic mismanagement and lengthy delays occurred, not with the operations handled by the federal government or even with BERC, but with a municipally funded private agency staffed largely by efficiency-minded businessmen. But as Mayor Jackson well knew, complex procedures and inordinate delays translated into fewer municipal expenditures for direct relief.[51]

The elimination of BERC and the Pecksniffian policies of the ECA ignited citizen protest throughout the city. The Citizens' Alliance held a mass meeting to denounce the ECA's relief application form, resulting in the deletion of a few of the more personal questions. Alliance member Rev. W. Owings Stone addressed another crowd of over 6,000 unemployed citizens protesting the ECA's policies. Stone embarrassed the association when he read aloud an eviction notice, written on ECA stationery and signed by chairman Cleveland Bealmear, a former BERC official and a successful realtor. Continued Citizens' Alliance protest caused the ECA to relax its strict requirements on the personal property allowed to relief recipients; they were no longer forced to give up their jewelry or radios. The alliance also petitioned the state legislature and the city council, demanding that the ECA help more people and that its name be changed from "charity" to "relief." In response to this pressure, city council member Daniel Ellison introduced a resolution urging the ECA to assist all those in need and to refrain from automatically excluding single people, married couples without children, and families cut off from the WPA because of federally mandated quota reductions. The city council passed the resolution unanimously and the ECA made "minor changes" in eligibility, extending "the possibility of relief to a few more people." With less success, the city's popular politician Thomas D'Alesandro championed the alliance's request for a name change: "The name should be relief not charity," he affirmed; "the people are not looking for charity, but work." But the mayor had carefully selected the ECA's name to reflect his own attitudes toward municipal relief responsibilities.[52]

Constant pressure from organized citizen groups brought minor improvements in the local administration of relief and a few conciliatory remarks from the mayor—but the protests did not effectively alter the behavior of the county legislators in the state's General Assembly. Before the special session convened in March 1936, a number of county senators prepared for the fight, denouncing what they termed "the terrific overhead and unnecessary expense of the present relief set-up" and vowing to "discontinue all taxes" for relief purposes.[53] The special session produced more wrangling than relief, and the city-county struggle continued into the 1937 legislative session. On the defensive and in the minority, Baltimore's representatives in the legislature proposed meeting with Mayor Jackson to "thrash out the relief problem" and to devise a plan that would prevent the counties from "leaving the city saddled with the entire burden of relief unaided by the State." But Jackson, eyes firmly fixed on the governor's chair, was disinclined to jeopardize statewide support and refused to put forth any plan drafted solely by the city's representatives. His characteristic inaction deeply disturbed Baltimore's senators and they labeled the meeting "futile." Without a plan or mayoral leadership, the city's senators found themselves isolated and ineffectual. The relief bill that finally emerged failed to meet the needs not only of the direct-relief recipients but also of those entitled to assistance under the social security provisions. Moreover, in order to raise the money for relief the assembly called for the legalization and taxation of bookmaking. Community and church groups attacked the bill, and Baltimore's legislators complained that county leaders forced them to "take this relief bill, bookies and all, or go back to Baltimore without a relief bill." Reacting to the community outcries, Governor Nice vetoed the bill and called the legislators back into session. After another round of fighting, they produced the same inadequate bill but without the bookmaking provision.[54]

At the national level, the federal government provided for unemployment insurance, aid to the needy, and old-age pensions with the passage of the Social Security Act in 1935. For the jobless, the act established a fund to be administered largely by the states, based on contributions from employers and employees. Matching federal funds were also made available for assistance programs for dependent children and disabled citizens. And a pension fund was created for the elderly, to be drawn from the tax contributions paid by workers and their employers. But because the federal Social Security programs were only gradually implemented and encountered stiff opposition at the local and state levels, they failed to alleviate substantially the city's burden of direct relief. Mayor Jackson ridiculed the Social Security Act and ignored its provisions, while the state legislature only reluctantly passed enabling legislation. Both the city and the state opposed abandoning the state's stringent residency requirement of fifteen years in order to conform to federal guidelines for the pension program. Moreover, the legislature refused to pass the necessary legislation for participation in the unemployment insurance program during its regular session, forcing Governor Nice to call a special session in late 1936 in order to meet the federal government's 31 December 1936 deadline. And when, in mid-December, the legislature finally passed the unemployment insurance bill, it rejected the pleas of the Baltimore delegates and set the employer-employee taxation level at the minimum established by the federal government. The new law, lamented one city delegate, "doesn't give the workingman a square deal." The terms of the enabling legislation were, however, very generous to certain political leaders; indeed, the laws were so calculatingly drawn for patronage purposes that the federal government delayed approval of all the programs until more satisfactory and less partisan arrangements were secured. Finally, even after receiving federal approval, the state assembly consistently refused to allot sufficient funds for the security programs. In 1936 the state provided funds for only 150 cases of aid to dependent children, but the city's Department of Welfare had already approved aid for 750 mothers with dependent children. Also hard-hit were the pensioners: throughout the decade the state never assisted more than 15 percent of its over-65 population, while other states were giving aid to more than half of their elderly citizens.[55]

The state's participation in the unemployment insurance program, moreover, initially offered more confusion than relief. The recession of 1937 threw additional people off their jobs, but they received neither direct nor work relief: WPA quotas were full and all state funds for direct relief were exhausted by the summer of 1937. The city was facing yet another relief crisis. Thousands of ineligible applicants crowded the local offices of the state employment service to register for unemployment benefits. The local director complained that he was "swamped with applicants" who erroneously believed that "registering will help get them a job." Some fell into the "uncovered" categories, such as domestic service, but most had simply not worked the requisite three-quarters of the year in order to receive the insurance payments. Even those eligible for benefits, some 30,000 Baltimoreans by 1938, did not receive them, for they remained misinformed or uninformed of the necessary procedures, which required an initial application and two renewal claims in successive weeks. On 25 January 1938 Robert Dorsey, an unemployed railroad worker, became the city's first recipient of unemployment compensation. Waving his check for $10.50, he announced that although the rent was "two weeks past due, . . . I'll be looking for the gas man. He's supposed to turn off the gas today." But throughout the first months of 1938 the distribution of checks did not proceed smoothly. Delays left needy families without assistance for weeks, while others received checks with incorrect names. In one instance, "good Jewish, German, Polish and English names began coming out of the [printing] machine with Irish prefixes" and surnames were revised to read

O'Steinmetz and O'Schultz. The difficulties in the program exacerbated the city's relief problems when desperate families applied for direct relief to tide them over until their checks arrived.[56]

The confusion surrounding the Social Security programs frustrated the jobless, families with dependent children, and pensioners—but their requests that the city establish information centers for the programs were rebuffed by Mayor Jackson, who disavowed all responsibility for the new assistance programs. Instead, the PUL organized offices throughout the city to explain the purposes and procedures of the programs. The recipients increasingly became, to the dismay of one local official, familiar with their "rights" under the Social Security program.[57]

Mayor Jackson made clear his intention to avoid the Social Security problems but called a meeting of ECA members and former BERC officials to discuss the city's direct relief responsibilities. Two of his closest advisors suggested that he abolish the ECA and incorporate all relief activities into the welfare department under Judge Waxter. Jackson's once intense opposition to such a plan weakened when he was persuaded that it would produce substantial savings. The same financial considerations that had earlier made him reject the proposal now made him accept it. But his underlying attitudes required adjustment, and he conceded that providing public assistance had become a permanent municipal responsibility.[58]

In June 1937 the city's Department of Public Welfare assumed responsibility for the ECA's relief cases. In keeping with the city's relief practices, Waxter began the program with a "purge," accepting only 75 percent of the relief burden of the ECA. The Citizens' Alliance immediately protested, urging those who had been released to reapply for aid. Alliance members even accompanied them to the welfare office, and over 90 percent of those who reapplied were granted assistance. The purge had been made merely in order to provide temporary savings for the city. But Jackson continued to demand cost reductions while declaring that "the truly needy will not be allowed to suffer in Baltimore." And purges of the rolls continued throughout 1938 and 1939.[59]

Moreover, with the waning of the New Deal, neither the 1938 gubernatorial campaign nor the 1939 mayoral election stirred sympathy for the unemployed. Indeed, many politicians and organized taxpayers had become weary of the relief issue. In 1938, for example, Jackson lost political support from the Taxpayers' League when he borrowed $2 million for unemployment relief; no longer could he boast, as he had since 1933, that the city had not borrowed for relief purposes. And when Jackson suggested a tax increase the following year the league sprang into action, denouncing the proposal and all the "chiselers" on the rolls. The mayor even received a threatening note warning him not to raise taxes: "If you do," read the card, "you won't live long." Rather than focus on the problems of the jobless, Jackson emphasized the need for greater efficiency in government. And the twin themes of efficiency and administrative reorganization figured prominently in both the gubernatorial campaign of 1938 and the mayoral election in 1939: promising a cost-saving consolidation of governmental departments, Democrat Herbert O'Conor won the governor's chair; in 1939 Mayor Jackson won reelection as well as support for the permanent adoption of a city plan to promote organized and efficient municipal development.[60]

Despite political neglect of the relief issue, Waxter still faced serious problems in the welfare department. He was accustomed to providing minimal relief and to conducting periodic purges, but by March 1939 he could no longer remain silent about the city's relief practices and the state's refusal to help. He warned that state funds for the year had already been spent and that further "cuts [in relief cases] are inadvisable." He called Maryland "one of the most backward states in the Union in respect to social work" and demanded that it break its tradition of "inhuman insensitivity . . . to the needs of the distressed citizens of Baltimore. . . . The Baltimore situation," he lamented, "is tragic." Legislators from rural counties objected to Waxter's condemnation, saying that the city's relief problem resulted not from the state's actions but from the refusal of the local private agencies to accept their responsibilities, from the greed of the city's wealthy citizens who refused to contribute money toward relief, and from the presence of "large numbers of Negroes" who, after having sampled the pleasures of "relief allotments, refused to work any more." The sides had been drawn once again. "The old issue of the Maryland counties versus Baltimore," noted the *Sun*, has been "never more clearly delineated than on the subject of relief." A state senator from Baltimore agreed, informing his fellow legislators: "You see this thing from a county viewpoint, and we see it from the viewpoint of a big city that knows if relief is suddenly cut off it will have such riots and civil commotion as it has never seen before."[61]

The threats of civil disorder brought neither increased sympathy nor financial support from the state legislature. Indeed, even within the city, a number of neighborhood associations persuaded one city council member to restrict the relief rolls by sponsoring a bill to increase the residency requirement for assistance from one year to three years. And reports that the federal government had distributed through its surplus commodity program quantities of herring roe to the needy angered certain groups in the city, who objected to giving "such a delicacy" to "reliefers." The struggle, as Waxter recognized, was not merely between the city and the counties. By the end of the depression decade, state appropriations for relief had fallen below the 1936 level, whereas the nation as a whole ranked above its 1936 figure. Consequently, the city was forced to take a greater share of the burden—but rather than meet that responsibility fully, the city purged its rolls and reduced its relief population, despite the 15 percent unemployment rate, to a mere 7 percent of the total population by 1938; in 1939, Baltimore claimed the lowest relief burden of any major city. Waxter conceded that the relief reductions resulted more from purges than from improvements in the city's employment opportunities, and he could hardly dispute the findings of a 1939 study of twenty-nine cities that called Baltimore's relief situation woefully inadequate. But the statistics and the purges little bothered Jackson, who inched toward his own version of social responsibility, calling in 1939 for his first "progressive budget" to meet relief and social needs.[62]

The development of the city's public welfare system involved the interplay of administrative policies, social attitudes, political traditions, and economic resources. Baltimore only reluctantly adopted its relief responsibilities, and, although even Jackson reported that he had become more "socially-minded" as the New Deal years wore on, the city's grudging commitment to helping those without work remained inadequate. The state, too, haltingly accepted the widened welfare responsibilities thrust upon it by the federal government. A concern for efficiency, and not for the unemployed, accounted for the incorporation of relief programs into the regular state budget in 1939, but the step also reflected the state's recognition of the permanency of social welfare; special sessions would no longer be necessary in order to provide relief.

Administrative changes at the local and state levels did not, however, result in adequate care of the unemployed. Programs and offices had been established but without sufficient funding. Indeed, the municipal acceptance of direct relief responsibility actually resulted in decreased assistance for the jobless. Citizen groups redoubled their efforts to halt that deterioration; even as late as 1939 a new unemployed group, called the Citizens' Committee on Relief, joined with the PUL and the Citizens' Alliance to lobby state and local authorities. It appeared that citizen participation had come full circle—in 1931 the Citizens' Emergency Relief Committee had raised money for the unemployed, and in 1939 the Citizens' Committee on Relief emerged to help the jobless. But in fact, significant changes had occurred. The membership and the function of these groups evolved in accordance with the city's development of a public welfare system. In 1931, the Baltimore Association of Commerce led in raising funds for the private agencies; in 1939 few business leaders could be found in organized citizen groups. Although Jackson's business associates managed the distribution of relief between 1933 and 1937, other businessmen shied away from public welfare responsibilities. Nothing came, for example, of the meeting of the Retail Merchants Committee called to "take the lead in helping the Government frame a wise [unemployment insurance] law."[63] To be sure, the influence of Baltimore businesses on the politics of relief remained significant. In 1936, for example, the realtor-dominated Taxpayers' League urged Mayor Jackson to consolidate relief responsibilities in order to trim costs, making his subsequent decision to do so in 1937 politically palatable to key segments of the business community. The sorry performance of the state legislature and its slipshod approach to budgeting for relief prompted the Baltimore Association of Commerce to begin lobbying in 1936 for a more permanent and efficient treatment of unemployment assistance—a recommendation fulfilled by Governor O'Conor in 1939.[64] Still, the voluntary activities of business leaders, never substantial, fell off sharply as the decade wore on. Repudiated by community groups for their "fixed ideas" about relief, businessmen, and especially members of the BAC, no longer dominated relief organizations.[65]

By the end of the 1930s, a diverse coalition of representatives from private agencies, social workers, Socialists, labor activists, religious leaders, and the unemployed themselves led the relief organizations that were no longer regarded as either emergency or temporary in nature. Like the city's permanent acceptance of relief responsibility, these citizen groups regarded their function as also permanent: to demand respect, recognition, and sufficient care for the unemployed. They knew that their job was difficult, for although social welfare had become a public responsibility, city commitment remained weak and relief funding inadequate.

The emergence of the city's public welfare system from the private charities through business domination to municipal control hardly represented a linear development of increased social responsibility. And that fitful transition reflected more than a change from "businessman to bureaucrat."[66] The private agencies remained important even during the period of business domination, and after 1937 they worked with the Department of Welfare to provide comprehensive social services. The shape that the city's welfare system took in the 1930s had at least as much to do with the views and organizational approaches of private agencies and social workers as it did with the budget limitations imposed by the BERC businessmen. In 1937, the private agencies organized the Baltimore Council of Social Agencies with the welfare department as a member agency, and the city, still devoted to the tradition of private charity, simultaneously sabotaged and strengthened that tradition by partially funding the new council with city money. The Great Depression had strained old formulas and forced new ones. The federal government expanded its authority in public welfare but also encouraged citizen participation among groups traditionally neglected by the city's political system. The city also widened its sphere of social responsibility to ensure at once the municipal acceptance of public relief and the continuation of private assistance.

CHAPTER 3

Policies and Programs

The New Deal in the City

As the New Deal unfolded in 1933, with the passage of the Federal Emergency Relief Act and the National Industrial Recovery Act, city officials immediately studied the legislation to determine what Mayor Howard Jackson termed "the opportunities offered Baltimore." Governor Albert Ritchie agreed that Maryland should get its "fair share" of federal assistance, frankly adding, "we ought to get all we can get."[1] But their flash of enthusiasm vanished before the sobering realities reported by Harry Hopkins as head of the Federal Emergency Relief Administration: he informed them that federal money would generally be available only on a matching basis, that federal funds alone would not meet public needs, and that the states must continue to meet their relief responsibilities. Financing unemployment relief, however, appealed to neither Jackson nor Ritchie, and neither moved rapidly toward satisfying federal demands in exchange for federal money. All too often, the federal government had to coerce the city and the state into providing assistance for their needy.[2]

The National Industrial Recovery Act, designed to bring employers under codes regulating hours, wages, and working conditions, alarmed local and state leaders, for it signaled a new level of government-business cooperation. Maryland's senators voted against the bill and Mayor Jackson publicly questioned the growing powers of government. The Baltimore *Sun*, although generally solicitous of business interests, sharply denounced the National Recovery Administration (NRA) as a dangerous departure from American tradition and a "far-reaching step in the direction of a controlled national economy." Moreover, the *Sun* questioned the efficacy of the "control of industry by vested interests in that industry" and the degree of governmental assistance provided to business leaders, noting that "for all the lip service they have given these many years to the ideal of free business and individual enterprise, they outclass any other group . . . in their pursuit of governmental care and sustenance."[3]

But the enlarged role of government did not bother many businesses or consumers; the public endorsed the NRA enthusiastically. Over 250,000 people turned out for an August parade in support of the NRA and cheered wildly as Baltimore's NRA chairman, Paul Malone, promised to fight unemployment. Employers pledged to follow NRA guidelines and consumers promised to patronize only businesses displaying the Blue Eagle symbol of NRA compliance. One local manufacturer boasted that he had signed and returned his Blue Eagle contract within minutes of receiving it. According to the Baltimore *Afro-American*, blacks, too, welcomed the NRA. An unemployed black laborer, although he acknowledged that he had not benefited personally from the Blue Eagle, added that "it is [still] a great help to the people." The executive secretary of the Baltimore Urban League praised the NRA for its potential in black communities, calling it "the finest organizational opportunity we have had in half a century." (One black worker interviewed by the paper, however, dismissed the program as "only for the white people.")[4]

Baltimore businesses eagerly grasped the self-regulatory opportunities provided by the NRA. Stressing the need to move from competition to cooperation, the Baltimore Association of Commerce initiated statewide meetings to bring together commercial, industrial, and labor interests. For local businesses, cooperation readily translated into higher prices. The Cleaners and Dryers Association, for example, kept "in line with actions of other trades under the national industrial recovery act" by boosting its prices. Practically no business remained untouched by the Blue Eagle; the NRA facilitated cooperative organization among traditionally highly individualistic businesses. Black barbers in the city, for example, joined to form the Master Barbers' Association, designed to increase efficiency, improve sanitation procedures, and standardize services and prices. The barbers also, of course, voted to increase prices across the board. Black beauticians rose to "the opportunity and spirit of the N.R.A.," establishing a trade association, increasing prices, and upgrading their job description to "hair work."[5]

Business cooperation did not, however, tend to promote increases in wages. Employers denounced nationally imposed wage codes as detrimental to industrial recovery, and in certain industries NRA wage standards were routinely defied. In Baltimore's garment industry, code violations occurred frequently—in one instance they even required the Department of Justice to intervene.

The job of ensuring NRA code compliance belonged to Arthur Hungerford, who had impeccable New Deal credentials: his early days as a *Sun* reporter made him appreciate the limits of investigatory action as compliance director; his quintessential 1920s career as a publicity expert provided invaluable lessons on selling NRA compliance; and his leadership in Roosevelt's 1932 Maryland campaign made him a reliable New Deal Democrat. He was sincere, yet superficial.[6] From the outset, Hungerford simply expected local cooperation in NRA code enforcement and naively adopted the policy that "compliance is the objective of this office rather than punishment." Failing to realize that persistent noncompliance required punitive measures, Hungerford was unable to prevent area businesses from violating NRA codes. Moreover, despite repeated violations on the part of some of the city's largest companies, Hungerford insisted on blaming only small businesses for the failure of the program. While dismissing serious abuses by large manufacturers as "unintentional," he charged that small businesses were most antagonistic to the spirit of compliance and bitterly denounced them for minor infractions. But in some sense Hungerford's accusation was correct: certain small businessmen were more vocal in their opposition to a program they derisively dubbed "National Run Around" and "National Ruin Administration," whereas large manufacturers, however guilty of noncompliance, praised the program and its director. Hungerford was an advertising man himself, but he proved unable to resist the ingratiating overtures of the city's leading industrialists.[7]

By May 1935, when the Supreme Court declared the NRA unconstitutional, local violations had become frequent and flagrant. One survey ranked Maryland fourth in the nation for "chiseling" on wage and price standards. Hungerford and his staff, however, blamed the state's poor record on decisions at the regional and national levels. After more than a year of recording noncompliance, Hungerford had finally begun in early 1935 to press for legal action against repeated offenders—but the regional NRA urged him to reconsider a number of cases, and the litigation division, suggesting that his charges were not adequately substantiated, rejected all "cases which do not stand a first class chance of going through successfully." Hungerford suspected, perhaps correctly, that the NRA's litigation division worked vigorously to prosecute only the cases initiated by regional or national offices and not those started at the local level. In any event, the combined effect of such restricted attitudes and decisions was to limit the impact of the NRA on Baltimore's workers and to leave business participation in the program merely voluntary and sporadic.[8]

Title II of the National Industrial Recovery Act provided for public works construction, a program that Mayor Jackson endorsed as an appropriate means for dealing with unemployment. Jackson applauded Harold Ickes of the Public Works Administration for his fiscal caution and his insistence on accepting only "useful" projects—according to PWA guidelines, those that cost over $25,000. Determined to "get our fair share" of PWA matching-grant funds, Jackson proposed a building program that totaled $16.1 million; but legal obstacles that limited the city's borrowing abilities forced a downward revision of the proposal to only $1.7 million, thereby seriously reducing the impact of the PWA on Baltimore's jobless. At the state level, further complications that necessitated a special session of the legislature, along with city-county rivalries, served to reduce the state's PWA proposal and to delay implementation of the program for months. By November 1933 only 200 men in the entire state had received PWA jobs.[9]

The upcoming elections of 1934, especially the contest for governor, also delayed the effective operation of the program, as certain officeholders attempted to use the program to ensure reelection. Authorities at the PWA strongly objected, noting, "We are perfectly aware that stalling these projects off until campaign time, when making jobs and allocating projects would be most useful, probably has occurred to some politicians as a very nice stratagem, but we are just as much aware that in the meantime, our only purpose—the providing of work for thousands of Maryland men now unemployed—is being defeated."[10] In January 1934, when Ickes discovered that only 11 percent of possible PWA work was under way, he threatened to cancel nearly $134,000 in allocations unless immediate action was taken to improve the situation—and yet in 1934, only sixty-eight men found work in Baltimore on PWA construction.[11]

Relations between PWA administrators and state and local officials continued to deteriorate. State Roads Commissioner E. Brooke Lee indignantly denied the "political" charges and intimated that the real problems lay in administrative difficulties at the national level. Local officials complained of their inability to find suitable unemployed men for PWA construction projects, despite Baltimore's unemployment rate of over 20 percent. They also attacked what they regarded as the PWA's troublesome legal division, with its "red tape" and overzealous young lawyers determined to scrutinize every PWA project. State and city officials further concurred in attributing construction delays to the short supply of materials and equipment.[12]

But in large measure, Baltimore's leaders simply resented any federal supervision and bristled at having to submit municipal projects for government approval. Federal officials recognized the problem, and although they frequently protested the behavior of the local administration they still attempted to accommodate the city's concerns and to respect local authority. Even President Roosevelt personally placed the PWA legal division "at the disposal" of local officials in order to expedite their receipt of federal funds. In 1935 the FERA allowed Baltimore to combine all construction projects into one PWA project, giving the city added financial flexibility and complete authority over both engineering design and construction work. Finally, the national administration also permitted Baltimore to combine PWA and Works Progress Administration funds for large construction projects—the only such arrangement allowed a major city in the nation.[13] Such federal capitulation to local demands suggests that national officials attempted to placate city leaders for political reasons and in an effort to hasten public works construction. Yet, ironically, the relaxation of federal authority resulted in fewer WPA projects and enabled local officials to politicize the programs while simultaneously maintaining their distance from, and hostility to, the New Deal administration.

With public works projects hardly beyond the planning stages and with local relief policies riddled with problems, the city's unemployed faced a difficult winter in 1933–34. For them, the Civil Works Administration—created in November 1933 as a temporary emergency work-relief program—was, as one unemployed laborer exclaimed, a "godsend." Headed by Harry Hopkins, the CWA was administered by the local and state FERA staffs. Harry Greenstein, director of the Maryland Emergency Relief Administration, became the CWA state administrator, and the Baltimore Emergency Relief Commission received responsibility for the city's CWA program. Hopkins allocated 40,000 CWA jobs for Maryland's unemployed, with about half of the quota assigned to the city. Given the city's unemployment rate, Hopkins expected that BERC could easily fill the first 8,700 jobs by his 15 December 1933 deadline—but, citing excessive federal regulations and a lack of job materials and equipment, among other "stumbling blocks," BERC failed to meet the deadline and bitterly denounced federal authorities for pressuring the city for more rapid implementation. Officials at CWA headquarters, labeling the excuses as "bunk, absolute bunk," urged BERC to assist the unemployed and even to "set the rules aside" if they "interfere with the human purposes" of the program. Despite such overtures, the city made little progress. In early January, with half of the quota still unmet, an infuriated Hopkins ordered a "national CWA probe" of Baltimore and threatened to cut off all CWA funds.[14]

But the reasons for the delay had already been supplied to Washington. At the outset, city and state authorities registered their disapproval of the CWA program, particularly its emphasis on rapid employment of the jobless. They warned Hopkins that the "necessity of speed . . . implicit in the program of Civil Works" would result in "eliminating all of the safeguards which are essential." The rapid placement of large numbers of unemployed men, they continued, could not be done "without waste, inefficiency, and possible dishonesty." They called the payroll procedures "a danger which gives us grave concern" and, denying responsibility for the ultimate outcome of the CWA, urged the federal government itself to implement the program. Given such a hostile environment and such disdainful policy makers, the quota problems, phony excuses, and consistent delays in Baltimore were hardly surprising.[15]

State CWA administrator Greenstein largely supported the city in its refusal to provide rapid employment. A Baltimorean himself, long active in the city's Jewish charities, and a former Progressive, Greenstein cherished efficiency and usefulness but regarded unplanned relief as counterproductive. He concurred with the local CWA board's decision to approve only projects that were "pre-eminently desirable and socially useful"—and, despite the national CWA's publicly stated goal, the rapid employment of jobless men did not accord with their definition of "socially useful." Indeed, Greenstein upheld Baltimore's conservative policy even after acknowledging that it created "a very serious situation in the City which has made it next to impossible for them to provide work for their allotment of men."[16]

The sharp rise in unemployment among seasonal workers, however, forced BERC to rely on the CWA. Moreover, city-state-national wrangling over relief finances further encouraged BERC to use the federally funded CWA jobs to meet the rising relief demands. The CWA not only provided jobs for those on BERC's relief rolls but also increasingly hired the unemployed who were not on the relief rolls. At its peak, the local CWA employed nearly 22,000 men—an impressive figure, but one to be balanced by the finding that many men worked but a week on the CWA payroll. And yet, no sooner had the city finally met its quota in mid-February than national commitment to the program wavered with the prospect of advancing warm weather. Citing the traditional fears of climbing costs and public handouts, Roosevelt ended the program, as William E. Leuchtenburg notes, "as quickly as he could." Hopkins obligingly reduced the CWA work week and slashed payrolls, and at the end of March 1934 the CWA was abandoned altogether.

A variety of problems plagued the CWA throughout its brief and difficult existence. Communication snafus between Washington, D.C., and Baltimore delayed essential instructions and rulings for weeks, as important letters arrived at the wrong offices. Baltimore CWA officials attempted to subvert national wage scales by reclassifying work descriptions at lower rates. Complaints from the Baltimore Federation of Labor about the unusually small number of skilled workers on the payroll (under 5 percent) resulted in a state investigation and an order from MERA that the city hire more workers at the skilled rate. Federal officials uncovered instances of illegal or unauthorized use of CWA funds, including the improvement of a private Hebrew nursing home—a finding of much concern to Greenstein as the state's CWA director and a long-time official of the Associated Jewish Charities. The government also found that Mayor Jackson, who never relented in his assault on the program, used CWA money to insure building equipment through his own insurance firm. Projects sponsored by the CWA and workers on them came under attack from a number of observers. Some state legislators, for example, bemoaned the number of "coloreds" on the payroll and publicly censured a program that would aid black families on relief before helping white war veterans, even though the latter group had not been on BERC's rolls. The state chairman of the Garden Club of America led a campaign to give landscaping work along the highways to "graduates of agricultural colleges" and not to ordinary laborers. Mayor Jackson and BERC complained about spending money on "made work" instead of major construction works and ultimately abandoned as too expensive the city's rat-catching program—a project suggested by federal authorities and praised by local health officials.[17]

The CWA workers themselves criticized the city's management of the program while simultaneously praising Roosevelt for creating it. They particularly objected to BERC officials who, they claimed, treated them as charity recipients rather than as employees of a federal works program, and they maintained that their president better understood their predicament than did local officials. Dissatisfied with BERC's probing inquiries and endless "red tape," prospective CWA workers protested the delays in implementing the program and instances of what they said were "job-selling" and "favoritism," especially the "preference given to those of the Roman Catholic faith in selecting employees under the C.W.A."—and it seems clear that the designs of local politicians did indeed figure heavily in the awarding of 20–30 percent of the CWA jobs, and that Catholics, who accounted for only 24 percent of the city's relief recipients, received over 50 percent of the total CWA jobs. Moreover, despite the racial concerns of state legislators, Baltimore's blacks, who made up about 42 percent of the city's total relief population, received but 28 percent of the CWA jobs.[18]

Women were even more underrepresented in the program. Either as heads of households or as widowed singles, in the winter of 1933–34 they accounted for almost 20 percent of Baltimore's relief load but received only 0.4 percent of the CWA jobs. Ignoring the suggestion of Eleanor Roosevelt to remember the "forgotten woman" by mandating a quota for women, the CWA merely adopted from the FERA the division of "Women's Activities" and required each state to appoint a women's director. Greenstein filled the position in Maryland with the energetic and competent Dr. Emma Ward, but he did little else to encourage the employment of women. And BERC officials focused almost exclusively on unemployed men: ninety-one projects, from archival assistance to mosquito control and rat catching, were created for men—and only one for women, employing but ninety-six workers. The few women who received CWA employment suffered sex-based wage differentials and complained that their low wages made it difficult "to support [their] families." Still, in that single project Ward managed to establish a substantive work program for the manufacture of mattresses; she even allowed the women workers to sell the mattresses in order to buy the materials that BERC failed to supply. But the very success of the project—the quality of the work and the competitiveness of the price—prompted local manufacturers to charge interference with free enterprise. Greenstein concurred and closed the shop, leaving, as one displaced woman worker lamented, "no work program [for women] in Baltimore City." Denied the work-relief opportunities provided to men, unemployed women were tied by convention and necessity to direct relief and to the home. In reviewing the progress of the CWA in February 1934, Harry Hopkins appropriately excluded women from the record, saying, "We haven't been particularly successful in work for women."[19]

William E. Leuchtenburg's finding that the CWA "proved immensely popular—with merchants, with local officials, and with workers" does not fully apply to Baltimore, where local officials, relying on class- and sex-biased definitions to determine public welfare, intentionally limited the efficacy of the program. As early as January 1934, the *Sun*, echoing the sentiments of city officials who objected to make-work, pronounced the CWA a "flop," citing "chiseling and graft" as the chief culprits. The state planning commission later pointed to the CWA as "the only exception" to the generally useful New Deal construction programs in Baltimore; CWA work, the commission declared, was unfortunately "limited almost wholly to man-made jobs involving mostly common labor" and therefore "did not benefit the community." Mayor Jackson agreed completely. For them, providing work relief for unemployed "common laborers"—both men and women—was not adequately serving the public's interest.[20]

The difficulties that the CWA faced in Baltimore were not altogether atypical. In Boston, too, according to Charles H. Trout, the CWA "encountered tough going" as city-state rivalries produced quota problems; had local and state officials worked with Hopkins to implement the program, "10,000 additional Bostonians would have gotten federal jobs." Still, compared to Baltimore, Boston officials proved more resourceful and responsible in working with the CWA.[21]

With the dissolution of the CWA in March 1934, the FERA took over work-relief responsibilities until the creation of the Works Progress Administration in 1935. When Hopkins became chief of the WPA, he attempted to correct some of the problems he had faced under the FERA. Trying to promote more state-federal cooperation by creating greater state loyalty to the WPA's programs, he assumed the power to name state administrators instead of relying on governors' appointees as under the FERA. In Maryland, at the suggestion of Senator Millard Tydings, Hopkins appointed John Mackall as the WPA administrator.[22]

Mackall had long been employed on the State Roads Commission, serving as its chairman from 1920 until 1929, when a scandal left him tarnished if not convicted. Further controversy surrounded his brief tenure as state WPA administrator. Mackall completely rejected the work-relief focus of the WPA and attempted to merge the entire PWA program into the WPA, declaring that he would not supervise projects unless they were of "lasting benefit"; WPA funds, he argued, should be used primarily to build roads and bridges and not to provide work relief. He early complained that the direction of the WPA represented a "retreat to the c.w.a. Program" and in June 1935 he offered his resignation. Anxious to get the WPA started in Maryland, Hopkins persuaded Mackall to reconsider and assured him that

Washington would be sympathetic to his concerns. However, despite Hopkins's assurances, the national WPA office rejected the city's WPA proposal, which emphasized major construction projects. Moreover, Mackall's efforts to combine the PWA and the WPA provoked the wrath of Ickes. New appropriation acts and the reorganization of relief in 1935 left few local officials clear about the national programs; indeed, not even BERC fully understood the differences between the WPA and the PWA. Yet local officials were very receptive to Mackall's request that they withdraw their proposals from the PWA, which required a state-local contribution of 55 percent, and resubmit them to the WPA under Mackall, who promised full federal financing. An irate Ickes publicly lambasted Mackall as "irresponsible," alluded to his scandal-ridden "highways job," and denounced him for ignoring the local PWA office in an attempt to "run the whole show" in Baltimore. Under fire and disdainful of the prospect of running a program designed primarily to provide work relief, Mackall again offered his resignation. Eager to be rid of the controversy, Hopkins unhesitatingly accepted it.[23]

State engineer Francis Dryden replaced Mackall at the WPA but inherited all his problems. Local officials continued to withdraw projects from PWA consideration and resubmit them to the WPA. Dryden complained to Hopkins of the projects "all piled in on me," and Hopkins instructed him not to touch them "with a ten foot pole." In a conciliatory move, Dryden approached PWA State Administrator Abel Wolman and together they issued a compromise statement urging that project applications be submitted to both the PWA and the WPA.[24]

Although Baltimore managed to combine PWA and WPA funding for its large construction projects, Dryden still faced other difficulties—such as delays in filling quotas, WPA worker strikes, program inadequacies, and eligibility problems. Like the CWA, the WPA got off to a very slow start. This time, however, local opposition to the program did not account solely for the delay. Indeed, the traditional interpretation that the WPA was less popular than the CWA does not apply to Baltimore. To be sure, workers on relief preferred the higher CWA wages to the WPA security payments, and the *Sun* roundly condemned the WPA (as it had the CWA) out of dislike for Roosevelt. But relief officials and local politicians overwhelmingly favored the WPA because the local version of the program promised major construction work of lasting benefit, not merely make-work for "reliefers." Yet despite their endorsement, their own bureaucratic ineptitude and insistence on politicizing the program slowed the local establishment of the

WPA. Even Mackall, who had little interest in relief work, complained at the time of his resignation in August 1935 that federal and local officials "squable [*sic*] over who is to do the Maryland relief program while 30,000 employables remain unemployed." Baltimore, which was carrying 80 percent of the state's relief burden, received but 50 percent of Maryland's 25,000 job quota. By late September only two WPA projects had been started in the city, providing about 100 men with work-relief jobs.[25]

Responsibility for transferring the able-bodied unemployed to the National Reemployment Service (NRS) for certification for WPA jobs rested with BERC. In the midst of the recurring state-city financial crisis over relief, BERC began slashing relief rolls and payments and eagerly transferring clients to the WPA. Dryden deplored the relief cuts, explaining that he would not be able to absorb the employables that rapidly. He was sure, he added, that the local community supported his policy that relief jobs must not be "made work" but projects "of value." Foremost among Dryden's fears, however, was his belief that BERC sent both employables and unemployables to the NRS office for certification. Of the 17,000 men sent by BERC to the WPA, Dryden reported to Hopkins, "there are not more than 9,000 men who are employable and will respond to the call to go to work," and he erroneously claimed that there were simply "not enough [suitable] men on relief in Baltimore to fill the quota." In disbelief, Hopkins asked whether he had "squeezed the list dry." Dryden replied that although BERC still had a case load of over 20,000, he doubted whether he could find more than 7,000 qualified men from that group. He charged that BERC, in an attempt to evade its responsibility for unemployables, was attempting "to load them on our necks."[26]

Suspicious of local authorities, Hopkins and Dryden devised a relief plan that not only reflected their distrust of BERC but also indicated their own prejudices and preferences regarding relief clients. According to Dryden, BERC had certified for WPA work "2 or 3 thousand derelicts" and many "negro women domestics." Hopkins warned Dryden not to "start fooling around with work projects" for "derelicts" if they "turn[ed] out to be incompetent" or "handicapped fellows." To deal with the "women business," as Hopkins derisively called it, Dryden and Hopkins defied WPA rules concerning work relief for employables. Their joint effort in this matter provided a clear indication of their hostility toward work relief for women; they especially objected to aiding black domestics, who, after all, were accustomed to inadequate wages, low status, and poor working conditions. And their effort provided an important example of cooperation between local and national administrators to limit the effectiveness of a New Deal program. That these limitations fell disproportionately on *employable* black women, whom they had placed in the same category as *unemployable* men (male "derelicts" and "handicapped fellows"), further illustrates their notions about the real purposes of the WPA. Hopkins instructed Dryden to "put about a thousand or so to work and then say that is all the projects we got so we can't use any more." He reassured Dryden, who was worried about violating the president's executive order prohibiting discrimination on WPA projects, that "they can't prove you are discriminating against anybody" if some were provided with jobs. But Hopkins not only wanted to restrict the number of women on relief, despite unfilled quotas, he also attempted to pay them less than the WPA security wage because, he explained, it "is more than they can earn on the outside." Tempted to adopt market considerations and prevailing prejudices, Dryden ultimately decided against the reduced wage rate, fearing that its adoption would provoke serious protest from the then 8,000-strong organization of the unemployed, the Peoples Unemployment League, and from organized labor. Instead, he suggested following a safer course: to rely on a "certain group" in BERC who had promised to "kick off [the relief rolls] a bunch of these domestics," thereby making them ineligible for certification for WPA jobs. Hopkins seemed mollified by such assurances but stressed that Dryden should still vigilantly screen all WPA applicants.[27]

Together, then, Hopkins and Dryden shaped the general outlines of the WPA program for Baltimore. The result was a program that emphasized public works and not work relief, that was hampered by delay, and that favored white males. Although the federal government established some of its own projects in the city, most WPA money funded large construction projects that more properly belonged under the PWA—and yet Hopkins failed to challenge Dryden's insistence on sizeable public works projects. Already familiar with the city's attitudes toward such work-relief programs as the CWA, Hopkins allowed the WPA to depart from its mission in order to placate municipal authorities and avoid much of the bitterness that had characterized city-federal relations.

The emphasis on major construction projects slowed implementation of the program; but for the first time, it was the federal government that could not move fast enough to satisfy local demands. Mayor Jackson, who had earlier denounced the national administration for "reorganizing" too rapidly and for not offering sufficient guidelines for the CWA, now complained that "too many officials and rules" stood in the way of construction progress. He assailed Dryden for parks left unfinished under the CWA, for the inadequate supply of construction materials, and for Dryden's inability to provide the necessary workers. With obvious indifference to the needs of the unemployed and with his attention firmly fastened on the requirements of a particular project, Jackson demonstrated his narrow view of the WPA: "Take a sewer job," he complained to Dryden, "we need forty laborers and five timber men. You can give us the laborers but you can't give us the timber men because you don't have them on the relief rolls." This, he added, was no way to "run a construction job." Jackson's limited, simplistic perspective on relief shocked even Dryden, who regarded the WPA as more than a collection of "construction jobs" funded by the federal government. When Jackson proposed that he and Dryden "take the responsibility and run the [WPA]" in Baltimore, Dryden brusquely declined the offer, warning the mayor that "orders from Washington will not be violated."[28]

The transitional period from the FERA to the WPA in late 1935 was particularly difficult for the jobless. Baltimore's insistence on large construction projects that required extensive planning and materials, together with the mayor's determination not to "spend a dollar" for direct relief, meant that the unemployed received neither WPA jobs nor BERC assistance. The delay in starting the works program alarmed BERC officials, who, although they recognized that "we have got to put people to work [on the WPA] or we will be in a hell of a fix," continued to aggravate the problems by accelerating the transfer of employables to the program. In fact, BERC even extended its hours of operation, and anxious relief recipients, as many as 3,000 a day, lined up for blocks, "waiting night and day to get jobs." Dryden shared the local commitment to major projects, but he still refused to resort to make-work, declaring that "it would be foolish" to expect all employables to be working on WPA jobs by 1 November 1935, when FERA money ran out. "There will not," he explained, "be sufficient projects of sufficient value by that time." Misled by BERC and angered by the delays, the employable jobless faced the winter months with neither direct relief nor WPA jobs. In need of food and heating coal, they turned in large numbers to private agencies for handouts. As reports of suffering grew more frequent, the PUL and other groups took to the streets, protesting the situation and canvassing the city for private contributions. With the exception of Mayor Jackson, all the major officials at the state and local levels appealed to Hopkins to provide additional funds during the "relief emergency"—and although the federal government had already terminated all FERA money to thirty-nine states, Hopkins again managed to compen-

The unemployed waiting for WPA *work assignments in December 1935.*
The line extended several blocks in each direction.
(Courtesy of the Special Collections Division, University of Maryland
College Park Libraries)

sate for state and local negligence with a grant of $859,000 for the month of November.[29]

The problems for the unemployed, however, remained serious. By January 1936, over 10,000 heads of households were still waiting for either their job assignments or their first WPA checks. Hard times forced neighbors to huddle together to conserve coal and restricted private relief agencies from providing much more than flour and beans. Families in the Hampden area of west Baltimore resorted to daily begging for food or money. Neighborhood grocers complained that they were no longer selling but giving away their food, and local bakeries witnessed lines of people begging for stale bread. One woman, a head of household who had been. certified for a WPA sewing project and who routinely combed her neighborhood for food scraps, declared, "I can starve and I won't do anything about it, I suppose. But when they starve my children, I'm going to fight." Both Mayor Jackson and Governor Nice vowed that no one would starve, but private agencies continued to report cases of malnutrition; BERC officials also conceded that their former "clients are begging" for food.[30]

Neighborhood organizations joined with the Peoples Unemployment League to protest the city's system of "starvation relief." They drew attention to the plight of the unemployed, forcing BERC to respond to the relief crisis. Because the PUL picketed Hopkins's office in Washington and BERC's headquarters, local relief officials agreed to "assist a few more cases" until the WPA was under way, indicating once again how the organized citizen groups worked to liberalize relief assistance in the city. Mayor Jackson, however, made no serious effort to alleviate the situation, offering instead a paltry $20,000 from a 1931 Citizens' Emergency Relief fund that, through municipal mismanagement, had been left unspent. Not until mid-1936 did a significant number of the employable jobless receive assistance from the WPA.[31]

Major construction projects accounted for over 76 percent of the city's WPA program. By combining PWA and WPA funding, Baltimore was able to launch an extensive street-improvement program, construct new bridges, tunnels, and sewers, improve harbor facilities, and build new schools and renovate others. The accomplishments were significant and, as the mayor had directed, "of lasting benefit." In 1938 the state planning commission praised the WPA as a "program of entirely worthwhile projects" where "a maximum of results were obtained for each dollar expended." By June 1939, the WPA had spent nearly $38 million in Maryland, completing about 170 miles of roads and constructing 18 bridges, 84 playgrounds, 17 parks, 72 miles of water lines, and more than 500 buildings.[32]

But the dominance of major projects meant that very little WPA money funded either cultural activities or smaller work-relief projects—programs that found greater support in other cities. Moreover, the prejudices and priorities of local officials shaped the programs that were funded. Political favoritism too often figured in local hiring policies, and municipal authorities tended to neglect cultural activities, finding publicly funded theatrical and orchestral performances to be impractical and ephemeral. Dryden did little to correct the situation although he early acknowledged that, unlike other cities, Baltimore had failed to initiate or support a municipal relief orchestra under the WPA. As in the 1935–36 relief crisis, organized activities of citizen groups brought at least marginal concessions from the city, and a thirteen-member orchestra was allowed to organize under the WPA and perform weekly concerts. Still, the record was poor. In the entire city in 1936, only eighteen musicians (including the orchestra members) and two dramatists received WPA jobs relevant to their talents. The Baltimore Artists' Union appealed directly to President Roosevelt for assistance, complaining that area artists had been "completely ignored by local authorities" and urging greater federal intervention. The presentation of the Federal Theatre's production "One-Third of a Nation," delayed until 1941, required considerable community involvement to overcome local obstacles. Even the Federal Writers' Project encountered serious opposition from city officials, and federal intervention and supervision were necessary for the publication of its guidebook to Maryland.[33]

Baltimore also failed, unlike other eastern cities, to establish a "light work" project for unemployed workers who were unable to perform heavy, manual labor. Officials at BERC insisted that these workers were employable and therefore a federal responsibility, but Dryden dismissed them as "handicapped physically" and ineligible for WPA employment. To assist this group of workers "thrown on the junk heap," the PUL and private charities cooperated with the state's director of the National Emergency Council to provide work-relief and rehabilitative projects that allowed the workers to acquire some limited skills.[34]

Women particularly suffered from the city's "pick and shovel" emphasis in work relief: not only were they ineligible for construction work, but their household skills were routinely devalued or ignored by local officials. Unlike the CWA, however, the WPA at least specifically required that women receive work-relief jobs—but Harry Hopkins insisted that the percentage of female employment on the WPA in cities and states across the nation never rise above 16, which represented the national average. In Baltimore, where women accounted for about 25 percent of the heads of households on BERC relief rolls by 1935, they received but 10 percent of the WPA jobs. Moreover, despite the earlier complaints of women leaders, female groups, and the CWA workers themselves, the WPA did not correct the problems caused by the gender-prescribed projects that characterized the CWA. For example, the WPA officials charged with devising "suitable projects" for women referred to their task as "project trouble," and, rather than retrain women or find appropriate projects for those who had clerical or manufacturing skills, they simply established sewing rooms throughout the city. As a consequence, the sewing room quickly became a "dumping ground" for Baltimore's jobless women.[35]

By November 1936, the city had three sewing projects (two white, one black), employing about 900 women. They labored at a rapid pace, turning out more than 30,000 garments per month for distribution to needy families on relief. Unless they were discharged for inefficiency, for engaging in radical activities, or as a result of federally mandated quota reductions, women in the sewing rooms rarely left their jobs for employment in private industry. "The commercial possibilities of their acquired skills," explained

Sara Ginsburg, a WPA economist, "are not great." As Baltimore's garment industry continued to decline, few women could realistically expect to secure sewing jobs.[36]

The ambiguity surrounding the purpose of the sewing rooms further restricted the effectiveness of the projects as a relief program. For such officials as Dryden, the sewing rooms represented a charitable service, modeled after the nineteenth-century workhouses for the poor—but these same officials demanded the strict application of scientific methods and efficiency standards designed to make the sewing rooms resemble the garment factories of private industry. Charged with the daily enforcement of production quotas were the female supervisors, who tended to regard their "primary goal" as "training [women] for private industry." These supervisors, unlike Dryden and his associates, did not regard the sewing rooms as a form of charity and instead staunchly defended the right of employable women to work relief under the WPA. Although they conceded that prospects of outside employment for the "sewing women" were quite small, the supervisors still treated their workers as employees, regularly discharging aging women with failing eyesight or those who simply could not "keep up." "If we allowed them to take things easy," explained one WPA supervisor, "they could never make the adjustment in a commercial plant." Some of the supervisors even refused the workers' request that they be trained as cutters—one of the highest-paying jobs in the garment industry—and instead brought in WPA men to serve as cutters, following industry's practice of reserving that position for men. The sewing rooms, insisted the supervisors, must conform to the standards and traditional divisions of labor set by private industry; only then would the women workers be able to find employment. Obviously not an experiment in social reform, the sewing rooms from the outset limited their relief activities to the loyal and efficient worker. In December 1936, for example, an evaluation of productivity records led to the overnight dismissal of 5 percent of the sewing women. But to the surprise of Dryden and his staff, the discharged women, some of them PUL members, joined forces with other league supporters to protest the firings. Confronted with hundreds of women outside his office and besieged with adverse publicity for discharging older women, a sheepish Dryden pledged to rehire "a few" of the workers. But throughout the decade, the sewing women suffered from the unsympathetic attitudes of WPA administrators, the application of efficiency standards, and periodic federal reductions in the WPA job quotas. In 1937 they even faced a total shutdown of the sewing rooms because the

The city's wpa *sewing project for black women, 1936*
(Courtesy of the Special Collections Division, University of Maryland
College Park Libraries)

federal government had grown weary of the city's refusal to provide any funding for the projects; a compromise of sorts was finally reached when Mayor Jackson reluctantly agreed to pay all supervisory costs of the sewing rooms, leaving the federal government to finance the bill for wages and materials.[37]

Employable black women found fewer opportunities in the predominantly white wpa sewing rooms than in domestic service. Local officials assumed that it was the destiny of black women to be servants and went so far as to attempt to recruit young black girls attending high school for wpa-sponsored domestic-training classes. National wpa officials echoed these sentiments, instructing their local counterparts that the most useful programs for the "employment of colored women" centered on the improve-

One of Baltimore's WPA *sewing rooms for white women, 1936*
(Courtesy of the National Archives)

ment of domestic skills. Even the black executive secretary of the Baltimore Urban League, although concerned about securing work relief for jobless women, frankly admitted his ignorance as to the kinds of WPA programs appropriate for black women—thereby underscoring the gender-based prejudice that all women faced.[38]

Depression conditions threw large numbers of black domestics off their jobs as middle-class white households cut back on expenses or turned to white women for service work. At least until the establishment of the WPA, the supply of houseworkers far exceeded the demand, and housewives often took advantage of their domestics. Employers increased the hours of service, widened the duties performed, cut wages, and, reversing a twentieth-century trend toward nonresident service, occasionally even required domestics to live in. The black women who retained their domestic positions suffered the most: their hours were longer, and their pay lower. Trained white servants received about $6 a week, but blacks earned as little as $3. "These private families," complained one Baltimore black domestic, "work the poor woman to death. . . . They have to work sixteen and seventeen hours a day," and their employers "put the work of three people on one and pay them less wages and they get no Sundays, no holidays of any kind. . . . They are harder on the colored woman," she added. "They seem to think that a colored woman have no feeling of tiredness."[39]

The deterioration in working conditions and wages encouraged household workers to seek employment elsewhere. "Our Negro girls," explained the local director of the National Reemployment Service, "will not work in private homes if they can get jobs as practical nurses, as helpers in nursery schools, as waitresses in restaurants, and as salad girls, pantry keepers, and kitchen workers in various establishments."[40] Both white and black domestics preferred the WPA sewing rooms to placement in private homes as servants. The sewing projects offered higher wages, shorter hours, and a predictable, if rapid, work rhythm that included a fixed time for lunch breaks and clearly stated production requirements.

Baltimore housewives complained of inadequately trained servants and criticized the federal government for placing their domestics in work-relief programs. One woman wrote Eleanor Roosevelt of the "servant problem," lamenting that "the courtesy and old spirit of service is lacking" and complaining that she had had to fire one domestic who refused to use the deferential title of "Miss" when addressing her daughters. The problem, she concluded, was that "too many prefer 'relief' to 'work.' " By 1937, requests from households for experienced workers had become so frequent that the NRS announced that Baltimore had "a serious shortage of trained domestic servants." But the issue was not an actual shortage of workers so much as a shortage of trained domestics willing to work long hours for miserably low wages. The local NRS director conceded that many domestics "failed to meet the critical requirements of Baltimore housewives" and that employers frequently became "indignant" when the NRS refused to place experienced white domestics in private homes for the "paltry sum" of $3–$5 per week.[41] Dryden was sympathetic to the housewives' demand for better-trained servants. Already familiar with WPA-sponsored domestic training classes in other cities, he determined to establish a project in Baltimore "to train young women of relief families for domestic service."[42]

This was one more attempt to ensure that a certain "class of people" was kept "available for domestic service."[43] Dryden and Hopkins had already constructed arbitrary quotas to limit the participation of unemployed black domestics in the WPA—a technique widely practiced in the South. And Dryden had been reluctant to establish work-relief projects for black women, saying that it "would be bad policy here in Baltimore."[44] But WPA training classes, he reasoned, would provide a supply of domestic servants and would face no serious opposition from local authorities. After all, in 1934 the FERA had sponsored a training class for "colored household employees" at Baltimore's Frederick Douglass High School, where young black women were instructed how best to serve white families. Across the nation, moreover, projects to train domestics proved extremely popular among local officials and middle-class families. Administrators at the WPA praised the program for its cost efficiency: the training period for the women was short, their placement in private homes was relatively high, and as trainees they received but 50 percent of the WPA's security wage for unskilled workers. By June 1940, nearly 18,000 workers had been trained, and 13,000 of them had received private employment.[45]

In Baltimore, Dryden's project to train domestic servants was well received. Both Mayor Jackson and members of BERC strongly endorsed the program (one relief official explained his support by saying that his own household had suffered too long without the services of a skilled domestic). Housewives applauded the project as a necessary service, local officials praised the classes for providing invaluable training, and the WPA used the program to improve public relations. One reporter who attended a special banquet prepared by the trainees commended the project for allowing black women to demonstrate their abilities as "naturally" good cooks.[46]

Only the trainees themselves objected to the program. Handled by the city's Department of Welfare, the first classes were under way by early 1938; because of increased unemployment in the 1937 recession, the welfare director, T. J. S. Waxter, decided to establish a class for white trainees in addition to the one planned for blacks. Of the thirty black women, ranging in age from 16 to 41, only ten completed the classes—and of the ten, only five took jobs in private employment. Among the thirty whites, fewer than half finished the training and only two began work as domestics. For the second round of training, Waxter abandoned altogether the class for whites and was unable to fill the thirty seats for the black project. Through their attrition rates, open complaints, and frequent parodies on the housewives they were instructed to serve, the trainees expressed their dissatisfaction with the program. Clad in "maid uniforms," they were directed to be personally "clean, neat, [and] quiet" and to perform as "efficient servants for Baltimore housewives"—to cook, clean, launder clothes, serve meals, market, and take telephone calls politely. Their training further included religious instruction and advice on how to

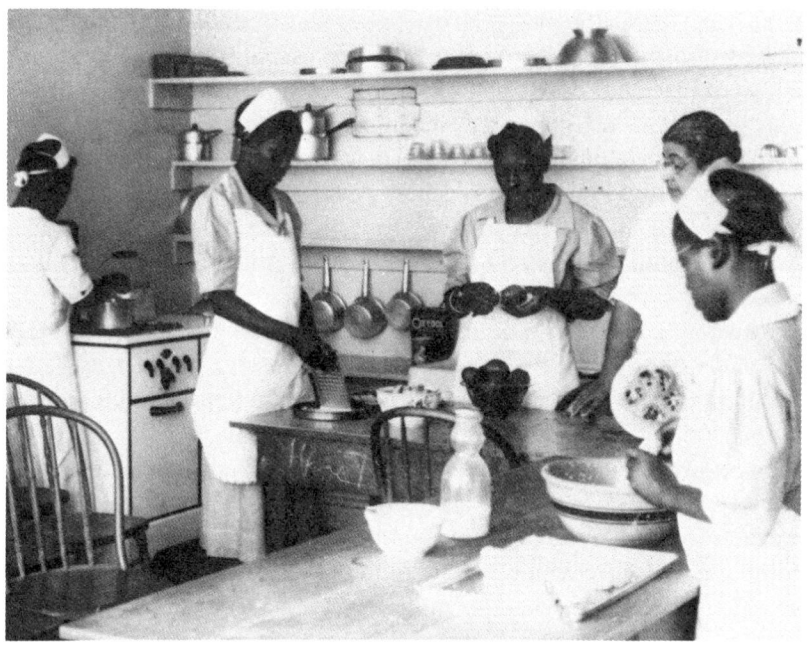

Baltimore's WPA domestic training class for black women, 1938
(Courtesy of the National Archives)

"get along" with children and pets in the household. Finally, WPA supervisors reminded them of their status not merely as workers but as servants, their obligation to be inconspicuous in the household, and their responsibility to be modest in dress (they were not allowed to wear jewelry) and demeanor. Issues of power and control not only defined the instruction given the trainees but also informed the image of the female employer as portrayed by WPA supervisors. Rather than present housewives as employers responsive to market considerations and eager for efficient workers, WPA officials pictured them as exploitative, capricious, and personalistic women with "certain whims that must be humored." To satisfy housewives, domestics were told, they must be not only hard workers, but personally pleasing to their employers.[47]

The nature of the training alternately angered and alienated domestics, but the situation for blacks was made still worse by the second-class treatment they received within the program. White trainees, for example, not only received a better facility for their instruction, but, if they refused employment offers at the end of their classes, they were not removed from the relief rolls. As the NRS director explained, the service had encountered serious "difficulty in getting [white trainees] to consider the kinds of jobs available"; it therefore delayed placing them until appropriate homes were found. Black domestics, however, did not receive similar consideration: upon completion of the training, should a black domestic refuse her job assignment she was "cut off relief and left to fend for herself."[48] Furthermore, when black houseworkers complained that live-in arrangements separated them from their families, a local WPA employment director coldly responded that depression conditions required such sacrifices. Rather than leave their children, some women turned to other relief programs, including aid to dependent children, in order to maintain their homes and support their families.

Both white and black women in Baltimore, then, thoroughly repudiated the WPA training program—an otherwise popular program that satisfied traditional notions about race, class, and gender in the labor force. One local WPA supervisor did, however, concede that a series of *Evening Sun* articles published in 1938, exposing the harsh conditions of domestic work, had served to heighten the participants' dissatisfaction with the program and with household service in general. Moreover, according to the supervisor, the purpose and nature of the instruction, and especially the emphasis on deferential behavior, often collided with the democratic messages from Franklin and Eleanor Roosevelt in the White House. "The President and Mrs. Roosevelt have been wonderfully just, kind, and humane to the poor of America," wrote one domestic worker, enclosing with her letter clippings from the *Sun* series on household service. But the "autocrats" who challenged Roosevelt were exploiting the domestics—a condition, she asserted, that could be remedied not by training classes but by a union. Only then would President Roosevelt be able to end the inequalities he decried in his radio broadcasts.[49]

Employable black men, traditionally excluded from the building trades, also suffered from the city's emphasis on major construction in its WPA program. And, as was the case for black domestics, Roosevelt's orders against discrimination on works projects did not protect unemployed black men from the racist policies of local officials. Citing local prejudice, Baltimore's WPA office initially refused to sponsor special projects for black men. Relief practices followed by BERC further restricted the program for blacks. The city's one-year residential requirement and, more importantly, its general refusal to assist single individuals fell disproportionately on black men as recent migrants to Baltimore. They were unable to qualify for BERC assistance, and they were usually unable to be certified for WPA jobs.[50]

Yet, thanks to the efforts of activist groups, some blacks did benefit from the works program—and for those families, the WPA often meant survival.[51] In 1937, for example, at the insistence of the Committee for Industrial Organization, blacks received WPA work on the construction of the Montebello tunnel system. Leaders of the CIO and representatives of the PUL routinely blasted the local WPA for racial discrimination, and regularly demanded more jobs for blacks. Although local officials tried to discredit such groups, often by citing their alleged ties to the Communist party, they still grudgingly acceded to minor demands. For example, blacks received WPA work on short-term paving projects in the city or on other jobs that were not of long duration. In another instance, the combined efforts of the CIO and the PUL forced the city to create a project for "unemployed white-collar blacks."[52]

The WPA also encouraged community organization among blacks, thereby underscoring the ability of the federal government to enhance simultaneously its own sphere of authority and the tradition of self-help at the local level. As Harvard Sitkoff notes, the WPA gave "blacks their first sense of being a part of things, of really being included."[53] Baltimore's black organizations sent petitions and letters to local and national WPA offices, demanding fairer treatment. Jobless blacks joined together to form a new organization, the Baltimore City Colored Unemployed. Its members worked to remind government officials that the "colored group is the true 'forgotten man' " and to demand administrative representation in the WPA, which, "packed with white citizens only," offered "no chance of fairplay" to the unemployed blacks in the city.[54]

Black women successfully organized to ensure that their children benefited from the WPA nursery-school program and to compensate for the inequalities in the program. Although blacks received five schools and whites four, the resources were not allocated equitably: black schools were smaller and more crowded, and some were "without playspace" altogether. Moreover, whereas both black and white schools depended heavily on volunteer efforts and special fund-raising activities, in the black schools inadequate funding forced their community supporters to raise money for coal, heat, and light—necessities that were automatically supplied to the white schools. Aggressive citizen action among black residents served to transform one nursery school "located in one of the worst sections of the

Howard Street WPA *"pick-and-shovel" project for black men, 1936*
(Courtesy of the National Archives)

city" into a project that won praise, not only from local and national WPA officials, but from foreign visitors as well. The black commitment to the nursery program among both mothers and fathers fairly shocked local WPA administrators, who scarcely disguised their incredulity in their reports. Particularly noteworthy was the construction, in one of the nursery schools, of a sitting room that was initiated and completed solely by the parents themselves. "Many parents," one WPA official observed, "dropped in" frequently to "sit and read or just to sit and watch the children."[55]

Finally, black Baltimoreans organized to persuade the city to comply with federal guidelines and establish a separate WPA "Division of Recreation for Colored People" to be staffed, they insisted, by unemployed blacks. By early 1936, Dryden had fulfilled their demand by creating a separate division with 150 employees, of whom 135 had been relief clients. Committed to the "sincere belief that hobbies have a strong influence in building morale," the division turned to neighborhood groups for cooperation in promoting "club organization" around interests ranging from "folk and interpretive dancing" to clay modeling and embroidery. It also supervised twelve recreation centers and eighteen play yards and sponsored the "lighted-school house"—a program of adult evening courses designed to enhance learning abilities and cultural awareness. And, to link recreational and educational activities, the black recreation division organized local councils composed of neighborhood residents and the principals of the schools where the play yards were located. The response was overwhelming and community participation far exceeded the division's expectations. Even before the more active summer months, between 1 January and 1 June 1936, 224,493 children used the play space and 40,121 adults attended the recreation centers and "lighted-school" program. The WPA's recreation division represented a major improvement for blacks. Before its establishment, only 3 of Baltimore's 248 staffed "play stations" had been available to blacks. The privately run but municipally subsidized Playground Athletic League of Baltimore had in fact earlier admitted that the "chief exception" to the city's adequate recreational facilities were "playfields for colored boys and girls." Federal money and support, then, enabled black residents to improve upon the city's record, to increase the number of recreational centers, and to use them more fully. Such interaction between federal programs and the citizen action they encouraged made possible many of the innovations achieved at the local level.[56]

But even limited gains for blacks in the works program met with resistance from whites. Fears of economic competition as well as strident racism accounted for their hostility. Whites complained of assisting "gin drunk niggers who will not work" with "money from white people who work and pay taxes."[57] One of the city's magistrates, George Eckhardt, publicly charged that many blacks who received assistance were not needy and that most of the traffic violators in his court were "WPA darkies." He further claimed that a visit to BERC headquarters would show "darkies coming in taxicabs and going in taxicabs." These charges were denied by BERC, which explained that even white WPA workers rarely owned automobiles and that relief rolls and allotments had been cut so severely there was little opportunity for misuse of funds.[58]

Baltimore received much of what it wanted from the WPA by reducing its effectiveness as a work-relief program and by minimizing its significance for groups that were traditionally neglected. Yet local officials continued to attack national programs and policies. Mayor Jackson rarely tired of demanding more federal assistance while simultaneously denouncing the government for its encroachments on local prerogative. He criticized certain work-relief projects as unnecessary make-work but also took credit for those same projects, including the preparation of a city atlas, the cataloging of collections at the Baltimore Museum of Art and the Enoch Pratt Free Library, and the completion of an economic survey for local businesses.[59] Even at a celebratory meeting of the WPA's Division of Women's Activities, Jackson appalled his audience of WPA officials and women workers with a diatribe against the "whole philosophy of the work-relief program." Members of the audience found his speech "discourteous, uncalled for, anti–New Deal, and unsympathetic toward the Administration's program in general."[60] Aware of the mayor's antics, federal authorities suspected Jackson Democrats of allying with Republicans to distribute "violently anti-Roosevelt" leaflets among the city's WPA workers. The "skillfully-worded [and] expertly printed" handbills charged that the WPA was run by a "Communist dictatorship in the United States."[61]

Further damaging to federal-local relations and to the WPA program in general were job quota reductions and restrictive policy changes made at the national level. In 1936, when the WPA had been operating for only a year, Hopkins was concerned about mounting costs and ordered a job quota reduction of over 25 percent. Mayor Jackson denounced the action but refused to aid the dismissed workers, saying that unemployment assistance was a federal responsibility. Apprehensive that work relief might become habit-forming, national WPA officials subsequently ordered all workers employed for more than eighteen consecutive months to be dismissed for at least thirty days and to be recertified before receiving WPA employment again. Akin to the city's own "purges," this ruling worked particular hardship on such WPA employees as the sewing women who were unable to secure private employment. The director of Baltimore's welfare department repudiated the policy change, declaring, "I am against throwing these old people to the dogs for thirty days"—but he also affirmed that the city would not assist them during that period. In 1938 the WPA "tossed a bombshell into Baltimore's relief situation" when it disqualified all WPA workers eligible to receive unemployment compensation.

In that instance the city was forced to supplement the "starvation" benefits of $3 to $6 per week.[62]

The federal government also began to question its singular financial arrangements with the city. Because an unusually large percentage of WPA money was expended on project materials rather than on relief—over 30 percent instead of the mandated 10 percent—WPA authorities insisted that Baltimore share some of those costs. Municipal officials consistently refused until the federal government threatened to withdraw all funds, and then they offered a compromise plan that required only a modest local contribution.[63] Intergovernmental relations remained so shaky that suspicious local authorities even refused to sign the necessary sponsor's agreement for a costly construction project, afraid that the federal government would suspend its funding and obligate the city to finance the project.[64] Angry WPA authorities reminded city officials that it was they who had insisted on using WPA money for substantial projects. Nevertheless, local leaders continued to place the national government in an impossible situation by insisting on increased federal assistance while decrying "constant meddling from Washington."[65]

Fears of federal encroachment did not, however, figure into the popular criticisms of the WPA. Although WPA workers and PUL members, for example, objected to the federally imposed quota reductions, they directed most of their complaints at local officials and frequently called for greater federal supervision of municipal policies. Numerous civic groups specifically requested that the federal government oversee the city's WPA to ensure that local officials fulfilled "the necessary requirements to obtain the funds." As one citizen group explained, "Because [the] WPA is so important to the welfare of our unemployed citizens, it is vital for the people of a community to know whether or not this resource is being utilized to the full by local authorities."[66] Numerous letters to local papers and national officials indicated that many Baltimoreans believed that local authorities failed in this task. One WPA worker himself perfectly captured popular sentiment when he wrote, "The W.P.A. was a God send through our President [but] from what I can see here, it does not seem to be carried out here locally as intended by our President."[67]

Few New Deal programs received as hearty a welcome as the Civilian Conservation Corps (CCC). In Baltimore in March 1933, "news of the reforestation camps proposed by President Roosevelt broke like a ray of sunshine upon the homeless and transient men sheltered from yesterday's cold and snow at the Salvation Army's central bureau." Unemployed steam shovelers, painters, pile drivers, mechanics, barbers, and chefs—all greeted the announcement with shouts of "Sign me on!" The prospect of leaving the city or state to work in CCC camps little bothered these eager volunteers. Native Baltimorean August Gill explained, "I'd go anywhere. I'd go to hell if I could get work there."[68]

Yet the CCC program was not intended to rescue the homeless men found in the city's shelters. Rather, it was designed to assist young men and their families on relief while simultaneously conserving the nation's forests and natural resources. Although nationally this was a highly popular combination, on the local level the CCC encountered a number of difficulties. The program was administered initially by the city's private relief agencies, and it began slowly, divided in its management and often weakened by idiosyncratic supervision. Its military character, for example, particularly rankled Anna Ward, executive secretary of the Family Welfare Association, who reluctantly and only minimally supervised the program in Baltimore. The city's allotment of volunteers was divided among the private agencies, but Ward delayed filling even the first monthly quota, maintaining that because the CCC represented only a small part of her duties, she would not allow other services "to slide in order to devote full time to reforestation." Federal officials complained about the delay, attributed it to Ward's pacifism, and attempted to reassure local administrators that the CCC camps were not part of a general military training program. Ward ignored their protests, welcomed a PUL demonstration at her office against the role of the War Department in the program, and firmly informed federal officials that local problems in filling quotas resulted not from her actions but from a decline in enthusiasm among volunteers who feared they were being "train[ed] for the first draft."[69]

Other Baltimore charity officials found too lenient the federal rulings concerning eligibility. They interpreted the federal directive that the CCC enroll only young men from families whose case histories were familiar to the agencies to mean that only worthy or "good young men" from respectable families should be allowed to participate in the program. As one FWA official declared: "We want enrollment in the conservation camps to be looked upon as a privilege and an opportunity." The integrity of the program, the FWA insisted, would not be sacrificed in a hurried attempt to fill quotas; it acknowledged that some families would suffer from the delays, but it believed that the necessary caution would serve the greater goal of weeding out the unworthy and ensuring that only proper families benefited from the efforts of honorable young men.[70] Reports from the Jewish Social Service Bureau should have served to quash fears about approving unworthy volunteers for CCC service. Bureau workers found its applicants eager to work and to help their families: "The greatest trouble we are having," observed one official, "is to keep them from sending all their money home [from the CCC camps]. It's hard to convince some of them that they will need a little bit of the $30.00 monthly wage."[71] Still, not one agency met the first quota deadline set for early April 1933. The record did not improve when BERC took over nominal control of the CCC in September, because the actual administration of the program remained unchanged, and for the remainder of the decade Baltimore had difficulty meeting its CCC quota.[72]

While white quotas went unfilled, black youths were denied the opportunity to participate in the program. In response to repeated complaints and protests by the Baltimore Urban League, federal officials launched investigations that revealed that as late as mid-1936 not one black youth in the entire state had received CCC employment, and that neither the city nor the state had even bothered to establish a "quota for colored boys." Continued protest by the Urban League and the federal intervention it provoked finally persuaded state officials to organize two camps for 500 black youths. But that did not help the 248 young blacks from relief families sent by the league to apply for CCC enrollment; BERC even denied them application forms, claiming that it "did not have the time to investigate their cases." More pressure and protest from the Urban League prompted city officials to meet at least part of the quota for blacks, but their minimal efforts remained a source of concern for the league and for federal officials who continued to denounce the quota as inexcusably low and to urge the establishment of more black camps.[73] The racial hostility followed Baltimore's black CCC members to their camps. In 1938, for example, several CCC black youths from Baltimore were wounded by a shotgun blast at a prayer meeting in Chestertown, Maryland.[74]

The state as a whole also experienced serious difficulty in complying with CCC quota schedules. By early June 1933, with only a week left to meet the final deadline, both the city and the counties still needed recruits. State CCC recruitment officer Paul Beisser explained the failure by simply repeating the city's defense: inappropriate applicants and an overburdened relief administration. Following the city's policy, Beisser stressed the need for good men and "refrained from just opening up the flood gates."[75] State FERA administrator Harry Greenstein, although usually sympathetic to local prerogative, lamented the city's and the state's lax performance in the CCC program. Two years later, in 1935, Greenstein regretfully observed that only one-third of the state's quota had been filled. In particular, he urged city officials to follow federal guidelines and reduce their "red tape," explaining, "We cannot afford to lose the opportunities of CCC enrollment for Maryland."[76]

Further complicating the CCC situation were communication problems uncovered only after federal intervention and a number of local investigations. To their embarrassment, city officials found the explanation for the unusually high absentee rates for approved volunteers: the CCC applicants had never been informed of their acceptance![77] Although this problem was ultimately resolved, it had still further restricted the relief role of the CCC.

Frequent field visits to Baltimore by federal officials resulted in little improvement. As late as 1939, federal authorities urged the city to be more "lenient" in "its interpretation of the purpose" of the CCC program.[78] They particularly disliked the city's CCC selection official, Anita Faatz. They complained that "she has no vision whatsoever concerning the possibilities for service involved in the responsibility for CCC selection"; that she lacked the "spirit and understanding" characteristic of the New Deal and essential to her work, regarding her position as "merely another job"; and that "her personality is unfortunate." "The more visits we can make to Baltimore the better," reported one official—but, he added, "as long as Miss Anita Faatz has control of the operation of the selection program, I doubt we will get very far very fast."[79]

The difficulties in Baltimore's CCC program outraged national officials, who recorded them in a report that labeled Maryland "one of our worst states from the point of view of attitude . . . and general inattention to the selection program."[80] When national authorities sharply rebuked the city for its delays and unmet quotas, phlegmatic local officials casually responded that their efforts represented the "time and care [necessary] to insure proper selection of boys for CCC enrollment." But federal CCC administrators noted that neither the incomplete and inaccurate applications they regularly received from the Baltimore office nor the city's alarmingly high discharge rate among volunteers reflected careful CCC processing procedures.[81]

Undoubtedly, city and state officials deserved criticism for obstructing the effectiveness of the CCC program. Their actions and inaction minimized the significance of the CCC both as a relief and as a conservation program. And yet, limited evidence also suggests that in a few instances local initiative liberalized the program. Complaints against a federal ruling that prohibited boys in training schools from participating in the CCC, for example, won a reprieve for those who had been sent to the schools out of "dependency, not delinquency."[82] Moreover, field reports indicate that federal officials often evaluated the success of a program more by its appearance than by its accomplishments. Concern for proper forms, neatly typed, with the appropriate signatures, for instance, figured more prominently in federal-local correspondence than did the city's shabby performance in regard to CCC participation.[83] Federal officials singled out Faatz not only because of her obvious administrative shortcomings and lack of New Deal vision but also because she was neither congenial nor deferential and she demeaned the program by filling out CCC forms in pencil.

Although Baltimore's unemployed benefited less from the CCC than they should have, the program still had some accomplishments. Its few recruits often worked outside the state, generally going first to Fort Humphreys, Virginia, where they underwent what was called "basic training." The work of the CCC was divided into two categories: "capital expenditures" involving highway construction and reforestation, and "make work" consisting primarily of "poison plant and rodent eradication." Maryland had no national forests, and so the principal CCC efforts involved reforestation in the state parks; most projects took place outside the city's confines. At the peak of the CCC in 1935 the state had thirty camps with about 20,000 corpsmen, but that number steadily declined in the latter part of the decade. Accomplishments of the CCC included the construction of 166 miles of telephone lines in forest areas, 188 miles of truck trails, and more than 300 miles of firebreaks; CCC workers also labored on drainage and mosquito-control projects on Maryland's Eastern Shore and planted more than half a million trees by 1936. Finally, the *Sun* and a few officials claimed that the program had transformed "callow" city youths into "strapping, clear-eyed, suntanned youths," who prospered in "an atmosphere of wholesomeness" characterized by "strict military discipline" and daily hard work.[84]

Some "CCC Boys," however, saw the program in a different light. They complained about the military discipline or what they called "Army life" at the camps and objected to the overcrowded conditions. One corpsman described the sleeping arrangements among men "packed somewhat like sardines" as unbearable. For many volunteers the chief attraction of the CCC was "plenty of food," and when food was in short supply they went on strike to protest the shortages. At one Maryland camp, military supervisors fired tear-gas shells at CCC corpsmen when they refused to return to work; the tear gas, the officers reported, had "a quieting effect" on the strikers.[85] The overall appraisal of the CCC program by the state's National Emergency Council director, Arthur Hungerford, contained little else but condemnation of the city's role. He censured local officials for their inability to fill CCC quotas and for their consistent failure to make full use of the program. He openly doubted the validity of their explanations and instead placed the blame squarely on their mishandling of the CCC program. He asserted that local relief officials had never fully appreciated the value of the CCC as a relief program. Their antimilitarism, he concluded, had cost the city's young men dearly, for according to his estimates Baltimore received but 20 percent of the statewide quota.[86]

Another program designed for the nation's youth, to give them "a definite stake in the life of their time," was the National Youth Administration (NYA). It had its origins in the FERA student-work program but became part of the WPA in 1935. Although officially administered through the WPA, the NYA had its own state administrator, who worked with area directors to coordinate projects that kept students in school and to provide training for youths out of school and unemployed. Like other New Deal programs in the city, the NYA took shape slowly and sporadically. And when exasperated federal officials demanded an explanation of the NYA's "considerable difficulty in getting underway in Maryland," they heard the usual refrain: too few materials, inappropriate clients, and an overburdened relief administration. A number of citizen groups protested the inaction. Their activities, along with a harsh letter from the NYA's national office demanding the immediate establishment of a local office, pushed Baltimore toward at least partial compliance. But national NYA officials continued to denounce the city's and the state's "inattention" to the program and to urge greater local-federal cooperation and communication.[87]

To delay the entrance of the nation's youth into the job market, the NYA encouraged higher education by assisting students between the ages of 16 and 24. Unlike the CCC, the NYA did not require eligible students to be members of families receiving relief. However, the college-aid component of the NYA was not particularly successful in Maryland because throughout the 1930s nearly half of all students left school after the eighth grade— accordingly, of all the state's students annually assisted by the NYA, only 17 percent were part of the college-aid program. And local and state officials took few steps to encourage higher education; indeed, in 1935 the state spent only $50,000 of $90,000 provided by the federal government to assist high-school students in preparation for college.[88]

The local NYA focused slightly more attention on the out-of-school work program. In implementing this program, the city tightened federal requirements, generally giving jobs to needy students whose families received relief assistance. Youths who participated in the program received one-third of the WPA security wage. Baltimore's first NYA work project, repairing toys for poor children, began 30 November 1935. Other projects were soon started, including a health survey at the Johns Hopkins School of Hygiene; by the end of 1936, 760 youths were working at sixteen projects scattered throughout the city.[89] Boys learned a variety of skills, working at "tabulating projects" and building bus shelters for school children. Girls, however, were limited to lighter clerical tasks and to NYA sewing projects where they made or repaired clothes for needy children and where they were, in effect, trained for WPA sewing projects.[90] Although, based on its statewide quota, the NYA assisted the city's youth proportionately more than did the CCC, Baltimore still failed to receive its fair share of the program: Baltimore held nearly two-thirds of the state's unemployed youth, yet fewer than one-third of the Maryland students helped in 1936 by the NYA were from the city. Officials of BERC did not press for a greater share but in large measure simply ignored the program. Delays in establishing the local apprenticeship training program, for example, meant that the city never received its initial allotment of funds, for beginning in 1937 the federal government sharply cut money for the training program and reduced NYA quotas. Over the next three years the number of NYA students declined by half. It was only in 1939, when the federal government reorganized the relief system and placed new emphasis on defense, that the NYA received more support; fifteen new projects were then started and youth employment figures rose from 334 in 1939 to 1,196 in 1940.[91]

Black students, who surely would have been excluded in regular allotments, received special consideration because there was separate funding for them. Aubrey Williams, as national director of the program, and Mary McLeod Bethune, as head of the "Negro Affairs" section of the NYA, made sure that thousands of dollars went directly to assist black youths.[92] A receptive and sympathetic national office of the NYA aided the Baltimore Urban League in lobbying for black participation in Baltimore's program. The league first insisted that the state NYA fill the position of administrative assistant in charge of Negro Affairs. That demand grew out of the state's earlier refusal to appoint a black supervisor for the FERA's Emergency

Education Program for Negroes. More successful under the NYA, the Urban League secured the appointment and cooperated with the new administrative assistant to assure that students in the city's black colleges received necessary aid. As a result of their efforts, nearly 30 percent of the students assisted in the city's college-aid program in 1936 were black. In the out-of-school work program, almost 29 percent of the participants were black (although they usually received training for less desirable jobs, such as orderlies in city hospitals).[93]

Federal retrenchment of the program in 1937, however, particularly hurt the NYA's "Negro Affairs" section. The state NYA director immediately attempted to reduce the role of his black administrative assistant, questioning the significance of the job and slashing budgets for necessary office equipment and secretarial assistance. Vigorous protest from both the PUL and the Baltimore Urban League limited the proposed reductions, but declining federal support weakened the program's commitment to assisting blacks. By 1941, black students constituted only about 10 percent of the participants in the college-aid program.[94]

Coordination of the diverse New Deal programs in the state fell to the director of the National Emergency Council (NEC): Arthur Hungerford, former NRA compliance director and ardent New Dealer. At the national level, the NEC functioned ineffectually to reduce the confusion and conflict caused by Roosevelt's disparate emergency efforts. At the local level, Hungerford faced an impossible task. From his office in Baltimore, he attempted in vain to instill a sense of common purpose among local and state officials and to coordinate New Deal programs and policies. The WPA, for example, rejected his efforts to coordinate job placement with "delinquent borrowers" in order simultaneously to save homes and provide employment. Local officials even accused him of "spying" on the city for the federal government. And although he was recognized as the official spokesman for the New Deal and authorized to review all relevant speeches in an attempt to preclude political controversy, Hungerford never managed to quiet Baltimore's harshest critics of Roosevelt—most of them Democrats who specialized in vitriolic attacks on the New Deal. Ignored or disparaged by local leaders, Hungerford found greater success in working with those who supported the New Deal—the unemployed and the many citizen groups that organized to ensure the full and equitable implementation of New Deal programs. He considered his major accomplishment to be the establishment of city consumer councils, which conducted

surveys of Baltimore's food and fuel prices and lobbied for higher allotments to relief recipients. His attempts to reform relief practices and
strengthen the city's New Deal programs not only alienated local officials
but also tested the sympathies of federal officials, especially when he
admitted to having friends among the leadership of the Peoples Unemployment League and to having attended the PUL's state conference. National
NEC administrators expressed concern about Hungerford's ties and advised
him that "it would not be judicious" to continue his association with the
PUL—an organization that they regarded as Socialist, pure and simple. By
the end of 1937, Washington decided that the national office could handle
the field operations in Maryland and closed the Baltimore office.[95]

Baltimore's municipal leadership never fully supported the New Deal
and often actively undermined its programs and openly criticized its purposes. City officials followed the inconsistent but expedient course of
simultaneously disavowing local responsibility for unemployment relief
and challenging federal encroachments on municipal obligations. Only
when New Deal programs provided federal money without requiring
matching funds or policy initiatives did state and local officials respond
enthusiastically. What they wanted from the New Deal was a federally
financed old deal that catered to their traditional constituencies and enhanced political loyalties.

Federal intervention, although rarely sufficiently aggressive, encouraged citizens not protected by traditional politics to organize in order to
make local officials more responsive by threatening exposure to federal
authorities. The spectre of greater federal intervention, in short, raised the
stakes in society and consequently stimulated citizen participation in public affairs. Local and state officials grudgingly complied out of economic
necessity, but when they were able, as with the CCC and the NYA, they
preferred to ignore the programs rather than follow federal guidelines. In
very rare instances, such as in the case of public housing (discussed in the
next chapter), organized public protest prevented municipal inaction from
debilitating New Deal programs.

CHAPTER 4

Community Organization and Citizen Participation

Public Housing and the New Deal

Few issues generated more public concern in the 1930s than that of housing. Like such other cities as Philadelphia and Boston, Baltimore suffered from a housing crisis, especially for the poor. There was, for example, a serious shortage of low-cost rental properties. Blacks, who were isolated in two areas of the city by economic and geographic discrimination, suffered especially: one survey in the 1930s found that "practically no housing of any kind designed for colored use has been created in Baltimore since antebellum times." The depression-related problems of evictions and foreclosures only aggravated the situation. Before 1939, moreover, the city failed to benefit significantly from New Deal programs designed to encourage home ownership or provide low-cost housing for the needy. The Home Owners' Loan Corporation (HOLC), for example, created by the federal government to prevent foreclosures, failed in Baltimore to serve those most in need: homeowners struggling against foreclosure publicly criticized the HOLC for catering to bankers and business leaders, and the HOLC's intimacy with the local financial community not only provoked public protest but led to financial irregularities, culminating with an investigation of fraud in the city's homeowners' loan program.[1]

Local bankers also restricted the impact of the Federal Housing Authority (FHA), created in June 1934 to encourage homeownership and house construction by insuring mortgages. By 1937 only 1,665 mortgages had been insured in the entire state while the city's construction industry limped along, its building contracts down to a mere $12 million from over $50 million in the late 1920s.[2] Baltimore's reputation as a "city of homes" ironically further impaired the efficacy of the FHA program. A survey of Baltimore housing conducted by local architects and sponsored by the FERA-affiliated Maryland Emergency Housing and Park Commission found the city's percentage of home ownership at over fifty to be unnaturally high—the result, the study concluded, of greedy realtors and bankers who "exploited" city residents with the "constant campaign to 'own-your-own-home' " and encouraged the "over-selling of ridiculously small equities in jerry-built houses," which caused "not only a cumulative hardship on these so-called owners, but a tremendous load on mortgages in the writing off of unsafe mortgages." The FHA, of course, refused approval for such risky loans, but that did not deter local bankers and realtors from hustling ill-prepared "younger people to invest" in poor-quality housing.[3]

Realtors cooperated with businesses and local political leaders to thwart still another New Deal program for housing. Created under section 202(d) of the National Industrial Recovery Act, the Public Works Administration Housing Division provided funds for "slum clearance" and the construction of public housing. Before being replaced by the United States Housing Authority (USHA) in 1937, it built fifty-one projects in a number of cities. Philadelphia, for example, received two public housing projects, and Boston one.[4] Baltimore was initially slated for two projects, but ultimately failed to get any. Real-estate interests, a stubbornly anti–New Deal mayor, and racial considerations all worked to undermine the PWA's proposed projects for the city.

Officials in the PWA's Housing Division early targeted Baltimore for necessary housing reform. Preliminary studies of the city found "a ring of blighted residential tracts of the most serious importance and size." The center of the city, they noted, "was almost completely girdled with a belt of poverty, which, unless rehabilitated, will remain an increasingly serious menace to all properties inside and outside of this ring."[5] Certain areas of the city, concluded one member of the investigative committee, were "so poor" that "it would be hopeless to attempt any correction with the limited funds available. It would be like treating a small portion of a cancerous growth—no real lasting good could be accomplished."[6] After considerable

discussion and revision of proposals, the housing committee finally recommended and received federal approval for two slum clearance projects
for the city—one for whites in the Waverly neighborhood of northeast
Baltimore, and one for blacks along McCulloh Street, near the Harlem
Park area west of the central business district. Extensive interviews with
residents in both areas indicated substantial community support for the
proposed projects.[7]

Mayor Jackson, however, objected to the PWA's proposal, bemoaning the
prospect of federal intervention and insisting that the national government
pay a "service charge" on land developed for public housing. The federal
government, he snapped, would not be allowed to compete unfairly against
private enterprise in his city. Maryland's National Emergency Director
Arthur Hungerford criticized Jackson's demand for a fee and predicted that
it would result in the PWA's abandonment of the projects for Baltimore.
"With cities and towns all over the country fighting for these projects," he
declared, "there is no reason in the world why it [the PWA] should pay a city
for allowing it to establish the project."[8] But Jackson's position drew a
hearty endorsement from the city's Real Estate Board and from officials of
the Baltimore Emergency Relief Commission, a number of whom were
prosperous realtors in the city. Cleveland Bealmear, for example, a close
friend to Jackson and a member of both the Real Estate Board and BERC,
certainly placed his business interests above his relief concerns when he
joined Jackson to oppose federal housing programs; such programs, he
charged, constituted "unfair competition" and would "lessen individual
incentive" and "invite chiseling." Other realtors called public housing a
"permanent dole" and "un-American." The program, they warned, would
"destroy property values and the investments in mortgage loans and make
us a nation of tenants (with Uncle Sam as the landlord) instead of homeowners." Some challenged the entire notion of urban revitalization, maintaining that new houses would only be "contaminated" by poor people and
their "surrounding conditions." Finally, a few realtors even attempted to
inflame racial prejudice against federal housing by erroneously suggesting
that the federal government proposed to integrate blacks and whites in the
projects.[9]

Charges against the PWA Housing Division for allegedly attempting to
blur racial distinctions in city neighborhoods were not only false but ironic.
Indeed, during the lengthy federal-local negotiations about appropriate
sites for slum clearance, it had been the federal housing officials who
objected to a locally devised plan that placed both the white and the black

projects in the same area, separated only by an alley.[10] Nor did their opposition stem merely from their belief that the two projects in close proximity would deter white participation in the program. Rather, their routine observations, reasoned explanations, and careful recommendations all suggested that their racial attitudes scarcely differed from the local discriminatory views they encountered. They identified, for example, one section of the city as "having no other value except Negro residence" and pointed to another area plagued by "high rates of burglary and robbery" and where the "dirt and smoke nuisance is serious" as "only useable for Negro habitation." And the federal officials' reasons for accepting the two projects that they did rested firmly on racial and class bias. In the black project they hoped to transform an area populated largely by female domestics and laundry workers, and by relief families with "an astonishing percentage living together without benefit of clergy," into a more "desirable" neighborhood "occupied by [a] somewhat higher group." The white project promised even greater change, for it would alter the community by eliminating a row of houses where "white and colored live side by side," where the "colored families are of [a] higher type than the whites," and where "colored and white both shoot crap together"; all this would be accomplished in favor of a housing project for a "better class" of whites who could, of course, afford to pay slightly higher rents.[11]

Local housing officials found such arguments irresistible and enthusiastically endorsed the projects. Mayor Jackson's continued opposition to public housing surprised and disappointed them. C. W. Perkins, a state appointee who chaired the city's housing committee, had repeatedly reassured the Housing Division that the city would be "liberal enough to do what is necessary to carry out" the program; but Perkins had met too infrequently with the mayor and neither his earnest appeals nor his awkward position softened Jackson's attack on public housing.[12]

Municipal efforts to thwart the program, however, angered a number of groups in the city. First to react, the Peoples Unemployment League protested Jackson's position, gathered petitions, and staged demonstrations in favor of public housing. Organized labor urged Jackson to "rescind the service charge ruling in order to expedite the slum clearance project." Baltimore Federation of Labor president Joseph McCurdy denounced the realtors for "gumming the works," adding that "the working people of Baltimore are being robbed of millions of dollars' worth of employment opportunities."[13] Carl Murphy, president of the Baltimore *Afro-American*, sharply rebuked the Real Estate Board and "all white boards in town that do not want government help. . . . Our own group of people," he continued, "needs new low cost housing." Religious leaders appealed directly to federal administrators to avert the "gathering storm on the proposed slum clearance in Baltimore," to "cut through this [local] red tape," and to "get something done. . . . A decent housing program," they declared, "is an indispensable part of any social security program." Social workers lamented the city's refusal to "avail itself of federal aid in any outstanding [housing] project," complaining that "it is all of a piece with the characteristic civic conservatism of the community." Finally, to the astonishment and dismay of both Mayor Jackson and the Real Estate Board, the Greater Northeast Baltimore Association, a neighborhood association whose members included renters and owners, vigorously denounced municipal opposition to slum clearance and reported unanimity "among the people in favor" of public housing.[14]

But Mayor Jackson refused to budge from his position and continued to press for federal payment of a service charge. Further, he challenged the legality of the Housing Division's plans to condemn certain city properties, and a subsequent ruling by the Cincinnati District Court of Appeals confirmed his suspicions by denying the federal government the right to condemn properties for slum clearance. The local Real Estate Board also rejected the PWA's suggestion to use vacant lots for housing construction. Consequently the Housing Division quietly shelved its construction plans for Baltimore, thereby relieving the fears of area realtors but reviving the protests of slum-clearance supporters. The Greater Northeast Baltimore Association particularly objected to the "arbitrary manner" in which the projects were killed and denounced the PWA for succumbing to the pressure of businessmen while denying the organization "a voice in the matter." The association vowed to enlist the support of the larger community in an effort to bring the public housing projects "back to Baltimore."[15]

The possibility of public housing in Baltimore emerged again with the 1937 passage of the Wagner-Steagall Act and the creation of USHA, a public corporation under the Department of the Interior that provided funds for low-cost housing. Jackson instinctively repeated his opposition to federally subsidized housing and publicly opposed the establishment of either a local or a state housing authority. City realtors also renewed their earlier criticism of public housing. But neighborhood citizen groups proved less reflexive, and, after examining their earlier failed efforts at securing public housing, moved toward establishing a more effective and comprehensive organization. They pounced on the "backward-looking real-estate fraternity," held well-publicized meetings, sent petitions to the mayor and the city council, and invited planners and architects to address the public on the need for slum clearance and public housing. The message of one particular architect convinced the groups to agitate even harder for city participation in the federal housing program. Urging them to organize the entire city, he explained that federal programs would be implemented inadequately or not at all without public insistence and participation: "You are not," he warned, "going to get anything done in city planning until the public learns what other cities have done and begins to demand that Baltimore move in the same direction." Representatives of thirty-two black and white fraternal groups, religious and civic societies, and organizations of the unemployed agreed on the necessity for aggressive "citizen participation" and formed the Baltimore Citizens Housing Committee in order to secure the establishment of a racially integrated housing authority and to advise the city on housing needs.[16]

Mayor Jackson proved unable to ignore such widespread citizen action and appointed his own committee to study Baltimore's "blighted areas." His response represented not only a transparently political move but also a reassertion of local authority: he intended to make decisions on the basis of the findings of the committees he himself appointed, and he intensely resented an outside agency discussing the problems of his city. Prominent among the thirty-four committee members he selected were, of course, realtors and builders—the most outspoken critics of public housing. But, sensitive to other political pressures, he also appointed four blacks (two realtors, one attorney-realtor, and a banker), a number of architects, and selected members of the virtually inoperative Commission on City Plan— all rumored to be more sympathetic to federal-city cooperation. In appointing the committee, Jackson reminded the city of his belief that the successful treatment of blighted areas "can and ought to be accomplished by private enterprise." But he softened his stand by adding that the federal government might provide "public assistance"—"either administrative or financial or both."[17]

The Citizens Housing Committee responded to Jackson's appointment of a committee by stepping up its activities to urge the formation of a local housing authority under USHA. The "public housers," as they were called, gathered more petitions, strengthened their neighborhood support, inundated the city council with letters, and met the city's Board of Estimates to persuade them to participate in the federal program. They reminded local officials that, unlike other cities, Baltimore had missed its opportunity for public housing under the PWA, and they urged them not to allow real estate interests to dictate public policy. Responding to these appeals, in November 1937 Daniel Ellison—a long-time champion of liberal causes and the city council's lone Republican member—introduced legislation authorizing the creation of a municipal housing authority, as a necessary first step in participating in the USHA program. Not to be outdone, and aware of the mounting political pressure, Jackson announced two days later that after having reviewed his own committee's report he supported the establishment of a local housing authority. Unaccustomed to any city council initiative, Jackson simply ignored Ellison's bill and drafted his own. The *Sun* correctly noted that with the "backing of Mr. Jackson," the formation of the Baltimore Housing Authority (BHA) "is deemed certain." Jackson's reversal attracted little press attention but to the Housing Committee it represented the importance of citizen activism and the value of "community initiative."[18]

Once the creation of the Baltimore Housing Authority was assured, the Housing Committee began lobbying for black membership on the authority. Council member Ellison introduced a resolution recommending "the appointment of at least one member of the Negro race on the Housing Authority." Although it was defeated in the council by a vote of 15 to 4, the resolution, along with the persistent activities of the Housing Committee, signaled to Jackson the politicial significance of a black appointee. In December 1937 Jackson named the BHA's five-member board, appointing former PWA housing official C. W. Perkins as its head and including George Murphy, a black former high-school principal.[19]

Officials of USHA lavished praise on the Housing Committee for its actions, declaring that the federal agency supported the group because "the initiative" for public housing came from the "communities themselves." Indeed, USHA maintained that the appearance and activities of such voluntary local housing groups in response to the opportunities offered by federal legislation constituted one of the major achievements of the New Deal. Until 1933, administrators noted, "only a handful of unofficial housing agencies" existed, but by 1938 "at least forty private associations [operated] in the country." This proliferation of voluntary housing associations convinced USHA officials that the federal government could enhance, not dwarf, voluntarism and that laws alone could not solve housing needs—rather, "citizen interest in the local community" determined "the success or failure of the government's latest attempt to grapple with one of the country's greatest social problems."[20]

In Baltimore, USHA served as an important catalyst in neighborhood and tenant organization. Many citizens looked to the federal government for assistance and guidance, but they did not relinquish their community responsibilities. Federal programs like USHA promised a means of combating the traditionally dominant interests in the city. The prospect of working with the federal government actually served to strengthen their resolve to effect necessary changes in their communities. Consequently, community groups attempted to assert their local influence not by discouraging but by encouraging federal intervention in local policy making. And federal officials generally reacted favorably to the organizational efforts of associations like the Citizens Housing Committee. They especially encouraged and assisted groups that were formed to aid in the implementation of New Deal programs. But there were also real limits to federal support. Properly organized groups would complement the government's responsibility for the general public welfare by offering advice, providing information, and even by airing grievances—but they would not be allowed to set policy or to establish the agenda for reform. In the public housing projects, for example, USHA encouraged tenant organizations but also sharply prescribed their functions: they were directed to develop programs for "more constructive" leisure time, to establish day nurseries, and to attend to the neighborhood's educational and social needs; they would not, however, be allowed to decide rental rates, determine residency requirements, or make tenant selections. Neighborhood associations, too, might cooperate with federal officials in carrying out housing programs but were also removed from the locus of decision-making power. Still, federal pronouncements about government responsibility and social welfare represented at least partial efforts to reach out to new constituencies and contrasted sharply with the statements by local politicians that tended to disparage their efforts or to dismiss community organization as Socialist agitation. In all, despite these important restraints to their local power, many community groups found that federal programs offered them more opportunity for citizen participation and influence than did their own city government.[21]

Despite its local success and national support, the Citizens Housing Committee disbanded in 1938. Some members dropped out, believing that their purpose had been accomplished with the formation of the Baltimore Housing Authority. Others grew weary of battling the enemies of subsidized housing. And sentiment against the "public housers" had in fact increased: a municipal budget crisis along with an economic downturn in 1937–38 ignited landlord opposition to public housing, and area realtors and landlords found a convenient target in the "public housers" to explain their own economic woes. But a few Housing Committee members remained determined to continue the struggle for adequate public housing. They believed that the BHA needed constant citizen involvement and that tenants in public housing projects deserved representation in municipal affairs. Two issues, in particular, underscored the need for continued community organization and citizen participation—the delays in slum clearance and housing construction and the inadequate provision for the relocation of displaced residents persuaded these "public housers" to reorganize into a new group. Frances Morton, a former member of the Housing Committee, took the lead in forming the association. Author of *A Social Study of Wards 5 and 10 in Baltimore, Maryland* (1937), which had drawn considerable attention from the press and from city officials, Morton knew well the housing problems and needs of the city's poor. She gathered together a number of concerned citizens of diverse political backgrounds —some of whom had been active in the Housing Committee—to launch the Citizens' Housing Council (CHC). Active in 1938 and 1939 but not officially founded until February 1940, the council attempted to "promote better housing through research and community education."[22]

The CHC immediately turned its attention to the city's program for public housing. In early 1938, the BHA had won approval and praise from USHA for its plan to build five housing projects—three for black residents and two for whites. Nathan Straus, national chairman of USHA, called Baltimore's public housing plan "one of the best-rounded programs of all," and within a short time the federal housing authority raised the city's initial $5 million allotment to $18 million. In response to the hefty increase, the BHA announced the possibility of adding two projects for whites to the five already proposed. But, for a number of reasons, the BHA's ambitious plans did not readily become operative, prompting the CHC to investigate. The council found the administration of the program inadequate and forced the BHA to explain the delays and relocation problems. The BHA blamed lengthy title searches for the postponement of construction but also conceded that some residents had already lost their homes to "slum clearance" while the BHA was "still discussing plans to shelter them."[23]

Not until the fall of 1939 did the ground-breaking ceremonies occur for Baltimore's first public housing project—the Edgar Allan Poe apartments. Located near Harlem Park, the Poe project involved the construction of 298 housing units for blacks and required the city to raze 250 dwellings and relocate more than 3,000 residents. Tenants in the area complained

*Houses to be razed and residents to be relocated in Baltimore's first effort at
"slum clearance" under the United States Housing Authority, 1939
(Courtesy of the National Archives)*

that they had been misled by the BHA, that they had been promised "first
priority" in renting the new homes. C. W. Perkins, BHA director, denied the
charges and declared that the "only requirement" he intended to observe
was "rental to a low-income group." A CHC study found that over 50
percent of the residents had been forced to relocate themselves and that
more than 50 percent of the original residents were paying higher rents
with "no improvement in living conditions." To quiet council complaints
and to cultivate better relations with the "public housers," Perkins invited

The cleared site for Baltimore's first public housing project, the Edgar Allan Poe Homes, 1939. A total of 298 Poe units were built to house black families. (Courtesy of the Baltimore Sun)

the CHC to "assist" with the tenant selection process for the Poe project. Council members eagerly accepted the offer in order to provide "special consideration" for those who had been relocated and were "paying more rent than they are able to afford." Despite the intentions of the CHC, however, the Baltimore Housing Authority allowed only 111 of the former residents to be among the 1,300 interviewed for the project, and of those, only 47 were actually placed in the Poe homes when they opened in September 1940. The subsidized apartments, the BHA and CHC both conceded, still remained well beyond the financial reach of most of the city's poor, especially those on relief.[24]

But not all families had wanted to be either relocated or assigned new shelter in the Poe housing project—some were unwilling to leave their original homes and disrupt their neighborhood in the name of "slum clearance," and thirty families organized to stop the project. Many of these opponents of slum clearance were elderly residents, who had lived in their homes for more than twenty years; Sam Gordon, for example, a shoemaker, stood to lose his home and business of thirty-five years. Led by Minnie Smith, a fiery seventy-year-old resident, the group denied that their neighborhood was a "slum" and demanded that their homes be "reconditioned not destroyed. . . . Abrupt young men from the housing agency," they complained, "pester us to sell at a quarter their value the homes we cherish and love. When we protest they say the buildings will be condemned anyhow. That is not right; it is bureaucratic." When interviewed, other people in the neighborhood expressed similar preferences for rehabilitation rather than demolition, but they believed that protest was futile and resigned themselves to searching for new rooms and apartments. And neither the fears nor the threats of the residents halted the destruction of homes filled, according to one observer, with "faded photographs, pieces of crockery, and statuettes."[25]

The Housing Council's failure to support these residents resulted primarily from its middle-class commitment to urban renewal and "slum clearance." With the reorganization of the housing group in 1938–39, many of the neighborhood members had withdrawn from the organization, leaving self-described "civic leaders" to form the new council. As urban leaders they felt confident in their prescriptions for social ills, and as representatives of the middle and upper classes they found it difficult to identify a collection of deteriorating buildings as a neighborhood with beneficial social relationships. Even the Socialist affiliation of some of its members did not sway the CHC from its adherence to the then-standard approach toward slum clearance. The BHA, of course, regarded intransigent residents simply as obstacles to community progress and failed to comprehend why people were not more supportive and appreciative. The CHC was more sympathetic to the problems encountered by displaced residents, but it still generally supported the BHA in its vision of urban revitalization.[26]

The CHC regarded community education about public housing as one of its primary functions. It directed its efforts toward public-housing tenants, toward the larger community, and even toward BHA members. The task of securing support for public housing, never an easy one, grew more difficult as the BHA's construction plans expanded. In 1939, for example, a number of neighborhood and improvement associations in northeast Baltimore turned out to protest the BHA's program. A few of these associations had earlier supported, and even worked for, city participation in the public housing program, but the enlarged scope of the plan worried them as taxpayers. They declared they were "fighting a battle for the taxpayers of Baltimore" to "protest the tax load saddled on home owners and buyers struggling to get along." Although some of the improvement associations objected to "putting slum dwellers in or adjacent to our midst," most were primarily concerned about the possible tax burden.[27] Because the proposed housing additions involved projects for whites, the question of race did not emerge during the meetings attended predominantly by white residents. From its beginning, moreover, the BHA had worked to prevent "bitter opposition" among white residents by pursuing strict segregationist policies; for example, it early assured white residents that not only would new projects not be built on vacant lands to guard against "negro encroachment," but all public housing for blacks would be confined to "the worst Negro slum areas of the city."[28]

Members of the CHC joined with representatives of the Housing Authority to try to alleviate the financial fears of the neighborhood groups. But at one community meeting the supporters of public housing were unable to speak above the boos and hisses. Even the usually popular council member Daniel Ellison, who rose to "soothe tensions," was overwhelmed with "hoots of derision." Only Patrick Whalen, an activist CIO labor organizer, managed to quiet the crowd as he delivered an impassioned speech defending both Ellison and public housing. Still, the meeting ended on a "stormy" note.[29]

Not all neighborhood associations opposed the city's expanded housing program. Even in northeast Baltimore, a group of residents who continued to support public housing splintered off from the more established associations to form a Neighborhood Advisory Committee. This committee hoped to secure a project for the Waverly neighborhood, one of the areas earlier targeted for slum clearance under the PWA's Housing Division, and it received significant encouragement from USHA in 1939 when the federal government agreed to conduct another survey of the area to determine its prospects for assistance. Yet the responses of the organized citizens' groups to the BHA's plans—both the protests and the support—were ultimately without practical effect. The Baltimore Housing Authority moved ahead with its expanded housing program but refused to include the Waverly area, where blacks and whites lived in close proximity, as a possible site for slum clearance.[30]

Popular misconceptions and uncertainties surrounded the city's experiments in public housing. Members of the Citizens' Housing Council discovered, for instance, that they had to educate the BHA staff about "poor people." They tried to assuage the Housing Authority's fears about possible tenant damage to apartments, reassuring them, for example, that the residents would know that installed tubs were for bathing and not for use as coal bins. But the CHC found far more difficult the task of dispelling the "regular rumors circulating about housing projects"—rumors that discouraged eligible citizens from applying for housing consideration. The council held meetings and distributed leaflets to counter reports that "cement floors give you rheumatism" and that all furniture had to be purchased new before renting an apartment. Prospective tenants most feared that a contractual relationship with the government would limit their personal freedom and invite governmental supervision and regimentation; they believed, for example, that they would not be allowed to entertain guests, and that federal regulations would require "all lights to be out at 10 p.m." City landlords seeking to sabotage the projects heightened their apprehension by falsely claiming that public housing was "only for criminals or relief families" and that federal law mandated racial integration.[31]

To assist and encourage prospective tenants, the CHC, at the request of the BHA, held a "model demonstration" of an apartment at the Edgar Allan Poe project. Council members neatly arranged the apartment with furniture supplied by Goodwill charities and staffed the event with black hostesses in order to make the tour more "appealing" to black residents. The demonstration proved so successful that both blacks and whites stood in line for blocks to gain admission; more than 30,000 people ultimately visited the model home. Interested citizens inundated the BHA with applications for public housing, even forcing the authority to stop accepting requests altogether. As a result of the council's efforts, enthusiasm for public housing among low-income families increased substantially. In 1941, when the CHC held a "model demonstration" in one of the 700 units of the newly constructed project for whites, the BHA was once again overwhelmed by the volume of applications.[32]

At the suggestion of the BHA, the CHC also assisted with the organization of public-housing tenants. The USHA program called specifically for "resident participation" in the housing projects, and Baltimore's Housing Authority delegated to the CHC the task of promoting that objective. Council members found the tenants eager to become active in their new community and very receptive to the CHC's lessons on the merits of organization. The black residents of the Poe project, for example, early organized a Tenants' Council, which set as its first task the establishment of a nursery school for children of working parents. They also organized a Mothers' Club, a Men's Club, a Dramatic Club, an Arts and Craft Association, and nondenominational Bible classes. Club meetings were well attended; both men and women went to the meetings of the Mothers' Club, which supervised the nursery school, and the entire neighborhood enjoyed the performances

Residents inside their new Poe apartment, 1940
(Courtesy of the National Archives)

of the Dramatic Club and the crafts displayed by the Arts Association. Neighborhood spirit also extended to holiday seasons when tenants entertained the community with door-to-door caroling. The Tenants' Council perfectly fit the model of tenant organization preferred by the federal government, and approving representatives from USHA who visited the Poe project praised the residents for their creative community activism. Concerned with constructive leisure time, the Tenants' Council also engaged in such self-help ventures as sponsoring movies in order to raise money to buy draperies for meeting rooms and beds for the nursery. Moreover, the Tenants' Council attempted to build links to the larger community by requesting, for example, that the neighborhood school's Parent Teacher Association regularly meet at the Poe's assembly room. Thanks to the USHA program, the volunteer activities of the CHC, and the initiative of the tenants themselves, the Poe residents accomplished a great deal in a very short time.[33]

The coming of the war, however, interrupted these efforts at community building; it also cut short the effective organization of white tenants in the

Armistead Gardens project that opened in east Baltimore in 1941. Although the Armistead residents organized a Civic Club and published a newsletter entitled "Civic News," their concern for their neighborhood was not matched by government officials at either the national or local levels, and within a short time the entire project was sold to the Federal Public Housing Authority in order to house white wartime workers.[34]

As the Citizens' Housing Council became more institutionalized, it moved away from its role as intermediary between tenants and the Baltimore Housing Authority and toward its new objective of bringing about "a closer relationship between the social agencies in the city and the Housing Authority." This change tended to enhance the respectability of the council, to reduce its direct contact with public-housing tenants, and to direct the council toward encouraging what social workers referred to as "agency participation." By the early 1940s the CHC's goal of effective community organization had not disappeared, but the means to achieve it had been transformed. No longer concerned with "citizen" or "client participation," council members and social workers alike championed the new cause of "full agency participation" in the "day-by-day activities" of the community.[35]

When they first organized, the "public housers" had been derided as "too radical" and denounced for their "social action program." The Baltimore Association of Commerce railed against them for sponsoring schemes that would undermine free enterprise and for supporting what it termed FDR's "soak-the-thrifty tax program." Moreover, when council member Frances Morton approached the Johns Hopkins University Planning and Redevelopment Association about a possible merger with the CHC, the Hopkins group declined, explaining that the CHC was tainted by charges of radicalism and racial integration. Only when the Hopkins Association itself suffered from similar charges did it reconsider the offer.[36]

What ultimately brought the two groups together was the presentation of the Federal Theatre's play, "One-Third of a Nation"—the city's "most controversial" play of the 1941 season, if not of the entire decade. The Hopkins group initiated the project and appealed to the trustees of the Baltimore Museum of Art for the use of its volunteer drama club. But the play, which vividly depicted "slum life" and "slum clearance" and celebrated community initiative—even favorably presenting a rent strike—alienated the museum's trustees, who objected to what they regarded as ill-fated attempts to mix theatre and politics. Claiming that the play held "no particular meaning to Baltimore," the trustees broke with tradition by refusing to allow their club to participate in a community performance. A bewildered Hopkins group, unaccustomed to such pointed attacks, gratefully accepted the assistance offered by the CHC. Housing Council members personally appealed to friends among the trustees, pledged a $500 contribution to the museum, and deftly secured a reversal of the museum's negative decision. Moreover, the CHC, unlike the narrowly based academic association, enlisted the support of such other groups as the PUL, neighborhood associations, and labor unions. It also raised money for the performance, selectively appealing to such appropriate businesses as the Starr Wrecking Company for contributions. The PUL took puckish delight in assisting with a play that raised so many brows, but it found the Hopkins planners disappointing when they refused to schedule free performances of the play for the unemployed. Finally, the CHC worked assiduously to counter viewers' criticisms of the play. To charges that the play was overtly propagandistic and tended to "justify and speed up a rather fundamental change," the CHC recited the social merits and the community-wide benefits of slum clearance and invited urban residents to envision a city revitalized by housing reform and community initiative.[37]

The Hopkins Redevelopment Association genuinely appreciated the CHC's assistance and resolved to work with the organization. In April 1941 the Hopkins group reorganized to form the Citizens' Planning and Housing Association (CPHA); as expected, the CHC joined the new association. The CHC's merger with an academic group clearly suggested its increased professionalism. Although not yet sufficiently respectable to receive money from the Community Fund, which labeled the CPHA "too controversial," the new association moved further away from the organization of tenants and closer to the administration of social services. It never lost sight of its social action program—in 1941, for example, it campaigned for rent control, war housing for blacks, and postwar planning—but it provided little assistance to tenants at Armistead Gardens when they asked for CPHA support to persuade the federal government to make needed maintenance repairs. Instead, it increasingly devoted its time to coordinating efforts with social agencies and the city's planning commission.[38]

The CPHA fashioned its program out of a commitment to civic responsibility. The concept of citizen participation formed the basis for its involvement in housing and planning; but its particular type of involvement frequently meant that it straddled two opposing worlds. Denounced by members of the Baltimore Association of Commerce as "radical public housers" and denied Community Fund support for "controversial" programs, the CHC (and later the CPHA) also encountered criticism from tenants who felt that the housing group responded more to the causes championed in theatrical performances than to the problems experienced daily by public-housing residents themselves. And it was true that it took the production of a play *about* "slum life" to unite two groups that had been unable to join together out of common concern for the poor and their housing needs. It was also true that the housing group tended to measure progress by the construction of new buildings and placed little emphasis on the values and priorities of the residents.

The prospect of public housing in Baltimore precipitated a variety of organizational responses. Initially, realtors and business leaders joined to oppose the experiment, while some residents organized to prevent their own neighborhoods from falling prey to "slum clearance." The public-housing tenants themselves united to create the networks and provide the services necessary for a cooperative and successful neighborhood. Finally, the "public housers" evolved from an inchoate group that mobilized a community demand for a housing authority into a professional association that championed city planning and better social services, among them public housing. The typology of community organization developed by Jack Rothman helps to explain these approaches to community involvement. Rothman distinguishes among three types of community organization: locality development, social planning, and social action. *Locality development* describes neighborhood residents who organize to develop or improve their community by solving their own problems and satisfying their own needs; *social planning* refers to groups that attempt to address specific issues by initiating or coordinating community projects for the benefit of the entire community; and *social action* refers to groups that seek to acquire community control or substantive change by defining the issues, identifying the opponents, and mobilizing the residents to take direct action.[39]

The "public housers" exhibited all three types of organizational behavior. More importantly, however, they evolved from a popular organization to a more formal association. Initially, the Citizens Housing Committee represented a wide variety of groups; its purpose was to mobilize the community against realtor and mayoral opposition to the creation of a housing authority and to participation in federally sponsored public housing. When the Housing Committee was reorganized in 1938 to become the

Citizens' Housing Council, it lost some of its original racial and class diversity. Although it still represented disparate political views, the CHC fell more securely into the hands of concerned, white, middle- and upper-class professionals. Between 1939 and 1941 the CHC assisted in the formation of tenant councils, urging the residents, in effect, to practice *locality development*. And the Poe residents demonstrated their ability and willingness to satisfy their own cultural, educational, and economic needs. The CHC also engaged in *social planning*, encouraging and assisting one of the first comprehensive housing surveys in the city in an attempt to coordinate public housing plans and community needs. Finally, the council suffered from charges of radicalism not merely because it counted Socialists among its members but also because it had a *social action* program that vociferously attacked "backward-looking" realtors and "greedy" landlords, that urged tenants to organize, that promoted public housing, that exposed the evils of poor living conditions, and that successfully campaigned for legislation that would fine landlords for slum conditions.[40]

Although never as radical as its opponents charged, the CHC rarely missed an opportunity to castigate those who opposed housing reform. But at the same time, it became less concerned about grass-roots organization and more interested in improving social services. That tendency received formal recognition in 1940 when the CHC became an official member of the Baltimore Council of Social Agencies—an organization begun by the city's private charities but also partially funded by the city government.[41] And in 1941, when the CHC merged with the CPHA, it solidly became an organization that practiced social planning. The coordination of community projects and the improvement of social services better suited the reformist goals and professional orientation of the CPHA. To be sure, there would still be moments of social action, as in 1942 when the CPHA joined with other groups to support a demonstration by 2,000 blacks in Annapolis, demanding an end to racial discrimination in housing and hiring.[42] But those efforts reflected the group's humanitarian concerns more than its professional interests. In subsequent years the CPHA enhanced its respectability and its administrative influence, emerging as a professional and expert group dedicated to an efficient, rational, and more humane distribution of social services.

Community organization and citizen participation, although certainly not new historical phenomena, experienced significant growth in the 1930s. Depression conditions and New Deal programs combined to increase the level and complexity of citizen involvement in issues of social welfare. Citizen groups responded with enthusiasm to calls for both self-help and expanded governmental responsibility. As John Finbar Jones and John Middlemist Herrick note, "phrases such as citizen participation, lay leadership, and grass-root democracy attracted men and women at the very same time when social engineering, central planning, and national control were in vogue."[43] The USHA program, in particular, illustrates that type of attraction, for it combined national and local planning with substantial community organization. Citizen participation was not only necessary to combat Mayor Jackson's obduracy and for the ultimate establishment of the local Housing Authority, but it was also evident, if not always decisive, in practically every level of public policy making, from the planning of public housing to the construction of the projects. The CHC and the tenants' councils best represent the process by which federal initiative could encourage, transform, and also limit the voluntary efforts of citizen groups. The New Deal housing programs, although fully culpable for being neither free of racist proscriptions nor directed at those most in need, served to heighten community involvement and to at least strengthen local awareness of housing needs and social responsibilities.

CHAPTER 5

Organizing the Unemployed

The Jobless and the New Deal

In January 1933 President Hoover's Research Committee on Social Trends presented its findings from a detailed study of American life in the twentieth century. The committee found that "life has become disjointed and upset because the flow of credit was not synchronized with the flow of production; that machines were everywhere displacing workers; that we devote far more attention to making money than to spending it; and that the church and family have declined in social significance." Given these conditions, the report predicted "increased friction and strife between workers and employers" and warned that "violent revolution" could not be averted unless there was a "change in the distribution of income."[1] That same month a New York rabbi urged a U.S. Senate committee to provide unemployment assistance, explaining that "the unemployed are organizing in many parts of the United States" and that their effort "could easily translate itself into action you and I would regret."[2]

Fears of "violent revolution" haunted national and local leaders throughout the decade. In Baltimore, National Emergency Council director Arthur Hungerford often admonished Mayor Howard Jackson to help the jobless, warning that "hungry men become warlike."[3] As late as 1938, when the state's attorney general, Herbert O'Conor, entered the Democratic gubernatorial primary, he spoke less of the New Deal or his own record than of the "social unrest, discontent and dissatisfaction . . . in every community," pointing with alarm to the "battle flags" unfurled by the masses, and concluding that both the unemployed and the unsuspecting had been exploited "by insidious and anti-American influences."[4] In part these persistent fears stemmed from the daily display of dramatic disparities in wealth, as in newspapers that simultaneously featured soup lines and opera-goers, and the painful awareness of "poverty amidst plenty"; but in some measure they resulted directly from the actions of the unemployed themselves: the often desperate and usually isolated acts of violence taken by the jobless, and the more systematic and organized efforts sponsored by groups of unemployed workers. Although the spectre of violent revolution was probably more in the minds of local leaders than in the plans of the unemployed, acts of defiance by frustrated men and women out of work and protest activities of organized groups took on added significance in times fraught with tension and economic uncertainty.

The reversion to state responsibility for assisting the unemployable jobless precipitated protest throughout the nation in 1935 and 1936 and calls went out warning of revolution among the "restless" unemployed. The governor of Pennsylvania solemnly declared in the spring of 1936 that "we face revolution," and that summer more than 400 men, women, and children shouting "Fight! Fight! Fight!" took over the capitol building in Harrisburg to demand larger relief appropriations in the state budget. In Miami, over 1,500 people marched on city hall chanting "We are starving. We want food now." The wives and daughters of striking Louisiana and Arkansas railroad workers kidnaped a train to protest their inability to receive assistance; they defied guards, imprisoned the conductor, and occupied the train while it traveled thirty miles. Cutbacks in federal programs also brought people to the streets. In what was called the "bloodless battle of Pleasantville, New Jersey," nearly 100 women held the entire city council hostage and refused to release the council members until their WPA sewing project was restored. In St. Louis, the unemployed occupied the city's relief headquarters and attempted to take over city hall. Still others politicized the needs of relief recipients. In Huntington, Indiana, the jobless were in the unusual position of having as their leader the mayor of the city, C. W. H. Bangs, who went to jail rather than obey a court injunction to cease operating a municipally owned utility plant. In Detroit, women on relief rolls organized a strike against local grocers to protest high meat prices, causing "a score of meat dealers to close their doors under the force of feminine lines"; when a judge issued an injunction restraining the women from interfering with the grocers' business, one of the group's leaders took the struggle to the political arena where she was promptly elected to serve as a councilwoman from Detroit's Polish area of Hamtramck. Moreover, the strike against meat prices spread to Chicago and other cities.[5]

In Baltimore, local relief regulations and policies often frustrated the unemployed, who endured long lines, probing questions, and periodic purges of the rolls. Relief officials complained of occasional protests by their clients, of a general spirit of uncooperativeness among all "reliefers," and, as the decade wore on, of "aggressive behavior" by clients toward public officials. In 1933, one woman on relief attempted to have her social worker arrested for the "attempted starvation" of her family. Abandoned by her husband, she was unable to register for relief because she was already listed on the rolls—but because she was not the head of household she was also not allowed to collect the check drawn in her husband's name. Caught in a web of directives and requirements, she turned to the police for help. A local magistrate refused to charge the social worker, however; instead, he issued a warrant for the husband and lectured the hapless woman on the virtue of patience.[6] Procedural obstacles also produced more militant responses, as in the case of the Platzke family. This family of seven stunned an entire city as Baltimoreans read the *Sun* headlines: "Idle Family Holds Relief Agent Captive." The Platzkes' repeated requests for food had been denied because they were unable to "produce a card showing the record of food" purchased earlier. Desperate and hungry, they held hostage their relief caseworker from the Baltimore Emergency Relief Commission when she visited the family. Locking all the doors, Mrs. Platzke told the official, "We've been nearly starving for the past three weeks, and if we are going to starve, you are going to starve with us." After hours of deliberations and assurances of relief assistance, the Platzkes finally released the BERC caseworker, explaining that the only defense for their action was starvation. Officials at BERC decided not to press charges and instead placed the family on the relief rolls and provided emergency aid.[7]

Most alarming to Baltimoreans was the bombing of Mayor Jackson's residence in April 1936. Although the bomb injured no one, it shattered windows throughout the house just minutes after the mayor arrived home, prompting police to speculate that the bomb had been intended for the mayor himself. Jackson agreed and, like the police, suspected clients dropped from relief rolls or disgruntled WPA workers of the bombing. This incident occurred during the difficult transition from the FERA to the WPA. City police therefore investigated the unemployed and striking workers—

the kinds of groups they believed most susceptible to the radical influence necessary for such an act of violence.[8]

Less violent but more widespread were petty offenses committed by the unemployed. Grocers consistently complained of children stealing fresh produce from their stands, and organized looting of food became common. According to Baltimore police, "crime waves" accompanied the city's relief crises. In 1935–36 and again in 1937–38, city police extended their hours of duty in order to "halt the rising tide of burglaries." Even BERC's headquarters was burglarized. But the police could not prevent the activities of those they termed the "touring bandits": "small bands of negroes" who systematically robbed grocery stores of foodstuffs but rarely of money. Only an improvement in the relief situation, the police concluded, would stem the "burglary wave."[9]

Hard times led some people to engage in crimes that the police referred to as "depression crimes." So widespread was the illegal tapping of gas lines, for example, that the Baltimore Gas Light Company was forced to hire its own detectives because the city's police force simply could not investigate all those suspected of "stealing gas." According to both police and company representatives, gas tapping was "most common" among relief recipients. In one tragic incident a twenty-three-year-old unemployed day laborer named Alfred Satti was arrested for tapping gas lines. Delays in his relief payments, the gas company's refusal to extend credit, and the earlier death of his five-month-old son from pneumonia persuaded Satti to steal the gas in order to protect his wife and three-year-old daughter from the winter's cold. Recognized at one of the city's relief offices, where police regularly circulated descriptions of gas chiselers, he was immediately arrested. While in jail the despondent Satti hanged himself; officers found him clutching a crumpled photograph of his children. News of his death ignited the Peoples Unemployment League to protest the entire episode and thousands of jobless workers turned out to attend the funeral. A number of religious and fraternal groups joined the PUL to oppose the gas company's policies and to demand that Baltimore provide adequate assistance to the needy. National officials also denounced the city's excessive "red tape for relief" and its callous treatment of obviously destitute clients.[10]

But public sympathy for criminal activities, even those committed out of "necessity not malice," was hardly typical. Local judges generally meted out tough sentences to those convicted of "chiseling," whether they were defrauding the relief agency or the gas company. Chief Judge Samuel K.

Dennis, for example, called all such activities "dirty, despicable tricks" and affirmed that "inexorable punishment" would follow every instance of "chiseling." And these sentiments only hardened when the acts were linked to the activities of the organized unemployed.[11]

The isolated responses of the individual unemployed to their plight often suggested desperation and frustration, and their actions rarely resulted in substantive improvements in their condition. Only the protest activities of organized groups secured important gains, and even those were not always permanent. Still, the organized activities of the jobless, at least in the earlier years of the New Deal, reflected more a sense of hope than one of futility and brought recognition to groups traditionally neglected in society.

As early as 1930, Baltimore's Communists, cooperating with the Trade Union Unity League, attempted to organize the unemployed into councils. On 6 March 1930, Unemployed Councils across the nation held demonstrations to protest the lack of aid to the jobless. In Baltimore, about 300 women and men marched from the Communist party's headquarters to City Hall, a distance of a few blocks. Political leaders publicly treated the protest in a light-hearted fashion; the acting mayor even sported a red tie and red carnation. But also present, as directed by the mayor, were scores of heavily armed police with "supplies of tear-gas bombs in case of an emergency." Still, unlike many cities on 6 March, Baltimore remained free from violence between protesters and police, and the *Sun* dismissed the demonstration as comprising "only Communists and Negroes."[12]

The outcome was not the same a year later when the local Communist party organized a "Hunger March" on City Hall and then headed for the State House in Annapolis. Protesting the city's relief policies, especially the reliance on police to conduct eligibility investigations, about 200 marchers first presented their demands to Mayor William Broening, who directed them to the state legislature for appropriate action. In Annapolis, the "rioting hunger marchers," as they were described, interrupted a state legislative session, resulting in "a furious battle between the marchers and the police." Police arrested the marchers and beat several "so badly" that they required medical attention. The police justified their swift and violent response by claiming that one of the marchers had drawn a pistol, but the warden at the county jail discounted these reports, saying that "the only thing approaching a weapon found on any of the prisoners was a small pen knife." Even the state legislators entered the fracas, launching, according to the *Evening Sun*, "a volunteer Red Hunt with the energy of the war days" and seizing "an undersized citizen with a Near East face," fiercely

*The Hunger March protest meeting outside Baltimore City Hall on 6 March 1930
(Courtesy of Jacques Kelly)*

"pummel[ing] him" until he was "identified as thoroughly conservative and 100 per cent American by a newspaper reporter."[13]

Although the Communist party refrained from organizing hunger marches for the remainder of the decade, animosities toward radical activity did not disappear. Rather, as certain federal programs encouraged citizen involvement and as New Deal rhetoric raised expectations among the unemployed, the increasing assertiveness of relief clients annoyed local critics. Already contemptuous of public assistance, such critics particularly resented helping those they regarded as ungrateful and uppity. From their perspective, nearly all organized activities among the jobless constituted instances of radicalism, and the government's endorsement of some of those activities merely made matters worse. Such was the case, they believed, in the federal relief program for transients.

Few groups were more despised in the Great Depression than the home-less unemployed. Uniformly castigated as "loafers" attempting to "leech off" the city's coffers, transients encountered both public and police hos-tility. To counter this popular and political prejudice, national authorities early attempted to "educate" local communities about the "new type" of transient—a victim of uncontrollable economic forces. In 1931 President Hoover's Organization on Unemployment Relief supervised the prepara-tion of *A Community Plan for Service to Transients*, which instructed social workers to improve their treatment of transients and to inform local residents of the needs of the homeless unemployed.[14] Propagandistic ef-forts continued throughout the New Deal. The WPA, for example, issued a report that distinguished the transient from the "chronic wanderer—the hobo, the tramp, and the bum" and urged communities to be more tolerant of "needy strangers." Another New Deal study found public sentiment to be "savagely antagonistic to the transients, all of whom were commonly regarded as dangerous and worthless bums"; it directed relief officials to view the new transients not as tramps but as "pioneers—the most enterpris-ing and energetic people of their former communities."[15]

In Baltimore the usual problems of homelessness, aggravated by the depression-related problems of eviction and abandonment, were made still worse by the city's geographic location. Single males, many of them black, left their homes in rural Maryland and Virginia to find work in the city; and Baltimore's sagging shipping industry left stranded large numbers of homeless seamen, who crowded the docks in search of food and shelter. The sheer volume of needy transients quickly overwhelmed private re-sources, but the city refused to help the homeless and instead increased the residency requirements for relief assistance. In early 1933, Mayor Jack-son's Advisory Committee on Unemployment proposed that transients be "weeded out" of the city and recommended that Baltimore take stringent measures to ensure that "drifters shun [the] city."[16]

Given the scope of the problem and the refusal of local governments to assist the homeless, the federal government in 1933 took responsibility for transient relief. The Federal Emergency Relief Act of May 1933 provided for the establishment of the Transient Division of the FERA. Created in July, the Transient Division instructed the states to set up state and local tran-sient relief offices and to devise comprehensive plans for assisting all needy single persons or family groups who had not resided within the state's boundaries for at least one year. The financing would be part of the FERA grants to the states.[17]

During its brief period of operation—from 1933 until 1935, when the federal government returned responsibility for transient relief to the states and localities—the Baltimore transient administration experienced a number of serious problems. Municipal political indifference delayed implementation of the program. Moreover, city-state rivalries, federal-state clashes over funding, and local mismanagement sharply reduced its effectiveness once it was operational. The hostility toward transients took on especially ugly features when racism and antiradicalism fueled popular objections to aiding the homeless. And the activism of the transients themselves seriously alienated local relief officials, who blamed the New Deal administration for the aggressive behavior of the transient unemployed.

From the start, Mayor Jackson and BERC refused to cooperate with the local transient bureau. The bureau's staff—largely appointed by the national director of the transient program, William Plunkert—was initially unable even to get BERC's lists of transients who had applied for assistance. To force the city to participate in the program, a desperate Plunkert turned the local operation of transient relief over to BERC and ordered it to provide the assistance mandated by Congress.[18]

The hesitant approach to the transient program taken by BERC suited Mayor Jackson, who consistently opposed homeless relief. The commission's policies toward the transients also conformed to the city's restrictive traditions. For example, BERC faithfully followed the segregationist practices characteristic of Baltimore. The color line extended to the dining and recreation areas of the transient shelters, and when sleeping facilities were crowded BERC rented rooms for the "best [i.e., white] class of men" at nearby hotels rather than have "mixed" shelter accommodations. When space was a problem, as it usually was, BERC granted the recreational areas to the white transients and forced blacks "to crowd in the street," which both neighbors and police found "objectionable." During one emergency period of unusual overcrowding, BERC refused to assist black transients until the government provided a "negro building" or a "separate feeding place for the colored clients."[19]

By March 1935 nearly 40,000 males had registered for assistance with the city's transient bureau. About half used the program only for overnight lodging, but the sheer volume of clients meant that the city's shelters were almost always overcrowded. Baltimoreans who resided near the transient lodgings vociferously objected to the presence of the "loafers" and denounced BERC for bringing the "negro into our midst."[20] To quiet these complaints, the transient bureau established three camps and two farms outside the city, where the transients could, as one approving judge noted, "dig or die."[21] But even that experiment caused considerable controversy when Baltimore placed transient blacks at nearby Aberdeen, already the site of a military installation. Residents there protested the camp, claiming that the "negro bathing beach" that the transients had created for themselves prevented the residents from renting their homes during the summer; even though the transients were restricted to only a small fraction of the beach, the residents complained that their enjoyment of the waterfront had been impaired by having blacks in view. Moreover, they argued that the "colored transients" might "in their leisure time" cross the racial boundaries and "roam over the [entire] neighborhood making it unsafe for women to remain alone in one place."[22] Local officials reassured residents that the transients were closely supervised by military authorities and that their activities were carefully monitored. Indeed, the response, while perhaps soothing the fears of Aberdeen residents, alarmed liberal New Dealer Aubrey Williams when he learned of the problem; he worried that the combination of racism and regimentation might turn the transient camp into "some sort of prison camp."[23]

A spirit of self-help permeated the transient camps and farms. At Aberdeen, for example, black transients attempted to improve their living and sleeping quarters. Unlike the white camps, which had housing and toilet facilities, the Aberdeen camp offered only outdoor shelters, forcing the men to sleep without benefit of walls or heat. Outbreaks of disease— including spinal meningitis, which killed a number of camp residents— encouraged the transients to build their own facilities. As Army officials looked on, they scavenged area dumps for wood scraps and other building materials and built themselves new shelters and toilet facilities. They also attended to their own recreational needs, clearing an area for a small bathing beach and constructing their own golf course (the latter accomplishment generated particular excitement among the white military officers, who had assumed that blacks knew nothing of the game of golf). At all the camps the transients supplemented their rations with their own vegetable gardens, and the two transient farms became nearly self-sufficient. By mid-1935 the transients had become so successful at providing for themselves that the costs of the program declined.[24]

As long as the initiatives among the transients remained confined to this type of "constructive" self-help activity, officials praised their efforts. But when their activism challenged program regulations or questioned authority, the official reaction was considerably different. Such was the case in 1934 when Baltimore's homeless and jobless seamen attempted to take greater control over their relief project.

Although homeless seamen were officially regarded as transients, they were treated separately from the others. Local authorities strictly segregated the nearly 2,000 jobless seamen, believing that they were "less appreciative" and "more demanding" of public assistance and would have a negative influence on the other transients. Seamen on leave or without work had traditionally found lodging at the Anchorage, a building operated by the YMCA in the Fells Point area of the city. In early 1934, to address the growing problem of unaided seamen, the local transient bureau leased the Anchorage, hiring most of the YMCA staff to administer the relief program for the seamen. But the seamen strenuously objected to these actions. Bypassing both the local and the state transient offices, a committee of seamen marched into the national office in Washington, D.C., identified themselves as members of the Marine Workers Industrial Union (MWIU), and described a "situation [at the Anchorage] of rebellion and unrest verging on mutiny." They demanded a "new relief set-up" that would allow for democratic control, displace the hated Anchorage officials (all "grafters" and "hypocritical tyrants"), and ensure that the "benefits of their labor" went to the seamen and not to the YMCA—an association, they asserted, that had exploited them for years. Finally, they insisted that they be permitted to organize at "peaceable meetings," free from interference by the Anchorage authorities who regularly called in the police "to break up their meetings and jail their leaders."[25]

The seamen next returned to the shelter, taking over the Anchorage, ousting the officials, and establishing their own work-relief project. They then used the building and the assistance program not only to aid those without work, but also to launch a strike against the Munson shipping lines. The Anchorage became the strike headquarters and the location of the hiring hall for the city's seamen; all other shipping services, including the government's own Sea Service Bureau, were successfully boycotted. The men shipped out on a democratic rotation basis, but the seamen at the Anchorage made sure that the Munson ships did not move.[26]

The events in Baltimore's harbor thoroughly frightened federal officials, who were still reeling from the impromptu meeting with the delegation of seamen. Correctly noting that the MWIU was "a Communist affiliate," they urged local authorities to proceed cautiously and to minimize publicity. But city officials were angry, irritated by the seamen's attempt to circumvent their authority and the consequent implication that they were unable to handle their own problems. Instead of negotiating with the seamen, they preferred punitive action. Echoing these sentiments were local shippers and members of the Baltimore Association of Commerce, who demanded that relief be "withheld from radical leaders and strikers." The federal government, they charged, was "actually encouraging communism, mutiny through intimidation, voluntary idleness, and even violence." But to avoid "industrial warfare," the national transient office urged local officials to adopt a moderate position and specifically prohibited them from restricting the seamen's rights to free speech. Fearful of repercussions, national officials warned that the takeover of the Anchorage indicated not only widespread dissatisfaction with the system of relief but an attempt by the MWIU to displace the more conservative International Seamen's Union (ISU) on the city's docks. Relief officials in other port cities, they explained, had already reported that, as a result of the events in Baltimore, "radical seamen [were] aroused to similar activities." State FERA administrator Harry Greenstein concurred, observing that "the seamen situation in Baltimore has taken a critical turn, which may assume national proportions."[27]

Undaunted by such appeals, local relief officials, led by Mayor Jackson, refused to meet with the seamen and threatened police intervention. City businessmen intensified their attack on the federal government for aiding "radical, loafing" seamen. And the ISU joined this chorus of opposition, accusing the government of "subsidizing Communism through its relief system for seamen" and of supporting a program for "racial equality."[28] The charges that the national administration "subsidized reds" alarmed such national transient officials as Assistant Director Elizabeth Wickenden, who solemnly noted the government's peculiar position:

I feel that the tie-up of relief with industrial warfare cannot be too strongly emphasized in this case. The Marine Workers' Industrial Union, through its psychological or organizational hold over the unemployed seamen in Baltimore has been able successfully to prevent scabbing on striking ships. They are determined to maintain at any cost the organizational strength while the ship owners are even more determined to break it up. Relief is the weapon in each case and the relief administration is attacked on both sides.[29]

To ensure local cooperation, the federal transient bureau dispatched special investigators to Baltimore. Their report confirmed fears at the national level that the intransigence of local officials was prolonging the entire incident. One federal agent found the seamen justified in their complaints, remarked on their orderly and efficient administration of relief, and added that "my own personal opinions . . . closely synchronize with those of the so-called communists in this instance."[30] Finding the municipal authorities paralyzed by fears of communism and unwilling to deal with "low-type" people like the seamen, federal officials offered their own compromise plan, which called for the evacuation of the building and the establishment of a federally supervised work-relief project, and which upheld the seamen's rights to unionize and participate in local decisions about work projects and relief distribution. The seamen at the Anchorage accepted the proposal and relinquished control of the building. Greenstein praised the government for resolving the crisis but also demanded that chief administrator Plunkert assume complete responsibility for all transient relief in Baltimore. Plunkert rejected that demand, although he did reorganize the local office of the transient bureau, replacing a few of the officials who had been most resistant to resolving the "seamen situation" amicably.[31]

The defiant action of the seamen and their insistence on having a greater voice in the process of relief assistance produced among Baltimore's social workers a new attitude toward the homeless unemployed. The achievements made by the transients themselves through self-help activities at the camps and in their shelters encouraged a new respect toward them. Baltimore transient bureau employees affirmed, "We must respect the transient's viewpoint and realize that he can and will, if given an opportunity, help to solve his problem."[32] That recognition led to new studies of the needs and attitudes of the homeless, a concern for the "maintenance of the morale" of those whose "roots have been torn up," and regular meetings between relief workers and the transient unemployed.[33] Local social workers had finally come to accept the notions and suggestions first recommended by President Hoover's *Community Plan for Service to Transients.* City politicians, however, still had a long way to go.

The transients responded enthusiastically and candidly to the increased attention they were receiving. They stepped up their organizational activities, forming such groups as the "Colored Transients of Baltimore" to demand an end to the inequalities in the relief program. The homeless also commended their social workers for their new, "courteous" approach and particularly praised them for inaugurating a program that sought to match the skills of the transients with particular work-relief projects. This latter service, one transient declared, "has made possible my re-entry into nor-mal community life"; another credited his work-relief experience with preventing his "growing stale through inactivity." Efforts by transient offi-cials to boost morale, however, met with less acceptance and more suspi-cion. One transient said he had regained but "scattered pieces of my pride," while another challenged an official whose position, he asserted, was "inconsistent and untenable. . . . If, as he [the caseworker] affirmed, the fault was with the social situation, why was he wasting time on me, or, worse still, was he trying to adjust or reconcile me to an inadequate social order."[34]

Although such comments were hardly typical among transients, the reports of transient caseworkers still indicate a dramatic new awareness of, and among, the homeless as more thoughtful people than the stereotypical bum with a half-empty bottle. But the wider community beyond the local office of the transient bureau continued to harbor hostile feelings against those without jobs or homes. Near the seamen's shelter in east Baltimore, for example, a group of local businessmen organized to have the "foul, insulting, and disgraceful" seamen removed from the area. A number of American Legionnaires also threatened to "clean the seamen out," provok-ing fears among area residents of "civil war."[35]

Budget reductions in the transient program in late 1934 and its termina-tion in 1935 further strained transient-community relations. In one in-stance police battled with seamen for more than an hour after the sea-men protested over decreases in their food allowances.[36] Transients also picketed BERC headquarters to oppose the cuts, but BERC removed those who participated in the action from the relief rolls. The widening of the seamen's strike in the fall of 1934 to shipping lines other than Munson's alienated the Baltimore Association of Commerce, and BERC used the federal reductions as an opportunity to cut off all relief for the activist seamen. The MWIU protested BERC's practices, declaring that "seamen are being thrown off relief for complaining of rotten conditions" and that "others are being denied relief in [an] attempt to break [the] strike." The union requested federal intervention but this time received no assistance from Washington.[37] Even the ISU denounced BERC, claiming that the sea-men in Baltimore were "turning Communistic due to the starvation rations being issued here."[38]

In 1935 the situation for all the city's transients worsened when the federal government shifted transient relief back to the states and localities.

The municipal response was predictable: Mayor Jackson announced that he had no intention of going into "the transient business." The state WPA administrator, Francis Dryden, also denied responsibility for the transients, claiming that they were all either unworthy or unemployable and therefore ineligible for WPA work relief. And the city police department warned the homeless that all those who sought assistance or shelter at police stations would be searched and fingerprinted in an effort to identify possible criminals. For the transients, all these actions threatened the respect and recognition they had won through the FERA's transient program and reaffirmed their position as social pariahs.[39]

To protest these changes, the transients organized, simultaneously denouncing the New Deal for not providing adequate assistance and struggling to preserve the gains they had made under the transient relief program. The seamen derided a New Deal that gave bankers "millions of dollars" but denied them even "sufficient food." Other transients in the city united to form the Baltimore Transient Committee, which held protest rallies, gathered petitions, and picketed Dryden's WPA office. Even staff members of the transient bureau, anxious to protect their jobs, joined the transients appealing to Harry Hopkins and Aubrey Williams for continued federal support of the program. Hopkins responded by authorizing a WPA project for Baltimore's transients.[40] When Dryden failed to act on Hopkins's proposal the transients resumed their protests, making surprise visits to the local offices of the WPA and the state transient director and threatening similar actions in Washington. Aubrey Williams instructed Robert Van Hyning, the state transient director, to establish the work-relief project, but Van Hyning remained helpless to do so without the necessary assistance from city relief officials or from the WPA. "The city," he told Williams, "is on record as not wanting to take care of any of them." Nor could Van Hyning curtail the protests of Baltimore's transients or prevent them from traveling to Washington. "We have a very active Committee here and they will by no means drop the picture," he warned Williams.[41] Indeed, a delegation of transients arrived at Williams's office in February 1936, demanding a work-relief project and greater assistance for the homeless unemployed. Although Williams refused to meet with the delegation, he insisted that Baltimore establish the work-relief project or face other consequences. Within weeks, a small project was created for the transients. However, the Transient Committee ultimately fell apart, demoralized by the inadequacy of the relief system and powerless to demand more without the support of the federal government.[42]

Local authorities proved even less willing to assist the more troublesome seamen. The seamen's protests and petitions secured scattered WPA jobs for a few, but the city consistently refused to create a project solely for them. In late 1937 about 700 seamen turned out at Dom Polski Hall in Baltimore's Polish neighborhood to decry their predicament. They appealed to Mayor Jackson to assume his proper relief responsibilities and relieve "the deplorable conditions existing among the unemployed seamen."[43] The state's National Emergency Council Director, Arthur Hungerford, also called on the city and the federal government to remedy the seamen's "desperate" situation. Startled federal officials, warned by Hungerford of possible violence by the seamen, demanded the establishment of a WPA project for them. The head of the welfare department responded that Baltimore would attempt to fulfill the "wishes of federal officials," not by establishing a new project for the seamen, but by allowing more of them to be certified for WPA employment. He added, however, that "the city itself would take no responsibility for the seamen."[44]

No longer pressing for a more democratic administration of relief, the seamen by 1937 were merely begging for food. Gone, too, were the organized activities of the "Colored Transients" and of the Baltimore Transient Committee. They all had depended on the national transient program, which had provided the framework for assistance and mediation as well as the specific targets of their agitation. With the demise of the national program in 1935, the homeless unemployed, unable to advance their interests through conventional political means, confronted a hostile local community without the aid of the federal government. Both national authorities and city social workers lamented the subsequent deterioration in the conditions of transients. "It was very disheartening," commented one federal field reporter, "to see how those few who were left in Baltimore simply took to the road or began panhandling the local streets." Greenstein echoed these sentiments, saying that only a permanent program would permit "real progress in the care of the transients" and alter the negative "attitudes and prejudices" toward the homeless. A federal survey placed Baltimore among the worst examples of local treatment of transients and noted that "the care of transients has pretty well slipped back to the days before the F.E.R.A." and "hit-or-miss private aid is largely the rule."[45]

In order to secure adequate relief assistance, the unemployed found it necessary to organize and place constant pressure on both local and national officials.[46] One of the most active organizations of the unemployed in Baltimore in the 1930s was the Peoples Unemployment League, founded in January 1933 by a group of Socialists. The PUL expanded rapidly in the city, and became one of the strongest such organizations in the country.[47] It grew from 6,000 members with twenty-three locals in March 1933, to a peak membership in 1934 of 18,000 in thirty-three locals. Although its membership was never stable, throughout most of the depression decade the organization claimed between 8,000 and 12,000 members.[48] The success of the league in attracting members stemmed in part from its organizing methods, which paralleled the social and geographic organization of the city. The PUL most often used the neighborhood as its organizational base, and locals grew out of meetings held in the basements of community churches. The league also reached out to shelters for the homeless, to specific groups of unemployed workers, and to local branches of the YMCA. Locals, consisting of at least ten members, were scattered throughout the city and each local was allowed to manage its own affairs as long as it conformed to the general purposes of the PUL. The locals elected officers to represent them in the General Council, the "supreme power" in the league, which met every other week. The PUL also used committees to advance the interests of the unemployed and to win improvements in the relief system. Especially important were the Adjustment Committee, which attempted to resolve specific relief grievances of the jobless; the Mutual Aid Committee, which promoted self-help projects, including cooperative housing and barter arrangements; and the Legislative Committee, which lobbied for larger relief appropriations and, through 1935, for the passage of some sort of unemployment insurance program.[49]

Hard times and inadequate assistance, although they provided the necessary framework for organization, did not, of course, guarantee membership. And dedicated Socialists and liberal sympathizers alike often found recruitment burdensome. Broadus Mitchell, an active Socialist and faculty member of the Johns Hopkins University, crisscrossed the city on behalf of the PUL—but privately he complained of exhaustion, of speaking in "miserable halls filled with smoke," and he noted that his activities were "wearing if useful." After one afternoon session at a YMCA building filled with unemployed workers and their families, Mitchell wrote his mother: "I am going to quit going to places where the work is so hard. Try once to speak to women and children . . . and locomotive engineers in a wretched dirty little hall and see yourself go crazy trying to interest anybody."[50] But the indefatigable efforts of such Socialists as Mitchell, Elisabeth Gilman,

Frank Trager, Joel Seidman, and James Blackwell, along with those of activist ministers like the Reverends W. Owings Stone and Tracy Fenby, helped to swell the PUL's membership and to strengthen its position in the local political arena. Most importantly, the PUL, with the assistance of liberal black ministers and under the slogan of "Black and White, Unite and Fight," managed to forge an integrated coalition that constituted a major accomplishment in a city divided by color and bound by tradition.[51]

Officially nonpartisan, the PUL drew its strength from its role as the lobbying and bargaining agent for the unemployed. It agitated for the adoption of unemployment insurance, the abolition of child labor, and the provision of adequate aid to the jobless, including substantive work-relief projects. In addition to its appeal as a group that worked to satisfy the immediate needs of the unemployed, the PUL also benefited in important ways from the policies and the administrative structure of a number of New Deal programs. At the simplest level, the congregation of the jobless at relief offices or at work-relief projects afforded unprecedented organizational opportunities. Moreover, the rhetoric of the New Deal itself, especially the personal promises of the president, reflected a growing recognition of public responsibility for the victims of economic depression and contributed to rising expectations among the jobless—a development that social workers labeled as "increased assertiveness" and that unsympathetic politicians bemoaned as a sense of "entitlement." According to the Socialist party, the New Deal whetted the appetites of the unemployed: "It opened up their eyes and gave them some measure of understanding [of their predicament] for the first time."[52]

Significantly, the PUL capitalized on those New Deal programs that either required or encouraged community organization. When, for example, the Housing Division of the Public Works Administration slated the Waverly neighborhood for public housing, an active community group emerged to deal with the government. Organizers from the PUL assisted this group and, although Waverly never received a PWA housing program, the league won new recruits and two additional locals.

The organizational efforts of the PUL ironically benefited from the anti–New Deal policies of intransigent local officials. The obstructionist efforts of city political leaders so often frustrated necessary programs that the unemployed were forced to organize in order to get a fuller share of New Deal relief assistance. This local political hostility to the New Deal also had another important consequence: it made national administrators more willing to deal with those concerned groups that endorsed the New Deal

and even greater federal intervention. To be sure, New Dealers, on principle, supported "constructive" activism on the part of the jobless to insure
against demoralization or a resignation to dependence on the dole, and
they also regularly cooperated with organized groups in an attempt to
channel the grievances of the jobless through predictable and controllable
administrative procedures. But in Baltimore those objectives were combined with a real need to deal more directly with the unemployed precisely
because of the refusal of local politicians to cooperate with the federal
government. Aubrey Williams expressed this sentiment when, upon meeting a PUL delegation, he indicated his pleasure at having finally met
someone from Baltimore concerned about the jobless. He reassured the
league that the Roosevelt administration was "very sympathetic with the
efforts on the part of the unemployed to better conditions."[53] In sum, the
behavior of local politicians, the objectives of the New Dealers, the practices of the PUL, and the structure of national programs—all helped to
legitimize the role of the PUL as the principal agency of the city's unemployed. "We were not," as one PUL leader later recalled, "a pariah
organization."[54]

Immediately after its formation in 1933, the PUL turned its attention to
the unemployed's specific grievances against the city's system of relief.
The league instructed the jobless on BERC's eligibility requirements and
application procedures and provided them with direct proof of the PUL's
effectiveness in relief matters: within a year, for example, it had won
additional relief from the city for 542 of the 600 cases it handled. The PUL
also established itself as a link between the unemployed and federal administrators, thereby forcing local-level leaders to deal regularly with the
league as well. Thanks to the information provided by PUL members,
federal officials were made aware of local practices that inhibited the
carrying out of certain New Deal relief programs. Civil Works Administration officials early knew of the city's opposition to their program, and
league members even managed to give federal authorities private memo-
randa written by BERC officials detailing their particular objections to the
CWA. Assisted by government officials and by the publicity that the PUL's
protests attracted, the league was able to ensure that the city minimized its
infractions against the CWA—forcing local adjustments in wages, providing some work relief for eligible blacks, and halting the city's practice of
sending CWA workers to break strikes in nearby states.[55]

The PUL also managed to alleviate the deleterious effects of BERC's
efforts in 1934 to sharply reduce its relief rolls. In one instance, BERC

sought to discourage relief applications by adopting a new questionnaire that contained a pauper's oath as well as extremely personal questions, but league petitions and demonstrations resulted in its modification; the "obnoxious questions and paragraphs," exulted one PUL member, "will be omitted."[56] Throughout the summer of 1934 the league protested BERC's "attack on relief standards," denouncing the "arbitrary removal" from the relief rolls of thousands of residents "without any provision being made for their care."[57] Explaining to federal authorities that local officials were "not especially social-minded," the PUL urged the government to take over the entire supervision of relief in Baltimore—a request that Harry Hopkins and Aubrey Williams politely refused.[58] The PUL's lobbying committee regularly visited the state assembly to demand more money for relief; they brought ample proof of hardship to legislators weary of public assistance and unsympathetic to the city's problems. But while the PUL's legislative activities became routine, the lobbying committee noted the conspicuous absence of the city's mayor, who not once appeared to appeal for additional appropriations.[59]

The reorganization of relief that began in the summer of 1935 presented the PUL with one of its greatest challenges. The termination of the FERA, the establishment of the WPA for the employable jobless, and the return of responsibility for aiding the unemployables to states and localities—all placed serious hardships on Baltimore's unemployed and taxed the resources of both the PUL and the private relief agencies. Because neither the state nor the city accepted its new responsibilities, the PUL turned most forcefully to federal officials, straining its welcome in Washington with frequent visits, telegrams, and periodic picketing. The insistent actions of the league had already produced warnings from Aubrey Williams: "If you take the position," he sternly told one PUL delegation, "that you have to force us by methods of publicity, coercion and demands obviously you cannot get far for the simple reason that . . . we hold the whip, and we have to keep the peace."[60] And when the league warned of "serious danger unless constructive action is forthcoming," federal officials became more disenchanted with the PUL, for it had, from their perspective, moved beyond the appropriate bounds of constructive organized activity among the unemployed. At one demonstration outside the FERA office in Washington in September 1935, Williams refused to meet with a delegation of the protesters and instead strongly criticized the PUL's disruptive actions.[61]

The abolition of the FERA made it especially difficult for the PUL to operate in the manner that federal officials endorsed. The termination not only withdrew relief from thousands of unemployable jobless, whom the city refused to help, but it also meant the end of FERA grants for self-help activities. Voluntaristic efforts became at once more necessary and more difficult, for groups like the PUL were no longer able to receive the small sums of aid that had allowed the remodeling of vacant buildings to house unemployed families, the widening of the league's barter program, and the initiation of a project in cooperative medical care for needy neighborhoods. As a result, the PUL relied more on private relief agencies to help the unemployed and conducted its own drives in the city to collect money, food, and clothing.[62]

Rebuffed by both local and national leaders, the PUL increased its presence in the community, hardening its rhetoric and staging more demonstrations. With sound trucks canvassing the city, league members defiantly declared that the "organized unemployed will not tolerate [relief] cuts" and warned of mass action by the jobless. The PUL even took its case to the city's more exclusive neighborhoods, prompting residents to complain of the threatening words they heard from the sound trucks. And, of course, the PUL protested almost daily at BERC's headquarters and at City Hall. To coordinate these activities, in the fall of 1935 the league established a Protest Committee—an important indication of its new reliance on agitation.[63]

Although much of the PUL's militancy resulted from the problems caused by the dissolution of the FERA, it also stemmed directly from the organizational opportunities presented by the WPA. Members of the PUL used work-relief sites to organize during lunch breaks, to distribute leaflets before and after working hours, and to encourage WPA workers to behave as unionists with the PUL acting as their representative. The placement of Baltimore, along with midwestern cities, in the WPA's Wage Region II classification provided an issue around which WPA workers rallied, with the PUL as their chief advocate. Calling for a reclassification of Baltimore to the higher-paying Eastern region—where it more properly belonged, given the city's cost of living—WPA workers complained that large families were simply unable to survive on the $45 monthly security wage. The PUL gathered petitions for presentation to the state WPA administrator, Francis Dryden, and the WPA workers, many of whom were also PUL members, conducted slow-downs and work stoppages on the job. Threatening to follow the example of the WPA workers in Cumberland, Maryland, who were already on strike, Baltimore's WPA workers demanded that Dryden increase their wages. To indicate their determination and to register

During the relief crisis caused by the termination of the FERA and by state and local policies, the PUL agitated widely for assistance to the unemployed. Here the Reverend Tracy Fenby addresses an integrated crowd at Hopkins Place and Redwood on 11 September 1935.
(Courtesy of the Baltimore Sun)

sympathy for the Cumberland workers, the Baltimore WPA workers walked off their jobs on 18 October 1935.[64]

The Baltimore Federation of Labor threw its support behind the WPA workers. Fearing that the WPA scale would depress wages in private industry, Joseph McCurdy, the BFL president, urged workers not to accept WPA jobs if they were forced to take less money than they had received on BERC's relief rolls. At a mass protest meeting, McCurdy, with atypical fervor, praised the PUL's efforts. "The P.U.L. are called communists and radicals for protesting this rate of pay, so were our forefathers on Boston Commons, but now as then, right will prevail." McCurdy urged the workers not to allow the WPA to make "slaves of you men."[65]

Negotiations between Dryden and PUL members continued throughout November and early December, but the pressure for a wage increase did not fade, as Dryden had hoped. Instead, tensions mounted and relations between WPA workers and their foremen deteriorated. In one instance, when a foreman attempted to discharge some WPA workers for their PUL activities the entire crew physically assaulted him; at two other projects, workers threw down their tools when their foremen refused them permission to build fires for warmth. Finally, on 7 December 1935 more than 300 men went on strike, marching directly to PUL headquarters and demanding wage increases before they returned to work. One PUL leader explained their action, saying that he had "counseled patience while the negotiations were underway, but it seems that the men have tired under the waiting process."[66] President McCurdy of the BFL, alarmed by the strong bonds between the WPA and the PUL, agreed that there had been too much delay "in resolving the wage issue" but firmly declared that all strikes should be called by organized labor and not by any other organization.[67] Under fire from both the PUL and the BFL, Dryden eventually agreed to a 10 percent wage increase, raising the monthly wage rate for unskilled men to $49.50; for the semiskilled to $63.80; for the skilled to $79.20; and for the technical and professional workers to $86.90.[68]

The 10 percent increase did not, however, end the PUL's protests over wages or its attempts to change Baltimore's wage-region classification. Because over three-fourths of the city's workers received the wage rate of the unskilled, many of them with large families still found it difficult to provide for all their children. One local social worker published an article entitled "How Some Families Live on W.P.A. Wages," demonstrating "instances of acute suffering and serious health problems" among large families dependent solely on WPA security payments. He concluded that for families of six or more the wages fell short of allowing for a minimum subsistence by nearly $7.00 a month. Using such studies, the PUL finally persuaded BERC to supplement the WPA wages—an agreement that BERC made publicly in order to still criticism, but one that it effectively reneged on in practice.[69]

Nor did Dryden's wage raise help women working at WPA projects, for he simply refused to extend the increase to them. At one sewing project the women, as WPA workers and PUL members, organized to protest "this discrimination" against them, sending Harry Hopkins a strong indication of their displeasure and an appeal for a reclassification of Baltimore, which would automatically raise their wages.[70] But the problem of inadequate wages for WPA women and unskilled men continued. A survey found increased absenteeism from school among children of WPA families for lack of clothes and shoes; fully 78 percent of the children surveyed who were unable to attend school were from families on work relief. The PUL was never able to change the city's classification or to secure additional public assistance for needy families. The first task was nearly impossible, despite precedent for such adjustments, because Mayor Jackson himself never requested a classification change for Baltimore. And the second had been "resolved" by BERC's agreement to aid large families.[71]

The PUL campaigned to make the WPA a more equitable, just, and responsive work-relief program—objectives that often clashed with both Dryden's and Jackson's preference for substantial construction projects. For example, the league publicized the absence of quotas for blacks in the WPA and persuaded federal authorities to intervene locally to ensure that at least a few unemployed blacks received WPA jobs. Cooperating with the Baltimore Industrial Council (the local branch of the CIO), it secured WPA jobs for a number of black men in the construction of the Montebello tunnel system.[72] The PUL also vigorously protested federally mandated quota reductions, pointing out the disastrous consequences of the local decision to reduce the number of WPA employees by discharging the elderly and the less efficient workers. Demonstrations by PUL representatives at one WPA sewing project, which had dismissed a group of older women for being too slow on the job, brought enough newspaper attention that the local employment director, D. L. B. Fringer, promised to rehire some of the workers—but Fringer privately instructed local project supervisors to continue to "apply the efficiency standard" and release the "less productive women," and, apparently determined that these women should receive no help whatsoever, he even told relief officials that, should the women reapply to BERC for assistance, they should be rejected as ineligible for direct aid because they had been certified as employables.[73]

Efficiency standards and quota reductions allowed Fringer and his WPA supervisors to fire other undesirable workers. In early 1936, for instance, Fringer authorized the dismissal of more than 300 men described by their foremen as "troublemakers" and "agitators." He freely admitted that workers had been "fired by their supervisors for P.U.L. organization work," explaining that they had "talked Socialism and Communism to the [other] workers" and had encouraged laborers to "stall during work hours." This practice of "shirking by workers," WPA foremen explained, was simply a device to challenge their authority on the job. Members of the PUL complained that they were treated "like dogs not humans," but Fringer reminded the WPA workers of their status as relief recipients and declared he would not tolerate disciplinary problems caused by radical agitation.[74]

Nevertheless, the PUL continued its efforts to represent WPA workers as a union of work-relief employees. It pressed for collective bargaining rights, secured the adoption of an on-the-job steward system to reduce conflict between workers and supervisors, and won the reinstatement of sewing women who had been discharged for wearing their PUL buttons.[75] And when, in the fall of 1936, Aubrey Williams recognized the Workers Alliance—the national organization of the unemployed—as a collective bargaining agency for WPA workers, the PUL, as an affiliate, officially strengthened its bargaining role. Federal recognition of the alliance enhanced the local power of the PUL and forced local WPA supervisors to devise more surreptitious means to rid themselves of the disruptive "PUL'ers." For instance, PUL members complained to federal officials in Washington, D.C., that newly hired WPA workers were forced to sign blank discharge forms in advance; the supervisors later inserted fraudulent reasons for the suspension or dismissal of those who were found to belong to the PUL. The discrimination against activists did not diminish as the decade wore on. As late as 1941, workers requested a federal investigation into the WPA's dismissal of workers "on unproven and unfounded charges of Communism."[76]

In some respects local policies toward the organized unemployed and the WPA resembled those at the national level. Neither city officials nor federal administrators regarded WPA workers as traditional wage laborers. In particular, they never granted workers the right to strike. And WPA laborers never escaped their status as "reliefers." Commenting on a series of strikes in 1935, Harry Hopkins emphatically declared that "there is no such thing as a strike on a relief job. This is a relief program"—and workers "will not be on relief if they refuse to take jobs." President Roosevelt even refused to acknowledge work stoppages as strikes and referred to the strikers as "men who had returned to their homes." In 1939 he reaffirmed that position when he declared "You cannot strike against the government."[77] Yet certain national officials, particularly Aubrey Williams, were still more solicitous of the rights of WPA workers at the workplace than were either local officials or WPA foremen. Williams urged the adoption of grievance procedures and the job-steward system, and, as noted, he recognized the Workers Alliance as the bargaining agent of the unemployed—all policies that departed significantly from the local attempts to decimate the ranks of the activist unemployed through routine dismissals. Rather than deal with the PUL to create more efficient work-relief projects, as federal administrators recommended, local officials preferred more adversarial relationships and only grudgingly acceded to isolated league demands.[78]

In the latter part of the 1930s local WPA supervisors became less concerned about PUL membership than about radical sentiments in general. This change reflected the growing influence of the CIO. The Baltimore Industrial Council (BIC), with the assistance of PUL leaders, encouraged a shift in organizational allegiance among WPA workers. Although the PUL continued to act on behalf of the unemployed, its leaders, like chairman James Blackwell, increasingly worked to further the cause of organized labor. Blackwell was instrumental in organizing both employed and unemployed autoworkers into Local #239 of the UAW.[79] The PUL and the BIC also cooperated in demonstrations to demand more relief for the jobless. Not surprisingly, then, when Patrick Whalen as head of the BIC demanded in 1938 that the Department of Welfare recognize "union committees as proper agencies to investigate relief needs," the PUL rallied behind the proposal. The league agreed with the BIC that union members better understood the "needs of their fellow workers," and it recommended that the Department of Welfare grant the CIO permanent membership on its advisory board.[80]

Despite its successful cooperation with the BIC, the PUL encountered a number of difficulties in its efforts to represent the unemployed in the last years of the depression decade. The legislative attack on the WPA at the national level in 1939 particularly hurt the PUL: it reduced funding, instituted an 18-month rotation rule, and curtailed the payment of WPA funds to persons who advocated, or who belonged to organizations that advocated, the overthrow of the United States. These provisions simultaneously provoked the ire of the PUL leaders and undermined the strength of the organization. And the conservative backlash in Congress encouraged such local officials as Fringer to intensify their search for radicals. Division among the organized unemployed further weakened the PUL, as the issue of communism led the predominantly Socialist PUL to renounce its ties with the Workers Alliance in favor of association with a newly founded faction called the Workers Security Foundation.[81]

But the problems of the PUL, from within and without, did not distract it from its primary goal of assisting the unemployed. In 1938 and 1939, it held major demonstrations to protest "arbitrary cuts" from the WPA and to denounce what it termed the "Nazification of relief."[82] League members continued their visits to Annapolis and City Hall, always prepared with data detailing deprivation and hardship among the jobless and, on one occasion, even forcing legislators to sample the surplus canned food supplied by the government to relief clients (a "typical relief meal," exclaimed one lawmaker, "is not fit to eat"). The PUL also scheduled regular meetings with the Department of Welfare to discuss department policy and specific grievances.[83] The league continued to promote self-help activities. In 1938 it transformed its complex network of barter arrangements, which had been thriving since 1933, into a "cooperative store" completely staffed by unemployed workers. The following year it attempted to expand its program of "community-sponsored socialized medicine," which attracted the enthusiastic endorsement of neighborhood clergy. The PUL further widened its community basis of support, joining, for example, with neighborhood and religious groups to form the Baltimore Committee on Unemployment and Social Security in 1937, and in 1939 establishing the Citizens' Committee on Unemployment to protest the city's "purges of relief rolls." The league sought to assist the handicapped unemployed by devising plans to prevent their institutionalization and to provide for them a "normal life in the community." It also held "workshops" throughout the city to educate the jobless about the complex procedures involved in applying for Social Security programs.[84] The persistent dedication of the PUL did not escape the attention of friends and foes alike, and the variety of its activities led the BIC's weekly paper, the *Labor Herald*, to establish a separate column for the PUL—the "oldest and largest unemployment organization" in the nation, the *Herald* boasted.[85]

In large measure, the PUL's success as an organization of the unemployed depended directly on its ability to improve New Deal programs—to agitate for stronger programs at the national level, to lobby for larger appropriations at the state level, and to remove obstacles to implementing programs at the local level. Not until the federal government took an active role in the administration of relief did substantive organizations of the unemployed appear. Words of support, along with necessary assistance programs extended by the federal government, provided many jobless workers with the framework they needed to press for greater social commitment to, and public responsibility for, unemployment relief. As a result of those same factors, however, the PUL also confronted important limitations. The federal government rarely challenged seriously the priorities of local political leaders, thus minimizing the potential of New Deal relief programs; and national administrators refused to support the PUL when it attempted to participate in local policy-making decisions. Finally, from the perspective of PUL leaders, their efforts produced a supreme irony: the gains they won for the jobless, the improvements they secured for the relief system—all tended to bolster among their membership support for a New Deal they thought inadequate.

Throughout the 1930s, then, the PUL never abandoned its goal of community organization. To be sure, declining membership in the last years of the decade and the establishment of permanent relief programs resulted in fewer mass demonstrations and forced the league to redouble its lobbying efforts in an attempt to accomplish what protest meetings had earlier achieved. And scholars focusing on the national level, particularly on the Workers Alliance, have detected a transition from "local insurgency to national responsibility," pointing to alliance leaders who accepted administrative positions in the WPA as examples of those who became "collaborators in the process that emasculated the movement."[86] But such a linear model of change does not fully explain the evolution of the PUL in the 1930s. Whereas league members cooperated with the political system they hoped to transform, and some even abandoned their lukewarm Socialism in favor of the New Deal, most PUL leaders held firm to their difficult position of calling for a new social system while working to improve the conditions of the jobless. The league never lost sight of itself as a community organization; certainly it never fully made the transition from a *social action* group to a *social planning* association.[87] In 1935 James Blackwell had warned PUL members not to be deluded by "the man behind the smile" but to "see the Roosevelt administration as the ruthless and inhuman agency of decadent capitalism."[88] In 1939 the PUL announced that the "New Deal has tried and failed," staged a demonstration outside the Department of Welfare, and called for a new system of relief. But the Socialist leadership of the PUL made few converts among its members, who continued to believe that the New Deal offered a real solution to the economic depression of the 1930s.[89]

The PUL was extremely important not only in calling attention to the needs of the unemployed but also in revising administrative thinking and local policies concerning the rights of the jobless. And, as observed by one of its founders, it served to educate its own members by "getting white men and women to work with and under Negro men and women." League activities forced local officials to liberalize their attitudes toward "reliefers." With neither power nor recognition, the unemployed were able to shape the administration of relief through organization, using the tactics of public pressure and demonstration. The PUL won improvements in relief assistance, stopped more than a few evictions, publicized the racism and sexism that accompanied most relief programs, familiarized politicians with the daily predicament of the jobless, encouraged social workers to support the rights of the unemployed, provided food and shelter for those most in need, fostered interracial cooperation, and introduced thousands of workers to the importance of organization. Such accomplishments, although too often lost in the historical record, represented significant advancements in a city that did not even have a municipal welfare department until 1935.[90]

But by the end of the 1930s the task of the PUL in representing the unemployed became more difficult. The creation of a permanent system of relief, despite its incomplete coverage and inadequate funding, served to diminish the urgency of the problem. A 1937 survey found that 55 percent of the people polled believed that "many persons on the WPA . . . could get jobs if they tried," and a 1939 Roper poll showed that less than one-quarter of the sample thought the government should spend as much on the WPA in 1939 as it had in the previous year.[91] Public weariness with the problem of unemployment combined with a growing hostility toward radicalism to make the PUL's job more arduous. Finally, the league could no longer count on assistance from federal administrators, many of whom had turned their attention to foreign problems. By 1939 the PUL rarely sent delegations to Washington, for support there had all but disappeared; it now attempted to inch local and state authorities toward accepting the level of public responsibility earlier demonstrated by federal officials.

CHAPTER 6

The Struggle to Unionize

Labor Organization and the New Deal

The Great Depression and the New Deal intensified the drive for collective action among the city's workers. "When the New Deal arrived in the spring of 1933," Baltimore's *Sew-Sew News* declared in November 1939, "the women's garment workers reacted to it at once by launching one organization drive after another." Like the citizens who acted in concert to exert greater control over their neighborhoods, laborers organized both as workers and as members of their communities. Rooseveltian rhetoric legitimized labor organization, and local labor leaders used New Deal slogans to equate union membership with patriotic duty. Versions of the slogan, "The President Wants You to Join a Union," rapidly spread beyond the printed appeals of the United Mine Workers. In 1937, for example, Baltimore cab drivers struck under the banner "Roosevelt Said Organize." New Deal labor legislation also did much to encourage organization. Nationally, union membership climbed from 3.4 million in 1929 to over 8 million in 1939. Section 7(a) of the National Industrial Recovery Act passed in 1933 stated that employees "shall have the right to organize and bargain collectively through representatives of their own choosing." Inadequate enforcement of this provision under the NRA and the Supreme Court's subsequent decision invalidating the Recovery Act, however, made the passage of the Wagner Act in 1935 necessary for successful union recognition and collective bargaining. With the Wagner Act's National Labor Relations Board (NLRB), workers received an institutional voice in labor-management relations. Just as the federal government approved the organizational role of politically marginal groups such as transients and public-housing tenants, it also legitimized the union idea among workers and some of their bosses. The New Deal provided an important opportunity to organize the industrial work force; the sons and daughters of immigrant families sided with the union and with Roosevelt. The Committee for Industrial Organization spearheaded the drive to organize the unorganized, often linking its movement to the Roosevelt reelection campaign of 1936. And in sharp contrast to the past, the government did not attempt to halt the labor movement of the 1930s.

To be sure, the federal government preferred loyal Democrats to disruptive militants among the work force. As in the case of other organizing groups, there were real limits to the support provided by the government, which favored a role of "constructive activism" for all such groups— whether they be transients, or tenants, or the labor force. There was but vague sympathy for workers from President Roosevelt, and he became weary of labor's struggles when he proclaimed a "plague" on the houses of both labor and management in the Little Steel conflict. Even the Wagner Act often failed to check unfair labor practices; at its adoption, the Baltimore *Sun* felt it "safe to predict that the Wagner bill will be as ineffectual as was section 7(a)."[1] City employers, moreover, openly flouted the NLRB's actions until 1937 when the Supreme Court upheld the constitutionality of the Wagner Act. Yet worker militancy increased and demands for union recognition grew more adamant. The New Deal for labor offered important opportunities for organizing, and there was growing sentiment among workers that they should have the unions they believed their president wanted them to have.

The depression imposed great burdens upon Baltimore's working population. The 1930 census recorded 362,072 gainful workers in the city—28 percent female and 72 percent male; 22 percent black and 78 percent white. All were not affected equally, but as the city's unemployment rate exceeded 20 percent and overburdened relief agencies suspended their services, many workers experienced increasingly desperate conditions. Employers were accustomed to labor passivity, especially during hard times, and some attempted to capitalize on the labor surplus by reducing wages and extending hours; sweatshops in the garment industry increased in number, and conditions in other industries also worsened. Other employers, hampered by a declining demand, laid workers off or shut down their businesses entirely. The Baltimore and Ohio Railroad turned to the job-sharing system, reducing the hours and wages of the workers rather than laying off its employees. Bethlehem Steel, on the other hand, discharged more than 1,200 workers by March 1933 and then announced its opposition to a proposal for a state-sponsored unemployment insurance program.[2]

Baltimore's industries were for the most part small and aspiring. They certainly did not share the notion, slightly more common among big businesses, that there was a "harmony of interests" between employer and employee, albeit an unequal partnership in harmony. Even the city's largest firms rarely endorsed labor-management cooperation and, like their smaller counterparts, they believed that there was much to be gained from making extraordinary demands on unorganized workers, who felt threatened by the prospect of unemployment. In theory, at least, those demands were to be tempered by state social legislation regulating hours and working conditions; but in practice the abuses proved enormous and consistent. J. Knox Insley—Maryland's commissioner of labor and statistics, a long-time supporter of Governor Albert Ritchie, and an unlikely ally of organized labor—wrote Ritchie of the blatant disregard for labor laws shown by a group of the city's employers: "There are," he complained, "a relatively small number of companies . . . which, no matter what means of encouragement or persuasion have been adopted, seem to acquire no sense of responsibility in regard to these laws"—laws, he added, that, if observed, would represent "little inconvenience" to them. These companies, noted Insley, particularly defied the state laws governing hours of employment for women. Fearful of losing their jobs during hard times, the women workers were "at the mercy of unscrupulous employers." The major clothing firms of J. Schoeneman and L. Greif especially exploited their women employees in this regard, turning their factories in the 1930s into "depression sweatshops."[3]

Businesses also regularly ignored state laws concerning accident disabilities and workers' compensation. Although Maryland had passed an employers' liability law at the turn of the century, subsequent judicial decisions declared it unconstitutional, and vigorous lobbying on the part of the Merchants and Manufacturers Association delayed the provision of statewide accident protection until 1912. After that, organized employers effectively chipped away at the program, winning, for example, major victories in the courts in the 1920s that sharply limited the application of compensation laws. In 1931, the state, at the request of employers, even disallowed the "appearance of the claimant as a witness" to prevent the worker from prejudicing the jury "in his favor." Without adequate protection from depression-era employers, many workers endured long hours and unsafe conditions or attempted to organize to change their predicament.[4]

In September 1932 some 5,000 garment workers in Baltimore, responding to the call of the Amalgamated Clothing Workers of America (ACW), went out on strike to protest their low wages and long hours and to demand recognition of their union. The strike was at once a bold and a desperate move for the ACW, whose ranks had been decimated by the antiunionism of the 1920s. In Baltimore, the 1920s had also been a period of economic decline in the men's garment industry; the city dropped from third to fifth place among the nation's garment centers, and major manufacturers either closed their doors or relied more heavily on the smaller, intensely competitive contract shops.[5] Firms like Schoeneman's had their own contract shops, where working conditions and wages resembled those of the nineteenth century and where most of the employees were women. Greif, too, exploited the labor of women in its shops and factories, but it also relied on the work of women at home to produce its men's garments. The strike in 1932, which affected over 200 manufacturers and contract shops, brought clearly into public view the desperate plight of the women working in the city's garment industry.

Women garment workers turned out en masse to picket the shops and factories in the city but focused particular attention on the Schoeneman firm, notorious for its low wages and miserable working conditions. They clashed with police, who at Schoeneman's request attempted to reduce the number of pickets in front of his factory. Although hundreds of women were taken away to jail, others moved in to fill their places. One striker, Sara Barron, later recalled with pride that "we [women] were really the ones who had something to do with mass picketing" in Baltimore in the 1930s; "I was locked up thirteen times" in the 1932 strike, she added. Concerned citizens of Baltimore, calling the strike a "civic nuisance," demanded that Mayor Howard Jackson resolve the conflict. Jackson responded by forming a committee to investigate the situation and selected as its head Jacob Hollander, a professor at the Johns Hopkins University, an erstwhile Progressive, and a persistent proponent of "enlightened labor-management relations." Schoeneman, however, refused to participate in the inquiry and rejected all of Hollander's overtures for cooperation. Still, the testimony of the workers proved so damaging that Schoeneman hurriedly made improvements in one of his worst shops.[6]

Schoeneman's women workers complained of inadequate light and ventilation; of rodent and pest infestation so severe they were unable to store their lunches safely; and of intimidation by male foremen, who forced them to work overtime or lose their jobs, refused to allow them leave for personal or family sickness, and regularly harassed those whom they found attractive. Paid by piecework and not compensated for training new workers, the women usually averaged only $6–$12 a week for sixty hours of work; victims of hard times and scarce jobs, they often accepted the dictates of their employers. When the fastest, most efficient workers questioned the wage rates they were informed that $12 was "a decent salary for any girl to make." At the same time, the foremen fully realized that many of the women had families to support, and during slack times certain foremen laid off women with children before women who had unemployed husbands at home. As one woman explained, "I took my two babies over [to the foreman], and said, 'For God's sake, Mr. Raab, don't take my job away from me.' He said he couldn't help it. 'I have to let you off, there are women who have to keep their husbands.' "[7]

Conditions for the few men working at Schoeneman's were only slightly better, but the investigation showed that foremen were less likely to shout insults at, or make provocative comments to, the male workers. Moreover, the men were not forced to perform janitorial duties at day's end, whereas the women were required to sweep and "pick up" before going home.

The revelations about conditions in the garment industry served to increase public sympathy for the workers and to persuade many of the city's employers to recognize the ACW. That the workers were no longer "a body of illiterate immigrants" but "Americans to the core" received much attention. "It is not without significance," Hollander explained, "that the 150 young women who have been arrested [this day] for violating police regulations as to picketing and who were carted off to the station house should have sung during the period of their detention, not the 'Red Flag' or the 'Marseillaise,' but the 'Star-Spangled Banner.' " The testimony provided during Hollander's investigation by Sidney Hillman, president of the Amalgamated Clothing Workers, heightened the appeal to patriotism, and within a short time about 70 percent of the city's garment industry accepted the terms proffered by the ACW. Of Baltimore's major manufacturers, only Greif and Schoeneman resisted. And Schoeneman, rather than deal with the union or alter the conditions that had generated so much negative attention, simply moved his business to the safe, nonunion environs of rural Pennsylvania. Moving vans loaded with factory equipment discreetly stole away in the middle of the night.[8]

The failure of the workers to unionize either Schoeneman or Greif in 1932 foreshadowed the problems that organizing workers would face throughout the depression decade. Despite the apparent protection of the Blue Eagle or the NLRB, workers encountered serious local opposition to their organizational activities, including the dismissal of union agitators, the employment of strikebreakers, the use of police to restrain picketing and protect the strikebreakers, and the antiunion policies of a number of public officials. Employer hostility combined with judicial practices and police intervention to slow union recognition throughout the 1930s. New contracts usually meant new struggles; battles were fought and refought with gains only temporary and victories never complete. Assisted by trade unionists, Socialists, and Communists, workers challenged their bosses, demanded their "New Deal rights," and stood firm by their unions—all confident in the belief that their president sympathized with their predicament. "Mr. Roosevelt," explained one worker, "is the only man we ever had in the White House who would understand that my boss is a sonofabitch."[9]

Both business and labor applauded the establishment of the NRA. Union leaders like ACW vice-president Hyman Blumberg saw the program as an opportunity to eliminate permanently the sweatshop conditions in his home town of Baltimore. The NRA, he observed, would help maintain the "excellent morale" among the workers caused by the 1932 organizational campaign and would ensure that women garment workers earned at least $12.00 a week. "It is not much," he added, "but it would mean a lot [to them]." But Blumberg also feared that the NRA would strengthen organizational ties among antiunion employers and that they would use the codes to undermine union influence. In keeping with the Amalgamated's emphasis on labor-management cooperation, and to ensure for itself a prominent role in code deliberations, the ACW took the lead in holding the city's first "NRA conference" of workers and employers. Blumberg called for the standardization of prices, garments, and wages and warned that "competition at the expense of labor alone will be terminated." No longer, he declared, would Baltimore compete with eastern Pennsylvania for the "title of lowest wage center in the industry." The Clothing Manufacturers of Baltimore disliked what they heard but agreed to abide by NRA wage codes; Benjamin LeBow, chairman of the association, later declared of his fellow employers that "they are not a damned bit pleased with this, but they know they've got to go along with it." As a precautionary measure, the ACW called a twenty-four-hour strike in the men's garment shops, saying that workers would return to their jobs only for the "New Deal" wages of forty cents an hour.[10]

Unlike the ACW, the Baltimore Federation of Labor took little initiative in promoting labor-management discussion of wage codes. The federation, which represented about 7 percent of the work force at the start of the depression decade, largely accepted the decisions made at the regional and national levels and, although it supported that program, did not attempt to be part of the decisions affecting local NRA policies. Sidney Hillman later denounced the federation for its limited role in the NRA, saying that it actually "stood in the way of organization." The BFL did at least condemn businesses that failed to uphold NRA wage codes, placing NRA violators on its "We don't patronize" list published in its paper, *The Federationist*, as part of its campaign against employer "chiselers." But even those actions came after similar ones taken by Socialists in their paper, the *Maryland Leader*. And, unlike the Socialists, the BFL refused to support the "Buy Where You Can Work" program organized by the City-Wide Young People's Forum to force Blue Eagle businesses to hire blacks; only the Baltimore *Afro-American* and the *Maryland Leader* regularly published the names of noncomplying companies.[11]

The difficult job of enforcing wage and hour codes belonged to the NRA National Compliance Board and the compliance offices that were established in every state. In Maryland, Arthur Hungerford began his duties as state NRA compliance director in January 1934. Urging complete cooperation from labor and industry, Hungerford expected a tidy administration. He saw the New Deal, and particularly the NRA, as an opportunity to create a cooperative order and predicted that in such an environment labor and industry would naturally treat each other fairly.[12] Trapped by his own zealousness, however, Hungerford failed to realize that spirit alone proved inadequate in a sagging economy and that cooperation often had little place in the contest between industrialists and unionizing workers.

The absence of a national commitment to upholding either the NRA codes or the provisions of Section 7(a) made local enforcement problematic. Further complicating the job, from Hungerford's perspective, were the variety and number of codes to be enforced: nationally, the NRA ultimately approved codes for over 700 "industries," causing some firms to be affected by at least two different codes. Clothing firms in Baltimore consistently attempted to use the lowest-paying code for all their workers. Compliance enforcement was especially difficult in such shops as H. Borenstein and Sons, which operated one-third under the Men's Clothing Code and two-thirds under the Cotton Pants Industry Code. Hungerford pressed for local enforcement, but he soon realized that Baltimore business leaders were usually unwilling to discipline their fellow employers. He regularly complained to the national office about inadequate local cooperation but received little assistance. Moreover, he failed to realize that his own prejudices operated to enhance NRA violations. Hungerford disliked strikes regardless of the employer offense, rarely punished persistent violators, and consistently favored large businesses at the expense of smaller ones, even dismissing violations made by big businesses as "unintentional."[13]

As part of the NRA arrangement, industries were allowed to organize into trade associations, ostensibly to fulfill the Blue Eagle agreement about wages, hours, and trading practices. Hungerford rarely questioned the decisions of these industrial associations. When, for example, the Retail Automobile Trade Authority refused to report violations to the state NRA office, Hungerford merely referred to the authority as "our bad boy." And when the local Cotton Garment Code Authority ruled that employers needed to pay their workers only 25 to 35 percent of the money owed them because of wage-code violations, Hungerford refused to challenge the decision. He also did little to halt the employers' practice of forcing workers to record only forty-four hours on their work cards despite the greater number of hours actually worked. Finally, ignoring the overwhelming evidence of repeated employer abuses, Hungerford clung tenaciously to his antistrike sentiments, declaring that it was never necessary for workers to strike "to obtain their rights under the NRA."[14]

The most celebrated NRA case in Baltimore involved the Greif company, the nation's second-largest clothing manufacturer. The dispute provided poignant testimony of the continuing difficulties faced by garment workers despite unionization and New Deal legislation. Hostile to worker organization and government regulation, Greif announced plans to challenge the constitutionality of the NRA while it deliberately ignored the wage codes. Indeed, Greif not only refused to pay its employees the minimum wage established by the men's clothing code but changed from the piecework system to a combined hourly wage and quota system, with the daily quotas set so high that workers complained they had to begin work before the official starting time and skip lunch simply to meet the required production schedule.

Hungerford failed to respond to the charges, but the national NRA compliance office, which had repeatedly received complaints about Greif's operations in Maryland, Virginia, and Pennsylvania, launched an investigation. In April 1934, federal investigators visited all eight of Greif's plants in the three states, only to find that the company had destroyed its 1933 pay records. Moreover, company officials refused to cooperate with NRA authorities. These obstacles notwithstanding, the NRA ruled that Greif was guilty of depriving its employees of over $35,000 by not paying the code's minimum wage. In turn, company attorneys filed suit against the NRA, charging that the recovery program was illegal and that the men's clothing code had been framed in violation of the law and represented an attempt to force "all manufacturers into [the ACW] or out of business."[15]

While legal proceedings continued, the NRA ordered Blue Eagle labels withheld from the Greif company for its violation of the wage code. Company officials appealed to the Baltimore Association of Commerce, which denounced the NRA's move against Greif. Hungerford lamented the situation and noted that the BAC had not bothered to "secure the facts" before protesting on behalf of Greif.

In response to the absence of Blue Eagle labels, retailers began canceling their orders from Greif, bringing substantial financial pressure to bear on the company. By the end of August, Greif announced its willingness to abide by the decision of an impartial mediator chosen by the Department of Justice. The arbiter ruled that Greif had violated the wage provision of the code and suggested that the company eliminate the quota system and raise wages to a level more commensurate with those paid by other companies in the industry. The NRA agreed that in order to get the higher wages it would "not . . . press for [full] restitution of the fair wages" owed to employees— so that Greif repaid only a fraction of the money due the workers. Hungerford found the entire Greif case unfortunate and complained that the federal authorities had completely bypassed the state NRA office. Moreover, he feared that the introduction of the Justice Department further undermined the strength of the NRA in settling disputes and resulted in too-lenient decisions regarding wage restitution. "As soon as violators realize," Hungerford explained, "that if they thumb their noses at NRA and are carried to the Litigation Division, that a compromise will be made that would never have been considered in this office, very few of them will make adjustment." Hungerford himself, however, had failed to initiate an investigation of Greif.[16]

Even with federal NRA intervention, the city's workers' efforts to organize never fully benefited from Section 7(a). At the local level, Baltimore's chairman of the NRA Grievance Committee, Colonel W. D. A. Anderson, demonstrated his typical reaction to labor complaints in the late summer of 1933 when unionizing boot and shoe workers encountered a lockout by intransigent employers. The workers immediately protested by demonstrating outside the building only to be arrested by police and chastised by Anderson, who termed their actions unnecessarily belligerent. Like state and local NRA offices, the state's Office of Labor and Statistics also resented disruptive worker activities. Although the individual state labor commissioners changed from 1932 to 1937, the office remained uniformly hostile toward agitation; throughout the 1930s it repeatedly denounced "summary" action on the part of strikers, maintaining that workers should be patient with employers who forbade unions or decreased wages.[17]

More supportive of worker organization was the Baltimore Labor Relations Panel, which by 1935 held jurisdiction over all of District V, encompassing Maryland, Virginia, and Delaware. The panel's membership helps explain its sympathy to unionization: designed to have three representatives each from labor and business and an impartial chair, it in fact operated in its first months without full management representation, for by the end of July all of the three businessmen selected had resigned, complaining of too much work. And the chairman was Jacob Hollander, who had led the 1932 investigation of the Schoeneman sweatshops and well knew the abuses in the city's shops and the arrogance of some employers. Although he was in favor of business growth and worker stability, Hollander was a strong advocate of fair labor practices and, unlike Hungerford or Insley, was not easily influenced by the ingratiating advances of certain business leaders.

Hollander submitted monthly reports on the activities of the Labor Relations Panel, frequently noting a "great deal of friction" between management and workers in the city. Between late 1933 and September 1934 the number of reported strikes increased by 60 percent. In pursuit of industrial harmony, the panel spent most of its time attempting to reconcile employers to the idea of organization and arbitration. "Baltimore employers," Hollander complained, "are traditionally hostile to the idea of unionism," and they consistently refused to meet with the panel or comply with its decisions. Still, the panel managed to resolve a few disputes in favor of union recognition. The presence on the panel of Erwin Feldman, business representative and attorney for the Needle Trades Association of Baltimore, largely explains the successful settlements. He bargained with labor representatives and urged fellow business leaders to accept the panel's decisions. Feldman's activities, along with those of another panel member, Charles Kreindler, vice-president of the International Ladies' Garment Workers' Union (ILGWU), ensured that the panel's record was best in the needle trades. Other cases, however, although officially recorded as re-solved, occasionally represented an agreement between management and union officials without the consent of the rank and file. For example, Harry Cohen of the International Brotherhood of Teamsters, Chauffeurs, Stable-men and Helpers of America settled a trucking strike with a "verbal agreement with the Hampden Transfer and Storage Company"; the union's members, however, continued to press for a written contract that included recognition of their union, the closed shop, and wage adjustments. Not only were there differences between the rank and file and their union representatives, there were major policy divisions between the leadership and the organizers of the BFL. Although a few activists such as Cohen used the Labor Relations Panel in an attempt to secure protection of union rights, the BFL leadership generally avoided the tripartite arrange-ments involving government, business, and labor in favor of more tradi-tional voluntaristic approaches. The ACW and the ILGWU, both supporters of government intervention in labor-management relations, relied more heavily on the Panel to resolve their problems.[18]

"The big battle over the NRA," aptly declared the *Maryland Leader*, "boils down to *the right to strike*. Employers everywhere are challenging the right to strike under NRA." The *Leader* correctly realized that in a city hostile to unions, organization rarely occurred without a struggle. Before his death in 1933, BFL President Henry Broening asserted that the "NRA means nothing to workers unless they organize and enforce their rights under the law." Other labor officials viewed the NRA with even less opti-mism, and one local BFL delegate warned in 1934 that the NRA was "crumbling," making the rapid organization of workers essential to better working conditions. "Organization," concurred new BFL President Joseph McCurdy, "must be the watchword of labor."[19]

McCurdy's pronouncements notwithstanding, the BFL generally pre-ferred the policy of reaction rather than action. Anxious not to alienate employers or city officials, McCurdy refrained from initiating organiza-tional campaigns. The *Maryland Leader* frequently denounced the federa-tion's reluctance to organize the unorganized. When, for example, the *Leader* discovered the poor conditions and miserable wages in local paper box factories, it exclaimed, "One is at a loss [to understand] why the Baltimore Federation of Labor allows these workers to remain unorganized. The *Maryland Leader* is ready and willing to help in every way possible the Federation to organize these workers." But the BFL proved more responsive to competition than to cooperation. Indeed, a BFL delegate urged the federation to push unionization among the city's upholsterers only after learning that a "communist group was endeavoring to organize an industrial union among the upholsterers."[20]

Despite the sporadic nature of the BFL's efforts at unionization, workers spontaneously organized and demanded affiliation with the BFL; bakers at a Baltimore bread company, for instance, requested recognition from the BFL after having organized 98 percent of the workers themselves. Between 1933 and 1935, the BFL's Organizing Committee largely limited its activities to granting charters to self-organized workers desiring union recognition. And although the new labor movement was fragile in nature and vulnerable to outside attacks, it still represented a significant advancement, for by 1935 the federation counted 15–17 percent of the city's work force as members.[21]

Organizational activities in Baltimore did not depend solely on workers' initiative. Unions such as the ACW, the ILGWU, and the Baltimore Industrial Council (as part of the national Committee for Industrial Organization) all conducted vigorous campaigns in the city. Less formal but extremely valuable assistance came from a handful of iconoclastic BFL delegates and a few Socialists, many of whom belonged to the union of the unemployed, the Peoples Unemployment League. By cooperating daily in all organizational matters, these unions and individuals worked together to strengthen labor's drive toward union recognition. Socialist and PUL member Frank Trager, for example, worked particularly hard in the garment trades, where he assisted local ACW and ILGWU organizers. Socialists Elisabeth Gilman and Naomi Riches of the PUL centered their efforts on organizing women in all trades and frequently cooperated with BFL delegate Anna Neary in assisting striking women textile workers and arranging boycotts. Neary's own contributions ranged from organizing the Women's Union of Dressmakers to forming a Union Label League comprised of women workers and wives of union delegates and laborers.[22]

Frustrated by McCurdy's inaction, still other delegates rented halls, scheduled speakers to "educate" the workers, and issued pamphlets and advertisements promising improved working conditions with organization—all of which resulted in marked increases in union membership for coopers, printers, seamen, textile workers, butchers, and bartenders.[23] But even these efforts did not obscure the reality that the BFL, at least officially, more often responded to the plans of competing labor organizers or the activities of the workers themselves than it initiated any comprehensive policy of its own.

The BFL's refusal to deal with black workers further restricted its impact on labor organization. Racial tension had frequently disrupted the federation in the past, as in 1916 when a local of the International Longshoremen's Association (ILA) had split into separate white and black locals. In 1932, black longshoremen walked out of a BFL meeting rather than accept segregated seating arrangements. Other mixed unions, like the Ship Caulkers, avoided such a schism, but blacks remained outside the major activities of the union. Hard times and scarce jobs only exacerbated racial animosities. During the depression, white union bricklayers, for example, permitted white nonunion hod-carriers to serve them, sometimes even before the black members of the International Hod-Carriers, Builders, and Common Laborers; blacks, however, who made up 70 percent of the union, consistently refused to serve nonunion bricklayers, regardless of color.[24] The BFL did nothing to stop the practices of white bricklayers, refused to challenge those unions in the city that explicitly barred blacks from membership, and consistently rejected the appeals of the Baltimore Urban League to help organize black workers in the city. The executive secretary of the Baltimore Urban League, Edward Lewis, declared that the federation was dominated by "craft adherents who seek to keep out colored workers." One BFL official expressed the federation's attitudes in his declaration that the organization of blacks was "not essential to the success of the labor movement." On the other hand, the Urban League received considerable support from the Socialist party and the League for Industrial Democracy. Socialists Gilman, Trager, and Joel Seidman were especially active and repeatedly denounced the BFL's racist policies. The local CIO also officially challenged the racism common in Baltimore's unions. But even the Baltimore Industrial Council devoted its energies in the latter part of the 1930s to organizing unorganized whites; not until 1945 did black membership in local unions approach significant levels.[25]

One of the few unions to collide forcefully with the BFL's policies was the Baltimore Joint Board of the ACW. The board was comprised of elected leaders from ACW locals in the city and, according to the BIC's *Labor Herald*, it reflected not only the ethnic composition of clothing workers but also the more radical sector of the union. "In Baltimore," the *Herald* wrote, "we have an international grouping of [garment] workers," from Jews to "foreign-born colored peoples." Jews, Italians, and Poles figured most prominently in the membership of the Joint Board and were represented by such local leaders as Sara Barrinsky, Max Anslander, I. Chaikin, Victor Zappacosta, Joe D'Annunzio, Pasquale Piersanti, Hyman Titelman, Michael Skrakowski, Nathan Gershowitz, and Samuel Caplan. In the 1930s it was chaired by Ulisse De Dominicis, known as the "militant leader" in Baltimore's union of garment workers. Unlike Hyman Blumberg, who emphasized relieving worker exploitation through the standardization of products and cooperation with enlightened employers, De Dominicis talked less about cooperation than about "workers' rights" and establishing a "workers' world." Not reluctant to call a strike, De Dominicis spoke proudly of the Amalgamated's "army of clothing workers" as a disciplined "fighting" unit with a thorough understanding of the importance of workers' "industrial power."[26]

Under De Dominicis's leadership, the Joint Board made special efforts to organize blacks, maintaining that "colored workers in Baltimore are eager to organize." The ACW made some gains in the rag-picking industry, although "bosses [were] especially concerned with promoting race hatreds to preclude organization." With ACW assistance, the Rag Graders, an affiliate of the Textile Workers Organizing Committee, elected a black president. De Dominicis consistently complained of employers who exploited race issues in order to stifle organization, and he urged both that workers be reeducated and that legal measures be taken to prevent employers from making effective use of racial threats.[27]

When, after successfully unionizing many of the men's garment factories, the ACW turned its attention in the late 1930s to the cotton-garment sweatshops, the race issue was of considerable importance. Not only were wages "notoriously low," with salaries ranging from $4 to $12 a week, but color largely determined the wages. The sweatshops kept a firm hand on their employees by "play[ing] on race differences," pitting whites against blacks, and threatening to replace unionizing white workers with "colored ones" or to pay them "colored salaries." An Amalgamated organizer, Sara Barron, encountered serious difficulty in organizing black workers in the cotton trades; "they didn't trust us," she later recalled. She turned to the Baltimore Urban League, however, where she received considerable support for her organizational efforts.[28] Despite the efforts of concerned individuals to improve the situation, racism—and particularly employer manipulation of such animosity—continued throughout the 1930s as a serious obstacle to organizing workers in an industry characterized generally by exploitation, but where degrees of exploitation were determined by color.

The use of local police as strikebreakers constituted still another barrier to worker organization. City employers had traditionally used the police during labor unrest, and that tradition remained unaltered by the New Deal. Socialists and activist BFL delegates registered their complaints against police harassment to local, state, and national officials as well as to the employers themselves, but little came of their objections. Union officials particularly denounced the police commissioner's arbitrary rulings limiting pickets and his practice of dispatching large numbers of police to all the city's strikes. The commissioner responded that police were necessary for the protection of employers' property. In a 1935 garment workers' strike for union recognition, for example, the police, according to the *Maryland Leader*, did "everything possible to discourage the strikers." Organizers from the ACW joined with Socialists to condemn the police behavior: "In any other city, not more than one or two police would be assigned to a shop of this size," but "in front of this shop we see at times 16 or 17 policemen with a patrol wagon." This show of force, they argued, was not to prevent violence but "for the purpose of intimidating the strikers, to discourage them, and to encourage the strikebreakers. . . . In some cases," they added, "the policemen at the door even open the door for strikebreakers." Workers routinely complained that the police were too eager to use force, and newspapers regularly reported cases of strikers with bruised heads and blackened eyes. In 1934 in the Canton section of east Baltimore, striking longshoremen were driven off the pier by 500 police officers wielding clubs and using tear gas. In another instance, a city policeman, later reprimanded, wounded two black strikebreakers whom he mistakenly thought were striking truck drivers. The state's attorney general and future governor, Herbert O'Conor, condoned the city's police practices and even suggested the use of state police to protect employers and their property during strikes.[29]

By 1937 Baltimore could claim a dubious national distinction for the behavior of its police during strikes. On 9 March 1937 a subcommittee of the U.S. Senate Committee on Education and Labor (the La Follette Civil Liberties Committee) revealed a letter written by Charles L. Vietsch, the Baltimore manager of the William J. Burns International Detective

Agency. In the letter, Vietsch complained to Burns about the poor market for his business due to the competition from the Baltimore police department: "The way strikes are handled here in Baltimore by various manufacturing interests," he wrote, "is, of course, to import skilled labor to take the place of the strikers, then enlist the service of the Baltimore Police Department GRATIS to guard the plant and protect the strikebreakers, and the strike is over in a very short while." The police methods, he added, made employers disinclined to pay for strikebreaking services "although we have repeatedly and vigorously canvassed them for undercover service."[30] Some employers relied on both public and private assistance. Crown Cork and Seal, for example, used the city's police force to break strikes but also employed armed guards to prevent union officials from meeting with its workers. Bethlehem Steel responded to the campaign of the Steel Workers' Organizing Committee (SWOC) in June 1937 by hiring 300 "special police armed with guns and tear gas," but it also called upon local police to quell labor disturbances.[31]

Judicial decisions and practices further complicated the efforts at unionization. Local judges frequently issued injunctions against strikes and exhibited personal animosity toward workers and unions. In a bloody strike in 1936, for instance, cab drivers attempting to unionize were arrested for violating an injunction against the strike, fighting with police and strikebreakers, and destroying company property. They were sentenced to heavy fines and jail terms. A ruffian AFL organizer, Harry Cohen, spent nearly three months in jail for his role in the drivers' strike. The judge who sentenced him, Eugene O'Dunne, denounced all strikes as examples of labor radicalism. O'Dunne stated his philosophy of labor when he declared, "A man has a right to work for whom he will and what he will"; a union, he added, "has no right to determine the conditions under which other men may work." Another magistrate involved in the taxicab strike later warned truck drivers striking against a local firm that he would "invoke jail sentences" as he had during the cab controversy. Legislation passed by the state assembly in 1935 tended to slow the judges' inclination to issue injunctions against striking workers: it required forty-eight hours' notice to the defendants and a hearing involving both sides before an injunction could be issued. But one judge, Robert Stanton, even violated that law in granting an AFL union and an employers' association an immediate injunction against a militant CIO faction in the 1936 seamen's strike. Only after persistent complaints by I. Duke Avnet, a CIO attorney, did the judge temporarily rescind the order.[32]

Yet, despite racial animosities, judicial practices, and police interference, workers continued to organize. They responded to New Deal slogans, to the overtures of a small group of radical labor leaders, and to the passage in 1935 of the Wagner Act. Because the Labor Relations Panel under the NRA had not successfully protected workers' rights to join independent unions, the creation of a permanent National Labor Relations Board held special meaning for a number of trade unionists. Designed to curb unfair labor practices, the NLRB signaled official approval of unionization and promised workers and their unions a greater say in labor-management decisions. The burst of rank-and-file activism that had brought new members into the BFL fold and had helped raise the wages of skilled and semiskilled workers did not disappear in 1935—indeed, the number of worker-days lost through striking jumped 91 percent between 1934 and 1935. The pattern of labor militancy was not, however, the same in all of the nation's largest cities. Such urban centers as Boston, Detroit, and Philadelphia witnessed significant declines in worker activism in 1935; but the increase in idle workdays due to striking in Chicago was even greater than that for Baltimore, and Pittsburgh and Los Angeles also experienced increases. The number of general strikes rose as well, and Baltimore ranked third in 1935 among the ten largest cities in the number of such strikes recorded.[33]

Although the episodic nature of worker militancy was insufficient to guarantee durable trade unionism, it did give pause to local officials and employers. Commissioner of Labor and Statistics Henry Lay Duer duly recorded the undiminished activism of the mid-1930s, noting that "serious labor unrest" also marked 1936 and that "union recognition [again] figured more largely than wage increases in the strikes." The momentum, moreover, was maintained in 1937 when the Supreme Court upheld the NLRB and in 1938 when Congress passed the Fair Labor Standards Act, banning child labor and establishing minimum wages and maximum hours for workers in interstate commerce. The commissioner noted that workers "took serious steps toward organization" in their unprecedented campaign for union recognition, and he suggested that the prolabor Supreme Court decision and the Standards Act served to weaken local employer hostility to unions.[34]

The introduction of the CIO in Baltimore served to advance significantly the city's labor movement. More than the BFL, the Baltimore Industrial Council—the CIO's counterpart in the city—embraced the New Deal effort simultaneously to spark community organization and to accelerate the expansion of governmental power. Influenced considerably by the Amalgamated Clothing Workers, the BIC completely rejected the voluntaristic approaches to labor-management relations that characterized the BFL. Consequently, the BIC took a more active role in politics; for example, it campaigned hard for Roosevelt in 1936. It also relied more heavily on the labor machinery created by the federal government and enlisted the support of attorneys and sympathetic politicians to counteract local hostility toward union organization. For the BIC, labor organization became a community responsibility, and union members were expected not merely to pay dues but to vote Democratic, attend union picnics and lectures, protest fascism and economic concentration, and educate their families and friends in the "union way." Sara Barron of the Amalgamated later boasted of helping the CIO "get active here. . . . We were giving out pamphlets and talking to the people" about the Depression, about industrial organization, and about President Roosevelt. For workers on the waterfront and in the garment, steel, and auto industries, then, the CIO meant a "new deal" for the laboring classes.[35]

The spirit of the New Deal, the BIC's activism, and the reform sentiments of a few BFL delegates combined to make the BFL more progressive and aggressive in its organizational activities. With considerable fanfare, McCurdy launched in 1935 the BFL's campaigns to organize white-collar workers and to prevent wage cutting and "chiseling" by employers no longer bound by the invalid NRA. In 1936, for the first time in the history of the Baltimore Federation of Labor, a woman delegate, Lillian Sipple, became a member of the federation's traditionally male executive board. That same year the BFL took another unprecedented step in condemning "racial discrimination in union organizers." McCurdy himself, although a cautious labor leader, consistently endorsed the New Deal despite the mayor's disapproval, and became more outspoken against the mayor and the Baltimore Association of Commerce. From the former, he requested permission to organize municipal workers, and from the latter he demanded a revised employment insurance bill that did not smack of "toryism" and reflect "reactionary chambers of commerce and their allied interests." On a visit to Baltimore, federal reporter Lorena Hickok found McCurdy a "grand," "intelligent," and "thoroughly honorable" labor leader. The BFL called for public housing and worked with the Baltimore Museum of Art to create exhibits "of particular interest to labor," opening the museum to those in "all walks of life." At McCurdy's insistence, the *Federationist* reprinted a full-page resolution condemning as a "royal

Baltimore Federation of Labor president Joseph McCurdy opens a BFL-sponsored exhibit entitled "Labor in Art" at the Baltimore Museum of Art, 5 September 1938 (Courtesy of the Albin O. Kuhn Library and Gallery, University of Maryland Baltimore County)

slumming party" the proposed visit to Baltimore by the duke and duchess of Windsor with Charles Bedaux, the "arch-enemy of labor." Finally, and most importantly, the BFL moved toward industrial as opposed to craft organization—a change that resulted in an increased but not always harmonious membership. Significantly, however, in a few instances the BFL upheld the rights of less-skilled workers. For example, in 1937 a local of the Chemical Workers Union at a fertilizer plant in Canton protested the comparable wage scale of "laborers" who belonged to the International Longshoremen's Association. Class and craft tensions emerged as the chemical workers denounced the acceptance of "mixed" laborers into the BFL. Work disruptions forced the federation to settle the issue, and the BFL upheld the ILA's wage scale.[36]

Still, McCurdy remained uncertain about the BFL's new course of action. When, for example, the federation began organizing municipal employees, the city's chief engineer promptly fired the union leaders among the workers. Rather than challenge the firings, McCurdy backed down, and at a mass meeting intended for organizing municipal truck drivers he explained that unionization would have to be postponed. According to the *Sun*, "A mild uproar greeted the announcement." Workers booed and hissed, chanting "We've been sold out!" Others pledged to organize without union assistance: "You can strike if you've got the guts," shouted Frank

Jankiewicz, one of the workers fired for union activity. But most of the workers merely filed out of the hall. As they feared, the city fired more workers even while conceding that the city's rule concerning municipal employees and labor organization was unclear. McCurdy halted BFL organizational activities, requested the city to clarify its rule, refused to challenge the firings, promised no-strike clauses in union contracts, and waited for seven months until the city solicitor finally announced that city workers held the right to organize as long as union participation did not "interfere with their duties." In another instance, McCurdy wavered again, retreating from his earlier denunciation of the duke and duchess of Windsor for their association with "Bedauxism" and apologizing for being the "genesis" of their decision to cancel the trip. Indeed, it becomes clear upon closer examination that McCurdy preferred his cautious, limited policies and departed from them only when challenged.[37]

Activist BFL delegates regularly complained of inaction at the top of their organization. In 1936 Fred Rausch, secretary of the Baltimore Building Trades (one of the federation's largest affiliates), challenged McCurdy for the BFL presidency—marking McCurdy's first opposition since assuming office in 1933. Rausch had earned a reputation as a "militant delegate" from his organizational efforts in the SWOC, his chairmanship of Labor's Chest for Liberation, and his membership in the Baltimore Anti-War Committee and the Peoples Unemployment League. Rausch accused McCurdy of being out of touch with the reformist sentiments of city workers. He introduced resolutions insisting that the BFL engage more aggressively in worker organization, that the union assist those without jobs, and that McCurdy resign from the Unemployment Insurance Commission because it had denied the unemployed any representation on the commission. McCurdy responded sharply, criticizing unionists who confused unions with reform organizations, denouncing the "ravings" of "ultra progressives," and dismissing reports "going around to the effect that nothing is being done to organize workers in Baltimore." Militant delegates who challenged the BFL's leadership, moreover, often found themselves in "arrears" for payment of dues and "disbarred from the meeting of the Federation." Outside the BFL, McCurdy's chief antagonists were neither intransigent city officials nor hostile employers but new BIC organizers, unschooled in the politics of compromise, unwilling to move cautiously, and unable to accept McCurdy's halting approach to unionization. At the federation's 1936 convention, both types of challenges coalesced. Led by Rausch, activist BFL delegates attempted to win federation support for the BIC. After considerable debate among the 375 delegates, the proposed resolution to approve officially the Committee for Industrial Organization failed by only sixty votes. The presidential race was also closer than McCurdy had anticipated: he beat Rausch by only eighty-eight votes. When in 1938 the CIO was forced to break completely with the national Federation of Labor, disgruntled local BFL delegates, including Rausch, left the federation. With little remaining opposition, in 1939 McCurdy began his seventh term as president.[38]

Disaffected BFL delegates joined the ranks of the CIO, cooperating with Socialists, the ACW's Joint Board, and various textile organizations to unionize the city. The *Labor Herald*, the BIC's official organ after 1937, supported the CIO from the paper's inception in 1936. The editor was Charles Bernstein, former editor of the Socialist *Maryland Leader*. James Blackwell—a Socialist, United Auto Workers organizer, and chairman of the PUL—served on the *Herald*'s advisory board. The ties between the Socialist party and the BIC were extensive and intimate, as Socialists like Trager, Gilman, and Blackwell worked long and hard to assist the Industrial Council's organizational campaign. Within a short time, the BIC claimed to represent 35,000 members in the city and boasted of creating an alliance of workers, regardless of trades. Its emphasis on class organization departed significantly from the BFL's focus on the "union man."[39]

The conflict between the BFL and the BIC often became intense and bitter. Long regarded as one of the city's most important labor leaders, McCurdy attempted to preserve that reputation. He was not anxious to share his recognition and authority either with newly created organizations or, even worse, with successful labor leaders from the ranks of such "marginal" groups as the city's Socialists. Even antilabor judges like O'Dunne singled McCurdy out for praise as a responsible union leader who acted in the true "spirit of the sons of Maryland." The BIC, on the other hand, had neither respected leaders nor organizational tradition. From the start, the BIC was suspect, and it was frequently charged with being un-American. O'Dunne denounced the BIC and called the sit-down strikes among auto and garment workers "forms of unlawful confiscation." Still others in the city warned workers to "beware of the C.I.O. activities dominated by avowed Communists." McCurdy himself routinely blasted the CIO for its radicalism, directing workers to rally behind the BFL and the "Star Spangled Banner" and not the CIO, which, he said, "stand[s] for Communist International Organization." "Woe be to those," he warned, "who will do anything to drag down American standards and substitute the Red flag of Communism." At the BFL's annual meeting in 1937, McCurdy not only refused to seat CIO delegates but persuaded the convention to condemn the activities of the CIO for having brought "chaos, strife, dishonor, and ill-feeling into the labor movement" and for using sit-down strikes, which were "unlawful practices and un-American." The BFL even urged state legislators to pass anti-sit-down legislation in order to stop this "perfectly insane public disorder" where the strikers resembled a "disorganized unreasonable mess."[40]

Disagreements between the BIC and the BFL filled the pages of the city's newspapers. Much of this publicity intensified organizational competition, but at least some of it worked against the cause of unionism. As early as 1936, before the official AFL-CIO division, the *Sun* noted a "split in the ranks of organized labor" over the election in the sixth Congressional district. When Fred Rausch announced the Baltimore Building Trades' support of liberal Representative David Lewis, McCurdy, although a New Dealer himself, praised Lewis's opponent, Republican State Senator Harry LeGore, for his comparatively obscure labor efforts. All the unions affiliated with the federation had already officially endorsed Lewis; nevertheless, McCurdy acknowledged that the "term endorsement probably could be used to describe" his announcement. Occasionally, the workers themselves grew weary of the bickering, and in 1938 a group of waterfront seamen repudiated both the AFL and the CIO by creating an independent union. The new organization's secretary explained their action: "Our members feel they don't want to be used as powder in a fight between individuals."[41]

But, as the organization drives indicate, the rivalry between the BFL and the BIC scarcely resembled a mere personality contest. Moreover, the competition frequently served to enhance unionization.[42] Although McCurdy certainly exaggerated the BIC's radicalism, and the BIC understated the BFL's organizational efforts, there were substantive differences between the two groups. The Industrial Council, unlike the BFL, believed that genuine cooperation with employers resulted less from the policies of responsible union leaders than from the strength of worker organization. The CIO that emerged in Baltimore was strongly influenced by the labor-management practices long advocated by the ACW. Consequently, the BIC relied more than the BFL on the NLRB to redress grievances and protect unions, but at the same time it emphasized the need for workers to be prepared to strike against intransigent employers. Whereas the BFL only reluctantly called strikes and never condoned the sit-in, the BIC readily threatened work stoppages, actively encouraged workers to sit down on the job, and freely invoked the rhetoric of the New Deal to rally workers in the struggle between "haves and have-nots." Workers began to turn out with greater frequency and in larger numbers, suggesting an important shift from a skilled to an industrial basis of organization. In 1934, for example, the average number of workers per strike was 144; after 1935, however, that average jumped to over 300, and it remained there for the rest of the decade. The BIC also heavily relied on the organizational activities of Communists and Socialists, regularly cooperated with a variety of reform groups in the city, and urged the PUL to send "fraternal delegates" to BIC meetings in order to unite workers with and without jobs. Moreover, CIO affiliates regularly supported each other. The garment workers, for example, collected funds for striking seamen, taxi drivers, and auto workers, and Amalgamated organizers assisted with the campaigns in the steel and auto industries. As Sara Barron later explained, she was instructed to "get together your girls. You're all going out to give out a circular near the Fisher Body [for the UAW]." Finally, at CIO gatherings the topics of discussion included the dangers of fascism and war, the problems of racism and discrimination, and the urgent need to assist the unemployed. In contrast, the federation affiliates rarely cooperated and the BFL, at its meetings, routinely "read and filed" requests from city radicals to address its members, denied the PUL's request for "fraternal membership," and held occasional lectures on workers' compensation laws or showings of such consumer-oriented films as that provided by General Motors "demonstrating the new chevrolet."[43]

The differences between the BFL and the BIC were particularly well illustrated in two strikes. The first began in 1935, when activist BFL organizers urged taxicab drivers to strike following company refusals to bargain with their union or grant wage increases. In response to the strike, the cab companies hired strikebreakers and special police to protect them. One company president told a *Sun* reporter that "the men who are on strike are dead." Unionizing cabbies sabotaged the cars by breaking keys off in the ignition and smashing windshields. In turn, union leaders had their cars destroyed, and strikers were beaten when they tried to prevent taxis from leaving the garages. Company officials hired crews of ruffians to "cruise the streets" in taxicabs. Although they were not allowed to pick up passengers, they served to remind the strikers that the cars could be moved. The violence prompted the city police to dispatch additional units to the ga-

Workers throughout the city used the slogans of the New Deal and President Roosevelt to legitimize their organizational activities. In one of the city's most violent strikes during the Great Depression cab drivers attempted in February 1937 to unionize under the banner "Roosevelt Said Organize." (Courtesy of the Baltimore Sun*)*

rages to protect company property. It also moved McCurdy to seek an immediate settlement. An uneasy armistice resulted and many workers returned to their jobs, unhappy with McCurdy and their inability to win their demands.[44]

In 1936 the drivers struck again, shutting down one company entirely for laying off cabbies involved in union activities. Both BFL and BIC organizers supported the strike. As before, company officials refused to negotiate, snubbing even federal arbiters, and once again they hired strikebreakers to operate the cabs. But this time the drivers were more prepared and determined: they met the first cars attempting to leave the garages with bricks and tire irons. Violence erupted, lasting over an hour and halting traffic until, as the *Sun* reported, "police finally broke up the pitched battle . . . and the battered cars limped back to the garage." Despite gun-toting strikebreakers, the cabbies continued their attacks on the company's autos —concentrating their assaults on the owners' primary source of profit. By immobilizing the cars, the strikers hoped also to prevent the newly hired drivers from replacing them on the road. A worried governor helped arrange a temporary settlement for the holiday season, with strikers return-

In the city's cab strike, arrests of strikers were frequent, as were complaints of police brutality. The strike's leader, Harry Cohen, shown here as he was taken into custody in February 1937, was ultimately sent to prison for his role in the strike. (Courtesy of the Baltimore Sun)

ing to work; however, the company undermined that arrangement by using the truce period to create a company union and to distribute leaflets denouncing specific labor organizers. In January 1937 the drivers resumed the strike and the employers refused to negotiate, maintaining that the creation of the company union had resolved the issue. But one particular BFL organizer stood firm against the owners: a loud-spoken teamster named Harry Cohen told a group of "enthusiastic" strikers that "the war is on . . . and we're going to take the battle into our own hands. . . . Some of you will get in trouble," he warned, "but we will get you out." McCurdy declined to comment on Cohen's declarations but denounced the police as a "strike-breaking agency."[45]

More violence followed and one company official observed that the strike had "gone haywire." Police arrested strikers daily, and on 16 February 1937 Judge O'Dunne issued a warrant for the arrest of Cohen on charges of "instigating, fomenting, aiding and abetting riot, assault and disorderly conduct on the public streets of Baltimore City." O'Dunne also instructed company officials, McCurdy, and Cohen to meet with him to arrange a settlement of the strike. On 22 February the *Sun* pictured

O'Dunne and McCurdy together, announcing the end of the strike. But the drivers found little to cheer about in the settlement. McCurdy refused to challenge Cohen's arrest, saying only, "Thank God we live in America or he'd probably be hung by now." No concessions were made to the workers; in fact, McCurdy weakly conceded that "organization of the cab drivers may be deferred for the time being." The BIC lambasted McCurdy for his surrender and for abandoning the drivers. When Cohen was sent to prison for three months it was the BIC, not the BFL, that provided an attorney to defend him and that then organized the cab drivers to protest Cohen's imprisonment as a denial of workers' rights to organize.[46]

The second major strike involved the city's seamen and lasted from the fall of 1936 to February 1937. They struck for higher wages, more equitable shipping rotation policies, and better treatment on board ship. From the outset, the BIC supported the striking unions—the International Seamen's Union and a radical faction of the ISU, which had joined with city Communists to form the Marine Workers Industrial Union. With BIC assistance, during the course of the strike the groups joined together under the aegis of the National Maritime Union (NMU). Cooperating with the Socialists, the BIC also helped establish the Citizens Committee for Striking Seamen. The BFL, however, refused to support the strike or assist the strikers. McCurdy urged the seamen to abandon the strike, claiming that the "communists are back of it, there is no question about it." He even closed the city offices of the ISU and the ILA because of "radical activities." When the Citizens Committee organized a mass meeting to "educate the public" about the strike, McCurdy denounced the 1,200 people who attended as radical sympathizers; he rebuked Mayor Jackson and Governor Nice for sending official representatives and for thereby contributing to "riot in the city" and to legitimizing the efforts of "foreigners and Communists" who "inflame the passions of the people of Baltimore." But the Communist party denied initiating the strike, although it pledged $50.00 and a truckload of foodstuffs for the strikers. Indeed, one party member, Earl Dixon, told a group of seamen gathered at a Polish-American hall in south Baltimore, "We wish we had men of your nerve and pluck with us. You're the kind we want. I am proud that there are men like you willing to fight for what they believe is right."[47]

McCurdy's stern lectures to the seamen contrasted sharply with the enthusiastic support of BIC leader Patrick Whalen. McCurdy, conservative in appearance and cautious in his rhetoric, instructed workers to abide by their contractual agreements with the ship owners. His restricted appeal to legal obligations was no match for Whalen's passionate insistence on "justice." As a labor organizer and future president of the Industrial Council, Whalen, when not in jail, was a powerful orator who inspired the seamen and won the support of Socialists like Elisabeth Gilman and reform-minded attorneys like Avnet. When Whalen spoke, Avnet later recalled, he "ran sentences together, . . . mispronounced words, . . . [and] cursed profusely. . . . But his thinking was clear," Avnet added, and he knew the seamen and their problems. His audiences were always receptive, especially when he ridiculed labor leaders who had "ritzy" tastes and wore "clean shirts." The seamen, long accustomed to a rudimentary life of inconvenience, cheered enthusiastically. "I have been involved in strikes for years," Whalen allowed, "and I have slept in flophouses, under viaducts and in jails—with my comrades. We have no money, and to win this strike every man must expect to suffer the hardships of his fellows." Such talk may have alienated the impeccably dressed McCurdy and strengthened him in his belief that the strike was "dominated by the Communist party," but it also increased support and sympathy for the strikers. Gilman, for example—despite her past cooperation with the BFL and McCurdy—stepped up her campaign to assist the strikers, countering that "Reds did not dominate" the strike but that it was a genuine "rank and file movement" with legitimate grievances "against low wages and living and working conditions."[48]

McCurdy and the BFL failed to understand the importance of the strike to the seamen and the significance of community and solidarity among the strikers. During the strike, the seamen brought to the shore their orderly and fraternal way of life on the sea. Their organization adapted well to waging an effective strike and to unionizing under the NMU. Gilman noted this when she proclaimed the strike "the most orderly and best conducted I have ever seen," and the *Sun* remarked upon its "organization that moves with clock-like precision." Not only did the seamen carefully structure kitchen as well as picket duty, but their spirit of camaraderie also extended to black and Asian sympathy strikers. They unanimously passed a resolution to "treat all seamen as brothers and on an equality," regardless of race or color, and accepted as a member a West Coast Chinese cook who had been officially excluded from the maritime unions. Moreover, fifty seamen organized a march on Washington to participate in an anti-Nazi demonstration in front of the German embassy. They also organized their own entertainment, playing instruments and singing songs appropriate to their ethnic heritage. Finally, to ensure orderly behavior, they created a "court of

The Sun *reporter covering the 1936–37 maritime strike remarked on the "clock-like precision" that characterized the seamen's organization of their strike. The strikers rotated their duties, from picketing to preparing meals. Here seamen receive their midday soup at strike headquarters in November 1936. (Courtesy of the Baltimore* Sun)

justice" with fines and punishments for crimes ranging from drunkenness—the most common offense—to "scabbing," the most serious offense. Whalen himself conducted the hearings, and when he took the union card of a seaman who refused to join the strike, he was arrested for theft by city police.[49]

The BFL's refusal to support the strikers resulted in significant gains for the BIC on the docks. And when McCurdy joined with the hated ship owners in an attempt to secure an injunction against the strikers, the BFL became the enemy. The end of the strike in February 1937 provided wage increases and a victory for the CIO-affiliated National Maritime Union. Subsequent elections held by the NLRB further legitimized the CIO's power. Even some members of the city's traditionally conservative ILA left the federation for the NMU.[50]

To a large degree, then, the activities of the BIC, the radical agitators, and the ACW contributed to the general labor unrest in Baltimore during the years 1936 and 1937. An Amalgamated-led walkout in August 1936 protesting wage cuts closed six clothing firms, particularly affecting the infamous sweatshop of A. Abrams and Sons on Redwood Street in Baltimore's

During the course of the maritime strike, workers from a number of unions joined together in the National Maritime Union. Subsequent elections held by the NLRB put the union in the CIO column.
(Courtesy of the Baltimore Sun)

clothing district. Despite police interference and violence by strikebreakers who hurled bottles from the windows of the Abrams factory, striker enthusiasm remained high and the ACW firm. On 11 September workers returned to their jobs with their wages restored. Certain groups of municipal workers also began to organize, declaring that they had suffered long enough from the city's budget cuts, that they had tired of "Jackson's red arithmetic"—a phrase used to express their contempt for the "scandalously low wages paid by the city."⁵¹

Labor turbulence was especially prevalent in the year 1937, with sit-down strikes and hard-driving organizational campaigns among dressmakers and automobile, chemical, and cotton-garment workers. The CIO–United Auto Workers opened the year with a General Motors organizing drive and walkout at the city's Fisher Body and Chevrolet plant. Led by UAW organizer and PUL chairman James Blackwell, the strike immediately encountered difficulties. Mayor Jackson revoked Blackwell's permit to organize at the company's gates, claiming that the use of a sound truck would lead to employer-employee violence. The Fisher manager told the strikers that the plant would never close, and nonunion workers initiated a loyalty movement. They presented the company a declaration of support signed by 2,400 employees, expressing gratitude for the recent Christmas bonus and confidence in General Motors. In an attempt to discredit the union, the *Sun* catapulted these "loyal workers" into prominence by reporting their charges of UAW intimidation. When the "loyal workers" met to organize a march on Washington to demand that Secretary of Labor Frances Perkins intervene and end the strike, the UAW workers were forcibly barred from the meeting; a "free-swinging melee" ensued. The UAW's defeat of GM at Flint, Michigan, brought an end to Baltimore's strike, but the strikers returned to work without solid UAW support among the workers. Within days, company officials fired the union leaders, prompting UAW members to disrupt plant production temporarily.[52]

Testimony before the La Follette Committee in February 1937 altered the public understanding of the Fisher plant's loyalty movement. Fisher's plant manager, although he insisted that the movement had originated among the workers, conceded that its leader was a former Pinkerton employee and that the "loyal" leadership had been provided with the company's payroll list for mailing and propagandizing purposes. Union men, testimony further indicated, had been systematically threatened and terrorized on the job.[53]

National and local UAW organizing efforts continued full force. Local organizers told auto workers that Roosevelt supported unionism, that the "loyal workers" were corporate apologists, and that GM violated their rights as citizens. Appealing to their sense of patriotism and partisanship, the organizers urged workers to join the union as a way to support Roosevelt and their country. In June the UAW called a sit-down strike of 800 workers at the Fisher plant to protest the use of nonunion labor on the trim line and succeeded in mounting a 2,000-person picket-line. A quick settlement brought the rehiring of the union leaders, mutual control of assembly-line speed, an agreement on seniority rights, and wage increases.[54]

Signs of improvement in labor's situation seemed to abound in 1937. Seventy-five women garment workers conducted Baltimore's first sit-in in March 1937, launching the ILGWU's major organizational drive and ultimately winning union recognition and wage raises at a number of dressmaking shops. The Baltimore Joint Board moved into a larger and more modern headquarters, providing tangible proof of the ACW's success. In July the CIO called its first meeting to form a central labor body in Baltimore; the assembled delegates, according to the *Labor Herald*, represented over 50,000 members. Socialists reported increased attendance of laborers at the Workmen's Circle Lyceum in east Baltimore. And even the labor commissioner helped secure the closed shop for striking workers at the Baltimore Enamel and Novelty Company; at the settlement, he suggested that the employer take his employees to dinner as a "sign of good feeling."[55]

But there was also another side to labor's story. Persistent efforts on the part of auto workers and textile employees failed to achieve a closed shop. In 1938 the annual number of strikes declined for the first time since 1933, and the number of worker-days lost through striking dropped 55 percent from 1935. Further, despite the city's favorable ruling, not all municipal workers could organize; the Board of Fire Commissioners, for example, issued a "flat no" to firefighters attempting to affiliate with the AFL and instructed fire captains to confiscate union materials and turn off radios when labor leaders "went on the air." And the police department continued to interfere with striking workers. In 1939 the city police commissioner issued a new ruling requiring pickets to walk the length of the block "instead of shuttling back and forth immediately in front of the establishment where a strike is in progress"; police then freely arrested strikers for violating the order, charging them with "disorderly conduct by interfering with the passage of pedestrians." Notwithstanding their extensive organizational activities, the ACW and the ILGWU could not eliminate sweatshops, and strikes frequently brought only temporary improvements.[56]

Despite some labor victories, then, many employers refused to concede defeat and continued to challenge the unions, especially those connected to the CIO. In 1939, for example, one company owner declared, "We just won't recognize the C.I.O. Before I'll do that I will walk right out the front door and lock the place up for good." Even companies that had cooperated with the BFL refused to deal with the CIO. The Baltimore Labor Relations Board continued to encounter intransigent employers who fired union activists, refused to bargain collectively, intimidated workers, or posted "discriminatory material" on company bulletin boards. Some manufacturers who preferred "independence" to union "dictation" left the city; such was the case for the clothing company of S. Cohen and Sons. Both the Baltimore *Sun* and the *Afro-American* attempted to prevent unionization on their premises. The *Afro-American* organized a company union for "loyal" workers, whereas the *Sun* created "pressroom committees" to forestall unionization. The NLRB ruled against both papers, ordering the *Afro-American* to rehire union workers and calling the *Sun*'s maneuver "a sham imposed by the management upon the men." *Sun* owner A. S. Abell successfully appealed his decision; an Annapolis judge peculiarly concluded that there had been no "actual discrimination" despite "evidence to show that the superintendent of the pressroom made statements from which the men could infer that it was not to their interest to join the union."[57]

Labor leaders and the rank and file also provided sources of discontent. Denouncing BFL conservatism, the *Labor Herald* declared: "We must have stronger and more militant labor leaders, with broader vision, foresight, and courage." It continued, "Baltimore has a long way to go. Let's start now." But the BFL attempted to broaden its appeal by narrowing its vision. Its leaders turned increasingly to the issue of anticommunism to discredit the CIO movement in the city. In an attempt to recoup some of its losses on the waterfront, in late 1937 the BFL threw "its entire resources . . . to building up the maritime industry" in Baltimore for the federation. One BFL spokesman aptly described the situation: the AFL and CIO "are lining up for a showdown on the matter of control over maritime and allied unions." Federation-affiliated longshoremen launched the campaign, announced their intention "to war on the C.I.O. in the port of Baltimore," and staged brief strikes, forcing CIO men off ships and denouncing them as Communists. "Counting on anti-Communist feelings," the BFL announced, it hoped to entice the seamen to leave the NMU and join the revived Sailors' Union of the Pacific—a national union like the NMU but, according to the BFL, without the "radical leadership."[58]

Charges of communism against the CIO served the BFL well in 1938 and 1939. The BFL urged UAW members, for example, to support America, to "love their homes," to repudiate dictation by a "damned bunch of Communists," and to join an American union, not one dominated by foreigners. Following the lead of the CIO, the federation increasingly tied support of the BFL to Roosevelt; unlike the CIO, however, it declared any questioning of Roosevelt's labor policies to be un-American and part of a subversive conspiracy led by Communists. In February 1939, the majority of the members of UAW local #239 voted to bar from its meetings all "Communist members"—which ironically included the city's first UAW organizer, James Blackwell, a Socialist and an anti-Communist. The local also voted to support the conservative Homer Martin in the dispute at the national level but stopped short of repudiating the CIO or industrial unionism. The BFL intensified its antiradical campaign by using New Deal rhetoric reminiscent of that employed by UAW-CIO organizers in 1937, with the difference that it was directed against the radicalism of the CIO rather than the antiunionism of the employer. Leaders of the BFL urged workers to rally behind Roosevelt and the American flag. In June, local #239 voted overwhelmingly to "unaffiliate with the CIO" and join the federation.[59]

Even before the federation initiated its anti-Communist drive, the BIC had begun to moderate its tactics and programs. Socialist PUL members were no longer the chief organizers, as long-time union activists from the ACW and the ILGWU rose to top positions in the state's CIO organization. Moreover, as the CIO became successfully incorporated into the city's labor arbitration process, strikes grew less frequent and sit-ins even rarer. The state's CIO director, Frank Bender, requested national permission to compete with the BFL in industries already organized by the federation as craft unions and even attempted to attract white-collar municipal workers by appealing to their middle-class interests. Fearful of losing the recognition it had achieved, the CIO attempted to modify its strike tactics and to remove itself from the radical ties that the BFL was using to discredit it. Even the ACW shifted its support within the local CIO away from Patrick Whalen and toward a more moderate leadership; the ACW's own militant leader, Ulisse De Dominicis, was by 1939 disavowing former friend and fellow labor organizer Whalen as a "tool" of the Communist party. The BFL's association of the CIO with communism also caused problems among Catholic workers, whose parish priests were by the end of the decade discouraging unionization, especially under the CIO banner. In the cotton-garment drive in 1939, local ACW organizers encountered "difficulty among the Catholic workers" and felt it necessary to distribute leaflets prepared by the national Catholic leader Father Francis Haas in support of labor organization.[60]

An ILGWU organizer, Angela Bambace, believed that the city's workers were themselves at least part of the CIO's organizing problem. In a 1937 *Labor Herald* article entitled "Wake up, Workers of Baltimore," Bambace cited the absence of working-class awareness as an obstacle to unionization: "Class consciousness is still a strange word among the Baltimore dressmakers" and workers in general. "In Baltimore," she added, "people crawl. Nothing moves, and the earth is still flat." *Labor Herald* editor Bernstein concurred. Although he acknowledged that Bambace's article had caused "very unfavorable comment and a good deal of resentment," he queried, how "can one help [but] draw the conclusion that Baltimore is not in the 20th Century cycle, when one observes and sees that many labor failures have recently taken place in the city." He added that "nothing encouraging ever seems to happen in Baltimore."[61]

In part, however, labor's failure to create the kind of worker solidarity that Bambace sought resulted from the priorities and practices of the labor leaders. The BFL rarely attempted to foster a sense of class consciousness; indeed, in its persistent attacks on the CIO it tended to divide workers. It never seriously promoted organization among blacks or women and often actually used race- and gender-based divisions to appeal exclusively to white male workers. The CIO, on the other hand, emphasized class unity above all other concerns in its organizational efforts and specifically denounced divisions caused by race, national origin, or gender. Pat Whalen called discrimination the work of "cowards . . . [and] the agents of reactionaries," and he reminded workers that "the theory of true unionism is not built upon any struggle against any workers because they happen to be born of a different color."[62]

But the class-based organization of the CIO only ostensibly removed the traditional barriers to organizing blacks and women, for it too often ignored those groups in its organizational activities. Although the CIO maintained its reputation as an organization "friendly" to integration, it rarely initiated drives at factories where blacks predominated, and it almost never challenged the all-white hiring practices of area employers. The workers in the production industries that the CIO sought to organize were predominantly white men. Although the ACW had organized women garment workers, the CIO did little to bring unorganized women into the fold. Indeed, CIO leaders ignored the overtures of black domestic workers who wanted to unionize in 1938, delaying much-needed assistance until 1941 when a local of the United Domestic Workers was finally formed. Furthermore, even within unions where women dominated the membership, men held nearly all the leadership positions—and in the case of the ACW, they deliberately prevented the formation of a "women's local" in Baltimore. Even Amalgamated leaders like Dorothy Jacobs Bellanca, who was indispensable to the organization of women in the city and who also recognized the "ever present tension between male and female workers," still maintained that working-class organization took precedence over women's particular concerns.[63]

Moreover, the CIO's emphasis on class in its organizational activities was occasionally expressed in the clichés of masculinity. Whalen, in particular, denounced his opponents as "cowards" and urged workers to protect their "manhood" by standing up to aggressive bosses. While such terms reflected an appeal to egalitarianism and workers' dignity, they also tended to exclude women workers from that appeal. Indeed, one CIO picket line of striking men featured signs reading "Restore Our Manhood: We Receive Girls' Wages."[64]

The discrimination that traditionally divided workers and segmented the economy also left black and women workers underrepresented in the new industrial labor movement. Certain CIO leaders recognized the problem, and a few even attempted to remedy it. But the primary direction of the new labor movement in the 1930s discouraged serious efforts at overcoming economic biases against women and blacks. And too often support for a class-based organization translated in practice into a union most hospitable to white male workers.

Still, the state of labor organization in Baltimore was not as grim as Bernstein or Bambace maintained. To be sure, labor's victories remained incomplete and insecure, but by 1938 such issues as seniority rights dominated labor-management discussions, suggesting at least a partial acceptance of unionization. The commissioner of labor and statistics reported fewer industrial disputes and noted that workers were winning union contracts without being forced to strike. Although compliance problems continued to plague the NLRB, employers increasingly accepted its decisions.[65]

The New Deal and the upsurge in labor organization helped to unite workers in a number of important and innovative ways. The revival of a labor press in the 1930s served to educate workers new to union membership about the value of organization. Such newspapers as the *Labor Herald*, the *Maryland Leader*, and even the *Baltimore Federationist* routinely reported union activities from CIO picnics to Lyceum lectures. The larger labor locals in the city published their own newsletters, which kept members informed and involved with the union. Activist women members of the ILGWU, for example, published the spirited *Sew-Sew News*. The cultural component of the city's WPA, albeit a rather anemic part of the program, served to bring workers symphony performances and museum exhibits. The CIO and the PUL cooperated with the FERA's Recreation Division and with USHA to widen recreational activities for unemployed workers and public-housing tenants; thanks to these New Deal programs and to the efforts of union leaders, workers throughout the city benefited from dances and theatrical performances while their children enjoyed the talents of WPA puppeteers. Both PUL and CIO organizers directed their activities toward the families of workers, connecting the family and the neighborhood to the cause of organization. Such activities strengthened workers' attachments to their union and fostered a spirit of cooperation and excitement previously often limited only to the drama of striking.[66]

Blacks, for example, responded favorably to the new industrial labor movement despite its obvious shortcomings. Religious leaders eagerly turned over their neighborhood churches for union meetings and not infrequently used their pulpits to discuss labor issues, keeping their congregations informed of boycotts, strikes, and other CIO activities. At Bethlehem

Steel, the Steel Workers' Organizing Committee made special efforts to organize blacks and directly linked its activities to the larger black community. Black and white workers cooperated to a degree unexpected in a city so divided by race. They joined together, for example, to write and perform a play that illustrated for fellow workers the value of organization to all laborers regardless of color. They performed the play for workers and their families, drawing large crowds at every neighborhood performance, and at the request of other steelworkers they printed and distributed copies of the play.[67]

The revitalized labor movement also provided new opportunities for women union members. Although the ACW and other CIO affiliates usually discouraged women from assuming their place as equals in their unions, the movement of the 1930s witnessed the increased participation of working-class women in strikes, in political activities, and in educational campaigns. Women garment workers, for example, placed their new activism in the context of loyalty to the Amalgamated and to Roosevelt—sentiments that were readily sanctioned by their union brothers. Significantly, women's voice in the labor movement of the 1930s contained few references to the inequalities they faced in the union and in society. They were fully aware of those inequalities, yet it was difficult, as Sara Barron remembered, to "speak up" at a time when society's concern focused on male breadwinners without jobs. Moreover, women workers, especially in the ACW, found the New Deal and the new labor movement professionally and personally rewarding. For Sara Barron, it meant new responsibilities as a regional organizer in the union—and it meant meeting Mary Dewson and Lorena Hickok and corresponding with Eleanor Roosevelt. Favored for her pluckiness, Barron was called on by union leaders to organize difficult shops. "Take Sara [with you]," Hyman Blumberg instructed a male organizer, "she's got a lot of nerve." Moreover, this reputation for toughness in the face of strikebreakers and armed police gave her pleasure at the same time that it facilitated her rise in the union and legitimized her role as an activist woman in the Amalgamated. "I always wanted to go picket," she recalled. "It was a lot of fun, a lot of excitement." In the depression, Barron affirmed, women workers "helped to make the union stronger. . . . The women in the shops, the executive board, our women were really wonderful." As loyal unionists, she recalled, they struck when necessary and "picketed plenty. . . . They could always count on us."[68]

Finally, the politicization of the work force in the 1930s was particularly influential in promoting a sense of trade-union culture. The reelection of

Franklin Roosevelt in 1936 provided the focal point for much of organized labor's activity. Women members of the ACW raised money, held dances, organized parades, and conducted door-to-door campaigns—all in support of FDR. And after Roosevelt's election labor groups celebrated throughout the city with victory balls, victory picnics, and victory parties. The president of local #28 of Baltimore's electrical workers hailed the election as a triumph of working-class solidarity. "When the rank and file make up their minds and act in concert," he exclaimed, "they can accomplish . . . results." The CIO established Labor's Non-Partisan League of Maryland, which published a magazine entitled *Labor Voter* and distributed more than 100,000 copies of its first issue. The league took an active role in the 1938 Senatorial primary campaign, joining with Roosevelt in an attempt to oust conservative Millard Tydings in favor of David Lewis, a long-time labor ally. Politics permeated all aspects of union culture in the 1930s, and, in certain instances, political awareness extended beyond personal allegiance to Roosevelt or the Democratic party. At a picnic of National Maritime Union members, for example, more than 500 seamen and their families joined together to eat and relax, but politics was so much a part of their concerns that as one of the "social" activities planned for the day the NMU sponsored a straw vote to determine workers' preferences in the upcoming 1938 gubernatorial election. Whereas over 50 percent divided their votes between the two Democratic candidates, over 47 percent "voted" for the Labor party "regardless of the candidate"—suggesting at least some endorsement of a working-class political movement.[69] Unions, then, successfully made politics an integral part of local activities, and the political efforts of Baltimore's workers, as will be seen in more detail, often forced those local politicians who were hostile to the New Deal to moderate their views at election time.

CHAPTER 7

Democratic Division

The Politics of Roosevelt
and the Party of Tradition

The partial efforts of the New Deal to reach out to new constituencies led to increased organizational activity at all levels of society. Citizen groups helped shape the city's welfare system and accelerate its lagging commitment to social responsibility. The unemployed organized to improve their status as clients in the emergent welfare state, and workers challenged their bosses and the city's traditions by bringing the union to the work place and the community. Central to all their activities was their growing attachment to the national Democratic party. Federal policy makers attempted not only to encourage and control these organizational energies but also to ensure their practical translation into voting for the New Deal and its leader, Franklin D. Roosevelt. And in ever-growing numbers, the New Deal encouraged the political participation of those voters who were often traditionally neglected by the city's political leadership. It was not enough, however, merely to vote for Roosevelt; organized groups held the larger responsibility of spreading the New Deal message—a job that took on added urgency in a city governed by Democrats hostile to the policies emanating from Washington. Thanks to their efforts, local leaders tempered their opposition to Roosevelt, mixing criticisms with less offensive observations about the New Deal and, on occasion, even claiming credit for some of its innovations.

The New Deal in Baltimore did not radically alter city politics. Traditional bossism had long since disappeared, with the deaths of state boss Senator Arthur Pue Gorman in 1906 and Baltimore city boss I. Freeman Rasin in 1907—but their absence led to a power struggle that lasted well into the 1940s. Factionalism, then, characterized the chiefly Democratic city in the 1920s and 1930s, and the New Deal and the politics of Roosevelt provided additional ammunition for the long-standing feud. More importantly, the New Deal made both local and state politicians aware of new constituencies and shifting political alliances within the city. Certainly, the politics and policies of the Roosevelt administration helped to politicize the economic discontent of the disadvantaged groups in Baltimore.[1]

At the death of Rasin, two of his chief lieutenants—John J. (Sonny) Mahon and John S. (Frank) Kelly—began a contest for control of the city's Democratic organization that lasted until 1921 and anticipated the intraparty rivalry that would characterize the Depression decade. Mahon, born of Irish immigrant parents, attended parochial school only briefly before entering the work force and the vagaries of city politics, ultimately pushing his way to the top of the machine. Kelly, too, had rather obscure origins; adopted at age nine, he had almost no education and later worked as a garbage-cart driver. In 1919 the Mahon-Kelly division cost the party the mayoral seat as the popular William F. Broening captured the position for the Republicans.[2]

Although the Republican triumph of 1919 did not extend to the city council, Democrats still feared that Broening's popularity might lead to the development of a genuine two-party system in the city. Without a pause, Baltimore's Democratic leaders raised the spectre of race in an attempt to curb possible enthusiasm for the Republicans: pointing to the election of two black council members under Broening's banner, city Democrats alarmed white voters by suggesting that the Republicans would appoint blacks to municipal offices to "handle the affairs of white people."[3] But a politically astute Broening moved to dissociate himself from black support, even allowing the KKK to march in Baltimore after Governor Ritchie had refused the Klan a parade permit. Broening's antiblack stance convinced the Baltimore *Afro-American* to urge black voters to reject their traditional party loyalties in favor of Democratic candidate Howard Jackson in the 1923 mayoral contest.[4]

To ensure a Democratic mayoral victory, Governor Ritchie called a conference of the Kelly and Mahon factions and arranged for Jackson, a popular Mahonite, to run for mayor while the other offices and patronage positions were divided equally between the two groups. Jackson handily defeated Broening and the Democrats swept the council, taking seventeen of the eighteen seats. The Republicans received support in a few German and native American wards in south and southwest Baltimore, in the Russian-Polish Jewish fifth ward, and, despite the appeals of the *Afro-American*, in the predominantly black fourteenth and seventeenth wards in northwestern Baltimore. Part of the Republicans' poor showing in the council resulted from the 1923 reorganization of the city council into a unicameral body with six districts, each selecting three members: the Democrats seized the occasion to place all the heavily Republican precincts into just one district, the fourth, thereby enabling the Democrats to carry easily the other five. Within the Democratic party, the outcome was not as equitable as Ritchie had planned. Although the Mahonites held the mayoral position, the Kelly group, led by Jackson's chief antagonist, William Curran of east Baltimore, took a majority of seats in the city council.[5]

In the 1930s, the struggle between Curran and Jackson would dominate city politics. The New Deal shaped the contest but rarely determined the outcome. An Irish Catholic, William Curran attended parochial school, graduated from the University of Maryland Law School, and served faithfully in the Kelly organization of the Democratic party. Often referred to as an intellectual and philosopher, Curran attempted to minimize his education and fondness for books, saying, "Don't get the idea I'm a scholar." Governor Ritchie once remarked that Curran was a "real if quiet genius."[6] Jackson had no comparable ethnic credentials and was not even a native Baltimorean—his birthplace was in Maryland's rural Harford county. Both men, however, held a strong commitment to advancing their own economic interests. According to one report, Curran profited enormously from "unsavory" connections growing out of his membership in a criminal law firm; Jackson used city and federal money to boost business for his own insurance company and represented, in the words of that same report, a "keen businessman without social vision."[7]

The mayoral campaign of 1927 indicated which of the two would emerge the more powerful in the Democratic rivalry of the 1930s. The mayoral race was between Republican Broening and Democrat Curran. At the urging of Governor Ritchie, Jackson had decided not to run again in 1927. He had come under a barrage of criticism as a result of his questionable financial dealings and his continual bouts with alcoholism—an inappropriate disease during Prohibition, except in dripping wet Baltimore.

Away from City Hall much of the time, he had become somewhat of an embarrassment to the party, and one of the city's most outspoken guardians of civic responsibility, Marie Baurenschmidt, publicly demanded that he "take the cure or resign."[8] But Jackson still managed to make his influence felt; his political supporters in the party campaigned against Curran, connecting him to criminal activities and to "Boss Kelly." A divided party once again resulted in a Republican victory, and Broening returned to office. Curran's defeat persuaded him to abandon the pursuit of elective office and focus his energies instead on securing control of the party in the city; but his inability to defeat a candidate who in an earlier election had been overwhelmed by his major competitor in the party suggested that Jackson, and not Curran, would have the political edge in the 1930s.[9]

Jackson was reelected mayor in 1931, 1935, and 1939—providing, however, only apparent continuity in a decade marked by persistent factionalism. In the 1931 race, Jackson, now "bone-dry," ran unopposed in the primary; both Curran and Ritchie conceded his considerable popularity, especially with the city's business community and with the *Sun* newspaper. Broening, linked to the depression and sensing defeat, declined to challenge Jackson and left the Republican nomination to a little-known candidate who lost by a large margin. Curran made sure, nevertheless, that one of his own won the comptroller's seat, and a group of independent ward leaders rebelled against both the Jacksonites and the Curranites to elect their own council president.[10]

As mayor, Jackson continued the policies that reflected the sentiments of the southern wing of the Democratic party and also resembled those of Ritchie at the state level. He regularly and viciously attacked the New Deal, referring, for example, to the "New Deal relief system" as "un-American, unfair to the people who receive it and unsound economically."[11] Uncooperative in federal-local matters, he consistently maligned the government for interfering in city problems and emerged in the 1930s as one of the New Deal's harshest critics. "He is openly out for the New Deal," observed one Democratic official, "and misses no chance to oppose and bitterly criticize it in public and private."[12] Yet Jackson was not above using the New Deal to his political or personal advantage—a tactic that was not lost on the Curranites. After publicly denouncing work relief, for example, he quietly arranged for WPA funds to be used to remodel his office. His oft-repeated contentions that "relief is not my job," that the "obligation of caring for the employables" belonged to the federal government, and that the state "is obligated to care for the unemployables" did not deter him from influencing the programs in the city, from packing BERC with his political favorites, and from using relief jobs to win votes. On one occasion, when Jackson attempted to push through the city council a relief construction bill, a Curranite council member actually stole the bill to delay the passage of a transparently "political ordinance" designed to assist a Jacksonite in a primary fight in the third congressional district.[13] And in the 1939 mayoral campaign, serious charges against Jackson's ward and precinct leaders prompted the state to investigate whether relief rolls had been "used to gather votes in the city"; but despite the testimony of a number of relief clients that they had been instructed to vote for Jackson "or be cut from the rolls," the state found the evidence "inadequate" and exonerated the mayor.[14]

Both the Jacksonites and the Curranites attempted to use the WPA for political purposes. State WPA director Francis Dryden complained that he was overwhelmed by requests from the feuding factions for work-relief projects that would extend their political influence. Dryden disappointed both groups when he pledged to "keep politics entirely out of the picture so far as possible." But although Dryden affirmed that he felt "under political obligation to no one," he tended in his policy decisions to favor the Jackson group, perhaps because he had to deal more with the mayor and perhaps because he hoped to soften Jackson's opposition to the New Deal.[15]

Jackson's systematic efforts to consolidate his political power were undertaken not merely to control the city's party but to secure the governor's chair—a goal that permanently eluded him. He was, as Curran aptly noted, "beside himself with an ambition to be governor."[16] Jackson made an unsuccessful bid for the party's gubernatorial nomination in 1934; this attempt won him only the enmity of Ritchie, who wanted another term as governor and resented the Jackson rebellion against the Ritchie organization at the state level. Moreover, Jackson's maneuvers to widen his appeal in the party backfired when he made friendly overtures to the Curran faction. William Curran seized the opportunity to boast complete control over the party in the city, announce a "new deal for Curran," and arrange an alliance with independent forces in the sixth district. Because Jackson refrained from repudiating Curran's grandiose claims his own supporters in the party became angry. Finally, after extensive political wrangling, he withdrew from the gubernatorial race and began preparation for the 1935 mayoral campaign.[17]

Emboldened by Jackson's difficulties, the Curranites resolved to challenge the mayor in the primary. They put forth businessman Charles E.

Maylan in an attempt to undercut Jackson's support in the business community and to counter his claims of a "business-like" administration. But Maylan was unknown in the city and did not receive the publicity he needed in the *Sun* papers; Jackson routed him in the primary and went on to defeat his Republican opponent in the general election. Furthermore, Jackson increased his hold on the council as Jacksonites took eleven of the seventeen Democratic seats. Still, one of Curran's supporters won the presidency of the city council.[18]

The Curran influence in the council, although a political irritant, did not generally affect the mayor's social or economic policies. In the 1930s the city council was, by its own admission, "usually docile." It merely responded to the mayor's initiatives and largely accepted the financial policies set by the city's Board of Estimates, which was under the mayor's control. The split in the council between Jacksonites and Curranites involved but slight differences on major policy issues; instead, both sides confined their abilities and energies to jockeying for political advantage. Occasionally council members threatened "an uprising," declaiming against their "loss of power" and their inability to serve their constituencies. Frank Busch from the sixth district, for example, complained that council members could not even command respect from their community, adding, "I figure myself [a] nothin'." Before his election to Congress in 1938, council member Thomas D'Alesandro declared, "If we had a real council we could tell the Board of Estimates what to do"; and after his election he claimed to be "more in touch with the city's unemployed" than he had been as a council member.[19]

Although the city council did little more than register its concern for the unemployed, after 1935 it nudged Jackson toward accepting more responsibility for those in need in the city. Despite some misgivings, the council had, at Jackson's insistence, approved in 1934 a "pay-as-you-go" policy for Baltimore, which effectively prevented the city from borrowing to meet relief needs and limited its participation in federal matching-fund programs—but the relief crisis of 1935–36 caused by the transition from the FERA to the WPA persuaded council members to pass an emergency resolution enabling the city to abandon this policy temporarily. Jackson nevertheless refused to borrow for relief purposes until 1938, when economic recession and inadequate state funding produced still another relief crisis in the city. As a whole, the city council consistently demonstrated more concern than the mayor for the plight of the unemployed, more interest in the possibilities offered by New Deal programs, and more determination to pressure the state to accept its proper share of responsibility for social welfare programs.[20]

In some measure the social conscience of the council stemmed from the actions of its lone Republican member, Jewish liberal Daniel Ellison. He lobbied long, hard, and successfully, for example, for the creation of the Baltimore Housing Authority. But in other ways the entire council was far in advance of the mayor, early calling, for instance, for a separate municipal welfare department. Council members also responded more directly to the state budget-making process and regularly met with the city's delegation to the general assembly in order to devise ways to increase allocations for relief in the city. When in 1937 the state assembly approved a budget that not only grossly underestimated relief needs but also legalized bookmaking, the city council rose in protest. Jackson, however, predictably removed himself from the controversy, saying nothing of the inadequate appropriation and addressing the issue of bookmaking by asserting, "As Mayor of the City, I feel whether or not bookmakers operate here is none of my business."[21]

Jackson's inaction brought sharp rebukes from certain council members—particularly from the Curranites, but also from the Democratic independents in the council who joined with the Curranites to demand that the mayor present the state with a "list of needs" and a plan for "raising relief money." Jackson refused to do either, fearful of alienating county support in his pursuit of the governorship. Council members scoffed at him for being a "silent Mayor," and Curranites regularly scored him for "stoop[ing] so low . . . to make political capital out of the hunger of our people."[22]

Occasionally, moreover, the city council acted to block the mayor's typically unilateral approach to municipal policy making. Led by Ellison in 1936, for example, they defeated Jackson's attempt to place the full power for "administering, expending, and disbursing" relief funds in the hands of the Board of Estimates. The measure, as Ellison eloquently argued, would have allowed the board to use the Democratic-Jacksonite political clubs in the city to serve as relief centers. But Jackson's greatest challenge came in 1938 when he faced what the *Sun* termed "the most serious revolt in the history of the Council." The relief crisis forced Jackson not only to borrow money but also to propose dramatic cuts in the city's budget. Targeted for layoffs, city employees appealed to council members, who forced Jackson to reconsider his plans before they finally approved a much-reduced municipal budget. The reaction shocked Jackson, long accustomed to an acquiescent council.[23]

After his reelection as mayor in 1935, Jackson immediately began preparation for the 1938 gubernatorial primary. City professional and business groups early endorsed his plans for higher office. Jackson's reputation for fiscal conservatism pleased not only key segments of the business community and the *Sun* papers but also outspoken white middle-class taxpayers, who believed that nearly all relief assistance went to undeserving blacks. Despite his anti–New Deal stands, he could also count on at least lukewarm support from organized labor, especially the Baltimore Federation of Labor. Although Jackson was never an enthusiastic supporter of organized labor, he knew and respected the BFL president, Joseph McCurdy—whereas William Curran, as a devout Catholic, often denounced organized labor from a fear, especially after 1936, that radicalism propelled the movement. Still, Jackson also realized that he could not rely on continued labor support without some concessions to the New Deal Democrats, for in 1934 Governor Ritchie had been defeated by a "New Dealish" Republican and in 1936 the city registered overwhelming support for FDR. And the mayor had to consider the position of the Curranites, who, except for the antilabor position of William Curran himself, were slightly more in support of New Deal social programs than were the Jacksonites. In short, the political situation in the city represented an odd mixture in which the mayor denounced the New Deal but not organized labor, while the Curranites decried union activities but upheld certain New Deal policies.[24]

State and local politicians judged the defeat of Ritchie and the election of Republican Harry Nice as governor in 1934 to be a victory for the New Deal and the final step in the decline of Ritchie's power in the state. Between 1930 and 1934 Governor Ritchie had alienated important constituencies in the party. His failure to win the Democratic presidential nomination in 1932 hurt his standing at home and signaled the decline of his popularity—indeed, it represented the first real setback for the confident and ambitious Ritchie. His life, from his Richmond birth into a distinguished family to his 1915 election as Attorney General and his four consecutive gubernatorial victories, had led him to take for granted the success most available to bright, young lawyers from prominent families. But Ritchie's botched handling of the banking crisis angered city and rural voters alike. His dispatchment of armed guards to the Eastern Shore to stop a spate of lynchings and disperse a white mob injured his traditional support among the Shore's racist Democrats.[25] His refusal to endorse the

1933 unemployment insurance bill seriously damaged his following in Baltimore; long-time supporters repudiated him for his "sorry performance," and even the *Sun* chastised him for his inaction.[26] And the intensity of Ritchie's biting invective directed against the New Deal disturbed even those who shared his states-rights views. Democratic leaders became anxious about Ritchie's fifth-term aspirations.[27]

To complicate matters for Ritchie, Mayor Jackson entered the 1934 gubernatorial primary and vowed to revive the anti-Ritchie forces he had earlier marshaled. Prominent leaders in the party such as Senator Millard Tydings, a personal friend of Ritchie, attempted to bridge the division by suggesting a compromise candidate, but Ritchie balked at the plan and pledged instead to fight Jackson. Unable to arrange a settlement, Tydings and others endorsed Ritchie, leaving Jackson with little significant support in the party leadership and forcing him to withdraw from the race. As the primary neared, Jackson fell into line and endorsed Ritchie—who, as expected, triumphed over his opponent, a virtually unknown physician from Frederick. The victory margin was not as great as the Ritchie forces had hoped, however, prompting the *New York Herald Tribune* to suggest a growing New Deal strength in Maryland. The following day, Ritchie unexpectedly endorsed Roosevelt, and the state party's subsequent platform pledged "one hundred per cent support of the New Deal."[28]

But Ritchie's Republican opponent, Harry Nice, called for "A New and Square Deal for All" and accepted his nomination to the tune of "Happy Days Are Here Again," exclaiming that "Our fight is not against the Democratic party, but against the Democratic machine."[29] The *Baltimore Post* noted the apparent irony of the Republicans' "more New Dealish than the Democrats" approach: "To find the Republicans cashing in on the popularity of a Democratic President and to find the Democrats, that is, the Ritchie organization Democrats—weakened by the success of their party nationally, would be a curious paradox. Yet it is one which the Annapolis administration seems to have been at pains to bring about and which the Republicans would be foolish not to formalize."[30] During the campaign, Nice repeatedly told the voters that Baltimore's incomplete New Deal resulted from the ideological differences between Ritchie and Roosevelt—differences, he falsely claimed, that did not exist between the president and himself.[31]

The Ritchie forces recognized the political need to embrace the New Deal, however belatedly. Senator Tydings toured Baltimore, saying that a Republican vote meant an anti-Roosevelt vote. Joined by fellow U.S.

Senator George Radcliffe, Tydings announced in October that the president had just made available PWA funds to modernize the Chesapeake and Ohio canal west of Washington, D.C. Ritchie surely strained his credibility when he simply abandoned his earlier objections to New Deal programs, broadcasting his support, for example, of the NRA—a program that he had earlier repudiated. He also enlisted the aid of administration Democrats, and despite their understandable bitterness toward Ritchie, they obligingly endorsed him. Postmaster General James A. Farley called Ritchie "one of the most outstanding Democrats," and Harold Ickes swallowed his pride to refer to the state's PWA program as one of the most efficient and conscientious in the nation.[32]

When the final vote was counted, Nice still edged Ritchie by 253,813 to 247,664. In its analysis of the Ritchie defeat, the press labeled Baltimore "the slaughterhouse": even though Ritchie won the city by 20,000 votes, this represented a dramatic decline from 1930, when he had carried Baltimore by 66,000 votes, and it ensured his loss in the state as a whole. An indication of the nature of the election as a protest against Ritchie was that while his total vote shrank by about 37,000 from his 1930 tally, the Republican Nice picked up only an additional 8,000 votes over the 1930 Republican total, suggesting that many people simply refused to vote. The Baltimore *Afro-American* claimed credit for Ritchie's defeat; it had endorsed the Socialist candidate Broadus Mitchell, explaining that the city's blacks were tired of Ritchie's anti–New Deal policies and his racist practices. The *Sun* attributed Nice's victory to the desertion of the newer immigrant wards in the central and eastern sections of the city. In the heavily Polish-American second ward, the voting percentage for Ritchie decreased from 83 to 64 percent in 1934; in the Italian-American third ward, from 76 to 64 percent; in the central city or "downtown" fourth ward, from 75 to 54 percent. In the predominantly black fourteenth and seventeenth wards Ritchie's percentages decreased from 44 to 36 percent and from 31 to 18 percent, respectively.[33]

The presidential race in 1936 underscored even more dramatically the growing popularity of the New Deal in Baltimore. When, for example, the *Sun*, traditionally a Democratic newspaper, repudiated the president and urged its readers not to reelect Roosevelt, it aroused a storm of protest, including an unprecedented number of letters to the editor and citywide boycotts of the paper. Marie Baurenschmidt, a popular spokeswoman in the city, faulted the paper for its inability to recognize one of the nation's greatest presidents, and Baltimore voters circulated petitions to protest that "the *Sun* has gone Benedict Arnold."[34] William Curran denounced the *Sun* for demonstrating a "Herbert Hoover type of mind" and accused it of "rationali[zing] an ancient Toryism."[35] Organized labor, especially the Amalgamated Clothing Workers, dismissed the *Sun*'s declarations against Roosevelt and the New Deal as predictable for a paper committed to conservative fiscal policies, state sovereignty, and business interests. But labor leaders also warned that similar "traitorous" acts by local political leaders would not be tolerated. On a visit to Baltimore, Mary Dewson of the Women's Division of the Democratic Party found the women garment workers to be "organized, aroused, and 100% for Roosevelt. . . . If Mayor Jackson of Baltimore," she noted, "does anything against the election of President Roosevelt, the Amalgamated workers there will remember it and manifest their displeasure the next time they have a chance at the polls." Jackson, she concluded, "has nothing to gain and everything to lose if he does not stand by the Democratic Party this fall."[36]

Party leaders and political indicators predicted a strong showing for Roosevelt and the New Deal in November. The city election board reported in October a "record number" of residents registered to vote in the presidential election. Curran observed a "decided Roosevelt swing" in the wards where "the laboring classes live," but he added that the president "has shifted too far to the left to suit the conservative element" in the party outside the city. Others suggested that the president might capture Baltimore's Jewish vote, which represented about 15 percent of the registered voters, and that he had a good chance of breaking the traditional Republican allegiance among the city's nearly 50,000 black voters, who accounted for approximately 14 percent of the electorate. One state Democratic leader noted that "the colored race is more in favor of our Party than they have ever been," adding that he had received many "requests from them desiring to organize, cooperate, and have headquarters in various sections of the city."[37]

The increased political activism among black residents attracted considerable local attention. Baltimore's blacks, although discriminated against in nearly every New Deal program, had still felt the effects of a more active and compassionate federal government. Government initiatives had heightened their political awareness and they fully realized that the national administration, and not the local government, offered them the best hope for a "new deal." Their political activities, however, also inflamed the passions of local Democratic leaders, who preferred the traditionally white Democratic party. Curran, for example, attempted to discount the political significance of the community activities among black voters, calling blacks "too ignorant and too shifty" to be relied upon and telling national party leaders that "Republican election day money" will hold the black vote "in line for Landon."[38]

But Roosevelt's campaign workers expected more difficulties from the established elites in the city. "The Democratic vote that will go to Landon," declared one observer, "is the business vote"; members of the Maryland Bar Association, he added, would also oppose Roosevelt, and he predicted a poor showing in the wards "inhabited by people with a dollar in the bank."[39] And indeed, in the May primary, although FDR scored an impressive victory, an anti–New Dealer named Colonel Henry Breckinridge carried twenty-three of the city's precincts—all located in the "most exclusive" urban neighborhoods, including Guilford, Homeland, Roland Park, and "uptown apartment sections."[40] Curranites warned the administration of possible "trickery" on the part of Mayor Jackson, who in an effort to displace the Tydings organization might conclude that he would be "better off with a Republican president." Finally, the Rooseveltian policies that alienated the business groups also troubled some of the city's Catholics, among whom existed, according to Curran, a "large following" for Father Coughlin, the popular and outspoken anti-Semitic critic of the New Deal. "The Coughlinites," Curran concluded, "are very well organized with a group of earnest workers who know how and who do play the game of precinct politics."[41]

Organized citizen groups campaigned vigorously for Roosevelt. At a Labor Day picnic, George Berry, as president of the Non-Partisan League, delivered a stirring oration in favor of Roosevelt and a thinly veiled threat to possible detractors—including Mayor Jackson, also seated on stage. The comment reportedly caused "Jackson's face [to] turn a vivid red." In October the ACW held its last in a series of mass rallies; thousands of workers lined the streets to hear Roosevelt's praises sung by Sidney Hillman, Hyman Blumberg, and David Dubinsky. "We had all kinds of parades," Sara Barron of the Amalgamated fondly recalled.[42] Women's groups accelerated their efforts at community organization, holding neighborhood meetings and political luncheons. Eager to serve the Rooseveltian cause, these groups loyally followed the "advice" of male political strategists who urged them "to confine their activities to campaigning among women." They worked hard to increase the voter registration among women and to counter the local anti–New Deal sentiment among such leaders as Jackson. At one women's meeting, when Jackson praised the upsurge of organization among women but made no mention of his "support" of Roosevelt, the group publicly chided the mayor for slighting the president, and he received thereafter "much unfavorable comment" from a number of women's groups.[43]

The outpouring of support and affection for FDR persuaded Jackson of the necessity to move closer to the party of Roosevelt. When, for example, members of Jackson's own faction such as Vincent Palmisano, Democratic nominee from the third Congressional district, heartily endorsed the president, Jackson demonstrated "uncharacteristic support" for FDR. The action was not lost on the *Sun*, which satirized his gesture in a prominently displayed cartoon.[44] Such gestures represented Jackson's attempts to widen his appeal in the party in anticipation of his 1938 gubernatorial bid. Indeed, one of Jim Farley's political "feelers" found local leaders more concerned with the upcoming governor's race than with the presidential election: "Jackson," he said, "is wild to be governor, and it is difficult to keep this issue out of the campaign."[45] The mayor's unrequited ambition to be governor and his recognition of the need to be less hostile to the New Deal were, however, also balanced by his fear of losing his traditional sources of support in the party. One political leader aptly summarized Jackson's predicament: "Mayor Jackson's attitude is one of carrying water on both shoulders. He pretends ostensible support of Roosevelt and a desire for his election, while at the same time he hopes and expects support of the public utilities, bankers, and industrialists in his fight for the Governorship in 1938."[46]

Roosevelt's victory was a decisive one in Baltimore: he won 68.3 percent of the major-party vote. Wards twenty-seven and twenty-eight, populated by the city's "better circumstanced people," offered FDR some resistance, but the ethnic and working-class areas registered strong support and organized labor celebrated for nearly a week after the election. The city's three Jewish locals of the ACW sponsored a "victory ball" held at the Italian Gardens to show the multi-ethnic and genuine working-class support for Roosevelt.[47] Roosevelt had increased his total vote by 31 percent from 159,928 in 1932 to 210,249 in 1936, despite the anti–New Deal sentiments of local political leaders and the *Sun*'s endorsement of Landon. Although the ecological data preclude precise statements about voting behavior, the results in certain wards suggest important trends in the party of Roosevelt, particularly when compared to Jackson's mayoral vote in 1931 and 1935.[48]

In the heavily Catholic first, second, and third wards, Roosevelt ran well in both 1932 and 1936. Polish-Americans largely controlled the local

Democratic clubs in the first and second wards, while Italian-Americans held a firm grip on the political machinery in the third. In 1932, FDR received 76 percent, 86 percent, and 86 percent of the vote from these three wards, respectively; in 1936, his percentages remained the same for wards two and three but increased to 81 in ward one. This electoral experience contrasted sharply with Jackson's in the 1931 and 1935 mayoral contests. In wards one, two, and three, Jackson won impressive victories in 1931, receiving 76 percent, 82 percent, and 81 percent of the ward votes; but his percentages fell markedly in 1935, to 57, 64, and 71, respectively. In the city's total vote, too, FDR gained strength while Jackson lost support. For the *Sun*, the reason for this divergence was clear: Jackson had suffered from his refusal to endorse the New Deal.[49]

The voting record of the predominantly black fourteenth and seventeenth wards further suggested the local political significance of the New Deal. Of the two wards, the seventeenth held the larger percentage of blacks with 88 percent, compared to almost 70 percent in the fourteenth. These wards had long traditions of voting allegiance to the Republican party. It was not surprising, then, that in both mayoral elections Jackson lost both wards; but his anti–New Deal policies may have diminished his chances even further, for his vote in these wards actually declined by over half between 1931 and 1935 whereas Roosevelt's support increased between 1932 and 1936. In 1932, FDR won 42 percent of the vote in the seventeenth and 48 percent in the fourteenth; in 1936, he captured 48 percent in the seventeenth and actually carried the fourteenth with 55 percent. That Roosevelt was able to break the solidly Republican voting of one "black ward" and make a respectable showing in the other simply dazzled local Democrats, who for years had watched city Republicans turn out the black vote with the same tactics that Democrats used among the white ethnic groups. The belief among city Republicans that the New Deal was altering voting alliances among blacks had prompted them to redouble their political efforts in wards fourteen and seventeen in 1936. They even mailed $5.00 checks to all black ministers in those wards, urging them to remind their congregations to vote Republican—but the effort was not especially successful, for a number of black ministers openly endorsed Roosevelt and indignantly responded that their pulpits were "not for sale."[50]

Local political observers also believed that Jackson failed to benefit from what was called the "relief vote." These voters, they maintained, had been created by new assistance programs and remained loyal to the New

Deal. Whether such a "relief vote" in fact existed is difficult to determine. But the findings of a social survey conducted in 1936 of wards five and ten—areas characterized by growing black populations and a disproportionately high relief load—combined with voting returns for mayoral and presidential elections, offer some suggestive comparisons.

Located near the central business district, wards five and ten formed one of the city's oldest areas and originally served as "a good German and Irish residential section." After the turn of the century, the southern and eastern sections of the wards were transformed, according to the survey, into a "typical slum" occupied by a "steadily increasing percentage of Negroes." By 1936, fully 25 percent of the wards' population received unemployable assistance from BERC—nearly twice the average for the city. The wards also contained large numbers of single black males who had migrated to the city in search of jobs, and who either did not qualify for aid or were routinely purged from the relief rolls. By the end of the decade, blacks constituted about 69 percent of the population in ward five and 47 percent in ward ten. In the 1932 and 1936 presidential elections, both wards supported Roosevelt; his strength remained about the same in ward five but jumped 20 percentage points in ward ten. The 1931 and 1935 Jackson votes, however, showed a decrease of 10 percentage points in ward five and 12 points in ward ten.[51] These returns, although minimally useful in analyzing voting behavior, were nonetheless important in shaping the perceptions and plans of local political leaders. Convinced by leaders of his faction that he was not receiving the "relief vote," Jackson aggressively canvassed the "reliefers" in his 1939 mayoral campaign. Indeed, he worked so aggressively in 1939 that relief clients complained of political intimidation.

Regression analysis of the electoral data from all of Baltimore's wards reaffirms the political trends suggested by the voting results already noted for a few distinctive wards. Although Baltimore was traditionally a Democratic city and remained one through the 1930s, the size and nature of the Democratic electorate changed importantly during the depression decade. In the 1931 mayoral and the 1932 presidential elections—before the emergence of the New Deal—black, ethnic, and poor voters were all relatively uninvolved in Democratic politics. The black vote was particularly small, and insofar as blacks engaged in politics they more often voted as Republicans: an estimated 59 percent of the blacks who voted in 1931 supported the Republican mayoral candidate. Poorer or working-class voters—as measured by those who rented their homes, or lived in houses in need of major repairs or without private baths—also remained outside the political process; an estimated 75 percent of those living in substandard houses, for example, did not cast a ballot in 1931. Of those few who voted, Jackson won 72 percent of the vote from residents of substandard homes and an estimated 57 percent from renters. Ethnic groups were more politically active than either blacks or poor voters and were solidly Democratic: Jackson captured approximately 92 percent of the ballots cast by ethnic voters in 1931. For the 1932 presidential election, Roosevelt received about the same percentages as Jackson had in 1931 in all categories of voters; as in 1931, the turnout was very small for poor and black voters. By 1935 and 1936, however, the political situation showed signs of important changes under way. In the 1935 mayoral contest voter turnout actually declined, and Jackson lost substantial support among black, ethnic, and poorer voters. Roosevelt and the New Deal, on the other hand, inspired in 1936 a higher turnout rate than in 1932, and FDR scored important victories among those same groups who constituted the emergent New Deal coalition. By 1936, then, diverging patterns of political participation suggested that Mayor Jackson and President Roosevelt were attracting different constituencies within the Democratic party.[52]

Jackson suffered politically from the local split in the party as the rift between the Curranites and the Jacksonites continued to widen. After 1935, he fought bitterly and openly with the newly elected president of the city council, a Curranite named George Sellmayer. In 1936 the two groups were so divided that they established separate headquarters for the Democratic party, marking the first time in the city's history that Democrats supporting the same ticket were serviced by two presidential campaign offices.[53]

But despite such division, Jackson believed that his traditional Democratic allegiance and his own party coalition would enable him to capture the governor's chair. And to insure his place in the 1938 contest, he announced his candidacy unusually early: in June 1937, almost fifteen months before the Democratic primary. Jackson hoped to replace the disintegrating Ritchie organization, a result of Ritchie's 1934 defeat and subsequent death in 1936, with his own coalition. His appeals to a number of Ritchie's former lieutenants did win him an early endorsement from several leading Democrats, but his endorsements alienated another Ritchie associate, Howard Bruce, Maryland's member of the Democratic National Committee. Bruce admonished the party leaders who "for years fattened on the Ritchie administration" and then immediately arrogated to themselves the power to name the next governor—a power that Bruce apparently believed belonged to him, for he suggested that Attorney General Herbert R. O'Conor or state senate president Lansdale Sasscer run for the office. Following Bruce's advice, both men entered the race.[54]

Of the two, O'Conor presented the greater threat to Jackson. He held the support of a newly formed Bruce-Curran alliance and, as a Baltimorean, was popular in the city. O'Conor appealed to Catholics and to "New Deal voters"—groups among whom Jackson had lost support. In the primary, O'Conor celebrated his ethnic and religious heritage, limiting Jackson's appeal in the city's Democratic electorate. When Jackson campaigned in the Catholic wards he detected a distinct lack of enthusiasm for his candidacy: "Where formerly the good Catholic parishoners had been the soul of cordiality to me, now a certain coolness sprang up between us. . . . I knew what it was," he explained; "one of their boys was running against me."[55]

During the primary campaign Jackson's caustic comments about the New Deal betrayed no trace of his earlier tentative steps toward endorsing the party of Roosevelt. Instead, he extolled the virtues of balanced budgets and pledged to put the state, like the city, on a "pay-as-you-go" basis. O'Conor, however, indicated his support of the president's programs and, more importantly, asserted that the state desperately needed a governor who would cooperate with the federal government and not meet President Roosevelt's every move with "carping criticism." Sensitive to the Catholic vote, O'Conor also balanced his moderate New Deal positions with frequent tirades against the evils of radicalism and warned of the dangers of invidious communism. His portrayal of workers and the unemployed in the city as unwitting dupes in an "anti-American" campaign disturbed the CIO and the PUL, whereas his claim that workers had "unfurled their . . . battle flags" annoyed the BFL. Despite O'Conor's comments, however, organized labor could no longer support Jackson, even reluctantly. Furthermore, such Curranites as Thomas D'Alesandro ignored O'Conor's and Curran's reservations and warmly embraced the New Deal, especially its assertion of labor's right to organize. The Jackson faction had no prolabor counterpart to D'Alesandro, and Jackson himself had so angered the BFL by his efforts to block the organization of municipal employees that the federation immediately endorsed O'Conor and the Curranites. The mayor's record, explained BFL president Joseph McCurdy, "is unfriendly to organized labor." Jackson's futile effort to combat McCurdy's announcement by staging a "Jackson-for-Governor Labor Committee" prompted other unions to denounce the mayor for "parading under fake pretenses."[56]

Jackson's mayoral record and his political practices came under fire in the campaign. Both O'Conor and Sasscer linked Jackson to "machine politics" and suggested that he would extend the hold he had on Baltimore's party to the state. And both faulted the mayor for his failure to represent the city in state budget negotiations. O'Conor excoriated him for his sorry performance during the city's relief crises. Jackson responded by sharpening his attacks on New Deal spenders and portraying himself as an efficient, businesslike mayor. The *Sun* assisted him with his image by running a cartoon entitled "Clothes Make the Man," depicting Jackson in the "100% businessman's suit" and the handsome O'Conor in the "Clark Gable Playsuit" with the caption, "Herbie Emotes His Way into the Hearts of Lady Voters."[57]

The primary race was a close one and, as expected, the party convention had to decide the nomination rather than perfunctorily endorse the winning candidate in the nonbinding popular primary. The identity of the Democratic nominee remained in doubt for weeks while convention delegates cast and recast their ballots. Finally, the crucial Prince George's county delegation decided to vote as a unit, giving O'Conor the necessary votes to win the gubernatorial nomination.[58]

The race that followed between Democrat O'Conor and Republican Nice, running for reelection, appeared tranquil after the tumultuous Democratic primary. Nice could no longer appear more New Dealish than the Democrats, and in 1938, given the trouble in the Roosevelt camp, he felt no political obligation to do so. Rather, he asked, "How does O'Conor stand on the New Deal? . . . As for me," he boasted, "I'm against it." The *Evening Sun* had already observed Nice's "startling" transformation from a supporter of the New Deal to "one of the most outspoken G.O.P. critics of Rooseveltian policies."[59] O'Conor generally minimized the New Deal as an issue in the campaign, focusing instead on the need for greater efficiency and less patronage in government. Although he promised not to sacrifice education or welfare programs, he vowed to manage the state more economically than Nice had. The *Sun* apparently believed him, for it endorsed O'Conor, despite his leanings toward Roosevelt, as the candidate more likely to reduce the state's level of indebtedness.[60]

On 8 November 1938 the voters placed O'Conor in the governor's chair. He won seventeen of the state's twenty-three counties and captured 59 percent of Baltimore's vote. O'Conor's Catholicism helped to return the ethnic wards solidly into the Democratic column after Ritchie's debacle in 1934. Still, O'Conor's percentages in wards one, two, and three were not as great as they had been for Ritchie in 1930, and they were lower than

than those given to FDR in 1936 (77, 83, and 63 percent for O'Conor in 1938; 81, 86, and 86 percent for Roosevelt in 1936). Curranites attributed O'Conor's poor showing in certain wards to Jackson's refusal to endorse him. But he had also failed disastrously in the predominantly black fourteenth and seventeenth wards, receiving but 27 percent and 14 percent, respectively; he had not been able to capitalize on the inroads made by FDR in 1936 when he won 55 percent and 48 percent of the votes in the fourteenth and seventeenth wards. O'Conor's ties to white ethnic groups and the state's traditional Democratic party combined with his limited support of the New Deal to make him less attractive to the "black wards."[61]

O'Conor's deemphasis of the New Deal in 1938 resulted not only from his own political preferences but also from Roosevelt's slightly weakened position in the state. The voters particularly objected to FDR's efforts to defeat Senator Tydings, whom Roosevelt denounced as a "betrayer of the New Deal." Cries against federal intervention rang out all over the state, and Tydings managed to benefit from this public indignation. Indeed, he had cleverly used the New Deal from the start, insuring loyalties and cementing ties within the party through New Deal patronage. Yet Tydings figured among Roosevelt's most troublesome critics; he voted against the National Industrial Recovery Act, the Agricultural Adjustment Act, the Tennessee Valley Authority, and the Wagner Act and abstained on the Social Security Act. He opposed the administration on eighteen of twenty-five major policy questions and led the attack on FDR's plan to expand the Supreme Court. For these reasons, Roosevelt sought to replace Tydings with a more amenable New Dealer, ultimately settling on David Lewis, a scrappy sixty-nine-year-old Democratic congressman from western Maryland. Lewis had been a miner in his youth, had pushed for the state's adoption of workers' compensation legislation, and commanded the respect and admiration of workers in the city and the counties. First elected to the House from his predominantly Republican district in 1910, Lewis served three terms and then returned in 1930 to serve another four. His political experience was extensive and his commitment to the New Deal, especially for workers, was unwavering.[62]

Tydings fully exploited his "underdog" status as an intended "purge" victim and, with the aid of the *Sun*, launched a vicious attack on Lewis. Front-page editorials referred to Lewis as a "federal not a popular" candidate, and Tydings even managed to win the support of Senator Radcliffe, long regarded as a personal friend of Roosevelt. In the race for the Democratic nomination, Tydings focused on two issues: unwanted federal intervention, and Lewis's links with organized labor, which, Tydings insinuated, resulted from his communist sympathies. "If you want a CIO Senator," he repeated throughout the campaign, "don't vote for me."[63]

Organized labor in Baltimore worked actively on Lewis's behalf. Patrick Whalen, representing the Baltimore Industrial Council, urged workers to "put a real liberal like Davey Lewis in office" and get "rid of [antilabor] torpedoes like Tydings."[64] Lewis also received the backing of the CIO's Labor Non-Partisan League, which officially blacklisted Tydings. The league told workers in its paper, the *Labor Voter*, to fight against Tydings and support Roosevelt and Lewis. Lewis particularly attracted the support of Baltimore's more radical workers. Auto workers affiliated with the Communist party, for example, endorsed Lewis in their publication *The Baltimore Auto Worker* and vowed to unseat Tydings: "We Communists in the auto industry . . . pledge to do everything in our power to cooperate with other forces to secure the defeat of Tydings." Steelworkers at Sparrows Point declared, "Put Senator Tydings in cold storage. When the capitalists get control of the country again then it will be time for Senator Tydings to come out of cold storage and get elected again to the Senate."[65]

As the campaign grew more fierce, the entire New Deal was put on trial. Lewis attacked Tydings for practicing "Tory Republicanism" and affirmed that Social Security "is here to stay." Tydings, however, claimed that the New Deal ran counter to the "Maryland view." But he was careful not to dismiss Roosevelt's policies entirely, for he well knew that many voters continued to support certain New Deal programs. Instead, he hammered away at Lewis's alleged ties to communism, conceding that "I do not say Mr. Lewis is a Communist," but adding that "if the Communists were to endorse me as they did Mr. Lewis I would be looking at myself in a mirror."[66] When he campaigned in Baltimore Tydings moderated his views slightly, eliminating the attacks on the New Deal from his speeches and restricting his criticism of Roosevelt to the issue of presidential encroachment in local affairs. Moreover, he also shrewdly retreated from his vigorous antilabor stand, explaining that he disliked only the CIO and its radicalism but recognized the important need for organized labor along the lines of the BFL. Confident of the support of BFL president McCurdy, Tydings hardly expected the announcement from AFL president William Green that "warmly endorsed" Lewis, praising him for his consistent prolabor record. "It looks as though Senator Tydings has endorsed the American Federation of Labor," Green observed, "but, unfortunately, because of his record, the

American Federation of Labor has not endorsed him but has given its endorsement to Congressman David J. Lewis." McCurdy, waging his own struggle against the CIO in Baltimore, refused to comment on Green's statement and continued to support Tydings.[67]

The Curranites in the city also endorsed Tydings. William Curran personally led a "whispering campaign," canvassing the homes of Catholic voters and warning them against labor radicalism and creeping secularism. The Curranites deceived the voters by claiming that Lewis opposed all forms of religious education and alarmed them by emphasizing the support he had received from city Communists.[68] Even Jackson, long excluded from the Tydings-Curran coalition, urged his supporters to vote against Lewis and radicalism and for Tydings and home rule. Very few Democrats in the city strayed from the Tydings line; only Thomas D'Alesandro, seeking the nomination in the third Congressional district, repudiated the anti–New Deal Democrats and openly endorsed Lewis in the 1938 primary.[69]

Although D'Alesandro operated within the Curran camp, his political positions reflected a discernible but limited trend among younger politicians toward greater independence from the city's two Democratic factions. And although most aspiring politicians accepted the "political axiom" that the "machine vote generally controls a primary election," the contest between D'Alesandro (a Curranite) and Vincent Palmisano (a Jacksonite) demonstrated that not even Jackson could always guarantee victory for "one of his boys." Not that Jackson did not try, for he exhausted nearly every trick of the trade to secure Palmisano's renomination. The mayor openly defied the Democratic State Central Committee by appointing the ward executives and, through them, the polling-place employees—a violation of the committee's appointive power. He even leaned on the local printer, whose final ballot for the primary listed Palmisano's name in "bold, large black type" and D'Alesandro's in smaller and slightly blurred print. Nevertheless, D'Alesandro managed to defeat Palmisano, edging him out by a few hundred votes. The election, according to D'Alesandro, represented a victory for the New Deal, organized labor, and President Roosevelt.[70]

Yet the city's voters also gave anti–New Dealer Tydings the Democratic nomination for the U.S. Senate. Winning 57 percent of the city's vote, Tydings could thank both Curranites and Jacksonites for their political efforts. But the Tydings victory, as the Jacksonites reluctantly admitted, represented a repudiation, not of the New Deal, but of federal meddling in local politics. The *Sun* touted the Tydings renomination as proof that when the president "frowns, . . . the world need not end." Yet Tydings polled not only fewer votes than Roosevelt but also fewer than O'Conor, and his antilabor position had cost him, the *Sun* conceded, two of the city's six legislative districts.[71]

Licking his wounds from the gubernatorial primary, Jackson turned his attention to the upcoming mayoral election in 1939. Having been stung by charges of "machine politics," he delayed announcing his candidacy in an effort, he said, to withhold "a target from the opposition." He also attempted to demonstrate that his reelection as mayor would depend, not on his political grip on the city's party machinery, but on his popularity and his record. In a much-publicized stunt, he urged the voters themselves to decide whether he should file again for the Democratic mayoral nomination. Although Jackson's representatives offered no written testimony or proof whatsoever, they claimed that thousands of people visited City Hall to affirm their support and still more telephoned their allegiance to the mayor.[72]

The Curranites, convinced that Jackson was most vulnerable to charges of machine politics, decided to focus on that issue in the primary. To dissociate their own faction from similar charges, they selected a political novice, Charles H. Buck, to challenge Jackson. Buck's first campaign speech underscored the new emphasis: he called for strengthening the merit system, declared that civil service and politics must be "divorced completely," and criticized the mayor's preoccupation with patronage, which, he said, had deprived Baltimore of "a modern system of personnel administration."[73] Although Buck, "the businessman," refrained from specifically endorsing the New Deal, he carefully noted that the city had been woefully inadequate in dealing with the policies and programs of the national administration—a problem he attributed directly to the inefficient management of the city. The mayor's misplaced priorities, he argued, stressed political success before municipal efficiency. Buck's sentiments won him endorsements from a number of consumer groups, the expanding Citizens Civic League, and a variety of neighborhood and community groups. His appeals provided a sharp contrast with those of the mayor: "I am no politician," Buck declared. "I know nothing about ward or precinct politics. I am a Democrat. I am a businessman. This is the first political office I have ever sought."[74]

In previous elections, an opponent's claim to business efficiency would not have bothered Jackson. But in 1939, the mayor's financial record rested on shakier ground. The 1937–38 relief crisis had forced the city to borrow money in order to prevent, according to the director of the welfare department, "starvation among relief clients." Furthermore, Jackson's earlier insistence on major construction projects through the WPA program took its toll on the city when the federal government reduced funding and construction delays increased costs. In March 1939, the state planning commission declared that "the general prospects of the City are not especially encouraging" and cited the problems caused by escalating relief costs and "unbalanced and uncoordinated spending for public improvements." The situation was aggravated, according to the commission, by the city's failure to adopt and follow a rational municipal plan of development.[75] Buck reminded voters of the commission's findings and chastised the mayor for taking the city "past the safe borrowing limit of 7%" to a rate of indebtedness of 8.5 percent of the total assessed value of real estate and personal property. Members of the city council found ironic Jackson's political vulnerability in financial matters, for in the council the mayor had been known since 1934 as "pay-as-you-go Jackson."[76]

Not content to remain long on the defensive, Jackson blasted his opponent for inexperience and blamed the state for the city's need to borrow funds for relief. He noted that he had reduced the tax rate from $2.97 per $100.00 valuation in 1923 to $2.65, and he pointed to the economy measures he had taken for the 1939 fiscal budget—measures, the Curranites countered, that were "purely political," designed to eliminate city employees who had supported O'Conor in the primary. Undaunted, Mayor Jackson, without even mentioning the New Deal, proudly listed the public construction projects nearing completion in the city. He also tightened the reins of control over his wing of the party, instructed his lieutenants to warn relief recipients that their continued funding depended on his reelection, and astutely placed the popular city council member Richard O'Connell on his ticket as candidate for council president in an attempt to oust the Curranite incumbent, George Sellmayer. Finally, Jackson simply dismissed all the charges made by Buck, declaring that the real issue of the campaign was "a choice between this administration and the Curran political machine."[77]

In the April primary the choice was made for Jackson, who defeated Buck by more than 36,000 votes, carrying all but two of the city's wards. Moreover, O'Connell beat Sellmayer for the council presidency and, of the eighteen council members elected, fifteen ran under the Jackson banner. The 1939 primary demonstrated that, even though the Curranites had

Democratic mayor Howard Jackson votes in the municipal elections of 1939.
Although reelected, Jackson suffered significant losses in key sections of the city.
(Courtesy of the Albin O. Kuhn Library and Gallery, University of Maryland
Baltimore County)

enhanced their position at the state level through the election of O'Conor, the city's political machinery still belonged to the Jacksonites. In the mayoral election, however, Jackson faced stiffer competition from a popular Republican candidate, Theodore McKeldin—and although he was victorious, he was unable to regain the support he had once held. His vote totaled just over 109,000, down from over 120,000 in 1931 and 114,000 in 1935. In key ethnic wards, his percentage had declined; in ward three, for example, where he had previously been strong (81 percent in 1931; 71 percent in 1935), his vote fell to 58 percent. And the percentages in wards with expanding black populations, wards that showed a growing support for Roosevelt, were lower as well: in ward five, Jackson received 52 percent (down from 67 percent in 1931 and 57 percent in 1935); in ward ten, 60 percent (down from 82 percent in 1931 and 70 percent in 1935).[78]

To Baltimore Democrats, the *Labor Herald* asserted, the New Deal "means only to get on the band wagon and get a job from the Federal Administration."[79] But the *Herald*'s analysis of the real political significance of the New Deal did not go far enough. Local and state political leaders attempted to use the national programs not only for patronage but to cement political alliances and further their own careers. Such actions would not necessarily have harmed the administration had New Dealers at the national level early demanded loyalty in return for sharing the benefits of the party of Roosevelt. But instead, local and state politicians managed simultaneously to exploit and denounce the programs that served their political needs. A perceptive and sympathetic Baltimore attorney warned FDR as early as 1933 of the "unfriendly attitude of recent federal appointees in Maryland toward your administration." Local politicians, he continued, were "openly hostile" to Roosevelt's programs and concerned less with national policies than with "the election of local and Congressional candidates. . . . I am disturbed and alarmed," he added, "when I see the fortunes of the federal administration in this State placed in the hands and under the keeping of people who never have been and who never will be in sympathy with your ideas of Government."[80]

In 1936, a Curranite ward leader advised James Farley that the national administration had been too lax in its political appointments in Baltimore. He noted, for example, that "not enough political importance was attached to the employment of clerical, laboring and other personnel in the WPA," resulting in the establishment of a local WPA office full of appointments who "oppos[ed] the Federal Administration."[81] Labor leader Pat Whalen put the problem more bluntly when he exclaimed, "I cannot understand why the liberal New Deal supplies patronage to men whose one object is to destroy it. . . . If this is politics," he declared, "then I say, frankly, it is the dumbest politics I have ever seen." The New Deal administration in Washington, he noted, "had better stop worrying about the feelings of these old guard Democrats, and break up some of the machines that were built with federal patronage." Otherwise, he predicted, the New Deal in Baltimore and Maryland would continue "to be used as a Frankenstein, which instead of winning the support of the citizens is being used to discredit the New Deal."[82] For all such observers, FDR's attempts to remove Tydings represented too little too late. Indeed, even with the president's intervention, the national administration remained unable to prevent the wholesale discharge of WPA workers who actively supported Lewis in the primary election against Tydings.[83]

The voting returns demonstrate that Baltimore voters endorsed both Roosevelt and his Democratic opponents, but the party of Roosevelt was not the party of Jackson. Roosevelt attracted greater popular support and drew from voter groups that were steadily less attracted to Jackson. FDR's programs and policies not only won the support of black, ethnic, and poorer voters but attracted them to the polls in greater numbers. In presidential elections, voting by blacks doubled between 1932 and 1940; voting among ethnics increased by 40 percent; and among poorer voters, the rate of political participation increased approximately 50 percent. This mobilization of previously neglected groups in the city's Democratic electorate stood in sharp contrast to the mayoral elections, where the turnout rates for blacks and poorer voters remained nearly constant and low and where there was only marginal improvement among ethnic voters—a feature of local politics that helps to explain Jackson's continued electoral success. By 1940, FDR had captured 65 percent of the votes cast by Baltimore's blacks, 96 percent of those cast by ethnics, 75 percent of those cast by renters, and 97 percent of those cast by residents of substandard housing. But for Jackson, the percentages in all categories of voters declined throughout the decade. Ethnic support for Jackson's Republican opponent, for example, increased from 9 percent of Jackson's vote in 1931 to 50 percent in 1939. Among poorer voters, who gave Jackson a solid majority in 1931, the trend was the same: in 1935 they divided their votes evenly between Jackson and his Republican opponent, but in 1939 they actually cast more ballots for the Republican nominee. Moreover, whereas Jackson's voters in mayoral elections voted nearly unanimously for Roosevelt in succeeding presidential elections, many of those who voted for FDR were not attracted to the polls to support Jackson. Over one-fourth of those who voted for Roosevelt in 1936, for example, failed to vote in the 1939 mayoral election, and nearly another quarter voted against Jackson.[84]

This failure of local politicians to match Roosevelt's success among the groups that mobilized to form the New Deal coalition represented most clearly the dynamics of the decade's politics. These citizens found little to be gained by supporting the local Democratic party—as Josiah Henry, a Baltimore black, discovered in 1934 when he attempted to get the party's nomination as a state delegate: rejected and sharply rebuked by the Curranites, Henry got even less from the Jacksonites, whose hostility toward the New Deal was far greater. Jackson himself ignored the personal appeals of prominent blacks in the city to "induce Negroes to become Democrats" active in local politics. Not impressed with their documentation showing a "New Deal drift of the Negro" into the party of Roosevelt, Jackson refused their pleas for "recognition" and "patronage" and instead reasserted the primacy of tradition and exclusion in the city's Democratic party.[85]

The failure to create a local party hospitable to Roosevelt's New Deal programs and to his coalition enabled Baltimore's Democratic leadership to continue its traditions of local prerogative, fiscal conservatism, and white supremacy. But the party of Roosevelt had left its mark. Even Jackson finally bowed to popular political pressure in 1937 when he appointed a black to the Baltimore Housing Authority. Thousands of Baltimoreans, then, embraced the New Deal and judged their political leaders accordingly. And with the assistance of the national administration, these same citizens ensured that such issues as public welfare, patronage, economic planning, and governmental efficiency were at least introduced into the political debates of the 1930s.

CHAPTER 8

Baltimore,
the Great Depression,
and the New Deal

By the end of the 1930s there were a few signs of New Deal vitality in Baltimore, as the business of defense supplanted the politics of relief. In 1939, public housing made its first mark on the city with the opening of the Poe homes, and there were more projects scheduled to follow. There were also local repercussions from the attempted effort at executive reorganization at the national level. In the 1939 mayoral campaign, for example, Jackson called for reorganizing and revitalizing Baltimore's planning commission and for rationalizing and standardizing the practices of a number of city agencies and commissions—all to be done, he declared, in order to provide a more unified, better focused, and more efficient municipal government. That same year Congress reorganized the relief adminstration, placing new emphasis on defense. Such agencies as the National Youth Administration benefited from the change, for city youths were needed "to help turn the wheels of our defense effort." The NYA hired young men and women to work at the Glenn L. Martin aircraft factory, the Baltimore Marine Hospital, and the city's Fort Holabird; between 1939 and 1940 NYA employment rose by more than 250 percent.[1]

But other New Deal agencies fared less well. Under attack from congressional conservatives for allegedly promoting and condoning radicalism, the WPA underwent significant changes in 1939 that reduced its effectiveness as a work-relief program. In 1940, a syndicated editorial entitled "Death of the WPA" reported that cities throughout the country had stopped seeking additional grants, citing the expense for project materials as the chief reason; WPA assistance, it continued, had come to be regarded as a "real burden on local budgets."[2] That burden was aggravated in Baltimore by Mayor Jackson's use of WPA funds to finance major construction projects—a problem that the state planning commission observed in March 1939 when it criticized the mayor for extending municipal indebtedness beyond a safe limit in order to pay for public improvements. In 1941 the state WPA administrations of Delaware and Maryland were consolidated to effect personnel reductions; the following year federal officials decided that the war had solved the unemployment problem and drew up plans to "liquidate the Maryland program." On 30 April 1943, the WPA officially closed the doors of its offices in Baltimore.[3]

Mayor Jackson, apparently emboldened by the conservative backlash against the New Deal, hardened his stand against the Roosevelt administration in 1939 and 1940. The New Deal, he maintained, had contributed directly to the increased radicalism and aggressiveness of workers and the unemployed and had also undermined the traditional ethic of hard work and individual enterprise. During Roosevelt's 1940 campaign, Jackson, no longer content merely to criticize features of the New Deal, publicly opposed the reelection of FDR—a position that cost him dearly. He not only received hundreds of irate letters and calls, he lost his job to a Republican in 1943. Jackson blasted Roosevelt for precipitating the "erosion of citizenship, the erosion of local governments, State, City, and County, by virtue of their dependence upon the national government, [and] the erosion of the moral fibre of the American people by their dependence upon government, rather than their own independence." The New Deal, he added, has "not been for the good of the American people. Our founding fathers," he asserted, "did not intend that we should have democracy, but a republic."[4] The *Sun* joined the mayor in his attack on Roosevelt and even requested the president to cancel his planned visit to Baltimore in 1940, prompting Governor Herbert O'Conor to denounce the *Sun* and personally appeal to FDR to attend a "rousing reception" in the city. Ignore your detractors, O'Conor urged Roosevelt, and reward "your loyal supporters" who, he reminded the president, "gave you a record-breaking majority in 1936."[5]

Local political opposition to the New Deal had served to limit the effectiveness of its programs in the city and to minimize the significance of its policies designed to strengthen public responsibility for the unemployed and the unemployable. Fearing the institutionalization of what he termed "emergency measures," Jackson, except in 1933 and 1938, avoided using municipal funds for unemployment relief, and he endorsed the WPA only after federal authorities allowed the city to reshape the program more along the lines of the PWA. In this respect, Jackson contrasted sharply with other big-city mayors. If the urban picture drawn by Mark Gelfand is correct, then Baltimore trailed far behind in terms of responsibility and leadership. According to Gelfand, the intensity of the Great Depression in the cities combined with the fiscal conservatism of the state governments to force mayors throughout the nation to take unprecedented steps in appealing directly for federal assistance—but Jackson did not take part in the municipal activism characteristic of such mayors as Frank Murphy of Detroit or Fiorello La Guardia of New York City, and even more conservative mayors like Boston's James Michael Curley, who merely "mixed radical rhetoric with older formulas," outdistanced Jackson in terms of sensitivity to the unemployed. La Guardia called the termination of the CWA "disastrous for cities," whereas Jackson, confronted with 22 percent unemployment, instead dismissed the entire program as unfortunate and misguided.[6] Jackson based his opposition to the New Deal on his faith in voluntarism, his preference for private over public initiative, and his long-standing commitment to limited government and fiscal restraint. However, his willingness to accept federal funds and his unbridled eagerness to shift the responsibility for relief onto the state and national governments suggested, not the limits of his ideological framework, but rather its utter bankruptcy.

New Deal programs throughout the 1930s consistently failed to meet the needs of the city's unemployed. And the depression took its toll on many Baltimoreans. The city's reputation for homeownership had been tarnished; the percentage of homeowners declined by one-fifth between 1930 and 1939. Still other city residents never found work or recovered from bankruptcy. Municipal obstacles to New Deal assistance programs too often forced them to fend for themselves. But in addition to local official resistance, financial constraints at the national level alternately restricted or eliminated necessary relief programs. Further, ideological limitations among federal leaders resulted in programs that, as historian William Bremer persuasively argues, produced "more relief than work, more charity than employment."[7] Unemployed women, in particular, rarely escaped the stigma of charity, and consequently a New Dealer such as Harry Hopkins felt justified in arbitrarily cutting off eligible women, secure in the belief that he had, through the establishment of sewing rooms and domestic-training programs, aided at least a few of the unfortunate women. Certainly, neither the federal nor the local government followed the advice of a Baltimore women's group to "come out for a square and new deal for [unemployed] women."[8] Federally mandated quota reductions after 1935 also meant that the number of available WPA jobs fell far short of the number of employables in need of work in Baltimore. And the policies of Jackson's small coterie of business friends and associates who directed the Baltimore Emergency Relief Commission made these problems much worse. They responded to rising rates of unemployment by slashing relief rolls, by devising new and sometimes costly means to detect possible fraud, and by blaming social workers instead of the state or local governments for the city's relief problems.

The "localization of federal programs," then, ensured that the New Deal would not alter the city in drastic ways.[9] Political traditions persisted and the local government only occasionally, and usually under duress, acted favorably toward Roosevelt and the New Deal. A border city with a strong Southern heritage, Baltimore (and its Democratic party) systematically excluded black residents from local political and economic activities. Neither the city nor the state made the predicament much easier for the jobless; relief eligibility rules remained stringent, and attitudes toward reliefers harsh. Periodic relief crises occurring as late as 1938 suggested that both the city and the state held rather stunted notions about public responsibility. The conservative "pay-as-you-go" approach to relief was referred to in other cities as the "Baltimore Plan." And the policies of Mayor Jackson made sure that Baltimore deserved its reputation for tight-fisted fiscal practices.[10] Out of the nation's twelve largest cities, Baltimore ranked sixth in the percentage of the vote given to Roosevelt in 1936, running ahead of such cities as Philadelphia, Chicago, Detroit, and Pittsburgh—and yet throughout the 1930s Baltimore's mayor remained antagonistic to the programs, architects, and spirit of the New Deal. Not even among the Curranites did a leader emerge to challenge Jackson and capitalize on the widespread support of Roosevelt in the city. Moreover, those few Curranites who, like Governor Herbert O'Conor, endorsed the New Deal did so with caution and restraint; they feared alienating the city's organized business community, from bankers to real estate brokers, and they also feared inciting the wrath of the violently anti–New Deal paper, the Baltimore *Sun*.[11]

The New Deal was not, however, without its effects on the city. To focus exclusively on the Roosevelt administration's inability to substantially alter political traditions and economic practices within a short five or six years is to ignore the complex changes that did take place. One of the most important transformations involved the interaction of state and local governments with the national administration. Before his death in 1936, former Governor Albert Ritchie issued his final complaint against the federal "dictation" of state policy and perceptively pointed to the emergence of a significant trend in the policies of both local and state governments; more and more, he lamented, "we look to Washington for a Federal yardstick to tell us how to conduct ourselves."[12] And throughout the 1930s, few observations annoyed state and local policymakers more than those made by federal officials suggesting that Baltimore and Maryland were backward or inefficient in administrative matters. Even rural legislators supported the reorganization of the welfare system in 1935 and the creation of a municipal welfare department in order to demonstrate to federal authorities that Maryland was not "primitive" in its administration of relief. These same legislators, although considerably less willing to fund relief programs, applauded themselves for modernizing the welfare system. Their feelings of pride—mingled with fears of the erosion of state power, which so often militated against a more receptive environment for the New Deal—encouraged them to fulfill the very federal recommendations they resented.

The establishment of New Deal programs and the evaluation of local policies by federal administrators served as necessary catalysts in reorganizing the city and state in important ways. It was the highly critical federal investigation of the city's relief system in 1934 that prompted the city council to adopt a resolution calling for a separate municipal welfare department to handle all assistance programs, and that helped facilitate the subsequent passage of state legislation creating the department. Further, the New Deal forced Mayor Jackson to recognize, as he did openly in 1938, that "relief . . . is now a public problem and permanently a public problem."[13] Federal complaints and criticisms also promoted modifications in the city's planning policies. Beginning as early as 1933, with the city's first PWA construction proposal, and continuing throughout the WPA program, federal authorities argued that Baltimore's public improvements reflected no coherent city plan and they strongly suggested adopting a systematic and scientific approach to urban development. Their findings did not go unnoticed. The state's Commission on Governmental Efficiency and Economy relied directly on federal reports to rebuke the city for its "uncoordinated spending" on public works. The city council resolved to urge the mayor to pass planning laws with "teeth" in them and to revive the Commission on City Plan, an organization created in 1910 as part of a burst of progressive energy but one that never functioned effectively. Jackson responded by appointing a committee to evaluate the planning group, and with its recommendations he placed on the 1939 ballot a proposal to reorganize the commission by substantially increasing its power and widening its representation to include more private citizens. He also publicly acknowledged the need for the "systematic development of the city along a carefully charted course." Voters agreed and overwhelmingly approved the establishment of a new planning commission.[14]

Changes were also made in another area of federal concern. The handling of all the city's recreational activities by the quasi-public Playground Athletic League particularly disturbed federal officials. They found inequalities in the distribution of services and equipment based on class and race, and they ridiculed the city for allowing the management of its recreational system to depend on the efforts of volunteers. The extension of recreational opportunities through the New Deal to the poor, the elderly, and blacks pointed up Baltimore's inadequate and inequitable administration of organized leisure activities. After considerable prodding from the federal and state governments, Jackson proposed and received in 1939 a completely public municipal department of recreation.[15]

Finally, federal complaints about Jackson's thoroughly politicized administration led to certain modifications in municipal organization. Although Baltimore, unlike a number of other cities, had been able through aggressive tactics to collect property taxes throughout the 1930s, its methods of assessment disturbed the federal government. Pointing to irregularities and inconsistencies in housing and commercial assessments, the federal administration suggested that Jackson restructure the assessment process. In 1939, under fire from Curranite opponents who relied on these federal charges, Jackson announced the formation of the Assessors' Association of Baltimore with its "ultimate aim" of standardizing assessments throughout the city. The Democratic mayoral primary in 1939 represented the culmination of the growing local concern about Jackson's "political machine," and federal complaints about Jackson's handling of municipal affairs even provided the Curranites with a platform. In that campaign the mayor's rival, Charles H. Buck, proudly proclaimed to be "free of political interference and politics," declared that "it was time the City Hall should be cleaned out," and called for the adoption of a "long-range scientific city plan."[16]

The intensity of the depression and the particular response of the Roosevelt administration to a decade of hard times served to transform the traditional functions of private relief agencies. Most agencies, with the exception of the Bureau of Catholic Charities, gladly surrendered the job of providing relief to the local and federal governments, but at the same time they expected to continue to serve the public and shape local relief policies. They resented the 1934 federal investigation of local relief, which suggested that the staffs of private agencies lacked the proper training for providing professional and efficient assistance. Attacked also by BERC, in an attempt to escape the consequences of its own managerial ineptitude, the private agencies rather suddenly lost the respect and recognition they were accustomed to receiving. As historian Robert Bremner notes, private agencies nationwide faced "difficult problems" as a result of New Deal programs. But in Baltimore, where public responsibility in the form of a municipal welfare department came late and where private agencies initially helped dispense federal funds, there occurred in some measure a struggle between private and public relief. The Family Welfare Association, for example, while celebrating its freedom from the responsibility for unemployment relief, also predicted in 1934 "many problems" in "defining the field in which it can best serve"; and in 1938 the FWA noted that it had "changed almost overnight from virtually a public agency to one that was entirely privately supported," adding that its "readjustment was not an easy one."[17]

The division between public and private agencies widened with the influx of professionally trained social workers and administrators into the public agencies. These professionals attempted to distinguish themselves from the private volunteers, often claimed the credit for "initiating the revolutionary reorganization of relief in this country," and restricted the duties of the volunteer to the "rudimentary" and "routine." Through their professional organization, the American Association of Social Workers, they often politicized their welfare responsibilities. In 1935, for example, the association officially decried the nation's "faulty distribution of wealth," and some social workers claimed that, unlike private volunteers, the "well qualified" caseworkers "were contributing to create a spirited, dynamic working class insistent upon a better social order."[18] Obviously, the federal government's prescriptions to remedy demoralization among the jobless through "client participation" in relief practices had affected the attitudes of the social workers themselves.[19]

But the New Deal also altered the concerns of the private agencies in the city. To be sure, neither private agencies nor citizen volunteers usually spoke of the need to mobilize the working class, but they did agree on the necessity for increased community involvement in all aspects of social welfare. In this regard, the interests of the private agency fitted perfectly into the cooperative public-private scheme envisioned by New Deal administrators. Federal authorities specifically recommended the use of volunteers in the FERA, WPA, and NYA programs as a means of establishing and maintaining community support for federal initiatives and projects. And overburdened trained social workers relied heavily on the efforts of private agencies and volunteer staffs throughout the 1930s. To minimize the distance between the public and the private, and to carve out a mutually acceptable role for the private agency, the city's private agencies joined together in 1937 to form the Baltimore Council of Social Agencies, with the Department of Welfare as a member agency. Further underscoring the public-private connection, the council received half its annual budget from the city and half from the private agencies.[20] The formation of the Council of Social Agencies reaffirmed Baltimore's long tradition of voluntarism, acknowledged the federal government's simultaneous endorsement of public and private responsibility, and testified to Mayor Jackson's personal commitment to the continuation of private assistance in an era of public welfare. The city's private agencies, reorganized and redefined, still retained a permanent, albeit diminished, role in the provision of social services.

The requirements imposed by the federal government in its establishment of public responsibility in Baltimore had reduced the influence of private agencies in the distribution of relief, and had ultimately forced the replacement of the business leaders who dominated the relief system with better-trained professionals, or at least with more appropriate political appointments. But Baltimore's particular response to the depression and to the federal government's demands also ensured that, even though a new system of welfare had emerged, by the end of the decade this system appeared neither startlingly novel nor fully responsible.

New Deal programs, from Social Security to public housing, challenged neighborhood groups to organize and to demand that the city participate more fully in social welfare programs. The WPA community projects in Baltimore, although somewhat limited in scope when compared to those in other major cities, still encouraged neighborhood involvement. One WPA archival project, for example, involving the collection and preservation of old photographs and community records, stimulated the neighborhoods of Hampden and Woodberry to join together and form their own historical society, the first of its kind in the city. In 1938 the *Sun* boasted of a "current of neighborhood spirit . . . seldom associated with part of a municipality." Increased federal attention and assistance did not, at least in the 1930s, displace community activism but, rather, inspired new forms to emerge. New neighborhood associations and consumer groups were organized; older ones were enlivened and expanded. In certain instances, moreover, neighborhood groups cooperated to a degree never anticipated, even crossing class and racial boundaries. Certainly the formation of the Citizens' Housing Council represents one of the best examples of such cooperation. United States Housing Authority officials openly endorsed the council's activities, dispatching federal representatives to its meetings in Baltimore and lavishing praise on its efforts. But the creation of the Housing Council underscores not only the significance of federal initiatives in transforming inchoate protests into a citizen activist group but also, in this case, the importance of community organization in altering municipal policy. Initially loath to support public housing, Mayor Jackson finally acquiesced in the formation of the Baltimore Housing Authority, and by early 1941 two public housing projects had been completed under the USHA program.[21]

The antibusiness rhetoric of the New Deal heightened Baltimoreans' awareness of their role as consumers. In the latter part of the decade, for example, the Belair Road Improvement Association narrowed its concerns to concentrate almost exclusively on what it regarded as excessive rates for gas and electricity in the city. With the assistance of other neighborhood groups, the Belair Association formed the City Civic Gas and Electric Committee to lobby for immediate rate reductions, to force an investigation of the pricing practices of the Baltimore Gas Light company, and to push for legislation providing for the municipal ownership of utilities. In early 1939 the committee secured the signatures of 40,000 city residents protesting the appointment of a "political crony" to the public service commission charged with evaluating gas and electric rates, and demanded a "consumer advocate," who would give Baltimoreans a "fair deal." The Consumers' Council of Baltimore, formed by Maryland's National Emergency Council director Arthur Hungerford and representing about forty associations—including trade unions, the Peoples Unemployment League, and fraternal and improvement groups—took up the cause of the Gas and Electric Committee and warned local politicians of its intention to make them more sensitive to consumer problems. The Consumers' Council distributed questionnaires to local policy makers to determine their positions on "consumer issues" and published its findings in the city's major papers.[22]

Other groups continued to agitate for better treatment of the unemployed. The PUL, along with neighborhood associations and labor unions,
established the Citizens' Alliance for Social Security in response to the
1935 federal legislation and to the failure of the city and state to assist all
those eligible for some type of aid. The Citizens' Alliance later expanded
its focus and membership and created the Baltimore Committee on Unemployment and Social Security to press for greater relief appropriations and
for a reduction in the lengthy application procedures, which too often
prolonged the hardship of families dependent on relief assistance. The
emergence of a public welfare system obviously did not cancel the need for
such community activity. Led by the PUL, these organizations rarely relaxed their vigilant watch over the city's relief practices, and by 1938 they
had become a regular feature of the city's welfare system.

The New Deal, then, not only brought welfare and recreation departments, a revitalized municipal planning group, and new streets, sewer
systems, bridges, and schools to Baltimore, it also transformed citizen
groups throughout the city. Interaction with the federal government enhanced political and economic awareness among Baltimore's residents.
Some citizens felt personal ties to the president and told him so in their
letters, which showered the White House in the 1930s. Others used their
vote to register their support. Workers, in particular, endorsed their president, who, they believed, understood their predicament with compassion
and upheld their right to improve their situation through unionization. Men
and women, blacks and whites, rallied behind Roosevelt, and he carried
even the stubbornly Republican and predominantly black seventeenth ward
in the 1940 election.

Labor leaders used New Deal programs and slogans to advance the pace
of organization in Baltimore. In the 1930s, unions, particularly those
affiliated with the CIO, relied heavily on the machinery provided by the
National Labor Relations Board to validate their bargaining voice at the
workplace and to legitimize their position among competing unions and
hostile city officials. And New Dealers, in turn, depended on the labor
unions to cement trade-union and political loyalities, thereby forging a
Democratic constituency that would support Roosevelt at work, at home,
and at the polls. The increased politicization of workers reinforced the
importance of the unions and of their activities in the community. Unions
affiliated with the CIO, particularly the Amalgamated Clothing Workers,
made politics an integral part of local union activities in an attempt to
extend the value of the union beyond the workplace. To be sure, more

radical unions like the National Maritime Union found the New Deal woefully inadequate and the Roosevelt administration less than enthusiastic in its support of organized labor. Still, the New Deal provided labor with new weapons, stiffened workers in their resolve to oppose the critics of unionism, and thoroughly challenged the local political environment. Consequently, even radicals like Pat Whalen campaigned for such liberal New Dealers as Davey Lewis.

However, the politicization of the work force also led to divisions within it, for the CIO and the federation drew different meanings from the local application of the New Deal. Following the lead of the ACW, the CIO embraced the government's initiatives to increase simultaneously government authority and community involvement, whereas the BFL only cautiously relaxed its voluntaristic traditions. For the CIO, the New Deal slogans perfectly matched its emphasis on the working class; for the BFL, these slogans took on more patriotic and coercive dimensions. Such divisions notwithstanding, the New Deal served to heighten concern about the ordinary worker, often celebrating the virtues of the downtrodden in art and theatre. And both the CIO and the federation in Baltimore could at least join together to support such WPA projects as the art exhibition entitled "Labor in Art" held at the Baltimore Museum of Art. One local CIO official heralded the project as an attempt to "unclass" art, and AFL president William Green, who visited the exhibit, called it a "symbol of new understanding of labor in the community."[23] That new understanding, many workers believed, resulted from the actions of the Roosevelt administration.

But organized groups also found the limits to government support. Associations of the jobless might unite to improve their conditions or to offer advice on certain relief practices, but they were not allowed to set policy or forcefully challenge federal directives. The PUL was early informed of its restricted role when Aubrey Williams warned that the government held "the whip." Organized transients tested the patience of the government, as when the seamen took over the Anchorage, and they ultimately witnessed the complete collapse of their assistance program when the federal government withdrew its support and returned that responsibility to the states and localities. Workers in WPA programs who attempted to organize and strike were often simply dismissed, and that policy largely conformed to national-level statements decreeing that reliefers were not workers but beneficiaries of government assistance programs.

Nevertheless, the federal government outdistanced local officials in its compassion for the jobless and its efforts to expand public responsibility—and therefore local groups that traditionally were ignored by major-party politics organized to support the changes that could and did result from a more active and positive government. As has been shown, municipal practices and policies thwarted the efforts of both the federal government and the citizen groups. But the New Deal's failure to reorganize society in a substantive fashion that would promote social solidarity, economic cooperation, and national unity, as some New Dealers wanted, resulted not merely from local obstacles to social reform. Rather, other New Dealers held a different vision and regarded the extension of federal authority as necessary to preserve individual political and economic rights. Their approach, as James Holt aptly argues, represented the "characteristic American way of defending the welfare state."[24] Ambiguities at the national level, then, made it more difficult for the New Deal to overcome the obstacles at the municipal level, where commitment to local prerogative, fiscal conservatism, and traditional politics all served to undermine the efficacy of federal relief programs.

This is not to propose, however, that had the New Deal been more radical the cities and states across the nation would have lagged even further behind.[25] Rather, this is to assert the improbability of a more radical New Deal but at the same time to suggest that had the Roosevelt administration more successfully politicized its programs, exerted greater control in local appointments, and made more demands on the state and local governments, more of the jobless would have received assistance and local politicians would have been less free to simultaneously denigrate and manipulate relief programs. Thanks to the efforts of organized citizen groups and to the intervention of federal officials, blacks, for example, received positions in the CCC, PWA, CWA, and WPA. And although the record is less clear for unemployed women, federal authorities did manage to secure two additional WPA sewing rooms for jobless women in Baltimore. These piecemeal efforts certainly benefited those groups most in distress but they also tended to create special-interest groups among the "have-nots." By failing to foster a communal sense of public responsibility, New Deal programs helped to divide the reliefers from the rest of society.

The coming of the war did not enhance the city's fitful acceptance of public responsibility. Unemployment declined to just under 10 percent in

1940 and continued to drop during the war years as opportunities in shipbuilding and aircraft construction swelled the labor force, and women, no longer accused of depriving men of jobs, were actively courted for wartime employment—but the invitation did not extend to blacks, who by 1940 represented 19.3 percent of the city's population (up from 17.7 percent in 1930), who still lived in substandard housing (as 70 percent of the city's blacks did in 1940), and who daily faced the effects of white discrimination. By 1943, for example, the Glenn L. Martin aircraft plant employed more than 20,000 workers but only 175 blacks, and yet the company continued to advertise for workers as far away as New Jersey. Only after a march of 2,000 city residents on Annapolis did the city and the state cooperate to provide some assistance to Baltimore's blacks. The march itself represented, in part, the effect on the black community of a decade of New Deal rhetoric and programs. As the vice-president of the Baltimore Urban League and the dean of Morgan State College, George Grant, explained in a letter to Roosevelt, the expectations of blacks had been lifted; there was hope where there once had been only resignation. "We know further," Grant wrote, shielding the president from any responsibility for the city's difficulties, "that you are caught in the web of traditional public opinion and are, therefore, restrained from taking steps which your heart dictates as just."[26]

The continued support for state sovereignty and local prerogative during the war years indicated that the struggle with the federal government was far from over. Governor O'Conor warned in 1943 that in order to reverse the trend of expanding federal authority, the state had to provide "convincing proof" of its ability to deal with the "impact of postwar problems before they get out of hand." Both the city and the state reaffirmed the need to intensify economic and social planning efforts in order to preclude either total subservience to, or dependence on, federal decisions.[27] The federal government in the Great Depression had become, as Governor Ritchie observed, the "yardstick" for measuring the progress of states and cities in handling their affairs. The war would not change that. The spectre of increased federal intervention had combined in the 1930s with the glaring inadequacies of the local administration of relief to help reorganize the city in permanent ways. The compassion of the New Dealers had pricked the conscience of local policy makers, and citizen groups organized to expand on those modest beginnings. But the policies of the Roosevelt administration and the political preferences of the municipal leadership meant that city leaders would mix old formulas with newer solutions and incorporate public responsibility into more traditional practices. The particular amalgam of social welfare that emerged pointed at once to the possibilities and limitations of the New Deal in Baltimore.

Notes

Abbreviations

ACW	Amalgamated Clothing Workers
ACWA	Amalgamated Clothing Workers of America Papers, Martin P. Catherwood Library of the New York State School of Industrial and Labor Relations, Cornell University (Ithaca, N.Y.)
BAC	Baltimore Association of Commerce
BCA	Baltimore City Archives
BERC	Baltimore Emergency Relief Commission
BFL	Baltimore Federation of Labor
BHA	Baltimore Housing Authority
BIC	Baltimore Industrial Council
CCC	Civilian Conservation Corps
CHC	Citizens' Housing Council
CPHA	Citizens' Planning and Housing Association
CPHAP	Citizens' Planning and Housing Association Papers, Baltimore Region Institutional Studies Center, University of Baltimore
CWA	Civil Works Administration
CWS	Civil Works Service
DNCP	Democratic National Committee Papers, Franklin D. Roosevelt Library (Hyde Park, N.Y.)
ECA	Emergency Charity Association
EPFL	Maryland Room, Enoch Pratt Free Library (Baltimore)
FDRL	Franklin D. Roosevelt Library (Hyde Park, N.Y.)
FDRP	Franklin D. Roosevelt Papers, Franklin D. Roosevelt Library (Hyde Park, N.Y.)
FERA	Federal Emergency Relief Administration
FWA	Family Welfare Association
ILGWU	International Ladies' Garment Workers' Union
JPCC	*Journal of the Proceedings of the City Council of Baltimore*
MHR	Maryland Hall of Records (Annapolis)
MSPC	Maryland State Planning Commission
NA	National Archives (Washington, D.C.)
NEC	National Emergency Council

NLRB   National Labor Relations Board
NRA   National Recovery Administration
NYA   National Youth Administration
PHA   Public Housing Administration
PUL   Peoples Unemployment League
PWA   Public Works Administration
RG   Record Group
SWOC   Steel Workers' Organizing Committee
UAW   United Auto Workers
USHA   United States Housing Authority
WNRC   Washington National Records Center (Suitland, Md.)
WPA   Works Progress Administration

Introduction

1. Patterson, *New Deal and the States*.

2. Trout, *Boston*; Blumberg, *New Deal and the Unemployed*. See also Biles, *Memphis*; Heinemann, *Depression and New Deal in Virginia*; Badger, *Prosperity Road*; Wickens, *Colorado*. In addition to the local and state studies found in Braeman, Bremner, and Brody, *New Deal: State and Local Levels*, there are a number of important works including Ingalls, *New York's Little New Deal*; Blakey, *Hard Times and New Deal in Kentucky*; Holmes, *New Deal in Georgia*; Coode and Bauman, *People, Poverty, and Politics*; and Judd, *New Deal in Vermont*. See also Lowitt, *New Deal and the West*.

Although dissertations continue to examine local developments of the 1930s, unfortunately there have been few monographs published that deal with specific cities during the Great Depression. For an important analysis of general urban developments during the New Deal, see Gelfand, *Nation of Cities*. Also see the still-useful collection edited by Bernard Sternsher, *Hitting Home*.

3. Braeman, Bremner, and Brody, *New Deal*, 2:ix. One of the few exceptions to this historiographical trend is Minton, *New Deal in Tennessee*, which concludes that the New Deal provoked a "revolution" in Tennessee.

4. Badger, "New Deal and the Localities," 104.

5. Maurer, "Relief Problems and Politics in Ohio"; Hunter, "Virginia and the New Deal," 132; Wickens, *Colorado*, 70–73. For another account of the economic experience in Virginia, see Heinemann, *Depression and New Deal in Virginia*.

6. Holmes, *New Deal in Georgia*, passim.

7. Trout, *Boston*, 321. One of the few exceptions to the general interpretation of the New Deal that emphasizes federal initiative and local or state obstructionism is Ingalls, *New York's Little New Deal*, which argues that the welfare state created in New York emerged from a philosophy of public responsibility within that state and refers to

Governor Lehman's policies as "the most comprehensive set of reforms ever enacted in New York" (p. 24). The peculiar spirit of reform in New York is also reflected in Bremer, *Depression Winters*.

8. Wickens, *Colorado*, 201, 388, 397, 400–401.

9. Trout, *Boston*, 315.

10. Heinemann, *Depression and New Deal in Virginia*, 172.

11. George Wolfskill, review in *American Historical Review* 89 (June 1984): 869.

12. See, for example, Susman, *Culture as History*, 159–61; Romasco, *Politics of Recovery*; and McElvaine, *The Great Depression*. McElvaine persuasively argues that FDR also won the allegiance of many people because of his polio—a factor, McElvaine suggests, that has been too little emphasized in recent years (see pp. 103–6). Another important issue in accounting for Roosevelt's popularity and linked directly to this author's concern for citizen involvement in the 1930s was the unprecedented letter-writing to both Franklin and Eleanor Roosevelt that occurred during the Great Depression. Significantly, both Roosevelts encouraged the correspondence from the "ordinary folk" and attempted to answer the letters promptly. McElvaine perceptively deals with this phenomenon in *Down and Out in the Great Depression: Letters from the "Forgotten Man."* The letters indicated, according to McElvaine, that many citizens "felt they knew the president personally" (p. 6).

Letters to Washington, D.C., from the unemployed in Baltimore were almost always addressed to the president or to Eleanor Roosevelt. Those indicating particular hardship or demanding corrective action were forwarded to local officials for some sort of remedy. Harry Hopkins even sent "follow-up" letters to make sure that the matters had been resolved. Local relief officials occasionally resented federal interference in relief matters and in a few instances attempted to penalize those of the jobless who appealed directly to the president for help. See, for example, *Evening Sun*, 13 April 1935.

13. Roosevelt quoted in James Holt, "American Anti-Statist Tradition," which discusses the cooperation theme of the early New Deal, 33–36.

14. Graham, "The Planning Ideal," 283. For an examination of the connection between the New Deal and community organization in public welfare, see Austin and Betten, "Intellectual Origins," especially pages 166–67; for the relationship between the New Deal and volunteer service, see Jones and Herrick, *Citizens in Service*, 94.

15. Nash, *The Great Depression*, 63. Louis Galambos offers the best discussion of the organizational theme in "Emerging Organizational Synthesis." Also see Israel, *Building the Organizational Society*. Of particular relevance to my approach to the organizational theme is Berkhofer, "Organizational Interpretation of American History." See also Graham, "The Planning Ideal," 257–99.

16. Coode and Bauman, *People, Poverty, and Politics*, 12, 16–19; Hawley, "New Deal and Business," 57.

17. Hawley, "New Deal and Business," 57; Nash, *The Great Depression*, 59. See also Leuchtenburg, "New Deal and the Analogue of War." For a discussion of the centrality of Progressive-era developments to the emergence of the modern, organized

state, see Skowronek, *Building a New American State*; for examinations of the failed efforts of the Roosevelt administration to create a more centralized government, see Graham, *Toward a Planned Society*, and Karl, *The Uneasy State*.

18. Roosevelt's quotation is from Holt, "American Anti-Statist Tradition," 36.

19. Holt discusses this failure of the New Deal when he writes, "but if 'learning about cooperation' meant learning what federal agencies could achieve, it was no longer clear how the individual citizen was supposed to express his devotion to the cooperative ethic other than by voting the straight Democratic ticket" ("American Anti-Statist Tradition," p. 36). The concept of "communalizing" New Deal programs is borrowed from Skocpol, "Legacies of New Deal Liberalism," 37. See also Skocpol and Finegold, "State Capacity and Economic Intervention."

I agree with Holt and Skocpol that the New Deal ultimately failed to legitimate its programs socially. But too little has been written about the *local* attempts within neighborhoods and among community groups at creating a more responsible society. An examination of such attempts will not only help explain Roosevelt's popularity and the willingness of people to write him of their predicament, it will also help account for the Democratic allegiance of key segments of the urban population. The administration's efforts, although limited, and perhaps ultimately even divisive through its creation of "special interest groups" among the poor, still served to provide an important link between the community and the federal government—a link that has yet to be fully explored.

Finally, perhaps still the best analysis of the ambiguities and confusion surrounding the New Deal programs and policy makers is Paul Conkin's *The New Deal*.

Chapter 1

1. *Evening Sun*, 1 January 1930.

2. Olson, *Baltimore*, 302. The Baltimore Association of Commerce, formed in 1924 through the amalgamation of a number of trade and manufacturers' associations, published a bulletin entitled *Baltimore*. For the BAC's comments concerning labor, see *Baltimore*, 13 (February 1920): 3. Arnold, "Suburban Growth."

Workers in Baltimore in nearly all occupations earned less than their counterparts in other major cities. Particularly low wages characterized the garment industry, where the predominantly female work force earned 50 percent less than women workers in Chicago, for example; see Hollander, *Report to Honorable Howard W. Jackson*, and Baltimore *Municipal Journal*, 9 January 1931. In letters to the *Sun* papers, workers denounced the BAC for "boasting to new industries just how little Baltimore people will work for"; see *Evening Sun*, 13, 23 September; 2, 3 October 1929. On her visits to Baltimore, Lorena Hickok frequently discussed the "low wages" paid to Baltimore workers; see, for example, Lowitt and Beasley, *One Third of a Nation*, 342, 343, 348, 349, 350, 351. For an examination of the disparity between black and white wages, see Reid, *Negro Community*, 16, 38–53.

3. U.S. Bureau of the Census, *Fourteenth Census, 1920: Population*; *Fifteenth Census, 1930: Population*; *Abstract of the Fifteenth Census*, 435, 437, 449; "Information Bulletin No. 2," *Baltimore* 19 (February 1926): 15; "Business Conditions in Baltimore as of December 1," *Baltimore* 19 (December 1925): 19; "Information Bulletin No. 3," *Baltimore* 19 (March 1926): 13. See also Dorothy Brown, "Maryland between the Wars," 697; Olson, *Baltimore*, 302–23.

4. *Baltimore* 19 (December 1925); Dorothy Brown, "Maryland between the Wars," 698–99; "Survey of Unemployment in Baltimore, February, 1930," *Monthly Labor Review* 30 (April 1930): 738–39; U.S. Bureau of the Census, *Statistical Abstract*, 790; *Fifteenth Census, 1930: Unemployment*, 29.

5. *Abstract of the Fifteenth Census*, 449; Reid, *Negro Community*, 15, 19, 23, 27, 29, 79, 130.

6. Reid, *Negro Community*, 148–53; Maryland, *Report of the Governor's Commission*, 85; Dorothy Brown, "Maryland between the Wars," 726; Olson, *Baltimore*, 325–37; *Abstract of the Fifteenth Census*, 435; "Report of the Associated Architects of Baltimore, Inc., to the Maryland Emergency Housing and Park Commission," PHA, Project Files, RG 196, Box 206, NA.

7. Garonzik, "Baltimore Neighborhoods"; Beirne, "Residential Growth"; "Report of the Associated Architects of Baltimore," PHA, Project Files, RG 196, Box 206, NA. See also Beirne, "Steadfast Americans." The persistence rate for Canton in the 1880s was a remarkable 75 percent, and for the entire period between 1880 and 1920, fully 30 percent of the residents stayed in the neighborhood.

8. *Fifteenth Census, 1930*; Olson, *Baltimore*, 325.

9. The average percentage of foreign stock in the ten largest cities in 1930 was 53.4; see Bruce Stave, *New Deal and the Last Hurrah*, 41. Based on ward-level population data, the index of dissimilarity for immigrant groups in Baltimore in 1940 was 30.2. *Fifteenth Census, 1930*; *Sixteenth Census, 1940*; Fox, "Social-Cultural Developments," 508.

10. See the news clippings on the KKK in the Vertical File, EPFL, including Sheldon Smith, "K.K.K. Empire Was Once Strong Here," *Evening Sun*, 20 January 1966. *Evening Sun*, 15 April; 9, 13, 19, 21 September; 22 June 1923; 25 February 1933; *Sun*, 9 September; 25, 29 October 1922; 16, 20 May; 19 August 1924; 3 June 1925; Dorothy Brown, "Maryland between the Wars," 714–15; *Catholic Review*, 24 November 1939.

11. Polish-American Roosevelt Democratic Club to FDR, 22 October 1936, DNCP, Official File, No. 300; FDR to Anthony J. Sochwrek, 28 October 1935, President's Personal File, No. 1945, FDRP. See also Chapters 2 and 7.

12. "Business Conditions in Baltimore Area," *Baltimore* 23 (April 1930): 9; "Baltimore Less Hurt," *Baltimore* 24 (February 1931): 43; Dorothy Brown, "Maryland between the Wars," 731.

13. *Fifteenth Census, 1930*; Reid, *Negro Community*, 55, 65–67; *Sixteenth Census, 1940*.

14. *JPCC*, 20 December, 1932, 812–13; *Sun*, 2 January 1933; 17 September 1930; 25 September 1936. See also *Sun*, 17 March 1930. The Gallup quotation is from

Bernstein, *A Caring Society* (p. 291); Bernstein notes that two important groups, women and blacks, went "uncared for" during the New Deal (286–87). Instances of legislative attempts to restrict work among married women can be found in Scimé, "Public Policy and the Married Working Woman," 4–6.

15. *Sun*, 27 February 1933; 25 September 1936; 28, 29 July; 12 March; 3 August, 1937; *Evening Sun*, 2 March 1937. In *To Work and to Wed*, Lois Scharf thoughtfully deals with the discrimination women faced in the 1930s; she also briefly discusses the inequalities within the New Deal programs (pp. 122–30). See also Blackwelder, *Women of the Depression*.

16. All relief comparisons are based on the data provided in BERC, *Annual Statistical Reports*. Also see Emergency Charity Association, *Annual Statistical Report*, 51, 58.

17. *Sun*, 12 April; 18 May; 27 June 1938. Between 1935 and 1937, the divorce rate rose 22 percent; see *Sun*, 2 January 1938.

18. Reid, *Negro Community*, 130; *Sun*, 25, 27 May 1937.

19. Mayor Jackson's attitudes toward public relief are more fully analyzed in Chapter 2, and his political activities in Chapter 7.

20. Reid, *Negro Community*, 216–18; Baltimore *Afro-American*, 27 April 1923.

21. Frank N. Trager to the author, 24 October 1975; Joel Seidman to the author, 17 November 1975; *Maryland Leader*, 22 June 1934; Reid, *Negro Community*, 190–93, 210.

22. William Curran to James A. Farley, 4 September 1936, Farley Correspondence, Box 1095, DNCP; Mary W. Dewson to Millard Tydings, 22 September 1936, Women's Division, Box 81, DNCP; *Sun*, 31 January 1934; Dorothy Brown, "Election of 1934."

23. The *Worcester Democrat and Ledger-Enterprise* (12 December 1931) defended the 1931 lynching as an example of "heroic methods of treating such varmient [*sic*]." See also Dorothy Brown, "Maryland between the Wars," 719.

24. Chepaitis, "Albert Cabell Ritchie," 39; *Sun*, 23 March 1920; *Fourteenth Census, 1920*; *Fifteenth Census, 1930*.

25. "Judge Coleman's Charge to the Jury," United States District Court, 17 February 1928, Vertical File, EPFL; Dorothy Brown, "Maryland between the Wars," 710–13.

26. *Sun*, 21 March; 2, 3 April; 26 May; 19 October 1933; Olson, *Baltimore*, 331–32.

27. Elvove, "State Bank Failures in Maryland," 36–54; Maryland, Bank Commissioners, *Twenty-Fourth Annual Report*, 18–19.

28. *Sun*, 29 January; 27 February; 4, 7, 8, 12, 24 March 1933; "WCAO, Saturday Evening, 25 February 1933," Ritchie Executive Papers, Box 4(b), MHR.

29. *Sun*, 3, 4, 8, 10, 12 March 1933.

30. Maryland, Bank Commissioners, *Twenty-Fourth Annual Report*, 18–19; *Maryland Leader*, 25 March 1933; *Sun*, 14, 17, 21, 22, 25 March 1933.

31. *Sun*, 31 March; 13 April 1933.

Chapter 2

1. "Mayor's Message to City Council of Baltimore," *JPCC*, 28 June 1937, 298.

2. "Survey of Unemployment in Baltimore, February, 1930," *Monthly Labor Review* 30 (April 1930): 738–39; Maryland, Commissioner of Labor and Statistics, *Thirty-eighth Annual Report* (1929), and *Thirty-ninth Annual Report* (1930); Baltimore Social Service Exchange, *Executive Report for 1929*, and *Minutes of Meetings*, August 1920–January 1932; *Evening Sun*, 18 March 1932; FWA, *Annual Report for 1929*, 7, 9.

3. FWA, *Annual Reports*, 1929, 1930, 1931; *Evening Sun*, 2 December 1930; "Report of Unemployment Relief Situation in Maryland, October 23, 1931," President's Organization on Unemployment Relief, No. 620.1, RG 73, NA; Kimberly, "The Depression," 19. A number of studies have documented the collapse of private resources; see in particular Schwartz, "Unemployment Relief in Philadelphia." For a fuller explanation of the Baltimore situation, see Argersinger, "From Charity to the Dole." Baltimore's 19 percent unemployment rate in 1931 was disputed by FWA social workers, who claimed that it did not include all the jobless blacks in the city.

4. *Evening Sun*, 12 March; 2 May 1930; 2 January; 3, 17 February; 9 March 1931; Reid, *Negro Community*, 127; Jones, "Charity But Not Work"; Gibson, "Family and Child Welfare Agencies," 132, 140; Cahn, *Man's Concern*, 21, 22.

5. *Sun*, 13 May 1933; 8 February 1936.

6. *Evening Sun*, 14, 25 February; 24 March; 31 December 1931; *Municipal Journal*, 6 March; 4 September 1931; Cahn, *Man's Concern*, 22.

7. *Evening Sun*, 1 January 1929; 27 January, 11 April 1930.

8. *Evening Sun*, 10 June 1930; 12 March 1931; 4 September 1930; Baltimore, *Mayor's Message*, 26 May 1930; Baltimore, Municipal Commission on Employment Stabilization, *Report of the Municipal Commission*, 2–3. The Stabilization Commission's membership included representatives from the business, social service, religious, and academic communities.

9. *Municipal Journal*, 31 July 1931; *Sun*, 1 January; 21 March 1933; *Evening Sun*, 4, 6, 17 September 1930; *Maryland Leader*, 26 September 1931; Baltimore, Municipal Commission on Employment Stabilization, "Report on the Shorter Work Week," and "Unemployment Insurance." Also see reports in Governor's Correspondence–Ritchie, Unemployment Insurance, MHR.

10. *Evening Sun*, 18 March 1932; Ritchie, "Unemployment Relief—If Business will do nothing about it, Government will," 30 July 1931, Ritchie Executive Papers, Box 8006, MHR; *Municipal Journal*, 16 May; 14 November 1930; 24 April; 15 May 1931; Baltimore, Municipal Commission on Employment Stabilization, *Report of the Municipal Commission*, 3. For a fuller discussion of Ritchie's role in the failure of unemployment insurance, see Argersinger, "Baltimore: The Depression Years," 300–302.

11. Baltimore, *Mayor [Broening] Report*; *Municipal Journal*, 24 April; 15, 22 May; 13, 31 July; 14 August 1931; *Evening Sun*, 6 March; 3 April; 6, 17 September;

1, 3, 4, 8, 22 December 1930; 6 February 1932; *JPCC*, Sessions 1931–32, 1093; Harry Greenstein to Howard Jackson, 14 August 1931, Jackson Administrative Files, RG 9, Series #19, E 50–7, Box 218, BCA.

12. Bogue, *Report of a Study of Needs*, 9; Reid, *Negro Community*, 195; *Evening Sun*, 1, 28 January; 16 December 1931; 1, 13 January; 19 March; 15 February 1932.

13. *Evening Sun*, 15, 22, 26 March 1932; 30, 31 January; 1, 2 February 1933.

14. *Sun*, 4 November; 1, 4, 8 December 1932; Kimberly, "The Depression," 50–51.

15. *Sun*, 15, 16 December 1932; 4 April 1933.

16. "Emergency Work Bureau–Placement Record," March 1933, Jackson Administrative Files, RG 9, Series #19, E 50–7(31), Box 217, BCA (for other reports, see Box 216); *Evening Sun*, 30, 31 January; 1, 2 February 1933.

17. *Sun*, 5, 21 June 1933.

18. *Sun*, 21 June 1933; BERC, *First Annual Statistical Report*, 2.

19. BERC, *First Annual Statistical Report*, 2; Waxter and Euchtman, "Administration of Public Welfare," 20–21. BERC did, however, increase the relief family's weekly budget from just over $1.00 to $2.71 per person; see *Sun*, 24 July 1934; 1 September 1935. Estimates of the number of people out of work varied widely and were not consistent even in BERC's own reports. I have used the more conservative figures, which probably underestimated the number of unemployed blacks. Compared to other large cities, Baltimore's rate of unemployment until 1932 was less severe; in 1930, for example, the national urban average was 16 percent, whereas Baltimore began the year at about 8 percent and closed the year with 12 percent unemployed.

20. BERC, "Baltimore Study," FERA, State Files (Maryland), RG 69, No. 400, NA; BERC, *First Annual Statistical Report*, 2; Manny and Clowes, *Analysis of the Relief Population*, 12; Baltimore Council of Social Agencies, "Analysis of Relief Expenditures," 30–32; *Evening Sun*, 31 January 1933; *Sun*, 22 June 1933. Although corporations no longer paid the salaries of relief administrators, the Associated Jewish Charities provided its top official, Harry Greenstein, to serve as director of the Maryland Emergency Relief Administration. From 1933 until 1936, when Greenstein resigned, the Jewish Charities paid his salary; see *Sun*, 8 February 1936.

21. BERC, "Baltimore Study," FERA, State Files, RG 69, No. 400, NA. A "case" referred to the household receiving relief; the average "case" represented about four people in 1933. Mayor Jackson contrasted sharply with other big-city mayors in his opposition to the CWA. For a fuller description of the CWA in Baltimore, see Chapter 3.

22. Robert Kelso to Harry Hopkins, 26 June and 1 July 1933, FERA, RG 69, No. 406; Alan Johnstone to the Unemployment Relief Commission of the Maryland State Board for Aid and Charities, 31 July 1933, FERA, RG 69, No. 127, NA.

23. A. C. DeLange to Harry Hopkins, 20 November 1933, FERA, RG 69, No. 460; FERA, "Special Folder–Baltimore Study," FERA, RG 69, No. 400, NA. Because FERA officials relied on earlier data they erroneously placed the relief load at 20 percent of the population. In fact, when the FERA finished its investigation, the level was down to about 15 percent; between May and July 1934, BERC reduced the rolls significantly.

24. FERA, "Special Folder–Baltimore Study," FERA, RG 69, No. 400; William J.

Plunkert to Harry Greenstein, 6 June 1934, FERA, RG 69, No. 420, NA. State and federal officials received letters from ministers, physicians, and members of the city's black communities citing inequalities in relief distribution. One physician complained to Governor Harry Nice that blacks received weekly relief allowances of only $1.70 per person, compared to the white standard of $2.70. He urged Nice to appoint a state official to "see after the interest" of blacks in the city. See David N. E. Campbell to Harry Nice, 24 May 1935, Governor's Correspondence–Nice, Relief Box 8064 (2), MHR. Examples of inconsistencies in the reports of private agencies can be found in the Jackson Administrative Files, 1933–34, RG 9, Series #19, E 50–7(3), Box 213, BCA.

25. Arch Mandel to Bruce McClure, 5 July 1934; Arch Mandel to Harry Hopkins, 15 October 1934, FERA, RG 69, No. 406; FERA, "Special Folder–Baltimore Study," FERA, RG 69, No. 400, NA; *Sun*, 14 July 1934. See also Mandel to Hopkins, 15 October 1934, and Mandel to Hopkins, 17 December 1934, Harry Hopkins Papers, Maryland–Field Reports, Box 58, FDRL.

26. Aubrey Williams to Arch Mandel, 29 May 1934; "Relief Expenditures in Maryland," 2 March 1934, FERA, RG 69, No. 406; "Summary Data Regarding State and Local Relief Funds," 1 June 1934, FERA, RG 69, No. 400; Arch Mandel to Harry Hopkins, 15 October 1934, FERA, RG 69, No. 420, NA; *Sun*, 1, 6, 15 March; 25 May; 14 August 1934; Baltimore Council of Social Agencies, "Analysis of Relief Expenditures," 36. In the fourth quarter of 1933, the city contributed 0.3 percent of the total relief expenditures, the state nothing, and the federal government 99.7 percent. The state's proportion improved to 37.7 percent in the first quarter of 1934 but dropped to 9.2 percent in the second; thereafter, the state kept its contributions between 13 percent and 23 percent.

27. *Sun*, 2 June 1934; Dorothy Brown, "Maryland between the Wars," 744; Eugene S. Leggett to Bruce McClure, 31 May 1934, FERA, RG 69, No. 400, NA. Mayor Jackson's public denouncements of the federal and state governments' failure to meet the city's relief problems angered Harry Hopkins. A few days before the June meeting, Hopkins suggested to Ritchie that they alone resolve the relief issue, adding, "I don't see any use of having the Mayor [present at the meeting], do you?" But Ritchie reminded Hopkins that "it concerns Baltimore City." See "Mr. Hopkins's telephone conversation with Governor Richey [*sic*]," Hopkins Papers, Telephone Conversations, Box 74, FDRL.

28. *Sun*, 2 June 1934.

29. Kimberly, "The Depression," 99–100; *Sun*, 9, 12 June 1934.

30. *Maryland Leader*, 22 September 1934; *Sun*, 3, 10, 21, 24 July; 1 August; 10 September 1934; George Frederick to Howard Jackson, 9 May 1934, Jackson Administrative Files, RG 9, Series #19, E 50–7(5), Box 214, BCA. In June Boston still had 16.9 percent of its population on relief but it had lowered its payments from $12.01 to $10.98. Other cities actually increased relief payments; Buffalo went from $12.66 a week in May to $13.06 in June.

31. "Conference: Peoples Unemployment League, Baltimore, Maryland, and Au-

brey Williams," 24 August 1934, FERA, RG 69, No. 460, NA; *Sun*, 31 July 1934.

32. *Evening Sun*, 1 September 1934; *Sun*, 31 July; 7, 10, 18 August 1934.

33. John Finbar Jones and John Middlemist Herrick in *Citizens in Service* argue that the intervention of the federal government into social welfare did not result in a decline in the number of volunteers but, in fact, "brought many volunteers into public agencies" (p. 22). The present study agrees with their findings that the New Deal actually encouraged citizen participation in the form of voluntary service, but it also argues that the New Deal changed the organization of relief so that volunteers no longer participated in the fields of family welfare and relief in the ways they had before 1933. Jones and Herrick also describe some of these adjustments made by private agencies; see especially pp. 41, 95, 98–99.

34. *Maryland Leader*, 1 April; 23 December 1933; 20 January; 8, 15 December 1934; *Sun*, 22, 23 August; 4 September 1934.

35. Arch Mandel to Harry Hopkins, 9 February 1935, FERA, RG 69, No. 420, NA; D. Luke Hopkins to Harry Nice, 20 March 1935, Relief Box 8064 (5); "Radio Address on Relief, Etc.," Governor's Correspondence–Nice, Relief Box 8064 (1), MHR; Ritchie, "The 'Fifty-Fifty' System of Federal Aid," 6.

36. "Radio Address on Relief, Etc.," Governor's Correspondence–Nice, Relief Box 8064 (1), MHR; telegram, Harry Hopkins to Harry Nice, 13 March 1935 (the same telegram was sent to Lansdale G. Sasscer, president of the Maryland Senate); Harry Nice to Aubrey Williams, 15 March 1935, FERA, RG 69, No. 401, NA; *Sun*, 10 January 1935.

37. Arch Mandel to Harry Hopkins, 10 April 1935, Hopkins Papers, Maryland–Field Reports, Box 58, FDRL; *Sun*, 19 December 1938. This same legislator freely admitted his persistent inability to distinguish the PWA from the WPA and his total ignorance of the funding mechanisms for these programs.

38. *Sun*, 18 January; 13, 18, 19 February; 8, 12, 19, 25, 28 March 1935; *Evening Sun*, 5, 18, 15 March 1935; Emanuel Gorfine to Harry Hopkins, 19 March 1935, FERA, RG 69, No. 401; Arch Mandel to Harry Hopkins, 10 April 1935, FERA, RG 69, No. 406.1, NA; Harry Hopkins to Harry Nice, 20 March 1935, Governor's Correspondence–Nice, Relief Box 8064 (5), MHR; Arch Mandel to Harry Hopkins, 10 April 1935, Hopkins Papers, Maryland–Field Reports, Box 58, FDRL.

39. R. C. Hall to Hopkins, 1 September 1935; Robert O. Bonnell, Edwin L. Leonard, and Sidney Lansburgh to Hopkins, 30 August 1935; Williams to Bonnell, 3 September 1935; Ruth Blakeslee to Aubrey Williams, 28 October 1935; Esther Lazarus to Hopkins, 5 September 1935; Harry Greenstein to Hopkins, 11 September 1935; Aubrey Williams to Greenstein, 13 September 1935, FERA, RG 69, No. 401; Frank Trager to Hopkins, 9 May 1935; James Blackwell to Hopkins, 10 August 1935; Elisabeth Gilman to Hopkins, 6 September 1935, FERA, RG 69, No. 453–60, NA; "Statement of Delegation Representing the People's Unemployment League of Maryland"; James Blackwell to Hopkins, 6 September 1935; "Minutes, Meeting of the Baltimore Unemployed League [*sic*] with Aubrey Williams, September 12, 1935,"

FERA, RG 69, No. 400, NA; Arthur Hungerford to Nice, 11 February 1935, Governor's Correspondence–Nice, Relief Box 8064 (1), MHR; *Evening Sun*, 27 May 1935; "Proposals on Relief," submitted by the PUL to BERC, 14 February 1935, Jackson Administrative Files, RG 9, Series #19, E 50–7(3), Box 213, BCA.

40. Harry Greenstein to Harry Hopkins, 11 September 1935; Aubrey Williams to Harry Greenstein, 13 September 1935, FERA, RG 69, No. 401; James Blackwell to Harry Hopkins, 10 August 1935, FERA, RG 69, No. 453–60; "Minutes, Meeting of the Baltimore Unemployed League," FERA, RG 69, No. 400, NA; Kimberly, "The Depression," 149; *Sun*, 13 September; 1 November; 1 December 1935. Governor Nice appointed the PUL chairman to his unemployment committee but his gesture failed to still the league's criticism. By December 1935, the PUL was denouncing the committee's failure to meet more frequently and Nice's refusal to call a special session; see James Blackwell to Harry Nice, 31 December 1935, Governor's Correspondence–Nice, Relief Box 8064 (5), MHR.

41. Esther Lazarus to Harry Hopkins, 5 September 1935, FERA, RG 69, No. 401, NA; Baltimore Emergency Relief Commission to Lazarus, 11 January 1936; Richard Cleveland to Harry Nice, 10 May 1935, Governor's Correspondence–Nice, Relief Box 8064 (5); D. Luke Hopkins to Harry Nice, 12 September 1935, Governor's Correspondence–Nice, Relief Box 8064 (1), MHR; *Sun*, 5 January 1936. By September 1935, BERC had reduced weekly relief budgets by nearly 28 percent, down to $1.95 per person; see *Sun*, 13 September 1935.

42. FWA, *Annual Report for 1936*; *Sun*, 16 November; 31 December 1935; 17, 18, 28 January; 7, 8, 10, 21 February; 3 March 1936.

43. *Sun*, 1, 5, 6 January; 3 March 1936; "Minutes of Joint Meeting of the Board of State Aid and Charities, Representatives of the Baltimore Emergency Relief Commission, and Mayor Howard W. Jackson," 7 January 1936, Governor's Correspondence–Nice, Relief Box 8064 (5), MHR. Especially active among the city's religious leaders was W. Owings Stone, a PUL member and the rector of St. Mary's Protestant Episcopal Church.

44. *Sun*, 6 January 1936.

45. Herbert R. O'Conor to Harry Nice, 5 January 1936, Governor's Correspondence–Nice, Relief Box 8064 (5), MHR; *Sun*, 6, 19, 25, 27 January 1936. Nice repeatedly told organized citizen groups that the city should borrow money to meet the relief crisis, saying on one occasion, "You must recollect that the City of Baltimore has spent comparatively little money for relief, and when it did borrow it was reimbursed by the state." See Nice to "Committee on Relief," Baltimore M. E. Preachers' Meeting, 29 January 1936; Nice to W. T. Dubel, 4 February 1936, Governor's Correspondence–Nice, Relief Box 8064 (5), MHR; *Sun*, 13 September 1935.

46. *Sun*, 18 December; 13 September 1935. Federal officials consistently pressured BERC to establish more work-relief projects; see, for example, Arch Mandel to Harry Hopkins, 15 October; 17 December 1934; 9 February 1935, Hopkins Papers, Maryland–Field Reports, Box 58, FDRL. BERC never established a substantive work-relief

program, offering instead jobs for white-collar workers. At its peak, the program employed only 4,000 men. National Emergency Council, *Report of the Proceedings of the Statewide Coordination Meeting*, 10; "Mr. Hopkins's telephone conversation with Mr. Dryden, this date," 8 November 1935, WPA, State Files (Maryland), RG 69, No. 610, NA. The term "unemployable" simply referred to those physically unable to work—but, in practice, men over 45 "considered unemployable by industry" and relief clients who had been on the relief rolls for a number of years were placed in the "unemployable" category. Rather than assist those who were spurned by private industry, the WPA merely adopted industry's standards. To "kill the prejudice against employing men over 45," the Community Fund established a Community Placement Bureau staffed by prominent business leaders and designed to find jobs for such "unemployables." BERC faced a more difficult task in attempting to persuade the WPA that clients on the city's relief rolls were receiving direct relief because of BERC's policies and not the recipients' inabilities; see *Sun*, 30 August 1935; 29 July 1937.

47. BERC, *Third Annual Statistical Report*, 1; BERC, *Financial Report*, 5; T. J. S. Waxter to George W. Strove, 6 January 1938, WPA, RG 69, No. 640, NA.

48. Maryland, *Report of the Committee on State Policy and Revenue*, 1–10; *Sun*, 5 March 1935; 4, 5, 6, 7 March; 3 April; 22 May 1936; Kimberly, "The Depression," 164–66.

49. BERC, *Financial Report*, 4; *Labor Herald*, 5 June 1936; *Sun*, 22, 29 May 1936.

50. *Sun*, 23 May; 6, 7, 10 June 1936; "Minutes," Special Relief Committee, 28 May; 5 June 1936, Jackson Administrative Files, RG 9, Series #20, A2–8(8), Box 230, BCA.

51. Emergency Charity Association, *Annual Statistical Report*; *Labor Herald*, 1 October 1937; *Sun*, 9, 10, 19 June; 1, 2 July; 21 August; 2 December 1936.

52. Citizens' Alliance for Social Security, "Relief Purge"; *Sun*, 13, 23, 24 June; 15 July 1936.

53. *Sun*, 12, 13 January 1936.

54. *Sun*, 30, 31 January; 1 February; 17 March; 7, 14, 15, 23 April; 5, 8 May 1936; 15, 21, 22 April 1937; *Evening Sun*, 16 March; 2 April; 5 May 1936; Kimberly, "The Depression," 311–12. Jackson was sorely disappointed with the 1937 relief budget; he had expected not only adequate operating funds but reimbursement for the city's $1.5 million outlay for the Emergency Charity Association (ECA). He received neither and immediately instructed the ECA to reduce its rolls. The divisions between Baltimore and the counties became so severe in the 1937 session that Baltimore's senators publicly attacked the "provincial" leadership of the state senate and urged the "ousting" of the senate's president; see *Sun*, 15 April 1937.

55. Lee L. Dopkin to John G. Winant, 9 December 1935, Governor's Correspondence–Nice, Relief Box 8064 (5), MHR; *Sun*, 18 January; 5 February; 20 March; 12 April; 20 May; 15, 20, 26 November; 12, 13, 17, 18 December 1936; 7 January; 29 August; 24, 30 September 1937; Baltimore, Department of Public Welfare, *Annual Statistical Report*. Beginning in 1936, in accordance with state legislation passed in

1935, the city Department of Welfare inaugurated its own old-age pension system. Surprise visits to the homes of a number of pensioners revealed devastating poverty; see *Sun*, 12 January 1936. To participate in the federal Social Security program, Maryland revised its system. Lump-sum payments to those citizens who were too old to qualify for assistance were begun in many cities in 1937; in Baltimore, in 1938.

56. *Sun*, 26 September; 31 December 1937; 3, 11, 25 January 1938; Maryland, Unemployment Compensation Board, *Second Annual Report*, 5–9.

57. *Labor Herald*, 1 June 1936; *Sun*, 26 September 1937; 25, 30 January; 12 February 1938.

58. *Sun*, 1 April; 18 May 1937.

59. Citizens' Alliance, "Relief Purge."

60. *Sun*, 18 May; 1, 4, 10 June 1937; 22 May; 15 June; 1 September 1938; 4, 11 May; 30 July 1939. It is probable that the administrative reorganization in 1939 at the state and local levels represented the filtering down of what Barry Karl has termed the "Third New Deal." Although that third phase fell prey at the national level to historical concerns about the power of the presidency and the balance of authority between localities and the federal government, it still provoked certain changes in Baltimore and Annapolis. Responding to federal criticisms, or in an attempt to preclude greater federal intervention, the city and the state attempted to "modernize" or "reorganize" their administrations; see Karl, *The Uneasy State*, 180–81.

61. *Sun*, 1 September 1938; 19, 22, 23 March; 8 November 1939.

62. *Sun*, 16 July 1938; 22 June; 28 November 1939. The results of the study were published in "Family Welfare and General Dependency," *Councillor* 4 (December 1939): 11–19. According to the survey, Baltimore relief programs spent, on a per capita basis, $4.26 for the WPA and the National Youth Administration program, $1.30 for the Civilian Conservation Corps, $13.31 for general public assistance, and $7.75 for relief programs. The other cities averaged, for the same expenditures: $18.32, $1.60, $30.18, and $10.26. Additionally, Baltimore continued to place more emphasis on direct relief, and it spent less than one-half as much as the other cities for work-relief programs.

63. *Sun*, 7 January 1935; 22 June 1939.

64. Adam J. Hazlett to Governor Harry Nice, 27 March 1936, Governor's Correspondence–Nice, Relief Box 8064 (1), MHR; *Sun*, 21 May 1936.

65. W. Owings Stone to Harry Nice, 3 December 1935, Governor's Correspondence–Nice, Relief Box 8064 (5), MHR.

66. See Berkowitz and McQuaid, "Businessman and Bureaucrat." I agree with their argument concerning the significant influence wielded by businessmen and bureaucrats but I also maintain that too little emphasis is placed on the organizational influence of private agencies and social workers in shaping welfare systems.

Chapter 3

1. *Sun*, 22, 23, 25, 27 May 1933.

2. Richard F. Cleveland to Albert C. Ritchie, 2 June 1933, Governor's Correspondence–Ritchie, Box 8006, MHR; *Sun*, 5, 7, 8, 12, 13, 16 June; 4 July 1933.

3. *Sun*, 19 May; 28 July 1933.

4. *Sun*, 19 June; 29 July 1933. Sara A. Whitehurst to Albert C. Ritchie, 25 October 1933, Governor's Correspondence–Ritchie, Box 23(a), MHR; Baltimore *Afro-American*, 26 August 1933. Within a month, however, a similar *Afro-American* survey found that the initial enthusiasm among blacks had dramatically diminished. Most responded to the question, "Just What Has the National Recovery Act Meant to You So Far?" with the reply "Nothing." One woman declared, "The N.R.A. has meant the same thing to me, no work for neither me nor my husband," and a Reverend F. F. King of south Baltimore observed that "the N.R.A. seems especially ineffective in the industrial districts that come under my [religious] supervision"; see *Afro-American*, 23 September 1933.

5. *Sun*, 16, 28, 30 June; 26 August 1933; Baltimore *Afro-American*, 15 April; 26 August 1933.

6. *Sun*, 11 September 1935; 18 August 1937; Kimberly, "The Depression," 117–22.

7. *Sun*, 30 August 1935; 18 August 1937; Biweekly reports, 25 May 1934, Box 412, and 9 November 1934, Box 180, NEC, RG 44, WNRC.

8. Arthur Hungerford to Donald Richberg, 18 August 1934, NEC, Box 180, RG 44, WNRC; "Weekly Report for week ending April 13, 1935"; G. R. Parker to Hungerford, 25 April 1935, NRA, State Files (Maryland), RG 9, No. 512, NA; *Sun*, 30 August; 11 September 1935; *Evening Sun*, 7, 18 March 1935. The post of Maryland NRA director was abolished in September 1935, but before its abolition Hungerford resigned to become the state director of the National Emergency Council. Frederic Lee, a former aide to Governor Ritchie, served briefly as the NRA compliance director. See *Sun*, 11 September 1935.

9. *Sun*, 11 September; 5, 11 November 1933; U.S. Federal Emergency Administration of Public Works, Press Release No. 7, 10 July 1933, Governor's Correspondence–Ritchie, Box 12 (d), MHR.

10. *Sun*, 11 January 1934.

11. E. Brooke Lee to Albert C. Ritchie, 11 January 1934, Governor's Correspondence–Ritchie, Box 12 (d), MHR; *Sun*, 11, 20 January 1934; BERC, *First Annual Report*, 44.

12. Lee to Ritchie, 11 January 1934; *Sun*, 9, 10 January 1934.

13. Maryland State Planning Commission (MSPC), *Appraisal*, March 1938 (no pagination); Franklin D. Roosevelt to Harry Nice, 22 December 1934; Nice to Roosevelt, 27 December 1934, Governor's Correspondence–Nice, Relief Box 8064 (2), MHR. See also the synopsis of correspondence dated 25 March 1935, in the same box.

14. *Sun*, 9, 10 January 1934.

15. Harry Hopkins to Richard Cleveland, 10 November 1933; Samuel Shannahan, Richard Cleveland, Sidney Hollander, William Garvin, and Harry Greenstein to Harry Hopkins, 11 December 1933, CWA, RG 69, No. 20, NA.

16. Kaplan and Schuchat, *Harry Greenstein*, 21–30; Harry Greenstein to Jacob Baker, 7 December 1933, CWA, RG 69, No. 20, NA.

17. Harry Hopkins to Richard Cleveland, 28 February 1934; Cleveland to Jacob Baker, 7 December 1933 (in this particular instance Cleveland received plans and directions for CWA projects in Norfolk); Arthur Goldschmidt to F. H. Dryden (CWA State Engineer), 21 February 1934; Bennet Schnuffler to Millard Tydings, 19 April 1934; Hopkins to Harry Greenstein, 24 November 1933; Watson to Corington Gill, 20 November 1933; Gustave Wirth to Hopkins, 17 January 1934; Greenstein to John Carmody, 24 January 1934; Dryden to Carmody, 26 January 1934; Greenstein to Carmody, 7 December 1933—all in CWA, RG 69, No. 20, NA; *Sun*, 18, 19, 23, 26 January; 14 February 1934.

18. Bruce McClure to Rev. Charles Walker, 18 December 1933, CWA, RG 69, No. 20, NA; all percentages are derived from the data provided in BERC's *First Annual Report*. For Mayor Jackson's personal requests for CWA jobs, see the Jackson Administrative Files, RG 9, Series #19, A15–3360(2), Box 202, and A15–3360(3), Box 203, BCA.

19. Hopkins's quotation is from Schwartz, *Civil Works Administration*, 179. Memorandum to Harry Hopkins, 6 December 1933; Viola Bassem et al. to Bruce McClure, 11 December 1933, CWA, RG 69, No. 20; "Transcript of telephone conversation between Emma Ward and Miss Owings" (undated); Ward to Ellen Woodward, 21 December 1933, FERA, RG 69, No. 453, NA; *Sun*, 31 January 1934; 4 September 1935. In addition to the CWA, the Civil Works Service (CWS) was established to provide employment for white-collar personnel in "relief offices and education." The CWS employed about 500 women in Baltimore, many of whom were "janitoresses" at relief office buildings. Despite the initial focus on white-collar workers, most CWS employees in Baltimore were not in white-collar positions, and the program was subsequently widened to include "sewing, gardening, canning, teaching, and other work in connection with the emergency education programs and personnel." Finally, the CWS, unlike the CWA, was funded by local, state, and federal money and the hourly wages were lower than those paid under the CWA. For a general description of the national program, see Schwartz, *Civil Works Administration*, 165–66. For Baltimore's experience with the CWS, see Ward to Ellen S. Woodward, 27, 31 December 1933, No. 453, and J. Warren Belcher to Harry Greenstein, 25 January 1934, No. 453.2, FERA, RG 69, NA.

20. Leuchtenburg, *Franklin D. Roosevelt*, 121–22; *Sun*, 23, 26 January 1934; MSPC, *Appraisal*, March 1938. Repeating the findings of the 1938 commission report is Kimberly, "The Depression," 80–82. The *Sun* rarely tired of denigrating the CWA. It resented both the degree of federal authority and the assistance to "common laborers" (about 90 percent of the CWA's projects involved manual labor). Because Hopkins

attempted to construct the program rapidly and because he had to overcome a number of local obstacles, the *Sun* was able to report regularly on bureaucratic snarls in the operation of the CWA. It did so with relish; see, for example, *Sun*, 18 August 1936.

21. Trout, *Boston*, 155–61. James Wickens notes similar delays in the establishment of the CWA in Colorado (*Colorado*, 80).

22. U.S. Federal Works Agency, *Final Report on the WPA*, 8; *Sun*, 8 August 1935.

23. *Evening Sun*, 18 July; 7 August 1935; Kirwin, *Herbert R. O'Conor*, 153; Kimberly, "The Depression," 141–44; John Mackall to Harry Hopkins, 19 May 1935, WPA, State Files (Maryland), RG 69, No. 610, NA; MSPC, *Appraisal*, March 1938.

24. *Sun*, 8, 9, 16 August 1935; "Telephone Conversation between Hopkins and Dryden," 15 August 1935, WPA, RG 69, No. 610, NA; Kimberly, "The Depression," 144–46; "Mr. Hopkins and Mr. Dryden," 15 August 1935, Harry Hopkins Papers, No. 74, FDRL.

25. *Washington Post*, 10 August 1935, in WPA, RG 69, No. 610, NA; MSPC, *Appraisal*, March 1938; U.S. Federal Works Agency, *Final Report on the WPA*; *Sun*, 2, 13, 24 September; 9, 13 December 1935. The urban-rural split in most states was usually 75 percent–25 percent, but county opposition in Maryland proved so strong that Baltimore officially received only 50 percent of the total WPA quota. In practice, however, Baltimore averaged between 50 and 55 percent of the state's quota, which at its peak stood at 27,000 jobs. Downward revisions of the quota beginning in 1936 meant that for most of the decade the city had between 7,000 and 10,000 jobs under the WPA. See *Sun*, 3 June; 12 December 1937; 9 May; 13 November 1938; and "Meeting of the City Delegation to the Legislature on February 21, 1936," NEC, RG 44, Maryland, Coordinating Correspondence, WNRC.

26. *Sun*, 2 September 1935; "Mr. Hopkins's telephone conversation with Mr. Dryden, this date," 8 November 1935, WPA, RG 69, No. 610, NA. Dryden's evaluation of the relief population resulted largely from his conviction that relief recipients who had been receiving direct assistance for a number of years were unemployable. This characterization worked an unfair burden on Baltimore's jobless because BERC's policy had consistently minimized work-relief programs in order to cut costs.

27. "Mr. Hopkins's telephone conversation with Mr. Dryden," 8 November 1935, WPA, RG 69, No. 610, NA. See also "Mr. Hopkins's telephone conversation with Dryden, this date," 17 December 1935, Hopkins Papers, Box 74, FDRL.

28. Raymond Kennedy to Governor Nice, 28 October 1935, Governor's Correspondence–Nice, Relief Box 8064 (1), MHR; *Sun*, 3 October 1935.

29. *Sun*, 2, 12 September; 1 November; 1, 3, 4 December 1935; Harry Hopkins to Harry Nice, 6 November 1935; Nice to Hopkins, 9 November 1935, Governor's Correspondence–Nice, Relief Box 8064 (5), MHR. See also Raymond Kennedy to Harry Nice, 28 October 1935, and Nice to Kennedy, 19 October 1935, Governor's Correspondence–Nice, Relief Box 8064 (1), MHR.

30. *Sun*, 1, 2 January; 16 February, 1936; Harry Greenstein to Harry Nice, 3 December 1935, Governor's Correspondence–Nice, Relief Box 8064 (5), MHR.

31. *Sun*, 1, 2 January; 16 February 1936; Arthur Hungerford to Harry Nice, 16 November 1935, Governor's Correspondence–Nice, Relief Box 8064 (5), MHR.

32. MSPC, *Appraisal*, March 1938; Maryland, *Report of the Committee on State Policy and Revenue*, 32–33; Dorothy Brown, "Maryland between the Wars," 752–53; *Sun*, 24 January 1937.

33. F. H. Dryden to Arthur Goldschmidt, 4 May 1935, FERA, RG 69, No. 451; Dryden to Colonel George D. Babcock, n.d., FERA, RG 69, No. 450, NA; "Status of Writers' Program Activities in Region III," 31 October 1940, WPA, RG 69, No. 651.317, NA; "Works Progress Administration–Federal Writers' Project," clippings, Vertical File, EPFL; *Evening Sun*, 11 January 1936; 2 May 1939; *Sun*, 29 January; 9 July, 20 October 1936. The local production of "One-Third of a Nation" is discussed in greater detail in Chapter 4. It should also be noted that federal authorities vigorously protested the staffing of such projects as the writers' program with political appointments instead of qualified writers.

34. "Coordination: Repairing Light Workers," 9 December 1936; "Report on Light Work," 9 January 1937, NEC, RG 44, Box 357, WNRC.

35. Howard, *WPA and Federal Relief Policy*, 278–85; Scharf, *To Work and to Wed*, 124; "Mr. Hopkins's telephone conversation with Mr. Dryden," 17 December 1935, Hopkins Papers, Box 74, FDRL.

36. Howard, *WPA and Federal Relief Policy*, 285; *Sun*, 14 February 1937; 1 December 1936.

37. "Mr. Hopkins's telephone conversation with Mr. Dryden," 17 December 1935; Scharf, *To Work and to Wed*, 124; *Sun*, 22 November; 1 December 1936; 14 February 1937. The problems associated with the WPA sewing rooms also applied to the earlier sewing projects established under the CWA; see Schwartz, *Civil Works Administration*, 170–71.

38. Ellen Woodward to Edward Lewis, n.d., FERA, RG 69, No. 453, NA. Local school administrators encouraged young black women to take domestic science classes in high school, even renaming the courses to avoid the social stigma associated with domestic service. At the all-black Dunbar High School, for example, domestic courses were relabeled "vocational technical" courses, thereby attracting, according to a news reporter, a number of unsuspecting young women; see *Evening Sun*, 23 May 1938.

39. Bertha Avery Smith to Mary Robinson, 22 May 1938, Women's Bureau, Household Employment Correspondence, RG 86, Box 925, NA; Helmbold, "Making Choices, Making Do," 289–91; Katherine Rutherford to Franklin D. Roosevelt, 12 July 1933, Women's Bureau, Household Employment Correspondence, RG 86, Box 926, NA. For a useful discussion of the traditional problems of domestics, see Katzman, *Seven Days A Week*, and "What is Wrong With Household Employment," 7 December 1939, Women's Bureau, Survey Materials on Publications other than Numbered Bulletins, RG 86, Box 561, NA.

40. *Sun*, 18 March 1937.

41. Mrs. Edwin C. Bosworth to Eleanor Roosevelt, 12 November 1934, Women's Bureau, Household Employment Correspondence, RG 86, Box 926, NA; *Evening Sun*, 14 May 1937; *Sun*, 3 July 1938.

42. Howard, *WPA and Federal Relief Policy*, 292; *Sun*, 10 January 1938.

43. Howard, *WPA and Federal Relief Policy*, 292.

44. "Mr. Hopkins's telephone conversation with Mr. Dryden," 17 December 1935, Hopkins Papers, Box 74, FDRL.

45. *Sun*, 19 August 1934; Howard, *WPA and Federal Relief Policy*, 128, 164, 278–94; Ellen S. Woodward, "W.P.A. Household Workers Training and the United States Employment Service," October 1936, Women's Bureau, Household Employment–General Articles, RG 86, Box 1718, NA. Unfortunately, historians have not fully investigated the domestic-training programs. Julia Kirk Blackwelder does, however, note the existence of a program for black women in San Antonio (*Women of the Depression*, 120–23).

46. *Evening Sun*, 18 March 1938.

47. *Sun*, 10 January; 13, 15 March 1938.

48. *Sun*, 16 June 1938.

49. *Evening Sun*, 16, 20, 23, 25 May 1938; *Sun*, 3 July 1938; Bertha Avery Smith to Mary Robinson, 29 May 1938, Women's Bureau, Household Employment Correspondence, RG 86, Box 925, NA.

50. Howard, *WPA and Federal Relief Policy*, 287–93.

51. Sitkoff, *New Deal for Blacks*, 70. Nancy J. Weiss also notes that although discrimination marred the performance of most New Deal programs, some blacks benefited from such relief programs as the WPA and were grateful for that assistance (*Farewell to the Party of Lincoln*, 210–14).

52. *Sun*, 17 August 1938.

53. Sitkoff, *New Deal for Blacks*, 70.

54. Petition, "Baltimore City Colored Unemployed" to Governor Nice, 24 May 1934 (copies sent to Frances Perkins), Governor's Correspondence–Nice, Relief Box 8064 (2), MHR.

55. Woodward to Lewis, n.d., FERA, RG 69, No. 453, NA; "Report of the Baltimore Emergency Nursery Schools"; "Report of the WPA Nursery Schools." In 1940, at the requests of white sponsors, the city took over the entire funding of three nursery schools (all white) in order to ensure proper care for the children. The black schools continued to operate with inadequate federal financing but energetic voluntary efforts.

56. William Burdick to Clarence Perkins, 4 April 1935, PHA, Project Files, RG 196, No. 208, NA; "Recreation Program of the Division of Recreation."

57. Pratt Thomson to Governor Nice, 30 March 1935, Governor's Correspondence–Nice, Relief Box 8064 (1), MHR.

58. *Sun*, 17 December 1935.

59. *Evening Sun*, 11 January 1936.

60. Izetta Jewell Miller to Francis H. Dryden, 13 April 1936, Hopkins Papers, Box 58, FDRL.

61. *Sun*, 23 June 1936.

62. J. Milton Patterson to George Betker, 2 March 1939, Governor's Correspondence–O'Conor, Box 8948 (4), MHR; *Sun*, 7, 31 March 1936; 18 April; 24 July 1937; 8 January; 13 November 1938; 8, 14 July 1939.

63. *Sun*, 31 October 1936; 20, 21, 22, 25 January 1937.

64. *Evening Sun*, 7 September 1937; *Sun*, 24 July; 22, 31 August 1937; Dorothy Brown, "Maryland between the Wars," 752–53.

65. *Sun*, 3 January 1938.

66. Edward Moore to Harry Hopkins, 1 July 1938; Doris Olds to F. C. Harrington, 7 May 1940, WPA, RG 69, No. 610, NA.

67. Lloyd Brooks to Mrs. Roosevelt, 22 October 1936, WPA, RG 69, No. 641, NA.

68. *Sun*, 26 March 1933.

69. *Sun*, 7, 8, 12, 19 April 1933.

70. *Sun*, 29 March 1933 (emphasis added). The president of the Johns Hopkins University early suggested that CCC work might be appropriate for his graduates, urging his students not to be "too selective" and to seriously consider the CCC program; see *Sun*, 14 June 1933.

71. *Sun*, 6, 8 April 1933.

72. For correspondence concerning the quota problems, see CCC, Selection Division, State File (Maryland), Box 1826, NA, especially the following letters: W. Frank Persons to Robert Fechner, 25 May 1936; Persons to J. Milton Patterson, 18 April 1938; and Patterson to Persons, 30 August 1939.

73. Baltimore *Afro-American*, 15 April 1933; Dean Snyder to Thelma Maddox, 13 October 1939, CCC, Selection Division, Box 1779, NA; Report, "Coordination," 26 May 1936, NEC, RG 44, Entry 28, Box 357, WNRC.

74. *Sun*, 15 December 1938.

75. *Sun*, 1 June 1933.

76. CCC, Local Bulletin #45, Bulletin from Harry Greenstein, 10 October 1935, Governor's Correspondence–Nice, Relief Box 8064 (1), MHR.

77. *Sun*, 19 April; 1 June 1933.

78. W. Frank Persons to J. Milton Patterson, 23 January 1939, CCC, Box 1826, NA.

79. Dean Snyder to Thelma Maddox, 22 April 1937 and 13 October 1939, CCC, Box 1779, NA.

80. Snyder to Maddox, 13 October 1939, CCC, Box 1779, NA.

81. Persons to Patterson, 23 January 1939; Patterson to Persons, 30 August 1939, CCC, Box 1826, NA.

82. Patterson to Persons, 18 April 1938, CCC, Box 1826, NA.

83. Especially see the letters written by Dean Snyder and W. Frank Persons in the CCC, Box 1826, NA.

84. *Sun,* 25 March; 16, 22 April 1933; 5 April 1936; 6 April 1937; "The Fifth Civilian Conservation Corps Anniversary in Maryland," press release in U.S., Civilian Conservation Corps, Vertical File, EPFL; Kimberly, "The Depression," 228–29; Dorothy Brown, "Maryland between the Wars," 746–47. See also Griffing, "The Educational Process in the CCC."

A number of CCC volunteers took the training courses offered as part of the CCC program. Corpsmen stationed at a CCC camp in Beltsville, Maryland, for example, attended special classes held at the University of Maryland College Park on a variety of subjects, including public speaking, dairy husbandry, and general chemistry; others learned basic reading, writing, and arithmetic skills. See CCC, *Report on Special Educational Projects.* Because the CCC program was limited by law to young men, a number of women asked where was the "she-she-she." Under the FERA and the WPA, the government established resident camps for women. Although no Baltimore women participated in the program, across the nation some 8,000 women did until the project was abolished in 1937. See Ware, *Holding Their Own,* 40–41.

85. "Clippings," CCC, Selection Division, Box 1687, NA; *Sun,* 28 June 1933.

86. "Coordination," 26 May 1936, NEC, RG 44, Box 357, WNRC; Kimberly, "The Depression," 229.

87. *Sun,* 28 September 1934; John J. Carson to John J. Seidel, 12 August 1935, FERA, RG 69, No. 401, NA; "Coordination," 7 July 1936, NEC, RG 44, Box 357, WNRC; Dorothy Brown, "Maryland between the Wars," 754.

88. *Sun,* 6 November 1935; 1 April 1936; "Meeting of the City Delegation to the Legislature"; Kimberly, "The Depression," 229–33.

89. "What is the NYA?" *Councillor* 1 (February 1936): 19; NYA, "Final Report, National Youth Administration for the State of Maryland," NYA, State Files (Maryland), RG 119, Box 3, NA.

90. "Meeting of the City Delegation to the Legislature."

91. U.S. Federal Security Agency, War Manpower Commission, *Final Report,* 32–56; NYA, "Maryland Student Work Program"; *Sun,* 1 April 1936.

An easy explanation of the city's lax attitude toward the NYA is not available. But, in large measure, BERC officials simply ignored the program because they were preoccupied with providing relief for unemployables and with transferring clients to the WPA. It is important to note, moreover, that BERC officials were also businessmen and attorneys who kept their professional interests very much alive during their tenure on the Emergency Relief Commission.

92. Hamilton, "National Urban League," 236.

93. Ambrose Caliver to Earle Bracey, 15 December 1934, FERA, RG 69, No. 430; Richard Brown to Ryland N. Dempster, 22 June 1936, NYA, RG 119, Box 104, NA; *Sun,* 1 April 1936.

94. Federal Security Agency, War Manpower Commission, *Final Report,* 51; Brown to Dempster, 22 June 1936, NYA, RG 119, Box 104, NA; NYA, "Final Report," 78, 86; Kimberly, "The Depression," 235–36.

95. Harry Hopkins to Harry Greenstein, 8 February 1934, CWA, RG 69, No. 20, NA; *Sun*, 13 August 1934; 12 December 1937; Weekly Report, 30 April 1935, NEC, Box 412; Eugene Leggett to State Director for the National Emergency Council for Maryland, 12 February 1936, NEC, Box 224; Leggett to Hungerford, 17 December 1935, NEC, Box 179; "Coordination: H.O.L.C. and N.R.S.," 9 January 1937, NEC, RG 44, Box 357, WNRC. See also Kimberly, "The Depression," 215–17, 223.

Chapter 4

1. Sanderson, "Houses and Baltimore"; *Sun*, 17 June 1933; 27 January; 28 February 1934; Kimberly, "The Depression," 237; Neverdon-Morton, "Black Housing Patterns," 31–34. For a discussion of Boston's housing situation in the 1930s, see Trout, *Boston*, 255–57; for Philadelphia, see Coode and Bauman, *People, Poverty, and Politics*, 200–223, and Bauman, "Safe and Sanitary."

2. U.S. National Emergency Council, "Narrative Review of Agency Operations, 1933–1938," September 1938, Vertical File, EPFL; Kimberly, "The Depression," 238; "Report of the Associated Architects of Baltimore, Inc., to the Maryland Emergency Housing and Park Commission," Public Housing Administration (PHA), Project Files, RG 196, Box 206, NA.

3. U.S. Public Housing Administration, *Slums and Blighted Areas*, 53; "Report of the Associated Architects of Baltimore."

4. Coode and Bauman, *People, Poverty, and Politics*, 201; Trout, *Boston*, 152.

5. "Report of the Joint Committee on Housing in Baltimore," PHA, Project Files, RG 196, Box 206, NA.

6. Homer Phillips to H. Tudor Morsell, 30 July 1934, PHA, Project Files, RG 196, Box 206, NA.

7. "Report of Meeting," 30 August 1934, PHA, Project Files, RG 196, Box 206, NA.

8. *Sun*, 24 October 1935.

9. Cleveland Bealmear to A. R. Clas, 11 June 1935, Box 207; Real Estate Board of Baltimore to Mayor Howard Jackson, 1 September 1935, Box 206; Philip Pitt to A. R. Clas, 12 July 1935, Box 206; Philip Poe to Horatio Hackett, 15 September 1935, Box 206—all in PHA, Project Files, RG 196, NA. Also see the report prepared for Jackson, "Report on Housing and Commercial Conditions in Baltimore: Constituting Studies prepared for Mayor Howard W. Jackson," by Wm. W. Emmart, October 1934, Jackson Administrative Files, RG 9, E 50–7(5), Box 214, BCA.

10. Through the Maryland Emergency Housing and Park Commission the federal government spent considerable time and money surveying areas for possible slum clearance. Particularly troublesome in making appraisals of properties was the city's peculiar tradition of ground rents. See folders numbered 2703.21 and 2703.23 in PHA, Project Files, Box 209, NA.

The housing committee initially suggested that the two projects be built in the

Waverly area, using a "buffer" of alley garages to separate blacks from whites. Federal housing authorities promptly rejected the proposal, claiming that only the "lowest" sort of whites would live so close to blacks and that it would be difficult to "protect the white project from the Negro." Robert Mitchell of the federal housing office declared, "You might keep the Negroes out for a while, but eventually they will emigrate to that section." Reassurances from local officials that encroachment would not occur because of the city's strict reliance on "covenant of the deed" did not dissuade federal officials from rejecting the plan. See "Report of Meeting," 30 August 1934, and E. H. Klaber to W. E. Trevveh, 2 April 1934, PHA, Project Files, RG 196, Box 206. For a description of the projects finally accepted, see Charles E. Reed to Horatio Hackett, 21 March 1935, PHA, Project Files, RG 196, Box 208, NA.

11. A. Jeannette Smith to C. D. Loomis, 20 September 1934, and "Report of the Joint Committee on Housing," PHA, Project Files, RG 196, Box 206, NA.

12. "Report of Meeting," 30 August 1934, PHA, Project Files, RG 196, Box 206, NA.

13. *Sun*, 24 October 1935; United Brotherhood of Carpenters and Joiners of America, Local #101, to Mayor Jackson, PHA, Project Files, RG 196, Box 207, NA.

14. Carl Murphy to A. R. Class [*sic*], 6 September 1935, Box 206; Rabbi Edward Israel to Arthur Hungerford, 6 June 1935, Box 207; Hungerford to Frank C. Walker, 8 June 1935, Box 207; Simon Moser to A. R. Clas, 15 February 1936, Box 210—all in PHA, Project Files, RG 196, NA; Sanderson, "Houses and Baltimore."

Baltimore nearly participated in the public housing program when several state-level officials attempted to override Jackson's objections. Also important in countering Jackson was the Associated Architects of Baltimore—a group of architects who participated in the federal government's investigation of city housing and then formally joined together in order to work with the Maryland Emergency Housing and Park Commission created by the governor in 1934; see "Outline of the Activities of the Associated Architects of Baltimore," PHA, Project Files, RG 196, Box 208, NA. For examples of Mayor Jackson's persistent efforts against public housing, see Jackson to the Maryland Emergency Housing and Park Commission, 3 September 1935, Box 206; A. R. Clas to Edward Kloppel, 18 September 1935, Box 206; Clas to C. W. Perkins, n.d., Box 206; Simon Moser to Clas, 15 February 1936, Box 210, PHA, Project Files, RG 196, NA.

15. Moser to Clas, 16 February 1936; Clas to Moser, 18 February 1936, PHA, Project Files, RG 196, Box 210, NA.

16. *Sun*, 17, 23 March 1937. W. T. Dürr discusses the origins of the housing group in "The Conscience of a City" (pp. 84–87).

17. *Sun*, 10 May; 21, 29 October 1937.

18. Dürr, "The Conscience of a City," 84; *Sun*, 1, 3 November 1937.

19. *Sun*, 27 November; 13 December 1937; Resolution 979, 29 November 1937, *JPCC* (1937–38), 631–32.

20. *Sun*, 3 February 1939; Gilbert T. Hunter, "The Functions of the Voluntary

Housing Association," 7 March 1938, Citizens' Planning and Housing Association Papers, Box 6, Folder no. 4, Baltimore Region Institutional Studies Center, University of Baltimore (hereafter referred to as CPHAP).

21. Seymour, "The Organized Unemployed," 1–3, 27, 39–40, 60–66, 108; Reed, "Efforts of Social Workers."

22. Dürr, "The Conscience of a City," 97–118; *Sun*, 3 February 1939; 23 January 1941; *Evening Sun*, 1 February 1940; Kaplan, "Citizen Participation," 14; Morton, *Social Study of Wards 5 and 10*; Morton to Yewell W. Dillehunt, 15 April 1940, CPHAP, Box 8, Folder no. 5. A copy of Morton's study, along with relevant clippings, can be found in the John Ihlder Papers, Box 107, FDRL.

23. *Sun*, 10 May; 24 June; 8 September 1938; 3 February; 1 June; 3 October 1939; J. A. Thomason to Philip C. Hamblet, 16 February 1939, NEC, RG 44, Box 323, WNRC. The Thomason letter noted that the "low-cost housing program . . . is lagging" in Baltimore. See also U.S. Housing Authority, *Annual Report, 1938*, 14.

24. Baltimore Housing Authority, *Annual Report*, 2, 14; "Citizens Housing Council of Baltimore—Suggestions for Tenant Selection," 15 April 1940, CPHAP, Box 8, Folder no. 5; Dürr, "The Conscience of a City," 88–92; *Sun*, 20 June 1938. The BHA charged $16.75 per month for a 3 ½ room apartment and usually disallowed WPA applicants for public housing, explaining that the rental fees would swallow up too much of their security wage. Few of the unemployed accepted that explanation, for the median rental rate in the city was $28.68, and black families could regularly expect to pay between $20 and $25. Some BHA officials also believed that subsidized housing should go to families not already on relief. Finally, the housing plan, as under the PWA, was designed to improve the area by introducing families with higher incomes into the development. Rental rates for the projects that opened in 1941 ranged from $17 to $23.50, depending on the size of the apartments. Public housing, then, did not accommodate the unemployed. A similar situation occurred in Boston; see Trout, *Boston*, 152–54.

25. *Sun*, 18 March 1939.

26. Morton to Dillehunt, 15 April 1940, CPHAP, Box 8, Folder no. 5; Kaplan, "Citizen Participation," 15; Dürr, "The Conscience of a City," 36–40.

27. *Sun*, 11 June 1939; George E. Muhly to Howard Jackson, 1 July 1939, Jackson Administrative Files, RG 9, Series #21, G1–74(3), Box 243, BCA.

28. BHA, *Annual Report*; *Sun*, 4 June 1939.

29. *Sun*, 7, 11 June 1939.

30. BHA, *Annual Report*, 11–12; *Sun*, 11 June 1939; 5 August 1945. Although Waverly did not become a site for slum clearance, it did receive support from another agency, the Federal Home Loan Bank Board (FHLBB). The FHLBB launched a pilot project in Waverly to explore ways to halt the deterioration of older urban areas and appealed to the principle of citizen participation, explaining that central to urban revitalization was systematic and "organized community housekeeping." See FHLBB,

Waverly: A Study in Neighborhood Conservation, and Gelfand, *Nation of Cities*, 122.

31. *Sun*, 4 March 1938; Citizens' Housing Council, *Annual Report*, 3 February 1941, CPHAP, Box 7, Folder no. 1.

32. Dürr, "The Conscience of a City," 92; CHC, *Annual Report* (1941), 2–3; *Baltimore Building Low-Rent Homes* (1939), in the Jackson Administrative Files, RG 9, Series #21, G1–74(2), Box 243, BCA.

33. BHA, *Annual Report*, 11–12. Also see clippings about the Poe project in the Ihlder Papers, Box 107, FDRL.

34. CHC, *Annual Report* (1941), 2–3; *Sun*, 5 August 1945. Individual issues of "Civic News" can be found in CPHAP, Box 8, Folder no. 5.

35. CHC, *Annual Report* (1941), 4–6; Pfeiffer, "Problems of Administration in Community Organization."

36. Dürr, "The Conscience of a City," 92; CHC, *Annual Report* (1941), 4–6. The play ran for a week; see *Sun*, 25 February 1941.

37. *Sun*, 1 March 1941. For clippings and letters concerning the play, see Box 7, Folder no. 1, and Box 31, Folder no. 1 in the CPHAP. Also see Dürr, "The Conscience of a City," 118–19. The Hopkins group still held its photographic exhibit at the all-white JHU Faculty Club; consequently, Robert Jackson, a black member of the Commission on City Plan, was unable to attend.

38. Kaplan, "Citizen Participation," 15–16; Dürr, "The Conscience of a City," 43, 97–119; *Sun*, 5 August 1945. One Armistead Garden tenant wrote, "the place is going to the bad very fast."

39. Jack Rothman, "Three Models of Community Organization"; Rothman, *Planning and Organizing*, 279–398. For my interpretation of the CHC and the CPHA, I found particularly helpful Fisher, "From Grass-Roots Organizing to Community Service." I also found useful in refining my notions about citizen participation Hawley's "American Quest for National Efficiency."

40. *Sun*, 6 March 1941; Dürr, "The Conscience of a City," 97–118.

41. CHC, *Annual Report* (1941), 4.

42. Lewis, "War Problems," 10–13; Kaplan, "Citizen Participation," 16. See also Box 108, containing CPHA reports and pamphlets, of the Ihlder Papers, FDRL.

43. Jones and Herrick, *Citizens in Service*, 94. Jane DeHart Mathews demonstrates that community involvement was hardly limited to issues of social welfare, for the federal government also attempted to reach out to new constituencies in its support of cultural programs ("Arts and the People," 323–27).

Chapter 5

1. *Sun*, 2 January 1933.
2. *Sun*, 5 January 1933.

3. "Report of Maritime Strike," 9 January 1937, NEC, RG 44, Box 357, WNRC.

4. *Sun*, 4 June 1937.

5. L. Glen Seretan (" 'New' Working Class") argues that "social banditry" and outlawry represented early stages of what he calls the "new working class." And it seems clear that depression conditions served to mobilize certain groups of the unemployed to engage in what they regarded as extralegal, as opposed to illegal, activities. For the examples mentioned in the text, see *Sun*, 15 April; 25 July 1936; 1 August 1935; 17 October; 5 December; 10 July; 12 May; 23 December 1936; 14, 24 March 1937; 10 April 1936.

6. Almond and Lasswell, "Aggressive Behavior by Clients"; Baltimore *Afro-American*, 12 January 1933.

7. *Sun*, 15 September 1934.

8. In August 1927 the residence of Mayor William Broening had been severely damaged by a bomb, which, the police said, was a protest against the execution of Sacco and Vanzetti in Massachusetts. For an account of the 1936 bombing of Mayor Jackson's residence, see *Sun*, 9, 10, 12, 13, 14 August 1936. As late as 1938 no one had been arrested for the crime; see *Sun*, 14 June 1938.

9. Bernstein, *Lean Years*, 421–22; *Sun*, 11 February; 1 April; 9 May 1936; 9 January; 27 February; 21 March; 30 May; 27 June 1938. The Baltimore Criminal Justice Commission verified the police reports, adding that more serious crime also increased by 14 percent in 1937. Even as early as 1930, moreover, the commission attributed a rise in assaults to unemployment: joblessness "naturally leads to increased friction both in the home as well as where men mingle in idleness." See the commission's *Annual Reports*, 1930–39. The quotation is from the *Eighth Annual Report* (1930), 3.

10. *Evening Sun*, 13 May 1933; William B. Cross to Harry Nice, 7 December 1935, and assorted clippings in Governor's Correspondence–Nice, Relief Box 8064 (1), MHR. See also *Sun*, 7, 9 December 1935.

11. *Evening Sun*, 21 May 1935.

12. Leab, " 'United We Eat,' " 302, 306; *Evening Sun*, 6 March 1930. See also Rosenzweig, "Organizing the Unemployed," 40–42.

13. *Evening Sun*, 19, 20 January; 31 March; 1 April 1931.

14. President's Organization on Unemployment Relief, *Community Plan*, 18.

15. U.S. Works Progress Administration, *Transient Unemployed*, 2; Reed, *Federal Transient Program*, 13–14, 28, 98. Other useful contemporary studies include Bristol, "Transients in Recent Reports"; Locke, "Unemployed Men"; and Culver, "Transient Unemployed Men."

16. *Sun*, 24 April 1933; Young, "New Poor," 240. For a fuller discussion of the transient relief question, see Argersinger, "Assisting the 'Loafers.' "

17. WPA, *Transient Unemployed*, 1–2, 12; Williams, *Federal Aid for Relief*, 147–48. A number of cities and states, including Baltimore, still objected to helping transients and intentionally delayed implementing the program.

18. Argersinger, "Assisting the 'Loafers,'" 231–32.

19. W. B. Kelly to William Plunkert, 23 June 1934, FERA, State File (Maryland), RG 69, No. 420, NA.

20. Kelly to Plunkert, 23 June 1934, FERA, State File (Maryland), RG 69, No. 420, NA; "Minutes of the Conference, Maryland State Transient Bureau, Division of Maryland Emergency Relief, March 12, 13, 1935," 8–10, EPFL.

21. "Minutes of the Conference, Transient Bureau," 6–19; *Sun*, 8 January 1938. The Baltimore transient office created one camp for black men and two for whites; it also established one farm for homeless families and one farm for white males.

22. Miriam Michael to Mrs. Roosevelt, 6 May 1934; Elizabeth Wickenden to Janet Long, 2 August 1934; Wickenden to Roberta Williams, 8 August 1934, FERA, RG 69, No. 420, NA.

23. "Minutes of the Conference, Transient Bureau," 7–10; M. E. Holcomb to Elizabeth Wickenden, 30 July 1934; Wickenden to Holcomb, 6 August 1934; Wickenden to W. B. Kelly, 28 June 1934; Janet Long to Wickenden, 20 May 1935, FERA, RG 69, No. 420, NA.

24. "Minutes of the Conference, Transient Bureau," 7–10.

25. Elizabeth Wickenden to William Plunkert, 2 April 1934, FERA, RG 69, No. 421, NA; "Minutes of the Conference, Transient Bureau," 6–10.

26. Wickenden to Plunkert, 2 April 1934.

27. Wickenden to Plunkert, 2 April 1934; Harry Greenstein to William Plunkert, 23 March 1934, FERA, RG 69, No. 420, NA; also see enclosures.

28. Joseph La Combe to William J. Plunkert, 22 April 1934; Frank R. Stockl to President Roosevelt, 15 March 1934, FERA, RG 69, No. 420, NA.

29. Wickenden to Plunkert, 2 April 1934.

30. "Report on Baltimore Seamen Situation by Mr. Harman," 2 April 1934, FERA, RG 69, No. 420, NA.

31. Harry Greenstein to William Plunkert, 2 May 1934; Greenstein to Aubrey Williams, 4 June 1934, FERA, RG 69, No. 420, NA.

32. "Minutes of the Conference, Transient Bureau," 8.

33. Elizabeth Wickenden to Janet Long, 13 July, 19 July 1934; Long to Wickenden, 20 July 1934, FERA, RG 69, No. 420, NA; *Sun*, 8 March 1936.

34. "Minutes of the Conference, Transient Bureau," 18–19.

35. "Notes Taken at a Meeting with Janet Long," 30 November 1934, FERA, RG 69, No. 420, NA.

36. *Sun*, 1 October 1934.

37. Marine Workers Industrial Union to William Plunkert, 10 October 1934, FERA, RG 69, No. 420, NA.

38. Lawrence Young to Department of Justice, 16 November 1934; Waterfront Unemployment Council to Plunkert, 30 October 1934, FERA, RG 69, No. 420, NA; *Sun*, 8 October 1934.

39. *Maryland Leader*, 25 January 1936; Corrington Gill to T. L. Spring, 18 October

1935; F. H. Dryden to Harry Hopkins, 19 September 1935; Charles Alspach to Robert Van Hyning, 28 October 1935; Alspach to Dryden, 24 September 1935, FERA, RG 69, No. 420, NA; *Sun*, 22 December 1935.

40. George Patterson to Franklin D. Roosevelt, 24 February 1936, FERA, No. 420; Robert Van Hyning to Judge Thomas J. S. Waxter, 24 January 1936; Van Hyning to Charles Alspach, 30, 31 January 1936, FERA, RG 69, No. 421, NA.

41. Wickenden to Alspach, 11 February 1936; transcripts of telephone conversations between Van Hyning and Alspach, 6, 12 February 1936, FERA, RG 69, No. 421, NA. NA.

42. Baltimore Transient Committee to Aubrey Williams, 11 February 1936; transcripts of telephone conversations between Van Hyning and Alspach, 6, 12 February 1936, FERA, RG 69, No. 421, NA.

43. D. Gillis to Howard W. Jackson, 3 December 1937, WPA, State File, RG 69, No. 641, NA. See also Benjamin S. Tongue to Governor Nice, 18 September 1935, Governor's Correspondence–Nice, Relief Box 8064 (1), MHR.

44. "Report on Maritime Strike," 9 January 1937, NEC, RG 44, Box 357, WNRC; *Sun*, 9 January 1938.

45. *Sun*, 8 September 1935; 8, 19 March 1936; 9 January 1938; Manfred Wilmer to Charles Alspach, 22, 24 April 1936, FERA, RG 69, No. 420, NA.

46. Albert Prago ("Organization of the Unemployed") discusses the important role of organized groups of the unemployed in improving relief systems and in securing unemployment insurance.

47. *Maryland Leader*, 14, 21 January 1933; Seymour, "The Organized Unemployed," 26–27.

48. *Maryland Leader*, 4, 11 February; 18 March 1933; Frank N. Trager to the author, 24 October 1975; "People's Unemployment League of Maryland," *Monthly Labor Review* 36 (May 1933): 1024–25. See also Rosenzweig, " 'Socialism In Our Time,' " 496–97.

49. According to Helen Seymour, the PUL in Baltimore modeled itself after the successful Chicago Workers' Committee ("The Organized Unemployed," 26–28). The PUL also closely resembled its counterpart in New Jersey; see MacNeil, *Seven Years of Unemployment Relief*, 209–17. MacNeil argues that the organized unemployed were important in advancing the system of public relief in New Jersey.

50. Broadus Mitchell to Mother, two letters undated, in the Samuel Chiles Mitchell Papers, Folder #135, Southern Historical Collection, University of North Carolina, Chapel Hill.

51. According to the director of the Baltimore Urban League, the integration of the PUL was a major triumph: "The history of this group of white and colored workers in a Southern city is unique" (Baltimore *Afro-American*, 1 June 1935).

52. "Conference: Peoples Unemployment League, Baltimore, Maryland, and Aubrey Williams," 24 August 1934, FERA, RG 69, No. 460, NA; McElvaine, "Thunder Without Lightning," 162.

53. "Conference: PUL and Williams"; Seymour, "The Organized Unemployed," 54–60.

54. Seymour, "The Organized Unemployed," 26–28; Rosenzweig, " 'Socialism In Our Time,' " 497. Although local officials were forced to deal with the PUL, they occasionally tried to discredit and undermine it.

55. Arch Mandel to Harry Hopkins, 17 December 1934; Clarence Whitmore to Jacob Baker, 25 July 1933, FERA, RG 69, No. 450; Viola Bassem et al. to Bruce McClure, 11 December 1933; Myron Jones to Walter Durr, 16 January 1934, CWA, State File, RG 69, Box 20, NA; Rosenzweig, " 'Socialism In Our Time,' " 497.

56. *Maryland Leader*, 14 April 1934.

57. *Sun*, 28 July; 4 August 1934; Frank Trager to Aubrey Williams, 3 July 1934; E. C. Andrews to Harry Hopkins, n.d., FERA, RG 69, No. 453–60, NA.

58. Trager to Williams, 3 July 1934, FERA, RG 69, No. 453–60; "Conference: PUL and Williams"; *Sun*, 28 July 1934.

59. *Sun*, 28 July; 4, 22, 23 August; 4 September 1934; *Maryland Leader*, 20 January; 3, 17 February; 5 May; 15 December 1934; 20, 27 April 1935; Frank Trager to Governor Nice, 18 February and 6 May 1935; Norman L. Trott to Nice, 27 February 1935, Governor's Correspondence–Nice, Relief Box 8064 (1), MHR.

60. "Conference: PUL and Williams."

61. Frank Trager to Harry Nice, 6 May 1935, Governor's Correspondence–Nice, Relief Box 8064 (1), MHR; "Minutes, Meeting of the Baltimore Unemployed League [*sic*] with Aubrey Williams, September 12, 1935," FERA, RG 69, No. 400, NA.

62. *Sun*, 1, 5, 6 January; 3 March 1936; "Minutes of the Joint Meeting of the Board of State Aid and Charities, Representatives of the Baltimore Emergency Relief Commission, and Mayor Howard Jackson," 7 January 1936, Governor's Correspondence–Nice, Relief Box 8064 (5), MHR; Seymour, "The Organized Unemployed," 44; Kerr, "Productive Enterprises," 5–13, 25.

63. *Evening Sun*, 14 June 1935; *Sun*, 27 September; 10 November 1935; PUL to Harry Hopkins, 17 August 1935; "Statement of Delegation to Mr. Francis H. Dryden, Works Progress Administration for the State of Maryland, from the Peoples Unemployment League of Maryland, Saturday, 17 August 1935," WPA, State File, RG 69, No. 641, NA.

64. *Maryland Leader*, 2 November, 21 December 1935; 11, 25 January; 1 August 1936; "Statement of Delegation to Mr. Francis H. Dryden," WPA, State File, RG 69, No. 641, NA; Harry Greenstein to Aubrey Williams, 29 October 1935, WPA, RG 69, No. 610, NA; *Sun*, 28 October 1935.

65. "Telephone Conversation between Hopkins and Dryden," 15 August 1935, WPA, RG 69, No. 610; "Report of a meeting of the Baltimore Federation of Labor, the PUL and WPA workers" [December 1935], WPA, RG 69, No. 641, NA.

66. *Sun*, 7 December 1935.

67. *Sun*, 9, 11 December 1935.

68. Harry Greenstein to Aubrey Williams, 29 October 1935, WPA, RG 69, No. 610, NA; U.S. Federal Works Agency, *Final Report on the WPA*, 21; *Sun*, 13 December

1935. See also the discussion of the threatened WPA strike in *Garment Worker*, 1 November 1935, 6.

69. F. H. Dryden to Corrington Gill, 21 July 1937, No. 640; Clyde D. Williams to Allen P. Goldsborough, n.d., WPA, RG 69, No. 641, NA; Roy L. Sloop to Harry Nice, September [?] 1935, Relief Box 8064 (1); "Minutes of Joint Meeting of the Board of State Aid and Charities and the B.E.R.C.," 2 December 1935, Governor's Correspondence–Nice, Relief Box 8064 (5), MHR; Bonnell, "How Some Families Live," 27; Hopkins, "Relief Supplementation," 8, 9.

70. Organized Women Sewing Workers to Harry Hopkins, 14 September 1938, WPA, RG 69, No. 641, NA.

71. L. L. Leith to Senator Millard Tydings, 14 January 1936; "Statement presented by delegation representing the organized WPA workers affiliated with the *Peoples Unemployment League of Maryland* to Mr. Francis H. Dryden, Administrator of Maryland Works Progress Administration at Baltimore on Saturday, 24 October 1936," WPA, RG 69, No. 641, NA; *Sun*, 6, 11 September; 16, 18, 24, 25 October 1936; Nels Anderson to L. L. Leith, 20 January 1936, No. 641; F. H. Dryden to Corrington Gill, 21 July 1937, No. 640; Gill to Dryden, 28 July 1937, No. 640—in WPA, RG 69, NA.

72. L. L. Leith to Senator Millard Tydings, 30 January 1936, WPA, RG 69, No. 641, NA.

73. James Blackwell to Harry Hopkins, 31 July 1936, No. 641; Elizabeth Mulholland to Howard C. Beck [April 1936], No. 610; Workers Alliance to Francis H. Dryden, 20 July 1939, No. 641.2—all in WPA, RG 69, NA; *Labor Herald*, 19 May 1939.

74. *Sun*, 18 February 1936; James Blackwell to Nels Anderson, 28 August 1936; Charles Yost to David Niles, 6 July 1938, WPA, RG 69, No. 641, NA.

75. *Sun*, 16 October 1936; 17 August 1938; "Statement of delegation to Dryden, 24 October 1936."

76. "Delegation from Workers Alliance of America, 429 Eutaw Street, Baltimore, Maryland, Met with Mr. N. H. Hogg," 26 July 1939; Patrick Whalen to Aubrey Williams, 22 December 1938; Pacific Coast Marine Firemen, Oilers, Watertenders and Wipers Association to Franklin D. Roosevelt, 22 June 1941, WPA, RG 69, No. 641, NA.

77. Howard, *WPA and Federal Relief Policy*, 222–27.

78. Ibid., 318–24. The purging of WPA rolls also took place in New York City; see Blumberg, *New Deal and the Unemployed*, 228–50.

79. *Sun*, 1, 9, 11, 20, 21, 22, 23 January 1937; *Labor Herald*, 27 May 1938.

80. *Sun*, 15 January; 8 July 1938.

81. Howard, *WPA and Federal Relief Policy*, 318–24; *Labor Herald*, 23 December 1938; 30 June 1939. In such other cities as New York, the changes in the WPA caused AFL-affiliated unions to lead strikes among WPA workers; see Blumberg, *New Deal and the Unemployed*, 246–47.

82. Workers Alliance to Francis H. Dryden, 20 July 1939, WPA, RG 69, No. 641.2, NA; *Labor Herald*, 19 May 1939; *Sun*, 21, 30 July 1939.

83. *Sun*, 25 March 1936; "Minutes of the Meeting of the Board of State Aid and Charities," 24 February 1939, Governor's Correspondence–O'Conor, Box 8948 (4), MHR.

84. *Labor Herald*, 7 January; 28 October, 23 December 1938; 20 January; 16, 30 June 1939; *Sun*, 14 May; 31 December 1937; 4 March 1938; 9 June 1939; Seymour, "The Organized Unemployed," 43–44. For a useful description of the evolution of self-help activities in the 1930s with particular emphasis on the role of federal aid, see Kerr, "Productive Enterprises." Kerr, however, erroneously claims (p. 23) that the active barter movement in Baltimore disappeared with the coming of the New Deal.

85. *Labor Herald*, 23 December 1938; 30 June 1939.

86. Rosenzweig, " 'Socialism In Our Time,' " 500–501; Piven and Cloward, *Poor People's Movements*, 76–77.

87. This typology of community organization is explained in Chapter 4. See Jack Rothman, "Three Models of Community Organization."

88. *Maryland Leader*, 16 February 1935. Even more moderate Socialists like Broadus Mitchell lamented that the New Deal held "little promise for needed change in the capitalist system"; see Mitchell to Mother, 9 August [?], Samuel Chiles Mitchell Papers, Folder #135, Southern Historical Collection, UNC.

89. *Labor Herald*, 14 July 1939. The Socialist party rarely attracted more than about 6,000 votes at the polls; see the *Maryland Manual* for the 1930s.

90. The quotation is from Frank Trager as quoted in Rosenzweig, "Organizing the Unemployed," 53. See also Rosenzweig, " 'Socialism In Our Time,' " 509.

91. Blumberg, *New Deal and the Unemployed*, 221–24; Seymour, "The Organized Unemployed," 44, 54–61.

Chapter 6

1. *Sew-Sew News*, November 1939; Green, *World of the Worker*, 170; *Sun*, 21 June 1935. Harry C. Boyte (*Backyard Revolution*, xii) notes the connection between the citizen movements and trade-union organization of the 1930s.

2. U.S. Bureau of the Census, *Fifteenth Census, 1930: Population*; *Sun*, 1 January 1933; Olson, *Baltimore*, 345. For a discussion of the collapse of voluntarism and private charities, see Argersinger, "From Charity to the Dole."

3. J. Knox Insley to Albert C. Ritchie, 19 July 1932, Governor's Correspondence–Ritchie–Labor, MHR; Bernstein, *Lean Years*, 164–65. An important exception was McCormick and Company. Its young president, Charles P. McCormick, largely avoided "labor trouble" in the 1930s because he practiced what he called "private ownership from bottom to top," spreading management and profits throughout the work force. He argued that strikes resulted from "mismanagement" and "dictatorial" control. See *Sun*, 23 November 1938.

4. Singleton, *Workmen's Compensation*, 12–17, 22–31, 68–70, 89, 98; Crooks, *Politics and Progress*, 194.

5. Argersinger, "To Discipline an Industry." For a useful analysis of the economic changes in the garment industry in the 1920s, see Fraser, "Sidney Hillman," 18–63. Also see General Executive Board Minutes, 30 August–1 September 1932, Amalgamated Clothing Workers of America papers, Box 165, Folder no. 17, Martin P. Catherwood Library of the New York State School of Industrial and Labor Relations, Cornell University (hereafter referred to as ACWA).

6. Hollander, *Report to Honorable Howard W. Jackson*; "Oral History Interview with Sara Barron."

7. Hollander, *Report of the Hearing of Strikers*.

8. Hollander, *Report to Honorable Howard W. Jackson*. The investigation led by Hollander also prompted the state commissioner of labor and statistics, J. Knox Insley, to conduct his own inquiry. Much less sympathetic to the workers and particularly ill-disposed toward the ACW, Insley dismissed the strike as an unfortunate misunderstanding and claimed that Schoeneman stood ready to remedy the problems. Schoeneman's abrupt departure from the city, however, left Insley in a somewhat compromised and embarrassed position. See Maryland Commissioner of Labor and Statistics, *Report of Investigation of Strike*.

9. Quoted in Leuchtenburg, *Franklin D. Roosevelt*, 189.

10. Maryland State Planning Commission, "Report on Men's Clothing Industry," 21; *Sun*, 27, 29 June 1933; Connery, *Administration of an NRA Code*, 9–18.

11. General Executive Board Minutes, 10–11 November 1936, ACWA, Box 165, Folder no. 22; *Maryland Leader*, 16, 23 September; 7 October 1933; 21 April 1934; Baltimore *Afro-American*, 16 December 1933; *Evening Sun*, 3 June 1935.

12. Biweekly Report, 25 May 1934, NEC, RG 44, Box 412, WNRC; Kimberly, "The Depression," 117–18.

13. Lyon et al., *National Recovery Administration*, 60–68, 87–98; Kimberly, "The Depression," 118–19; Arthur Hungerford to Donald Richberg, 18 August 1934, NEC, RG 44, Box 180, WNRC; "NRA Violation," ACWA, Box 249, Folder no. 2; "Other Cases Involving Discharge of Employees in Violation of Section 7(a)," *Monthly Labor Review* 39 (November 1934): 1155. For a useful discussion of the antilabor policies of the NRA's Hugh Johnson at the national level, see Bellush, *Failure of the NRA*, 85–135.

14. Hungerford to Richberg, 18 August 1934; *Maryland Leader*, 1 December 1934; "Wage and Hour Law–Rank and file letters," ACWA, Box 263, Folder no. 13.

15. *Sun*, 19, 26 July 1934; Connery, *Administration of an NRA Code*, 69; Kimberly, "The Depression," 122–23.

16. *Sun*, 26, 28, 30 July; 2 September 1934; Connery, *Administration of an NRA Code*, 74–75; Kimberly, "The Depression," 124; Biweekly Report, 26 September 1935, NEC, RG 44, Box 412, WNRC.

17. BFL, Minutes, 13 September; 1 November; 20 December 1933, Baltimore Office of the Metropolitan Council AFL-CIO Unions. Until 1939, when the department was reorganized, the labor commission was a "slipshod and loose-knit organization"; see *Sun*, 17 June 1937; 1, 2, 14 March 1938; 31 January; 16 February 1939.

18. "Report on the Activities of the Baltimore Labor Relations Panel, to August

17th, 1934"; "Report on the Activities of the Baltimore Labor Relations Panel, August 17th, 1934 to September 1st, 1934"; folders marked "Monthly" reports, "Weekly" reports, and "Daily" reports; Harry Cohen to Baltimore Labor Relations Panel, 7 August 1934—all in NLRB (Administrative File, Baltimore), RG 25, NA; "Industrial Disputes," *Monthly Labor Review* 39 (July 1934): 32, and vol. 42 (May 1936): 1305; author's interview with Jacob Edelman, attorney for the ACW, 18 June 1983.

19. *Maryland Leader*, 9, 16 September 1933; 10 March 1934. (Emphasis added.)

20. *Maryland Leader*, 8 July 1933; BFL, Minutes, January 1934.

21. BFL, Minutes, 30 August; 27 September 1933; 31 January; 23 May 1934. The BFL unfortunately did not indicate how much union growth took place between 1933 and 1935, but at the beginning of the decade the booklet published by city boosters, entitled *The Industrial Advantages of Baltimore*, called the city an "open shop town" and placed unionization of the work force at about 7 percent.

22. Frank Trager to the author, 24 October 1975; *Maryland Leader*, 20 May 1933; 21 April 1934; BFL, Minutes, 30 July 1930; 1 November 1933; 31 January 1934; 13 March 1935; *Sun*, 13 January 1938.

23. BFL, Minutes, 20, 27 September; 25 October 1933; 31 January; 29 August; 19 September 1934.

24. Reid, *Negro Community*, 59–62.

25. Baltimore *Afro-American*, 14 December 1935; BFL, Minutes, 22 November 1933; 11 July 1934; 27 March 1935; Reid, *Negro Membership*, 140; Ryon, "Ambiguous Legacy"; *Maryland Leader*, 19 August 1933; 23 June 1934; Chamberlain, "The Five Largest CIO Unions," 14, 120.

26. *Sun*, 14 August 1935; *Labor Herald*, 12 June 1936; 3 September 1937. At a CIO banquet honoring a labor editor, De Dominicis urged the editor to "write more sharp and incisive articles condemning the capitalist society until the day when it will be a workers' world"; see *Sun*, 29 November 1939. In 1939, Sara Barrinsky changed her name to Sara Barron at the request of friend and fellow ACW member Jacob Edelman; Edelman advised her to "get rid of the sky" lest she be labeled a communist (author's interview with Sara Barron).

27. *Labor Herald*, 3 September 1937; Reid, *Negro Community*, 60–63.

28. *Labor Herald*, 2 July 1937; "Oral History Interview with Sara Barron." For more discussion of the cotton-garment drive, see Newman Jeffrey to J. S. Potofsky, 5 April 1939, Papers of Joint Boards and Local Unions, ACWA, Box 57, Folder no. 6. For a later ACW drive to organize black and white workers in dry-cleaning plants, see Baltimore *Afro-American*, 19 August; 2 September 1939.

29. BFL, Minutes, 18 October 1933; *Maryland Leader*, 22 July; 9 December 1933; 10 February; 16 June; 28 July 1934; 30 March; 31 August 1935; 21 March; 11 April 1936; *Sun*, 21, 22, 23 May; 25 September 1936; Olson, *Baltimore*, 344.

30. *Evening Sun*, 9 March 1937. See also *Labor Herald*, 9 April 1937.

31. *Labor Herald*, 25 June 1937; Olson, *Baltimore*, 345.

32. *Sun*, 12, 14 November 1936; 19 January; 9, 14 March; 11 May; 6, 9, 31 October 1937. (The taxicab strike is discussed in greater detail later in this chapter.)

33. "Industrial Disputes," *Monthly Labor Review* 42 (May 1936): 1305, and vol. 48 (May 1939): 1119.

34. Maryland Commissioner of Labor and Statistics, *Annual Reports*, 1933–39. See especially *Forty-fifth Annual Report* (1936), 6; *Forty-sixth Annual Report* (1937), 9; *Forty-seventh Annual Report* (1938), 12–13. *Evening Sun*, 18 July 1937.

35. *Sun*, 22 June; 3 July 1937; 4, 18 August; 13 September 1939; author's interview with Jacob Edelman; "Oral History Interview with Sara Barron."

36. *Sun*, 3 June 1935; 7, 20 May; 5 December 1936; 22, 23 June 1937; 22 January 1938; Lowitt and Beasley, *One Third of a Nation*, 346.

37. *Sun*, 7, 8, 9, 18 July 1937; 22 January; 10 February 1938. For a discussion of the Bedaux system, see Egolf, "Limits of Shop Floor Struggle."

38. *Maryland Leader*, 30 May 1936; *Sun*, 21 May; 1, 4 August 1936; 4 May 1939; BFL, Minutes, 13 November 1935; 3 June; 22 July; 21 October; 23 December 1936; 6 January 1937. According to BFL minutes, after 1936, the leadership of the federation increasingly retreated into longer sessions of executive deliberations where no official minutes were kept.

39. *Labor Herald*, 27 May 1938.

40. *Sun*, 14 November 1936; 10, 14 March; 20 May; 15 September 1937.

41. *Labor Herald*, 12 March 1937; 22 April 1938; *Sun*, 30 September 1936; 25 January 1938. For another example of the adverse effect of BIC-BFL divisions on organizing workers, see *Sun*, 6 September 1937.

42. *Sun*, 4 March; 15 October 1937; 18 January 1938.

43. *Sun*, 20 May; 1 August 1936; 4 March 1937; 29 January 1938; "Industrial Disputes," *Monthly Labor Review* 42 (May 1936): 1305, and vol. 48 (May 1939): 1119; "Oral History Interview with Sara Barron"; BFL, Minutes, 5 June; 11 September; 6 November 1935; 7 April 1937.

44. *Sun*, 23 February 1935.

45. *Sun*, 13, 14, 16, 17, 19, 31 December 1936; 1, 5, 6, 19 January 1937; *Labor Herald*, 12 March 1937; 22 April 1938.

46. *Sun*, 1, 2, 3, 6, 8, 9, 10, 12, 13, 15, 16, 17, 18, 20, 22, 23, 28 February; 9, 14 March; 11 May; 9, 31 October; 10 December 1937; 2, 3 September 1938. Jacob Edelman of the ACW defended Harry Cohen.

47. *Labor Herald*, 13 November; 25 December 1936; *Sun*, 8, 16, 24 November 1936; 29 January 1938.

48. Avnet, "Pat Whalen," 250; *Sun*, 8, 16, 24 November; 13 December 1936. For a discussion of the seamen's relief situation, see Argersinger, "Assisting the 'Loafers.'" The portraits of McCurdy and Whalen tend to support the notion that AFL leaders were more conservative than their CIO counterparts; see, for example, Licht and Barron, "Labor's Men," 542.

49. *Sun*, 28, 29 November; 1, 3 December 1936.

50. *Sun*, 19 December 1936; 13 June 1937.

51. *Labor Herald*, 31 July; 21, 28 August; 4, 11 September 1936; *Sun*, 11 June 1937. In addition to those already mentioned, particularly active organizers included

SWOC agitators such as John J. Mates, who organized at Bethlehem Steel and the Standard Sanitary Manufacturing Company; see *Sun*, 10, 14 June 1937.

52. Maryland Commissioner of Labor and Statistics, *Forty-sixth Annual Report*, 8–16; *Sun*, 1, 9, 11, 20, 21, 22, 23 January; 23 February; 10 March; 10 June 1937; Dorothy Brown, "Maryland between the Wars," 757–58; *Labor Herald*, 26 March; 14 May; 18 June; 2 July 1937. See also Vertical File, EPFL.

53. *Sun*, 19, 24 February 1937; *Labor Herald*, 26 February; 12 March 1937; Dorothy Brown, "Maryland between the Wars," 758.

54. Dorothy Brown, "Maryland between the Wars," 758; *Sun*, 10, 14, 15, 16, 17 June 1937.

55. *Labor Herald*, 26 March; 16 April; 18 June; 30 July; 15 October 1937; *Sun*, 12, 17 March; 11 June 1937.

56. *Labor Herald*, 14 April 1936; 17 September 1937; "Industrial Disputes," *Monthly Labor Review* 48 (May 1939): 1119; "Weekly Report," week ending 16 February 1935; "Strikes Occurring in the Fifth Region During the Calendar Year of 1935," NLRB (Administrative File, Baltimore), RG 25, NA. See also the folder marked "Daily Reports" in the same file.

57. *Sun*, 15 July 1938; 13 September 1939; MSPC, "Report on Men's Clothing Industry," 142–43; *Labor Herald*, 14 April 1936; 17 September 1937; 23 March; 1 July 1938.

58. *Labor Herald*, 12 March 1937; *Sun*, 22 December 1936; 13 June; 3, 20 September; 9 November 1937; 25 March; 22 August 1938.

59. *Sun*, 6 February; 4 June 1939. For a discussion of the Martin controversy in the UAW, see Keeran, *Communist Party*, 189–92. For a larger discussion of communism and the CIO, see Levenstein, *Communism*, 78–123.

60. Ulisse De Dominicis to Sidney Hillman, 30 October 1939; Dorothy J. Bellanca to Mildred Jeffrey, 30 September 1939, Papers of Joint Boards and Local Unions, ACWA, Box 57, Folder no. 7. Baltimore's Archbishop Curley early warned that, "among the laboring classes," communism was "being spread from one end of the country to the other"; see *Sun*, 13 October 1936.

61. *Labor Herald*, 29 January; 12 March 1937.

62. *Labor Herald*, 29 January 1937.

63. Author's interview with Jacob Edelman; Ryon, "Ambiguous Legacy," 26, 29, 30; Milkman, "Organizing the Sexual Division of Labor," 125–28; Clippings and correspondence, "Domestic Workers," Vertical File, EPFL; "Brief on Household Employment in Relation to Trade Union Organization," by Jean Brown, 1938, Women's Bureau, RG 86, Box 1718, NA; Asher, "Dorothy Jacobs Bellanca," 200. For an extended discussion of the gender-based division in the ACW, see Argersinger, "To Discipline an Industry."

64. *Labor Herald*, 29 January 1937; *Sun*, 5 August; 14 October 1939; Montgomery, *Workers' Control in America*, 13–14; Milkman, "Organizing the Sexual Division of Labor," 126; Strom, "Challenging 'Woman's Place,'" 370, 378.

65. If the figures provided by the BFL and BIC are even approximately accurate, then by the end of the decade the two unions had organized about 20–25 percent of Baltimore's work force. This compares to a national average of 20.7 percent in 1939; see Troy, *Trade Union Membership*, 4–5. Boston, on the other hand, had 17 percent of its workers organized even before the New Deal; see Trout, *Boston*, 16–17, 198–226.

66. *Sew-Sew News*, 1939–40; *Labor in Art: An Exhibition*. An especially helpful analysis of trade-union culture in the 1930s is provided by Elizabeth Fones-Wolf, "Industrial Unionism."

67. Ryon, "Ambiguous Legacy," 20–24; *CIO News* (Baltimore), 30 January; 16 February; 13 March; 4 December 1939; "What Can the Union Do For Me? A Steelworkers' Play."

68. Argersinger, "To Discipline an Industry"; "Oral History Interview with Sara Barron"; author's interview with Sara Barron.

69. Mary Dewson to Millard Tydings, 2, 22 September 1936, DNCP, Women's Division, Box 81; *Journal of Electrical Workers and Operators* 35 (December 1936): 519; *Sun*, 17 August 1937; 16 July; 14, 15 August; 1, 3 September 1938.

Chapter 7

1. Edwin Rothman, "Factional Machine Politics," 5, 184–88; Arnold, "Good Old Days," 443. For an insightful examination of the electoral significance of the New Deal among economically disadvantaged groups, see Kleppner, *Who Voted?* 97–102.

2. Edwin Rothman, "Factional Machine Politics," 21; Arnold, "Good Old Days," 444.

3. *Sun*, 2 May 1919.

4. Baltimore *Afro-American*, 27 April 1923; Edwin Rothman, "Factional Machine Politics," 29.

5. Arnold, "Good Old Days," 445–46.

6. *Sun*, 15 September 1934; *Evening Sun*, 28 August 1927.

7. *Sun*, 28 September 1937; "Present Situation" [1934?], DNCP, Women's Division, Box 81.

8. Arnold, "Good Old Days," 446; Dorothy Brown, "Maryland between the Wars," 684.

9. Edwin Rothman, "Factional Machine Politics," 31; Dorothy Brown, "Maryland between the Wars," 685; *Evening Sun*, 17 February 1927; *Marylander*, 19 March 1927.

10. Edwin Rothman, "Factional Machine Politics," 86; *Sun*, 6 May 1931.

11. *Sun*, 14 December 1935.

12. "Present Situation," DNCP, Women's Division, Box 81.

13. *Sun*, 25 June 1936.

14. *Sun*, 2 January 1936; 7 April 1934; 14, 29 April 1939.

15. *Sun*, 28 August 1935.

16. William Curran to James A. Farley, 4 September 1936, DNCP, Farley Correspondence, Box 1095.

17. Edwin Rothman, "Factional Machine Politics," 86; *Sun*, 1, 6 May; 29 June 1933; 2 July 1934.

18. *Sun*, 15 August 1934; Edwin Rothman, "Factional Machine Politics," 102, 107; Arnold, "Good Old Days," 447.

19. *Sun*, 4 December 1938; 14 October 1936; 18 June 1939. All of the volumes of the *Journal of Proceedings of the City Council of Baltimore* for the years 1927–41 were examined.

20. *JPCC*, 14 November 1932, 541; 10 December 1934, 417; 11 February 1935, 417; 27 January 1936, 668, 1011–12; 16 March 1936, 847–48; 25 May 1936, 55; 6 July 1936, 182; *Sun*, 25 March 1936.

21. *JPCC*, 17 September 1934, 169; 25 May 1936, 55; *Sun*, 6, 9, 11, 12 April 1937.

22. *Sun*, 23 March 1937; 11 March 1936.

23. *JPCC*, 17 September 1934, 169; *Sun*, 20 October 1936; 4, 7, 16 December 1938.

24. *Evening Sun*, 15 February 1935; Edwin Rothman, "Factional Machine Politics," 162.

25. *Maryland Leader*, 8 April; 15 July 1933; 18 August 1934; Dorothy Brown, "Election of 1934," 416; *Evening Sun*, 25 February 1933.

26. *Sun*, 9 September; 9, 24, 31 March; 1, 4 April 1933; *Evening Sun*, 9 November 1932; Simon E. Sobeloff to Albert C. Ritchie, 22 December 1932; Ritchie to Sobeloff, 23 December 1932; Ritchie to A. H. S. Post, 5 April 1933—all in Box 8006; H. A. Wise to Ritchie, 5 May 1933 (Unemployment Insurance)—all in Governor's Correspondence–Ritchie, MHR.

27. Dorothy Brown, "Maryland between the Wars," 760–61; Edwin Rothman, "Factional Machine Politics," 90; *Evening Sun*, 18 April; 16 May 1934.

28. *Sun*, 2, 8, 29 July; 15 August; 6, 11, 21, 26 September 1934; *Evening Sun*, 2, 9, 13, 19 July 1934; Dorothy Brown, "Maryland between the Wars," 762–63.

29. *Maryland Leader*, 6 October 1934; Dorothy Brown, "Maryland between the Wars," 764; "The Political Platform of Harry W. Nice," Vertical File, EPFL.

30. Baltimore *Post*, 6 June 1933.

31. *Sun*, 24 October 1934.

32. *Sun*, 19 October 1934; Dorothy Brown, "Maryland between the Wars," 765. For a description of the campaign, see *Sun*, 23, 26, 30, 31 October 1934; *Maryland Leader*, 20 October 1934; Kimberly, "The Depression," 254; and White, *Governors of Maryland*, 266.

33. Percentages are based on data provided in the *Evening Sun*, 7 November 1934, and the *Maryland Manual*, 249. *Maryland Leader*, 21 July 1934; Dorothy Brown, "Maryland between the Wars," 767.

34. *Sun*, 20 August; 10, 13, 14, 19 September; 8 October 1936. One worker, disturbed by the antilabor sentiment in the *Sun*'s editorial against FDR, declared that,

"in my estimation, Roosevelt is the workingman's choice" (*Sun*, 13 September 1936). Numerous WPA workers also wrote letters defending Roosevelt and criticizing the *Sun*; especially see *Sun*, 19 September 1936.

35. *Sun*, 13 September 1936. See also *Sun*, 29 September; 30 October 1936; and Edwin Rothman, "Factional Machine Politics," 40.

36. Mary W. Dewson to Millard Tydings, 22 September 1936, DNCP, Women's Division, Box 81.

37. *Sun*, 8 October 1936; William Curran to James A. Farley, 4 September 1936; Gilbert Dailey to Farley, 10 September 1936, Box 1095, DNCP, Farley Correspondence; Curran to Sumner Welles, 18 September 1936, President's Official File 300, Box 43, FDRP.

38. Curran to Farley, 4 September 1936.

39. Curran to Welles, 18 September 1936; Curran to Farley, 4 September 1936; Dailey to Farley, 10 September 1936.

40. *Sun*, 5 May 1936. Roosevelt received 93,396 votes to Breckinridge's 17,041.

41. Dailey to Farley, 10 September 1936; Curran to Farley, 4 September 1936.

42. *Sun*, 18, 22 October 1936; Dailey to Farley, 10 September 1936; "Oral History Interview with Sara Barron." For a detailed description of ACW activities designed to get "families and friends" of union members "out to vote on Election Day," see Herbert Levy to Corinne Berger, 11 September 1936, and Mary Dewson to Millard Tydings, 2 September 1936, DNCP, Women's Division, Box 81.

43. Dailey to Farley, 10 September 1936.

44. *Sun*, 11, 12 September 1936.

45. William Stanley to James A. Farley, 12 September 1936, DNCP, Farley Correspondence, Box 1095.

46. Dailey to Farley, 10 September 1936.

47. *Sun*, 4 November 1936; I. Chaikin to Sidney Hillman, 14 November 1936, Papers of Joint Boards and Local Unions, ACWA, Labor Management Collection Division.

48. The author is familiar with the recent literature that discusses the problems of ecological data, but also see Ranney, "Utility and Limitations," 91–102. As will be seen, the author has also used regression analysis for all mayoral and presidential elections between 1931 and 1940.

49. Edwin Rothman, "Factional Machine Politics," 115; *Sun*, 8 May 1935; 4 November 1936.

50. U.S. Bureau of the Census, *Fifteenth Census, 1930: Population*, vol. 3, part 2, 1070; *Sixteenth Census, 1940: Housing*, 630; *Sun*, 7 November 1928; 6 May 1931; 9 November 1932; 8 May 1935; 29 October; 4 November 1936. For the GOP's efforts to influence black ministers, see *Sun*, 19 October 1936.

51. Frances H. Morton, *A Social Study of Wards 5 and 10 in Baltimore, Maryland*.

52. Regression analysis here followed the procedures outlined by J. Morgan Kousser ("Ecological Regression"). The percentages of renters and of those living in substan-

dard housing were used as surrogate measures for class. Some studies have instead used the average monthly rent; see, for example, Jeffries, *Testing the Roosevelt Coalition*. The percentage of ethnic voters is based on all foreign-born Baltimoreans combined with those of mixed parentage. Social and economic data are from the 1930 and 1940 census, interpolated for each election. Voting statistics are from the *Maryland Manual* and Baltimore *Sun*.

53. *Sun*, 4 November 1936; Edwin Rothman, "Factional Machine Politics," 102–13. For a sampling of the persistent sniping between Jackson and Sellmayer, see *Sun*, 20 November 1935; 18 April 1936.

54. *Sun*, 28 June; 1, 3, 4 July; 20 August 1937.

55. *Evening Sun*, 10 September 1937; *Sun*, 9 November 1938; Kirwin, *Herbert R. O'Conor*, 224–26.

56. *Sun*, 4, 28 June; 11, 12, 13 July 1937; 6 January; 13 March; 18, 19, 20, 21 August 1938.

57. Edwin Rothman, "Factional Machine Politics," 123; *Sun*, 2, 9 October; 16 April 1937; 2 January; 2 February; 3, 9, 11 September 1938.

58. *Sun*, 24, 14 September 1938; Edwin Rothman, "Factional Machine Politics," 123; Kimberly, "The Depression," 270.

59. *Sun*, 12, 14, 23 October 1938; *Evening Sun*, 8 June; 22 July 1935. Nice's unrelieved attacks on the New Deal attracted in one instance the criticism of both Republicans and Democrats. While on a Caribbean cruise in 1936, Nice declared that "a second Roosevelt Administration will bring the United States to ruin and bankruptcy." Both parties censured Nice for exporting partisanship; the Democrats called the comment "inexcusable," and the Republicans said it reflected "poor taste." See *Sun*, 25 May 1936.

60. *Sun*, 12, 14, 16 October 1938.

61. *Sun*, 9 November 1938.

62. Scholnick, "The President and the Senator," 17–18; *Sun*, 17 August 1938; Kimberly, "The Depression," 265–69; *Labor Herald*, 3 March 1939.

63. *Sun*, 10, 12, 22, 26, 27, 29 June; 5, 15, 17, 19 July; 13, 22, 24, 28 August; 11 September 1938; *Labor Herald*, 9 September 1938.

64. Patrick Whalen to Aubrey Williams, 29 September 1938, WPA, State Files (Maryland), RG 69, No. 641, NA.

65. *Sun*, 16 July; 14, 15 August; 1, 3 September 1938.

66. *Labor Herald*, 9 September 1938; *Sun*, 15 July; 16 August 1938.

67. *Sun*, 17, 19 July 1938.

68. Daniel F. O'Connell to Marvin H. McIntyre, 1 September 1938, President's Official File 300, FDRP, Box 43.

69. *Sun*, 28 June 1938; Thomas D'Alesandro, Jr., to Franklin D. Roosevelt, 26 January 1939, President's Official File 300, FDRP, Box 43.

70. *Sun*, 8 May; 30 August 1938; 12 April 1939; D'Alesandro to Roosevelt, 26 January 1939.

71. *Sun*, 14 September 1938; D'Alesandro to Roosevelt, 26 January 1939.

72. *Sun*, 1, 7, 8 March 1939.

73. *Sun*, 7, 19 February 1939.

74. "Communication from Commission on Governmental Efficiency and Economy, Inc.," *JPCC*, 22 March 1939, 1030–35; *Sun*, 3, 8 March 1939.

75. "Communication from Commission on Efficiency"; *Sun*, 15 June 1938.

76. *Sun*, 29, 31 March 1939.

77. *Sun*, 7 December 1938; 29 March; 10, 12 April 1939.

78. Edwin Rothman, "Factional Machine Politics," 123–27; *Sun*, 13 April; 3 May 1939.

79. *Labor Herald*, 24 March 1939.

80. Edward J. Colgan to Franklin D. Roosevelt, 18 August 1933, President's Official File 300, FDRP, Box 43.

81. Gilbert Dailey to James Farley, 10 September 1936, Farley Correspondence, DNCP, Box 1095.

82. Patrick Whalen to Aubrey Williams, 29 September 1938, WPA, RG 69, No. 641, NA.

83. *Sun*, 4 September 1938.

84. These estimates of voting behavior are derived from regression analysis of the 1931, 1935, and 1939 mayoral elections and the 1932, 1936, and 1940 presidential elections. For an explanation of the methods employed, see n. 52, above.

85. "Ways and Means of Building up the Howard W. Jackson Section of the Democratic Party"; "Patronage for Negro Democrats in Baltimore City," (1935), Jackson Administrative Files, RG 9, Series #20, A16, Box 231, BCA.

Chapter 8

1. Mack, "National Youth Administration." Barry D. Karl discusses the failed efforts at the "Third New Deal" to reorganize the office of the executive; see Karl, *The Uneasy State*, 177–81.

2. F. H. Dryden to Howard O. Hunter, 12 February 1940, WPA, State Files (Maryland), RG 69, No. 610, clipping enclosed, NA.

3. "Communication from Commission on Governmental Efficiency and Economy, Inc.," *JPCC*, 22 March 1939, 1030–35; Warren Belcher to George Field, 15 February; 30 April 1943, WPA, RG 69, No. 610, NA.

4. *Sun*, 30 August 1940. For the popular response to Jackson's announcement against FDR, see the Jackson Administrative Files, RG 9, Series #21, G1-1630, Box 244, BCA.

5. Herbert R. O'Conor to Franklin D. Roosevelt, 18 October 1940, President's Personal File, FDRP, Box 6844.

6. Gelfand, *Nation of Cities*, 23–70 (Mayor La Guardia's quotation appears on page 43); Trout, *Boston*, 62.

7. Bremer, "Along the 'American Way,'" 638, 642–43, 650–51, 652.

8. *Sun*, 23 May 1933.

9. The phrase "the localization of federal programs" is from Trout, *Boston*, 315.

10. See, for example, Stellhorn, "Depression and Decline," 113.

11. For a useful discussion of the political significance of the popular support of FDR in urban areas in 1936, see Bernstein, *A Caring Society*, 296–99; and Kleppner, *Who Voted?* 102–3.

12. *Evening Sun*, 12 June 1935.

13. *Sun*, 3 December 1938.

14. "Communication from Commission on Governmental Efficiency and Economy," *JPCC*, 22 March 1939, 1030–35; *Sun*, 11 April 1937; 13 April 1938; 3 May 1939.

15. "Report," 4 April 1935; William Burdick to Clarence Perkins, 4 April 1935, both in PHA, Project Files, RG 196, Box 208, NA; *Sun*, 3 May 1939.

16. *Sun*, 22 January 1938; 3 March; 27 December 1939. See also Chapter 7.

17. Family Welfare Association, *Annual Report for 1934*; Bremner, *American Philanthrophy*, 163; *Councillor* 1 (February 1936): 1; FWA, *Annual Report for 1938*.

18. Reed, "Efforts of Social Workers"; Jones and Herrick, *Citizens in Service*, 68. It should also be noted that social workers in Baltimore, while cooperating with and supporting the Peoples Unemployment League, strongly denounced Communists and deeply resented the seamen's actions in taking over the Anchorage building and establishing their own system of relief. The actions of social workers, then, suggested a certain ambivalence toward the changes they noted among their clients.

19. This conclusion receives a fuller exposition in William Bremer's thoughtful study, *Depression Winters*, which traces the influence of New York City social workers on the policies and programs of the New Deal.

20. Waxter and Euchtman, "Administration of Public Welfare," 16–19; "Public and Private Responsibility," 14–16; FWA, *Annual Report for 1940*; "Agencies Merge"; Maryland, Commission on Governmental Efficiency and Economy, *Department of Public Welfare*, 1; Pfeiffer, "Problems of Administration in Community Organization."

21. *Sun*, 13, 14 June 1938. Also see Chapter 4.

22. *Sun*, 4 March; 8 September 1938; 10, 17, 21 February 1939. See also Warbasse, *Cooperative Democracy Through Voluntary Association of People as Consumers*.

23. *Labor in Art: An Exhibition*.

24. Holt, "American Anti-Statist Tradition," 46.

25. Charles H. Trout suggests this for the Boston experience (*Boston*, 321).

26. Lewis, "War Problems"; Maryland, *Report of the Governor's Commission*, 57, 117; George C. Grant to Franklin D. Roosevelt, 28 January 1941, President's Personal File, FDRP, Box 6844. Grant's letter, along with the sentiments of a number of blacks in the city, tends to affirm Harvard Sitkoff's finding that the New Deal allowed for the "emergence of a new type of faith" (*New Deal for Blacks*, 1:83).

27. *Sun*, 10 April; 13 July 1943.

Selected Bibliography

Primary Sources

MANUSCRIPT COLLECTIONS

Annapolis, Maryland
  Maryland Hall of Records
    Executive Papers of Governor Harry Nice
    Executive Papers of Governor Albert C. Ritchie
    Governor's Correspondence. Official Correspondence of Harry Nice
    Governor's Correspondence. Official Correspondence of Herbert R.
      O'Conor
    Governor's Correspondence. Official Correspondence of Albert C.
      Ritchie
Baltimore, Maryland
  Baltimore City Archives
    Mayor Howard Jackson Administrative Files, Record Group 9
  Baltimore Office of the Metropolitan Council AFL-CIO Unions
    Minutes of the Baltimore Federation of Labor, 1927–39
  Baltimore Region Institutional Studies Center, University of Baltimore
    Citizens' Planning and Housing Association Papers
  Maryland Room, Enoch Pratt Free Library
    Minutes of Meetings, August 1920–January 1932, Social Service
      Exchange
    Vertical File
Chapel Hill, North Carolina
  Southern Historical Collection, University of North Carolina
    Samuel Chiles Mitchell Papers
College Park, Maryland
  McKeldin Library, University of Maryland College Park
    Albert C. Ritchie Papers
    Millard S. Tydings Papers
Hyde Park, New York
  Franklin D. Roosevelt Library

Democratic National Committee Papers
   James A. Farley Correspondence (1933–36)
   State File (Maryland, 1928–42)
   Women's Division (1933–44)
Harry Hopkins Papers
John Ihlder Papers
Franklin D. Roosevelt Papers: President's Personal File; Official File.
Ithaca, New York
   Martin P. Catherwood Library of the New York State School of Industrial and
      Labor Relations, Cornell University
   Amalgamated Clothing Workers of America Papers
Suitland, Maryland
   Washington National Records Center
   National Emergency Council, Record Group 44
Washington, D.C.
   National Archives
   Civilian Conservation Corps
   Civil Works Administration, Record Group 69
   Federal Emergency Relief Administration, Record Group 69
   National Labor Relations Board, Record Group 25
   National Recovery Administration, Record Group 9
   National Youth Administration, Record Group 119
   President's Organization on Unemployment Relief, Record Group 73
   Public Housing Administration, Record Group 196
   Public Works Administration, Record Group 135
   Reconstruction Finance Corporation, Record Group 234
   Women's Bureau, Record Group 86
   Works Progress Administration, Record Group 69

INTERVIEWS AND CORRESPONDENCE

Author's interview with Jacob Edelman, 18 June 1983.
Author's interview with Sara Barron, 1 March 1986.
Letter to the author from Broadus Mitchell, 19 September 1975.
Letter to the author from Joel Seidman, 17 November 1975.
Letter to the author from Frank N. Trager, 24 October 1975.
New York State School of Industrial and Labor Relations Library, New York City
   Division of Cornell University. "Oral History Interview with Sara Barron by
   Barbara Wertheimer, June 4, 1976, Baltimore, Maryland."

NEWSPAPERS AND PERIODICALS

The Afro-American (Baltimore), 1929–39.
Baltimore, 1925–35.
The Baltimore Federationist, 1930–39.
CIO News (Baltimore edition), 1939–40.
The Councillor (Baltimore), 1936–43.
The Evening Sun (Baltimore), 1929–40.
The Garment Worker (New York), 1935.
Journal of Electrical Workers and Operators (Washington, D.C.), 1936.
The Labor Herald (Baltimore), 1936–39.
Maryland Employment News (Baltimore), 1940–41.
The Maryland Leader (Baltimore), 1928–36.
Monthly Labor Review (Washington, D.C.), 1929–41.
The Municipal Journal (Baltimore), 1929–31.
The Post (Baltimore), 1929–33.
Sew-Sew News (Baltimore), 1939–40.
The Sun (Baltimore), 1928–41.

GOVERNMENT PUBLICATIONS

For publications that are not readily accessible, the location where the author consulted the publication is given.

Baltimore

Appropriations. *The Ordinance of Estimates*. Baltimore: n.p., 1929–40.
City Council. *Journal of the Proceedings of the City Council of Baltimore*. Baltimore: King Brothers, 1929–39.
Criminal Justice Commission. *Annual Report*. Baltimore: n.p., 1930–40.
Department of Public Welfare. *Annual Report*. Baltimore: n.p., 1935–42.
_____. *Annual Statistical Report*. Baltimore: n.p., 1937.
Emergency Relief Commission. *Annual Statistical Report*. Baltimore: n.p., 1934–36.
_____. *Financial Aid and Statistical Report: September 1, 1933, to June 30, 1936*. Compiled by Thomas E. Cosgrove, Jr. Baltimore: n.p., 1936.
_____. *Financial Report, Covering the Entire Period of Operations, September 1, 1933, to June 30, 1936*. Baltimore: n.p., 1936.
Housing Authority. *Annual Report*. Baltimore: n.p., 1940. (Consulted at CPHAP, Box 7, Folder no. 4.)
_____. *Low Rent Housing Survey: Baltimore, Maryland, 1941*. Baltimore: n.p., 1941.
Mayor [Broening] Report to the City Council on the General State of the City, 11 May 1931. Baltimore: n.p., 1931.

Mayor's Message to the Members of the City Council. Baltimore: n.p., 1930–39.

Municipal Commission on Employment Stabilization. *Report of the Municipal Commission on Employment Stabilization and the Municipal Free Unemployment Service.* Baltimore: n.p., September 1931.

———. "Report on the Shorter Work Week." Baltimore: n.p., December 1931.

———. "Unemployment Insurance: An Analysis of the Problem with Special Reference to Maryland." Baltimore: n.p., October 1932.

Supervisors of City Charities. *Annual Report.* Baltimore: Department of Charities and Correction, 1929–33.

Maryland

Bank Commissioners. *Twenty-Fourth Annual Report of the Bank Commissioners of the State of Maryland.* Baltimore: State Printers, 1934.

Commission on Governmental Efficiency and Economy. *The Department of Public Welfare, State of Maryland.* Baltimore: State Printers, 1948.

———. *Some Physical and Population Characteristics of Baltimore: An Analysis and Graphic Presentation of Factors to Guide in Sound City Planning and in Dealing with the Menace of Urban Blight.* Baltimore: State Printers, 1943.

Commissioner of Labor and Statistics. *Annual Report.* Baltimore: King Brothers, Inc., and Twentieth Century Printing, 1929–39.

———. *Report of Investigation of Strike Existing in Men's Garment Industry in Baltimore.* By J. Knox Insley. Baltimore: n.p., 14 December 1932.

Emergency Relief Administration. *Maryland's Emergency Relief Program: From April, 1933, through December, 1935.* Baltimore: Board of State Aid and Charities, 1936.

———. *Relief—A Challenge to Maryland: A Report of the First Twenty-One Months of Maryland's Relief Administration.* Baltimore: Board of State Aid and Charities, 1935.

Governor's Committee on Unemployment Insurance and Relief. *Report of the Governor's Committee.* Baltimore: n.p., 4 March 1935. (Consulted at Johns Hopkins University Library.)

Report of the Committee on State Policy and Revenue for Aid to the Needy. By William J. Casey. Baltimore: The Daily Record Company, 1936.

Report of the Governor's Commission on Problems Affecting the Negro Population. By Joseph P. Healy. Baltimore: n.p., March 1943.

Report of the Social Welfare Survey Commission of the State of Maryland. Baltimore: Board of State Aid and Charities, 20 December 1930.

Secretary of State. *Maryland Manual: A Compendium of Legal, Historical, and Statistical Information Relating to the State of Maryland.* Baltimore: State Printers, 1929–40.

————. *Message of Governor Albert C. Ritchie to the General Assembly of Maryland of 1931.* Baltimore: King Brothers, Inc., 1931.

————. *Message of Governor Albert C. Ritchie to the General Assembly of Maryland of 1933.* Baltimore: Twentieth Century Printing Co., 1933.

State Planning Commission. *An Appraisal of the Federal Works Program in Maryland, Including Such Agencies as: Federal Emergency Relief Administration, Civil Works Administration, Public Works Administration, Works Progress Administration.* Baltimore: State Printers, March 1938.

————. *Five Years of State Planning.* Baltimore: State Printers, 1938.

————. "Maryland Federal Public Works Program, 1924–1940." By Alvin Pasarew. Baltimore: State Printers, June 1941.

————. "Report on Men's Clothing Industry." By Abraham Imberman. (Sponsored by the Works Progress Administration.) Baltimore: State Printers, November 1936.

————. *Ten Years' Expenditures for Public Works, 1924–1933.* Baltimore: State Printers, 1936.

————. *Ten Years of State Planning.* Baltimore: State Printers, 1945.

Unemployment Compensation Board. *First Annual Report.* Baltimore: n.p., 1937.

————. *Second Annual Report.* Baltimore: n.p., 1938.

United States

Bureau of the Census. *Abstract of the Fifteenth Census of the United States.* Washington, D.C.: Government Printing Office, 1933.

————. *Fifteenth Census of the United States, 1930: Population.* Washington, D.C.: Government Printing Office, 1932.

————. *Fifteenth Census of the United States, 1930: Unemployment.* Washington, D.C.: Government Printing Office, 1931.

————. *Fourteenth Census of the United States, 1920: Population.* Washington, D.C.: Government Printing Office, 1921.

————. *Sixteenth Census of the United States, 1940: Housing.* Washington, D.C.: Government Printing Office, 1942.

————. *Sixteenth Census of the United States, 1940: Population.* Washington, D.C.: Government Printing Office, 1943.

————. *Statistical Abstract of the United States.* Washington, D.C.: Government Printing Office, 1929–41.

Civilian Conservation Corps. *Civilian Conservation Corps Program of the United States Department of the Interior, March 1933 to June 30, 1943.* By Conrad Wirth. Washington, D.C.: Government Printing Office, 1944.

————. *Report on Special Educational Projects.* Washington, D.C.: Government Printing Office, March 1937. (Consulted at EPFL.)

Department of Labor. *Trends in Different Types of Public and Private Relief in Urban*

Areas, 1929–1935. By Emma Winslow. Children's Bureau Publication No. 237. Washington, D.C.: Government Printing Office, 1937.

Federal Emergency Relief Administration. "New Cases on the Relief Rolls." By Howard B. Meyers. Washington, D.C.: Government Printing Office, 19 July 1934. (Consulted at Library of Congress.)

————. "Relative Effects of CWA and Private Employment on the Relief Loads in Five Selected Cities." By Howard B. Meyers. Washington, D.C.: Government Printing Office, 13 July 1934. (Consulted at Library of Congress.)

————. "The Relief Rolls and the Underemployed." By John H. Mueller. Washington, D.C.: Government Printing Office, 16 July 1934. (Consulted at Library of Congress.)

Federal Home Loan Bank Board. *Waverly: A Study in Neighborhood Conservation.* Washington, D.C.: Government Printing Office, 1940.

Federal Security Agency. War Manpower Commission. *Final Report of the National Youth Administration.* Washington, D.C.: Government Printing Office, 1944.

Federal Works Agency. *Final Report on the WPA Program, 1935–1943.* Washington, D.C.: Government Printing Office, 1946.

————. *Works Progress Administration. Final Report of the Federal Emergency Relief Administration.* By Theodore Whiting. Washington, D.C.: Government Printing Office, 1942.

Housing Authority. *Annual Report, 1938.* Washington, D.C.: Government Printing Office, 1939.

National Emergency Council. "Maryland State and National Reports." Washington, D.C.: Government Printing Office, 1933–38. (Consulted at EPFL.)

————. "Narrative Review of Agency Operations, 1933–1938." Baltimore: n.p., September 1938. (Consulted at Vertical File, EPFL.)

————. "The National Emergency Council: A Chronological Review of its Activities from November 17, 1933, through December 31, 1937." Baltimore: n.p., 1938. (Consulted at EPFL.)

————. *Report of the Proceedings of the Statewide Coordination Meeting of Federal Agencies Operating in Maryland, January 20, 1936.* Baltimore: n.p., 1936.

National Youth Administration. "The Maryland Student Work Program." *Report for 1939–1940.* Baltimore: n.p., 1941. (Consulted at EPFL.)

————. "A Special Report to the Advisory Committee of Baltimore City." By Ryland N. Dempster. Baltimore: n.p., 20 June 1938. (Consulted at EPFL.)

President's Organization on Unemployment Relief. *A Community Plan for Service to Transients.* Prepared by the National Association of Travelers Aid Societies. Washington, D.C.: Government Printing Office, 1931.

Public Housing Administration. *Slums and Blighted Areas in the United States.* By Edith Elmer Wood. Federal Emergency Administration of Public Works, Housing Division Bulletin No. 1. Washington, D.C.: Public Works Administration, 1935.

Works Progress Administration. *Organization and Procedures of the Maryland Board of State Aid and Charities.* Research Bulletin 9670. Washington, D.C.: Government Printing Office, July 1936.

———. "Reports of State Directors, Division of Women's and Professional Projects." Washington, D.C.: Government Printing Office, 1936. (Consulted at Library of Congress.)

———. *The Transient Unemployed: A Description and Analysis of the Transient Relief Population.* By John N. Webb. Washington, D.C.: W.P.A. Division of Social Research, 1935.

———. *Urban Workers on Relief, Part I: The Occupational Characteristics of Workers on Relief in Urban Areas, May 1934.* Washington, D.C.: W.P.A. Division of Social Research, 1936.

OTHER PRINTED PRIMARY SOURCES

"Agencies Merge." *Councillor* 3 (June 1938): 14–16.

Baltimore Chamber of Commerce. *Annual Report.* Baltimore: Hess Printing Co., 1932–43.

Baltimore Council of Social Agencies. "An Analysis of Relief Expenditures and Relief Caseloads in Baltimore City, 1931 through 1935." *Relief Bulletin No. 4.* Baltimore: n.p., 17 February 1936. (Consulted at Vertical File, EPFL.)

———. *Annual Report.* Baltimore: n.p., 1936–41.

Baltimore Social Service Exchange. *Executive Reports.* Baltimore: n.p., 1929–33.

Bealmear, Cleveland. "A Business Man Looks at Relief." *Councillor* 2 (June 1937): 12–14.

Bogue, Mary F. *Report of a Study of Needs and Resources for Unemployment Relief in Maryland.* Baltimore: Maryland State Conference of Social Work, 1932.

Bonnell, Robert O. "How Some Families Live on WPA Wages." *Councillor* 3 (December 1938): 27–31.

Bristol, Margaret Cochran. "Transients in Recent Reports." *Social Service Review* 7 (1936): 311–28.

Citizens' Alliance for Social Security. "The Relief Purge." Baltimore: n.p., August 1937. (Consulted at EPFL.)

Citizens' Emergency Relief Committee of Baltimore. "Report of the Citizens' Emergency Relief Committee of Baltimore to the Mayor and Board of Estimates as of October 1, 1932." Baltimore: n.p., 1932.

Citizens' Housing Council. *Annual Report.* Baltimore: n.p., 3 February 1941.

Culver, Benjamin. "Transient Unemployed Men." *Sociology and Social Research* 17 (1933): 519–34.

Emergency Charity Association. *Annual Statistical Report, 16 June 1936–15 June 1937.* Baltimore: n.p., 1937.

Fales, W. Thurber. "Population Changes in Baltimore." *Councillor* 6 (June 1941): 13–21.

"Family Welfare and General Dependency." *Councillor* 4 (December 1939): 11–19.

Family Welfare Association. *Annual Report*. Baltimore: n.p., 1929–40.

Fenn, Don Frank. "Relief Goes Back to the States and Localities." *Councillor* 1 (February 1936): 3–5.

Fringer, David B. "Local Labor and Defense." *Councillor* 6 (June 1941): 1–6.

Gallin, Leo. "Strictly Private." *Councillor* 1 (October 1936): 8–10.

Greenstein, Harry. "Defense and the Social Agencies." *Councillor* 5 (December 1940): 1–7.

―――. "Launching the Baltimore Council." *Councillor* 1 (February 1936): 1–3.

―――. "The 1936 Legislature in Retrospect." *Councillor* 1 (May 1936): 1–3.

Griffing, J. B. "The Educational Process in the CCC." *Sociology and Social Research* 19 (1935): 376–80.

Healy, Joseph P. "Problems Affecting Maryland's Negro Population." *Councillor* 8 (March–April 1943): 13–17.

Hollander, Jacob H. *Report of the Hearing of Strikers from the Schoeneman Shops in Connection with an Investigation of Conditions in the Clothing Industry Held at City Hall*. Baltimore: n.p., 13 October 1932.

―――. *Report to Honorable Howard W. Jackson on Working Conditions in the Garment Industry*. Baltimore: n.p., 24 October 1932.

Hopkins, D. Luke. "Relief Supplementation of WPA Wages." *Councillor* 1 (February 1936): 7–8.

Ihlder, John. "Housing." *Councillor* 2 (December 1937): 5–10.

Johnson, Charles Spurgeon. *The Negro in Baltimore Industries*. Baltimore: Baltimore Urban League, 1932.

Jones, Dewey R. "Charity But Not Work, Unemployment Still Bad, Urban League Makes Exhaustive Study." In *Pamphlets on Unemployment in the United States*. No. 56. Washington, D.C.: Government Printing Office, 1931.

Judge, Maria C. "Lack of Care for Transients." *Councillor* 1 (February 1936): 5–7.

Kerns, J. Harvey. "The Community Organizes to Meet Problems of Racial Tensions." *Councillor* 8 (September 1943): 11–13.

Labor in Art. An Exhibition of Paintings, Sculpture, and Prints Sponsored by the Baltimore Federation of Labor and Held at the Baltimore Museum of Art, September 5 through September 30, 1938. Baltimore: n.p., 1938.

Lewis, Edward S. "War Problems of Baltimore's Negro Community." *Councillor* 7 (September 1942): 10–16.

Locke, Harvey. "Unemployed Men in Chicago Shelters." *Sociology and Social Research* 19 (1935): 420–28.

Mack, Mary D. "National Youth Administration in the Defense Program." *Councillor* 6 (March–April 1941): 22–25.

MacNeil, Douglas H. *Seven Years of Unemployment Relief in New Jersey: A Report Prepared for the Committee on Social Security*. Washington, D.C.: Government Printing Office, 1938.

Manny, Theodore B., and Clowes, Harry G. *An Analysis of the Relief Population in Selected Areas of Maryland.* College Park: University of Maryland Social Research Studies, 1937.

"Meeting of the City Delegation to the Legislature Held on February 21, 1936." Baltimore: n.p., 1936. (Consulted at EPFL.)

"Minutes of the Conference, Maryland State Transient Bureau Division of Maryland Emergency Relief, March 12, 13, 1935." Baltimore: n.p., 1935. (Consulted at EPFL.)

Morton, Frances H. *A Social Study of Wards 5 and 10 in Baltimore, Maryland.* Baltimore: Baltimore Council of Social Agencies, 1937.

"Public and Private Responsibility for Social Welfare." *Councillor* 1 (October 1936): 14–16.

"Recreation Program of the Division of Recreation for Colored People and the Works Progress Administration, From January 1 to June 1, 1936." Submitted by Gerald E. Allen. Baltimore: n.p., 1936.

Reed, Ellery F. "Efforts of Social Workers Toward Social Reorganization." *Social Forces* 14 (October 1935): 87–93.

―――. *Federal Transient Program: An Evaluative Survey, May to July 1934.* New York: Committee on Care of Transient and Homeless, 1934.

Reid, Ira De A. *The Negro Community of Baltimore: A Social Survey.* New York: National Urban League, 1934.

―――. *Negro Membership in American Labor Unions.* New York: Alexander Press, 1930.

"Report of the Baltimore Emergency Nursery Schools Under the WPA." Baltimore: n.p., 1938–39.

"Report of the WPA Nursery Schools for the year 1940–41." Baltimore: n.p., 1941.

Ritchie, Albert C. "The 'Fifty-Fifty' System of Federal Aid, Why It Should Be Stopped." Address of the Seventeenth Annual Conference of Governors, 30 June 1925. (Consulted at Library of Congress.)

―――. "Which Shall It Be, a Government of Law or a Government of Men?" Pamphlet No. 208 in *Pamphlets on Prohibition in the United States.* N.p., n.d. (Consulted at Library of Congress.)

Sanderson, Ross W. "Houses and Baltimore." *Councillor* 2 (June 1937): 1–4.

Singleton, Evelyn Ellen. *Workmen's Compensation in Maryland.* Baltimore: Johns Hopkins Press, 1935.

"Statement of Delegation Representing the People's Unemployment League of Maryland to the Honorable Harry W. Nice, Governor, September 13, 1935." Baltimore: n.p., 1935. (Consulted at EPFL.)

Warbasse, James Peter. *Cooperative Democracy Through Voluntary Association of the People as Consumers.* New York: Cooperative League of the U.S.A., 1936.

Ward, Anna. "Public Assistance before the General Assembly." *Councillor* 3 (December 1938): 1–6.

————. "Statement Concerning Unemployment Relief, the Present Situation, and the Outlook for 1932." Baltimore: n.p., 1931. (Consulted at EPFL.)

Waxter, T. J. S. "The Relief Situation in Baltimore, June 1939." *Councillor* 4 (June–July 1939): 5–10.

Waxter, T. J. S., and Euchtman, Frieda B. "Factors Affecting the Administration of Public Welfare." *Councillor* 3 (June 1938): 15–22.

"What Can the Union Do for Me? A Steelworkers Play." Sparrows Point, Md.: n.p., April 1940.

"What Is the NYA?" *Councillor* 1 (February 1936): 19.

Williams, Edward A. *Federal Aid for Relief*. New York: Columbia University Press, 1939.

Young, Pauline V. "The New Poor." *Sociology and Social Research* 17 (January–February, 1933): 234–42.

Secondary Sources

Almond, Gabriel, and Lasswell, Harold D. "Aggressive Behavior by Clients toward Public Relief Administrators: A Configurative Analysis." *American Political Science Review* 28 (August 1934): 643–55.

Argersinger, Jo Ann E. "Assisting the 'Loafers': Transient Relief in Baltimore, 1933–1937." *Labor History* 23 (Spring 1982): 226–45.

————. "Baltimore: The Depression Years." Ph.D. dissertation, George Washington University, 1980.

————. "From Charity to the Dole: Baltimore's Response to the Problem of Relief, 1929–1933." *Journal of Historical Studies* 4 (1980): 65–87.

————. "To Discipline an Industry: Workers, Employers, and the ACWA in Baltimore." Paper presented at the annual meeting of the Social Science History Association, Chicago, November 1985.

Arnold, Joseph L. "The Last of the Good Old Days: Politics in Baltimore, 1920–1950." *Maryland Historical Magazine* 71 (Fall 1976): 443–48.

————. "Suburban Growth and Municipal Annexation, 1748–1918." *Maryland Historical Magazine* 73 (Summer 1978): 109–28.

Asher, Nina. "Dorothy Jacobs Bellanca: Feminist Trade Unionist, 1894–1946." Ph.D. dissertation, State University of New York at Binghampton, 1982.

Austin, Michael J., and Betten, Neil. "Intellectual Origins of Community Organization, 1920–1939." *Social Service Review* 51 (March 1977): 155–70.

Avnet, I. Duke. "Pat Whalen." *Phylon* 12 (September 1951): 249–54.

Badger, Anthony J. "The New Deal and the Localities." In *The Growth of Federal Power in American History*, edited by Rhodri Jeffreys-Jones and Bruce Collins, pp. 102–15. Edinburgh: Scottish Academic Press, 1983.

————. *Prosperity Road: The New Deal, Tobacco, and North Carolina*. Chapel Hill: University of North Carolina Press, 1980.

Bakke, E. Wight. *The Unemployed Worker*. New Haven: Yale University Press, 1940.

Bauman, John F. "Safe and Sanitary without the Costly Frills: The Evolution of Public Housing in Philadelphia, 1929–1941." *Pennsylvania Magazine of History and Biography* 101 (January 1977): 114–28.

Beirne, Randall. "Residential Growth and Stability in the Baltimore Industrial Community of Canton during the Late Nineteenth Century." *Maryland Historical Magazine* 74 (March 1979): 39–51.

_____. "Steadfast Americans: Residential Stability Among Workers in Baltimore, 1880–1930." Ph.D. dissertation, University of Maryland College Park, 1976.

Bellush, Bernard. *The Failure of the NRA*. New York: W. W. Norton, 1975.

Berkhofer, Robert F., Jr. "The Organizational Interpretation of American History: A New Synthesis." *Prospects* 4 (1977): 611–29.

Berkowitz, Edward, and McQuaid, Kim. "Businessman and Bureaucrat: The Evolution of the American Social Welfare System, 1900–1940." *Journal of Economic History* 38 (March 1978): 120–41.

_____. *Creating the Welfare State: The Political Economy of Twentieth-Century Reform*. New York: Praeger, 1980.

Bernstein, Irving. *A Caring Society: The New Deal, the Worker, and the Great Depression*. Boston: Houghton Mifflin, 1985.

_____. *The Lean Years: A History of the American Worker, 1920–1933*. Boston: Houghton Mifflin, 1960.

_____. *Turbulent Years: A History of the American Worker, 1933–1941*. Boston: Houghton Mifflin, 1969.

Biles, Roger. *Memphis in the Great Depression*. Knoxville: University of Tennessee Press, 1986.

Blackwelder, Julia Kirk. *Women of the Depression: Caste and Culture in San Antonio, 1929–1939*. College Station: Texas A&M University Press, 1984.

Blakey, George T. *Hard Times and New Deal in Kentucky, 1929–1939*. Lexington: University Press of Kentucky, 1986.

Blumberg, Barbara. *The New Deal and the Unemployed: The View from New York City*. Lewisburg, Pa.: Bucknell University Press, 1979.

Boyte, Harry C. *The Backyard Revolution: Understanding the New Citizen Movement*. Philadelphia: Temple University Press, 1980.

Braeman, John; Bremner, Robert H.; and Brody, David, eds. *The New Deal*. 2 vols. Vol. 1, *The National Level*. Vol. 2, *The State and Local Levels*. Columbus: Ohio State University Press, 1975.

Bremer, William W. "Along the 'American Way': The New Deal's Work Relief Programs for the Unemployed." *Journal of American History* 62 (December 1975): 636–52.

_____. *Depression Winters: New York Social Workers and the New Deal*. Philadelphia: Temple University Press, 1984.

Bremner, Robert H. *American Philanthropy*. Chicago: University of Chicago Press, 1960.

Brody, David. *Workers in Industrial America: Essays on the Twentieth-Century Struggle*. New York: Oxford University Press, 1980.

Brown, Dorothy. "The Election of 1934: The 'New Deal' in Maryland." *Maryland Historical Magazine* 68 (Winter 1973): 405–21.

————. "Maryland between the Wars." In *Maryland: A History, 1632–1974*, edited by Richard Walsh and William Lloyd Fox, pp. 672–772. Baltimore: Maryland Historical Society, 1974.

Brown, Josephine Chapin. *Public Relief, 1929–1939*. New York: Octagon Books, 1971.

Burns, James MacGregor. *Roosevelt: The Lion and the Fox*. New York: Harcourt Brace, 1956.

Cahn, Louis. *Man's Concern for Man: The First Fifty Years of the Associated Jewish Charities and Welfare Fund of Baltimore*. Baltimore: Associated Jewish Charities and Welfare Fund, 1970.

Chamberlain, Vivian E. "The Five Largest CIO Unions in Baltimore, Maryland, with Special Reference to the Negro." M.A. thesis, Howard University, 1945.

Charles, Searle F. *Minister of Relief: Harry Hopkins and the Depression*. Syracuse: Syracuse University Press, 1963.

Chepaitis, Joseph. "The First Two Administrations of Albert Cabell Ritchie, Governor of Maryland, 1920–1927." M.A. thesis, Georgetown University, 1965.

Conkin, Paul K. *The New Deal*. New York: Thomas Y. Crowell, 1967.

Connery, Robert H. *The Administration of an NRA Code*. Chicago: Public Administration Service, 1938.

Coode, Thomas H., and Bauman, John F. *People, Poverty, and Politics: Pennsylvania during the Great Depression*. Lewisburg, Pa.: Bucknell University Press, 1981.

Crooks, James B. *Politics and Progress: The Rise of Urban Progressivism in Baltimore*. Baton Rouge: Louisiana State University Press, 1968.

Dürr, W. T. "The Conscience of a City: A History of the Citizens' Planning and Housing Association and Efforts to Improve Housing for the Poor in Baltimore, Maryland, 1937–1954." Ph.D. dissertation, Johns Hopkins University, 1972.

Egolf, Jeremy R. "The Limits of Shop Floor Struggle: Workers vs. The Bedaux System at Willapa Harbor Lumber Mills, 1933–1935." *Labor History* 26 (Spring 1985): 195–229.

Elvove, Joseph T. "State Bank Failures in Maryland." M.A. thesis, University of Maryland College Park, 1936.

Fisher, Robert. "From Grass-Roots Organizing to Community Service: Community Organization Practice in the Community Center Movement, 1907–1930." In *Community Organization for Urban Social Change: A Historical Perspective*, edited by Robert Fisher and Peter Romanofsky, pp. 33–58. Westport, Conn.: Greenwood Press, 1981.

Fones-Wolf, Elizabeth. "Industrial Unionism and Labor Movement Culture in Depression-Era Philadelphia." *Pennsylvania Magazine of History and Biography* 109 (January 1985): 3–26.

Fox, William Lloyd. "Social-Cultural Developments from the Civil War to 1920." In *Maryland: A History, 1632–1974*, edited by Richard Walsh and William Lloyd Fox, pp. 499–589. Baltimore: Maryland Historical Society, 1974.

Fraser, Steven Clark. "Sidney Hillman and the Origins of the 'New Unionism,' 1890–1933." Ph.D. dissertation, Rutgers University, 1983.

Galambos, Louis. "The Emerging Organizational Synthesis in Modern American History." *Business History Review* 44 (Autumn 1970): 279–90.

Garonzik, Joseph. "The Racial and Ethnic Make-up of Baltimore Neighborhoods, 1850–1870." *Maryland Historical Magazine* 71 (Fall 1976): 392–402.

Garraty, John A. *Unemployment in History: Economic Thought and Public Policy.* New York: Harper & Row, 1978.

Gelfand, Mark I. *A Nation of Cities: The Federal Government and Urban America, 1933–1965.* New York: Oxford University Press, 1975.

Gibson, William. "A History of Family and Child Welfare Agencies in Baltimore, 1849–1943." Ph.D. dissertation, Ohio State University, 1969.

Graham, Otis L., Jr. "The Planning Ideal and American Reality: The 1930s." In *The Hofstadter Aegis: A Memorial*, edited by Stanley Elkins and Eric McKitrick, pp. 257–99. New York: Knopf, 1974.

_____. *Toward a Planned Society.* New York: Oxford University Press, 1975.

Green, James R. *The World of the Worker: Labor in Twentieth-Century America.* New York: Hill & Wang, 1980.

Hamilton, Dona Cooper. "The National Urban League and New Deal Programs." *Social Service Review* 58 (June 1984): 227–43.

Harris, Howell. "The Snares of Liberalism? Politicians, Bureaucrats, and the Shaping of Federal Labor Relations Policy in the United States, ca. 1915–1947." In *Shop Floor Bargaining and the State: Historical and Comparative Perspectives*, edited by Steven Tolliday and Jonathan Zeitlin, pp. 148–91. Cambridge and New York: Cambridge University Press, 1985.

Hawley, Ellis W. "The Corporative Component of the American Quest for National Efficiency, 1900–1917." Paper presented at the annual meeting of the Organization of American Historians, New York, April 1986.

_____. "The New Deal and Business." In *The New Deal: The National Level*, edited by John Braeman, Robert H. Bremner, and David Brody, pp. 50–82. Columbus: Ohio State University Press, 1975.

Heinemann, Ronald L. *Depression and New Deal in Virginia: The Enduring Dominion.* Charlottesville: University Press of Virginia, 1983.

Helmbold, Lois Rita. "Making Choices, Making Do: Black and White Working Class Women's Lives during the Great Depression." Ph.D. dissertation, Stanford University, 1983.

Holmes, Michael S. *The New Deal in Georgia: An Administrative History.* Westport, Conn.: Greenwood Press, 1975.

Holt, James. "The New Deal and the American Anti-Statist Tradition." In *The New Deal: The National Level*, edited by John Braeman, Robert H. Bremner, and David Brody, pp. 27–49. Columbus: Ohio State University Press, 1975.

Howard, Donald S. *The WPA and Federal Relief Policy.* New York: Russell Sage Foundation, 1943.

Hunter, Robert. "Virginia and the New Deal." In *The New Deal: The State and Local Levels*, edited by John Braeman, Robert H. Bremner, and David Brody, pp. 103–36. Columbus: Ohio State University Press, 1975.

Ingalls, Robert P. *Herbert H. Lehman and New York's Little New Deal.* New York: New York University Press, 1975.

Israel, Jerry, ed. *Building the Organizational Society: Essays on Associational Activities in Modern America.* New York: Free Press, 1972.

Jeffries, John W. *Testing the Roosevelt Coalition: Connecticut Society and Politics in the Era of World War II.* Knoxville: University of Tennessee Press, 1979.

Jones, John Finbar, and Herrick, John Middlemist. *Citizens in Service: Volunteers in Social Welfare during the Depression, 1929–1941.* East Lansing: Michigan State University Press, 1976.

Judd, Richard Munson. *The New Deal in Vermont: Its Impact and Aftermath.* New York: Garland, 1979.

Kaplan, Louis L., and Schuchat, Theodore. *Justice—Not Charity: A Biography of Harry Greenstein.* New York: Crown Publishers, 1967.

Kaplan, Robert S. "Organized Citizen Participation in Planning: A Case Study of the Citizens' Planning and Housing Association." M.A. thesis, New York University, 1965.

Karl, Barry D. *The Uneasy State: The United States from 1915 to 1945.* Chicago: University of Chicago Press, 1983.

Katzman, David M. *Seven Days a Week: Women and Domestic Service in Industrializing America.* New York: Oxford University Press, 1978.

Keeran, Roger. *The Communist Party and the Auto Workers Union.* Bloomington: Indiana University Press, 1980.

Kerr, Clark. "Productive Enterprises of the Unemployed, 1931–1938." Ph.D. dissertation, University of California, 1939.

Kessler-Harris, Alice. *Out to Work: A History of Wage-Earning Women in the United States.* New York: Oxford University Press, 1982.

Kimberly, Charles M. "The Depression and New Deal in Maryland." Ph.D. dissertation, American University, 1974.

Kirwin, Harry W. *The Inevitable Success: Herbert R. O'Conor.* Westminster, Md.: Newman Press, 1962.

Kleppner, Paul. *Who Voted? The Dynamics of Electoral Turnout.* New York: Praeger, 1982.

Kousser, J. Morgan. "Ecological Regression and the Analysis of Past Politics." *Journal of Interdisciplinary History* 4 (Autumn 1973): 238–62.

Kruman, Marc W. "Quotas for Blacks: The Public Works Administration and the Black Construction Worker." *Labor History* 16 (Winter 1975): 37–51.

Lamoreaux, David, with Eisenberg, Gerson G. "Baltimore Views the Great Depression, 1929–1933." *Maryland Historical Magazine* 71 (Fall 1976): 428–42.

Leab, Daniel J. " 'United We Eat': The Creation and Organization of the Unemployed Councils in 1930." *Labor History* 8 (Fall 1967): 300–315.

Leuchtenburg, William E. *Franklin D. Roosevelt and the New Deal: 1932–1940.* New York: Harper & Row, 1963.

———. "The New Deal and the Analogue of War." In *Change and Continuity in Twentieth-Century America*, edited by John Braeman, Robert H. Bremner, and Everett Walters, pp. 81–143. Columbus: Ohio State University Press, 1964.

Levenstein, Harvey A. *Communism, Anticommunism, and the CIO.* Westport, Conn.: Greenwood Press, 1981.

Licht, Walter, and Barron, Hal Seth. "Labor's Men: A Collective Biography of Union Officialdom during the New Deal Years." *Labor History* 19 (Fall 1978): 532–45.

Lichtenstein, Nelson. *Labor's War at Home: The CIO in World War II.* Cambridge and New York: Cambridge University Press, 1982.

Lowitt, Richard. *The New Deal and the West.* Bloomington: Indiana University Press, 1984.

Lowitt, Richard, and Beasley, Maurine, eds. *One Third of a Nation: Lorena Hickok Reports on the Great Depression.* Urbana: University of Illinois Press, 1981.

Lyon, Leverett S.; Homan, Paul T.; and Lorwin, Lewis L. *The National Recovery Administration: An Analysis and Appraisal.* Washington: Brookings Institution, 1935.

McCoy, Donald R. *Angry Voices: Left-of-Center Politics in the New Deal Era.* Lawrence: University of Kansas Press, 1958.

McElvaine, Robert S. *Down and Out in the Great Depression: Letters from the "Forgotten Man."* Chapel Hill: University of North Carolina Press, 1983.

———. *The Great Depression: America, 1929–1941.* New York: Times Books, 1984.

———. "Thunder Without Lightning: Working-Class Discontent in the United States, 1929–1937." Ph.D. dissertation, State University of New York at Binghamton, 1974.

Mathews, Jane DeHart. "Arts and the People: The New Deal Quest for a Cultural Democracy." *Journal of American History* 62 (September 1975): 316–39.

Maurer, David J. "Relief Problems and Politics in Ohio." In *The New Deal: The State and Local Levels*, edited by John Braeman, Robert H. Bremner, and David Brody, pp. 79–102. Columbus: Ohio State University Press, 1975.

Milkman, Ruth. "Organizing the Sexual Division of Labor: Historical Perspectives on 'Women's Work' and the American Labor Movement." *Socialist Review* 10 (January–February 1980): 95–150.

Minton, John D. *The New Deal in Tennessee, 1932–1938*. New York: Garland, 1979.

Mitchell, Broadus. *Depression Decade: From New Era through New Deal, 1929–1941*. New York: Harper & Row, 1947.

Montgomery, David. *Workers' Control in America: Studies in the History of Work, Ideology, and Labor Struggles*. Cambridge and New York: Cambridge University Press, 1979.

Nash, Gerald D. *The Great Depression and World War II: Organizing America, 1933–1945*. New York: St. Martin's Press, 1979.

Neverdon-Morton, Cynthia. "Black Housing Patterns in Baltimore City, 1885-1953." *Maryland Historian* 16 (Spring/Summer 1985): 25–39.

Olson, Sherry H. *Baltimore: The Building of an American City*. Baltimore: Johns Hopkins University Press, 1980.

Patterson, James T. *America's Struggle against Poverty, 1900–1980*. Cambridge: Harvard University Press, 1981.

―――. *The New Deal and the States: Federalism in Transition*. Princeton: Princeton University Press, 1969.

Pfeiffer, C. Whit. "Problems of Administration in Community Organization: Selection of Projects and Participation of Public Agencies." In *Proceedings of the National Conference of Social Work: Sixty-Eighth Annual Conference, Atlantic City, New Jersey, June 1–7, 1941*, pp. 577–86. New York: Columbia University Press, 1941.

● Piven, Frances Fox, and Cloward, Richard. *Poor People's Movements: Why They Succeed, How They Fail*. New York: Pantheon, 1977.

● Prago, Albert. "The Organization of the Unemployed and the Role of Radicals, 1929–1935." Ph.D. dissertation, Union Graduate School, 1976.

Ranney, Austin. "The Utility and Limitations of Aggregate Data in the Study of Electoral Behavior." In *Essays on the Behavioral Study of Politics*, edited by Austin Ranney, pp. 91–102. Urbana: University of Illinois Press, 1962.

Romasco, Albert U. *The Politics of Recovery: Roosevelt's New Deal*. New York: Oxford University Press, 1983.

Rosenzweig, Roy. "Organizing the Unemployed: The Early Years of the Great Depression, 1929–1933." *Radical America* 10 (July–August 1976): 37–60.

♦ ―――. " 'Socialism in Our Time': The Socialist Party of the Unemployed, 1929–1936." *Labor History* 20 (Fall 1979): 485–509.

Rothman, Edwin. "Factional Machine Politics: William Curran and the Baltimore City Democratic Party Organization, 1929–1946." Ph.D. dissertation, Johns Hopkins University, 1949.

Rothman, Jack. *Planning and Organizing for Social Change: Action Principles from Social Science Research*. New York: Columbia University Press, 1974.

―――. "Three Models of Community Organization Practice, Their Mixing and Phasing." In *Strategies of Community Organization: A Book of Readings*, edited by Fred M. Cox et al., pp. 25–45. Itasca, Ill.: F. E. Peacock, 1970.

Ryon, Roderick N. "An Ambiguous Legacy: Baltimore Blacks and the CIO, 1936–1941." *Journal of Negro History* 65 (Winter 1980): 18–33.

Scharf, Lois. *To Work and to Wed: Female Employment, Feminism, and the Great Depression.* Westport, Conn.: Greenwood Press, 1980.

Scholnick, Myron. "The President and the Senator: Franklin Roosevelt's Attempted 'Purge' of Maryland's Millard Tydings in 1938." M.A. thesis, University of Maryland College Park, 1962.

Schwartz, Bonnie Fox. *The Civil Works Administration, 1933–1934: The Business of Emergency Employment in the New Deal.* Princeton: Princeton University Press, 1984.

_____. "Unemployment Relief in Philadelphia, 1930–1932: A Study of the Depression's Impact on Voluntarism." In *Hitting Home: The Great Depression in Town and Country*, edited by Bernard Sternsher, pp. 60–84. Chicago: Quadrangle Books, 1970.

Scimé, Joy A. "Public Policy and the Married Working Woman in the Great Depression." Paper presented at the annual meeting of the Organization of American Historians, New York, April 1986.

Seretan, L. Glen. "The 'New' Working Class and Social Banditry in Depression America." *Mid-America* 63 (April–July 1981): 107–17.

Seymour, Helen. "The Organized Unemployed." M.A. thesis, University of Chicago, ● 1937.

Singal, Daniel Joseph. "Broadus Mitchell and the Persistence of New South Thought." *Journal of Southern History* 45 (August 1979): 353–80.

Sitkoff, Harvard. *A New Deal for Blacks: The Emergence of Civil Rights as a National Issue.* Vol. 1, *The Depression Decade.* New York: Oxford University Press, 1978.

Skocpol, Theda. "Legacies of New Deal Liberalism." *Dissent* 30 (Winter 1983): 33–44.

Skocpol, Theda, and Finegold, Kenneth. "State Capacity and Economic Intervention in the Early New Deal." *Political Science Quarterly* 97 (Summer 1982): 255–78.

Skowronek, Stephen. *Building a New American State: The Expansion of National Administrative Capacities, 1877–1920.* Cambridge and New York: Cambridge University Press, 1982.

Stave, Bruce. *The New Deal and the Last Hurrah: Pittsburgh Machine Politics.* Pittsburgh: University of Pittsburgh Press, 1970.

Stellhorn, Paul Anthony. "Depression and Decline: Newark, New Jersey, 1929–1941." Ph.D. dissertation, Rutgers University, 1982.

Sternsher, Bernard. "Great Depression Labor Historiography in the 1970s: Middle-Range Questions, Ethnocultures, and Levels of Generalization." *Reviews in American History* 11 (June 1983): 300–319.

_____. *Hitting Home: The Great Depression in Town and Country.* Chicago: Quadrangle Books, 1970.

Strom, Sharon Hartman. "Challenging 'Woman's Place': Feminism, the Left, and Industrial Unionism in the 1930s." *Feminist Studies* 9 (Summer 1983): 359–86.

Susman, Warren I. *Culture as History: The Transformation of American Society in the Twentieth Century.* New York: Pantheon, 1984.

Tomlins, Christopher L. *The State and the Unions: Labor Relations, Law, and the Organized Labor Movement in America, 1880–1960.* Cambridge and New York: Cambridge University Press, 1985.

Trout, Charles H. *Boston, the Great Depression, and the New Deal.* New York: Oxford University Press, 1977.

Troy, Leo. *Trade Union Membership.* New York: National Bureau of Economic Research, 1965.

Ware, Susan. *Holding Their Own: American Women in the 1930s.* Boston: Twayne, 1982.

Weiss, Nancy J. *Farewell to the Party of Lincoln: Black Politics in the Age of FDR.* Princeton: Princeton University Press, 1983.

White, Frank F., Jr. *The Governors of Maryland, 1777–1970.* Annapolis: Hall of Records Commission, 1970.

Wickens, James F. *Colorado in the Great Depression.* New York: Garland, 1979.

Zieger, Robert H. "Toward the History of the CIO: A Bibliographical Report." *Labor History* 26 (Fall 1985): 485–516.

Index